NEWS

The Politics of Illusion

Ninth Edition

W. LANCE **BENNETT**

University of Washington

Longman
Boston   Columbus   Indianapolis   New York   San Francisco   Upper Saddle River
Amsterdam   Cape Town   Dubai   London   Madrid   Milan   Munich   Paris   Montreal   Toronto
Delhi   Mexico City   São Paulo   Sydney   Hong Kong   Seoul   Singapore   Taipei   Tokyo

Executive Editor: Reid Hester
Project Editor: Toni Magyar
Senior Marketing Manager: Lindsey Prudhomme
Production/Manufacturing Manager: Pat Brown
Production and Composition Services: Sarvesh Mehrotra/Aptara®, Inc.
Cover Design Manager: Jayne Conte
Cover Designer: Karen Noferi
Cover Images: Obama image: Gordon M. Grant/Alamy
             Palin image: Muskopf Photography, LLC/Alamy
Printer and Binder: Courier Stoughton
Cover Printer: Lehigh-Phoenix Color

Library of Congress Cataloging-in-Publication Data
Bennett, W. Lance.
  News : The Politics of Illusion / W. Lance Bennett.—9th ed.
    p. cm.
  ISBN-13: 978-0-205-08241-4
  ISBN-10: 0-205-08241-6
1. Journalism—Political Aspects—United States.   I. Title.
  PN4888.P6B46 2012
  302.230973—dc22
                                        2010053150

1 2 3 4 5 6 7 8 9 10—COS—14   13   12   11

Longman
is an imprint of

www.pearsonhighered.com

ISBN-10:   0-205-08241-6
ISBN-13: 978-0-205-08241-4

CONTENTS

FOREWORD

Doris A. Graber, University of Illinois–Chicago

Throughout human history, politicians and laypeople have known and used the power of communication to achieve their goals. Nonetheless, social scientists have frequently ignored the news media in their analyses of how political systems function. Not so Professor W. Lance Bennett. In *News: The Politics of Illusion*, he has cast the spotlight on the major roles played by news media in the conduct of politics. He did so initially at a time when the study of news media impact had reached a historically low ebb. This is why the book that you are about to read was pathbreaking when it was first published in 1983. It continues to be a leader in the political communications field.

A NEW APPROACH TO NEWS/POLITICS STUDIES

The study of mass-media impact on politics withered in the decades following World War II because several narrowly focused research projects suggested that media had little impact on voting behavior. The crowning blow to the desire to study media impact on politics was a book by sociologist Joseph Klapper. Based on a massive overview of studies drawn from various social sciences, Klapper argued in *The Effects of Mass-Communication* (1960) that mass-media impact was minimal. The message to social scientists was clear: There was no point in wasting their talents on researching a trivial phenomenon.

In 1980, contrary to the then-prevalent wisdom, I authored a text titled *Mass Media and American Politics*. Observation of American politics had convinced me that the substance and framing of news stories affected the conduct and direction of political affairs in major ways. The finding that mass-media effects were minimal was obviously wrong. News effects had been undetected because researchers had focused only on changes in individuals' voting behavior. Other effects, such as learning new information or becoming disgusted with politicians, had been ignored, as had mass-media effects on the behavior of larger social units, like interest groups or the national government. My book was designed to give political science students an overview of the many instances in which news stories about politics had influenced political situations.

Three years later, in *News: The Politics of Illusion*, Lance Bennett took a different approach to cover virgin intellectual territory. Starting with the same premise that had guided my work—namely, that political news does affect politics—Bennett's book focused on what this means for democratic governance in the United States. Rather than outlining how news affects all phases of government, including the formation of public opinion, Bennett formulated basic questions designed to evaluate how well the news serves the needs of America's democracy. For instance, he asked what determines which stories get published and which are ignored. He inquired whether news choices enhance or diminish the quality of grassroots and elite discourse about politics; and he gathered data to discover whose interests were served by what is published or omitted and whose interests were harmed.

His concerns about news impact on the quality of American democracy led Bennett to explore aspects of news production and consumption that had hitherto received sparse scholarly attention from political communication scholars. For instance, Bennett focused on the informants journalists consult when they prepare news stories, because the predispositions and interests of news providers shape the perspectives of their accounts. Examining the human sources of news generates careful analyses of the substance, format, and presentation styles used by informants. It goes beyond concentrating on how journalists select news topics and how they cover them and beyond what politicians say and do.

Message studies are crucial because the political news stories that allow citizens to form opinions about politics are based largely on what individual politicians disclose to the journalists who interview them. In an age where the handling of media relations has become a science practiced by well-trained public relations professionals, scholars must examine how political images are framed to influence public opinion. They must also study how particular politicians manage to get their messages chosen for publication when so many individuals and groups compete fiercely for scarce media time and space, preferably in the most prominent spots and at the earliest moment.

Here is where the book's subtitle—*The Politics of Illusion*—comes into play. Bennett demonstrates that political images reported in news stories are artfully constructed visions of a reality that may have very little relation to what an unbiased observer might see. Yet audiences believe that the published stories reflect the reality of politics and act accordingly. Facts and perspectives that are never reported in available media, irrespective of their importance for the world of politics, elude audiences for whom this information may be crucial.

Bennett has definite views about the issues that he raises. That forces you, the reader, to be more critical than would be necessary when faced with a more descriptive account. Instead of merely asking whether the facts that he reports are accurate, you also must assess whether the inferences and conclusions that he draws from these facts are warranted. You must consider his underlying assumptions carefully and determine whether or not you share them. That is a challenging task, and Bennett invites you to tackle it. I happen to agree with most of Professor Bennett's interpretations, but recognize, as does he, that substantially different interpretations are possible.

To give just one example: Bennett believes that journalists have a duty to use the news to educate the public about the most important political problems facing the nation. He evaluates news quality based on that assumption. But is civic enlightenment really the media's mandatory responsibility and mission? Shouldn't various news venues, like nightly local television news, deliver to their publics what these publics want, as judged by their actual choices of television programs, even if these contradict the publics' professed preferences?

In the United States, news media are private business enterprises. It is the owners' prerogative to decide their businesses' mission within the limits set by public laws? No laws mandate that the news must educate the public. In fact, the Constitution explicitly prohibits Congress from making laws about what news media may report. Even television stations, which are subject to licensing regulations, are only required to "serve the public interest, convenience, and necessity." Civic enlightenment is not mentioned, although America's founders deemed it a priority.

Bennett does acknowledge that the likes and dislikes of news audiences play an important role in the news production system. He notes that many Americans avoid fact-laden news stories designed to educate them about major political issues and that they flock instead to light, entertaining news that allows them to relax, rather than stories that force them to think and likely worry about the affairs of the nation. As a political communication student and citizen, you need to ponder whether journalists should determine what audiences must know to perform their civic duties and construct the news accordingly. If journalists concentrate on "spinach news," it is questionable whether people will consume these stories that journalists deem good for their civic health but that citizens do not find palatable. When people have many other options for occupying their spare time, they are unlikely to attend to news that they consider dull, disturbing, or irrelevant to their concerns.

Wrestling with questions about what information news stories ought to feature is difficult because democracies respect clashing value preferences. News professionals and their audiences want unfettered choices. But journalists and the public also agree that democratic government requires a well-informed citizenry capable of judging the soundness of public policies. They know that the news media are the only institutions that can supply most of the public with readily available information about evolving political events. So what should it be—entertainment stories or unpalatable but important spinach news? You decide! The only compromise—making spinach news entertaining—is very difficult to achieve in many cases.

THE SEARCH FOR NEW THEORIES

Bennett's contributions to the study of politics go much farther than pioneering a critical approach to the media/politics interplay. *News: The Politics of Illusion*, in its various editions, has been a showcase for a number of theories developed and tested by Professor Bennett. Again, one example must suffice: the indexing theory. Not satisfied with merely reporting what kinds of subjects are covered or ignored by the news media and how stories are framed to feature the news from particular perspectives, Bennett has steadfastly explored the all-important "why" questions. Why are particular stories selected and not others? Why are certain frames chosen? Why, for instance, are the government's foreign policy decisions reported uncritically much of the time, and why are controversies about the wisdom of these policies featured at other times? It took painstaking research and analysis of the circumstances sur-rounding each type of coverage to develop indexing theories.

Bennett found that featuring controversy could not be blamed on deliberate or capricious choices by media personnel. Rather, journalists take their cues from political leaders. If credible spokespersons, such as members of Congress or established community leaders, challenge the policies, the news media will re-port their dissent. Absent such challenges, most news stories merely report the official version of events, as told by spokespersons of the incumbent administra-tion. This theory—that the reporting of conflicting views about public policies and events is "indexed" to the surfacing of conflict by widely known, credible sources—has been tested repeatedly by Bennett as well as many other scholars. So far, it has stood firm under most conditions so that, like all theories supported by solid evidence, it can be used as a guide to predict what is likely to happen.

A RECIPE FOR SCHOLARLY EXCELLENCE

What goes into the making of a pioneering scholar like Lance Bennett? First of all, one needs to be exceptionally curious about one's world. Next, one needs to fall in love with the scholarly discipline that is most likely to provide answers to one's burning questions. Lance Bennett fell in love with the world of politics and how it is shaped by the mass media. He earned his bachelor's, master's, and doc-toral degrees in political science from the University of California at Irvine and from Yale University. He received high honors for his academic accomplish-ments. The pattern of producing work of exceptional quality has continued ever since. Following his formal education, Bennett immediately embarked on a re-search and teaching career, most of it spent at the University of Washington.

By the time he wrote *News: The Politics of Illusion*, Bennett had already published numerous articles in scholarly journals as well as three important book-length studies dealing largely with the way people form their opinions about politics. An interest in public opinion leads quite naturally to an interest in the stream of information that people use to form their political views. Hence, the publication of *News: The Politics of Illusion*, along with more arti-cles that deal with media impact on diverse phases of politics.

Subsequently, Bennett focused his research and writing on elections—the showcase of democratic politics. In *The Governing Crisis: Media, Money and Marketing in American Elections* (1992), he analyzed the impact of news coverage, political spinning, and money on elections. He concluded that the American system of governance was in bad shape because the elec-tion message process is flawed. In fact, the political system was in crisis. Bennett's clarion call for election communication reform was followed by another groundbreaking work, *Democracy and the Marketplace of Ideas* (1997), a comparison of political communication in Sweden and in the United States coauthored with Erik Åsard. The book points to widely preva-lent, major flaws in the message systems that link governments and people in modern democracies. In 2007, this was followed by a major critique of the American press, based on a series of case studies. The title of the multiau-thored work heralds its subject matter: *When the Press Fails: Political Power and the News Media: From Iraq to Katrina.* In sum, Bennett is an unrelenting critic of news media performance and a knight in shining intellectual armor trying to rescue our endangered democracy. As mentioned, he has also written about other topics, like public opinion, the American court system, foreign policy, and American culture.

THE MAKING OF A "CLASSIC"

After contributing so amply to the political communications field and receiving multiple prestigious professional awards, many scholars would be tempted to rest on their laurels and merely embellish their pioneering works. Not so Lance Bennett. *News: The Politics of Illusion,* now in its ninth edition, is testimony to the fact that it takes persistent scholarly efforts over many years to produce a masterpiece that is widely acknowledged as a "classic"—a work of exceptional excellence. The interplay of news and politics represents a moving target for analysts. Assessments of the status quo therefore must be updated frequently. Lance Bennett has risen to that challenge repeatedly.

Over the two-and-a-half decades that separate the first and the ninth editions, much has remained stable in the interactions between the news and politics, but there have also been huge changes. Technological advances have moved American society from the age of broadcasting to the age of narrowcasting. Organizations that produce and disseminate news, as well as audiences for particular news offerings, are vastly different from what they were in the 1980s. The Internet has become the "giant gorilla" that looms over the new political communication landscape, forcing many adjustments. A host of newly popular terms like *surfing the Web, blogging,* and *digital divide* are obvious markers of the ever-changing media scene.

The hallmark of the ninth edition is its emphasis on the development of this new media system, its interaction with established media, and its impact on citizens' engagement with politics. As is his style, Professor Bennett spotlights the main issues raised by evolving technologies and asks profound questions about the likely impact on democratic governance. But he also shares his lack of certainty about forecasting outcomes because the dust stirred by major innovations has not settled yet. The established media, it seems, remain the chief gatherers and disseminators of news for now. Internet sources feed off of them, customizing their offerings for mostly young audiences with more narrowly focused interests and a penchant for interactive media. Subsequent editions will, undoubtedly, reveal much clearer pictures.

News: The Politics of Illusion is popular with students for many reasons, foremost among them being its iconoclasm that cuts through illusions to reveal reality, its focus on empowering citizens, and its clear writing style. In each new edition, Bennett reports his own latest research on the shifting political communication scene as well as the findings of other scholars. Bennett always tells it like he sees it—news/politics dynamics are complex, messy, and full of surprises and contradictions. The many brief case studies interspersed throughout the book—and changed or updated for each new edition—make it clear that Bennett's descriptions and analyses are based on events in the real world, rather than ideologically driven philosophizing. The author's conclusions are firm, but never dogmatic.

The book is written in smoothly flowing prose, free from the jargon that obscures so much social science writing. Bennett is critical, but never carping, praising the news system for what he considers its many strengths and condemning it for what he perceives to be its shortcomings. Unlike many other critiques of the American media system, this is not a depressing book that leaves readers wishing that they could escape to another planet because our political communication system is a hopeless mess that must be endured because cures are unavailable. Not surprisingly, when students tell me which of their textbooks they intend to sell at the end of a course and which they intend to keep, Bennett's book is usually in the "keep" category.

SOME QUESTIONS TO PONDER

This foreword ends with a small sample of the kinds of fundamental questions that are worth pondering while you study Professor Bennett's stimulating book. Such questions deserve your attention because they concern basic issues about what kind of media system will best serve American democracy at this point in history.

1. Most scholars agree that media can and often do perform important watchdog roles when public officials misbehave or policies misfire. But should journalists' judgments about the merits of policies be given greater weight than the judgments of politicians on the assumption that journalists are wiser, more objective, and more honest than politicians?

2. Can journalists who have never been elected by the public validly claim to be the voice of public opinion? Do they enjoy the kind of legitimacy that popularly elected politicians have because they were chosen by citizens to represent them? Do politicians forfeit the right to speak for the public if they are self-seeking and deaf to the voices of their constituents?

3. Are average Americans profoundly disinterested in politics so that the spike in attention to news that routinely occurs during political crises is merely a short-lived aberration? Or could it be that they are disinterested only when the substance of much of the news is irrelevant to their lives because it is, indeed, trivial or because its relevance is obscured by the pedantic way in which many political stories are told?

4. Are American journalists focusing their stories primarily on situations about which average citizens can do nothing, while neglecting situations that provide opportunities for citizen action? Unrest in Sudan may have large consequences for the lives of African people, but is far less consequential for average Americans. Should one therefore argue that it is more important for America's local media to focus on major local problems and forego news from abroad so that scarce resources of space and time can be devoted to arouse citizens to cope with their local needs?

5. Journalists organize their work by identifying the places—called "beats"—where they expect to collect news routinely. In practice, this has led to

a preponderance of news from selected government sources. Is such heavy emphasis on "official" sources a sound policy? Would you change it if you could? If so, what sources would you use, and what would be the consequences?

6. In periods of history when people distrust politicians because of numerous well-publicized scandals, should they distrust the news that features politicians' pronouncements? If so, should journalists act as a buffer and scrutinize and interpret politicians' pronouncements, rather than leaving it to citizens to examine politicians' words and draw their own conclusions?

Such problem-laden questions deserve your attention, thought, and judgment because a dysfunctional news system harms all citizens by impeding effective democratic governance. Bennett stresses that the three pillars on which our current media system rests include the public on par with politicians and journalists. Thus far, the public's voice has been mostly inaudible and, therefore, far less influential than it might be. You and your fellow citizens of all ages can change that. Learning about how the news system really operates is the first step. The authors of the books listed in the Suggested Readings have important things to say about our current news system and how it might be reformed. Read and reflect as you delve more deeply into the mysteries of political communication in our world.

SUGGESTED READINGS

Baum, Matthew. *Soft News Goes to War: Public Opinion and American Foreign Policy in the New Media Age* (Princeton, NJ: Princeton University Press, 2003).

Brader, Ted. *Campaigning for Hearts and Minds: How Emotional Appeals and Political Ads Work* (Chicago: University of Chicago Press, 2006).

Cook, Timothy E. *Governing with the News: The News Media as a Political Institution*, 2nd ed. (Chicago: University of Chicago Press, 2005).

Entman, Robert M. *Projections of Power: Framing News, Public Opinion, and U.S. Foreign Policy* (Chicago: University of Chicago Press, 2004).

Graber, Doris A. *Processing Politics: Learning from Television in the Internet Age* (Chicago: University of Chicago Press, 2001).

Hallin, Daniel C., and Paolo Mancini. *Comparing Media Systems: Three Models of Media and Politics* (Cambridge: Cambridge University Press, 2004).

Hamilton, James. *All the News That's Fit to Sell: How the Market Transforms Information into News* (Princeton, NJ: Princeton University Press, 2004).

Kellstedt, Paul M. *The Mass Media and the Dynamics of American Racial Attitudes* (Cambridge, UK: Cambridge University Press, 2003).

Patterson, Thomas E. *Out of Order* (New York: Alfred A. Knopf, 1993).

Schudson, Michael. *The Power of News* (Cambridge, MA: Harvard University Press, 1995).

Ward, Stephen, Diana Owen, Richard Davis, and David Taras, eds. *Making a Difference: A Comparative View of the Role of the Internet in Election Politics* (Lanham, MD: Lexington Books, 2008).

Weaver, David H., et al. *The American Journalist in the 21st Century: U.S. News People at the Dawn of a New Millennium* (Mahwah, NJ: Erlbaum, 2006).

PREFACE

Every edition of *News: The Politics of Illusion* reflects changes in the world of press-politics. The goal is to put the focus on how those changes affect the quality of American democray, measured in terms of how poiliticians communicate with the people, and how the people engage with the issues facing them. In the three years since the last edition, so much has changed that I have reframed much of the book to address the big news story about American democracy today: Journalism is in crisis. The term crisis is used too easily for too many things, but it seems appropriate for describing a press system that has lost roughly one quarter of the journalism jobs that existed in 2000. Dozens of prominent newspapers have folded, and many others are operating in or at the brink of bankruptcy. One result is that news organizations are less capable of investigating the stories they run. At the same time, the public relations industry that aims to spin journalists continues to grow. A national news magazine named public relations as one of the top careers in the otherwise down job market of 2011. As a result, the public gets less investigative reporting and more spin in the news that links politicians and the people in the governing process.

Much of the discussion about the journalism crisis is about how to fix the broken business model of the American press. However, there is an even deeper problem that may not be fixed just by restoring the flow of profits into news organizations: the stunning declines in public confidence in both the press and the political process, particularly among younger citizens. This companion crisis involves the credibility and relevance of the press, and the widespread perception that the mainstream media have become insiders in a corrupt system of government. Exploring these dual crises is a running theme in the ninth edition of *News*, as illuminated by updated examples, new perspectives from the academic literature, and case studies in each chapter that put the spotlight on key aspects of our mediated democracy.

As ever, the focus of the book is on the importance of news for governing the American democracy. One of the great puzzles of our time is why the news has become so important for governing even as it is losing the confidence and attention of many citizens. Among the core concerns of this book are how politicians and various interests compete to get their issues and positions onto the news agenda, who succeeds, and why it matters. In particular, it is important to understand why news organizations defer to some political sources over others, even when they try to be fair and balanced.

With the crisis of confidence in journalism and politics as a backdrop, this edition of *News: The Politics of Illusion* continues to explore the book's enduring focus on the close relationship between the press and government. Since the early days of the last century, with the rise of modern public relations, many influential politicians and intellectuals have regarded news management as an essential means of engineering the public consent they believe necessary to govern in a democracy. Others continue to believe that the news should act as a people's forum and a watchdog that checks the power of those who govern. In balancing these two models of the American press, I disagree a bit with how my good colleague Doris Graber has characterized in her foreword my core value bias in this book. I do not so much think that the press should educate the public about the issues of the day, as it should hold those in power accountable to some standards of honesty, transparency, and balance between the public interest and the growing influence of corporate and private influence (and money) in politics.

Both of these models of the news (as official public record and as watchdog of those officials) establish the centrality of news to governing, but one limits the role of the public in government and the other puts citizens at the center. This historic controversy about the ideals of public information in democracy is alive in every chapter of the ninth edition, illustrated with timely examples from the 2010 elections, the great health care debate, the rise of the Tea Party, and the news-making strategies of the many political interests involved with these and other important developments.

THE POLITICS OF ILLUSION

Filled with growing volumes of political spin, sensation, and insider buzz, the daily news sometimes provides, but increasingly does not offer, citizens a solid basis for critical thinking or effective action. At least this is what a good deal of evidence presented in this book suggests. Perhaps, it would be a happier prospect if the news were merely an entertainment medium—a sort of theater of the daily absurd hosted by friendly media personalities. Such a political information system would not be so worrisome if it did not have real effects on government decisions and people's lives. For example, was there a link between Iraq and the terrorist strikes of 9/11? The president and his chief advisors said so repeatedly in their news campaign in the fall of 2002 and winter of 2003 to go to war against Iraq. A majority of the American people believed them. The news media reported those administration claims largely for the record without challenging them. Today, many journalists lament that there were many areas on which the evidence (or lack of evidence) for those claims could have been challenged when it might have made a difference. Would Americans have gone to war just because Saddam Hussein was a very bad guy whom the world was better off without? We can't know the answer to that question now, but we can imagine that it would have been a different kind of national decision—one that would have raised fewer doubts afterward. Why was it so difficult for major news organizations to raise such crucial questions prominently before the war? What was the effect on public confidence in the press and government of raising them after the war, when it was too late to take back a fateful decision?

Or flash forward to the time of writing this edition: How did the press come to terms with the Republican claims in 2011 that they had a mandate from the people (which people?) to repeal the "Job-Killing Health Care Law" (how was it killing jobs?). Among the more creative efforts of journalists to sort out these political incantations involved journalists putting on their "sorting hats," as David Corn referred to the change of power in the House of Representatives as passing "Hagrid's gavel," and Peter Greir referring to the symbolic house repeal of the health care law as similar to Harry Potter casting a magic spell: "repairo governmentus overreacheum!"

This edition of *News* explores questions of why the press system as a whole seems to be operating with rules that make it so difficult to sort truth from fiction, and to challenge cases of political overreaching and credibility stretching. Before going further, I should also note that there are many cases of good investigative reporting that continue to put the spotlight on serious issues, and pressuring government and citizens to address them. The trouble is that such reports are relatively few in number compared with daily formula news that depends overwhelmingly on government officials to define and solve problems. This book is concerned primarily with the daily flow of politics— the routine communication between public officials, reporters, and citizens on which the quality of government and democracy depends.

Despite (or perhaps because of) their simplicity and familiarity, news images of the political world can be tragically self-fulfilling. Scary images of distant enemies can promote war or military interventions that in retrospect seem dubious (Vietnam, for example, and Iraq). Failure to report the full extent of real-life calamities can delay timely actions. Years of balancing news about human causes of climate change with sources who raised questions about the underlying scientific evidence may have dampened public urgency and political action. Dominant political images, when acted upon, can create a world in their own image—even when such a world did not exist to begin with. Media crime waves may have little connection to levels of crime, yet may lead to public policies that put more people in prison. Thus, the illusions of news become translated into political realities.

The proliferation of cable channels and Internet sites leaves traditional organizations increasingly desperate as they watch their market shares shrink. Such competition pushes once-serious news organizations toward sensationalism—with unattributed sources, rumor, and innuendo carrying many stories. This, in turn, directly foists journalists themselves into the news, as they first provoke and then judge the significance of story developments.

The creation of news drama can blur the connection between news and underlying political realities. Is it really significant that a presidential candidate used the wrong word to talk about a problem? What about the problem itself? On the other hand, issues that cannot be dramatized may not become news at all. Many journalists are beginning to raise questions about their own somewhat captive relationship—caught between corporate owners who demand more profitable content and politicians who offer little that is not packaged for public consumption. This bind often limits what journalists can report, even when they know more about the story.

As the crisis of citizen confidence in news and government deepens, many citizens are tuning out. Perhaps, the most disturbing trend of all is the flight of young citizens from conventional news sources. Those who try to keep up often find more perspective in late-night comedy than in the news itself. This edition of *News* examines these trends and looks at the future of citizenship itself.

WARNING: THE NEWS HAS NO DEMOCRATIC WARRANTY

It can be unsettling to take the news down from its democratic pedestal and see it as an often disjointed social, economic, and political production. Recognizing that there is no guarantee that the news will suit the needs of democracy raises a disturbing question: Why is there so little focused public (and formal government) debate aimed at defining and improving this most important product to better supply the information needs of democracy?

What little public debate there is may be focused on precisely the wrong issues: the alleged political biases of reporters and the call for more balanced or objective reporting. Yet, there is no acceptable solution for the bias problem because different individuals expect the news to conform to their own political views. The added irony is that ideological bias is one of the few information characteristics that people are generally aware of and able to correct on their own.

There is a ray of hope in the continuing signs that most people are disillusioned with both politics and the media these days. People clamor for more representation from government, for less filtered information, and for the right to have more say in political life. The big question—given the nature of the current information system and the personalization of citizen demands on government—is whether the public is truly capable of more direct democracy and whether they would like the results.

DEMOCRACY WITHOUT CITIZENS?

The case for more direct citizen control of government (even though digital technologies make it feasible, as noted in Chapter 8) is challenged by the low levels of information possessed by citizens on most issues. Many media scholars argue that an uninformed citizenry is hardly surprising given the fact that citizens are seldom portrayed as actively involved in the majority of issues in the news. The marginal roles for the public in media politics constitute what political communication scholar Robert Entman has called a "democracy without citizens." The marginalization of the public in the logic of political communication extends throughout all levels of government, at least down to the state level. Susan Herbst's interviews with journalists and political players (activists and legislative staffers) in the Illinois state capital revealed that the communication process was largely for the benefit of these inside players themselves and that they had only a dim sense of the existence of a larger public or what their information needs might be.

Why are citizens and their information needs often afterthoughts for politicians, journalists, and political insiders alike? There are many explanations, and we will examine them throughout the book. However, the overarching reason may be, as Thomas Patterson suggests, that journalists lack clearly defined political or democratic norms to help them decide how to cover the increasingly contrived and managed news performances of politicians. The fuzziness of news organizations' democratic responsibilities generally results in emphasizing strategy and conflict over details of problems and policies. Stories about winners and losers, insider deals, and political calculations promote cynicism, as Joseph Cappella and Kathleen Jamieson note.

It may not be possible to govern without the news, as Tim Cook has argued, but the evolution of the current news system may make such government less authoritative, less trusted, and less legitimate. For all their dysfunctional aspects, the news media—and the ways in which political actors and citizens use them—retain a major role in the American political system.

An information system that generally fails to inform seems an odd development in a digital age that could offer vibrant national discussions with direct communication to the centers of power, right from our desktops. As noted in the concluding chapter of the book, however, this technology cannot simply be switched on with the expectation that people will use it wisely or that changes for the better will automatically follow. On the contrary, the dangers of extreme political fragmentation, individual isolation, and ever more sophisticated political marketing urge us to think seriously about how we should use political information in the digital age.

Meaningful change requires people to better understand some of the underlying defects in the current communication system. In particular, change requires thinking more critically about how to inform people in ways that bring them together around programs of political action that might actually solve problems both in private life and in society. We will return to consider the possibilities for electronic democracy and, more generally, for better political communication, at the close of the book. If such active reforms are possible, however, it is important to build a basis for thinking sensibly about how to implement them. Above all, a better understanding of how the communication system operates might enable journalism schools, news organizations, government representatives, and citizens themselves to convert disillusionment into constructive responses. All of which returns us to the central concern of this book: understanding the continual interplay of news and politics.

A NOTE TO THE READER

- Why is a society that is so rich in information populated with people who are so confused about and alienated from politics?
- Is it possible or even desirable for journalism, as it is practiced in America, to be objective?
- Is the news mainly a propaganda forum for organized interests? Is it mainly a profitable product for the companies that sell it? Or is it a valuable citizen resource?

These are just a few of the questions you will encounter in this book. In the final analysis, it is up to you to draw conclusions. The goal of this book is to challenge comfortable myths by introducing evidence that invites new ways of thinking about our political information system. To stimulate your thinking, the book provides a perspective that is critical of the news—a perspective intended to provoke thought and reaction. I have chosen to present a broad, alternative point of view for a simple reason: there would be little gained by going over the story of the free press in America yet another time. As an American citizen, you already know by heart the saga of a free press and a free people. True, you may have forgotten a few characters or some of the episodes. Nevertheless, memorizing those missing facts once again would not change the plot about how the enduring struggle for freedom of speech and information has created the foundation for democracy in America. Because you know this story already, you should use it in thinking about the argument in this book. Don't feel that you must accept either the story of the free press or the perspective in this book in its entirety. Use the two perspectives to challenge each other and help you draw your own conclusions. After all, the capacity to think independently, without fear or insecurity, is the foundation on which our political freedom rests.

CHAPTER OVERVIEW AND NEW FEATURES

The thing that makes each edition of this book such a pleasure to write is that society, media, and democracy are in continual change. Thinking about these changes and how they affect our political affairs offers the motivation to continue this project and bring new ideas to these pages. In keeping with the spirit that unites all the editions of *News*, this ninth edition continues to follow the evolution of news, both as a social and economic product and as a key to understanding the American political process. The core organizational theme of how the press, public, and politicians interact in a (not always functional) political system remains at the core of the book. New discussions and examples address changes that define the news business, news audiences, and the turbulence of public life in recent years.

The general flow of the other chapters remains similar to the last edition. Chapter 1 introduces the American political information system and suggests that news is a constantly changing and evolving social construction built daily through the interactions of journalists, politicians, and citizen-consumers. Nothing highlights these themes of a changing news and political system than the journalism crisis that currently grips American democracy, and that is discussed in Chapter 1 and throughout this edition. I have continued to strive to make this opening chapter an accessible, big-picture look at how citizens, politicians, and journalists produce the American political process. This first chapter clarifies and expands a simple model of why the institution of the press, despite coming under fire from publics and politicians, remains a key to understanding politics and governance in the United States. The opening chapter also introduces a number of basic press-government concepts, such as gatekeeping, and explores how they work in the context of changing media and political environments.

Chapter 2 examines the underlying information biases of this news system from the standpoint of citizens interested in participating in the political process. This edition shows how the conventional wisdom that the press is somehow "liberal" distracts attention from other, more serious information biases that frustrate effective citizen engagement in political life. The discussion explains why the news is so often fragmented, dramatized, personalized, and preoccupied with authority and disorder—and why these information biases matter. The chapter explains these biases with contemporary illustrations aimed at providing students with examples that they can use in class discussions and analyses of their own. A new case study in this chapter discusses how the press came to a consensus that President Barack Obama had somehow "lost his narrative."

Chapter 3 addresses the question of how citizens process the political information that comes at them through the news media, and how news shaped by professional communication managers may influence public opinion in strategic ways. This discussion shows how news plots drive opinion polling and the interpretation of results, often creating misleading impressions of public thinking in the process. The ninth edition includes updated examples about polling surrounding the Arizona immigration law and President Obama's handling of immigration. Also included are reasons for public inattentiveness to the historic health care legislation, and why the Republican strategy of opposing this and almost all Obama administration initiatives during a time of national crisis did not hurt them. This chapter sets up the discussion of the press-politics system detailed in Chapters 4 through 6.

The middle chapters of the book take an in-depth look at the press-government interactions that produce the news. Chapters 4, 5, and 6 continue to dissect the ways in which politicians and the press alternately cooperate and compete in the odd symbiotic relationship that produces the daily news.

Chapter 4 shows how political actors attempt to control news content. The focus here, as in past editions, is to show how news management strategies work, and how they can go awry. The case study in this chapter examines how scientific consensus on human causes of global warming became a partisan and contested story in the news. A core feature showcases the Republican marketing guru Frank Luntz, illustrating his methods of strategic communication. The ninth edition also features new material on the failure of Obama administration communication strategies, and why White House lapses produced hostility from the press corps and a breakdown of the Obama 2008 campaign narrative of hope and change. This chapter shows clearly why the mainstream press still matters.

Chapter 5 explains how the everyday organizational routines and practices of journalism contribute to the information biases of the news. This look inside news organizations retains much of its familiar focus on the basic operations of American journalism, with new material on digital media and the impact of corporate pressures in the newsroom. The case study in this chapter explains why mainstream press reporting on the buildup to the Iraq War raised so few questions about the Bush administration case for the invasion. More contemporary examples include how political operatives aided the rise of the Tea Party in 2010 by using blogs and edited videos to feed FOX News charges of racism in the Obama administration. This example illustrates the increasingly short circuit between online information and mainstream news.

Chapter 6 deepens our understanding of the press system by examining how the journalism profession has evolved in the United States with fragile connections to the needs of democracy. A close look at the professional norm of objectivity (as defined by fairness, accuracy, balance, and detached, fact-based reporting) shows how this seemingly noble standard, as it is applied, actually contributes to the information problems with the news. Because Chapter 6 is largely historical in nature, the discussion of the origins of professional journalism norms and practices has not been changed much from the last edition. The historical origins of objective reporting continue to highlight this chapter. The case study shows why these reporting norms that seem so desirable actually limit the capacity of journalists to challenge deceptions and lies when they occur. The ninth edition includes an expanded discussion of the journalistic conflation of official sources with objectivity, showing how officials can spin online rumors and extremist allegations into news. This includes examples of political attacks and scandals aimed at Barack Obama (e.g., is he a real U.S. citizen?) that were based on little evidence, but remained big news in the media echo chamber.

Chapter 7 on the political economy of news continues to track the business and economic underpinnings of news as a commercial product. This chapter has undergone a major revision focusing on the economic crisis in the news business and how it affects the quality of public information. The ninth edition includes many examples of the news business in freefall, along with explanations of why this impacts the public value of news content. As with past editions, the goal of this chapter is to explain the economic, political, social, and technological forces that affect the production and consumption of news. The emphasis is on the business practices that create the information biases described in Chapter 2 and that help explain the transformation of news as tracked through the middle chapters of the book. Many examples illustrate how public information continues to be undermined by business interests. The role of the government in this economic makeover of news is discussed in an updated case study of the Telecommunications Act of 1996, which launched the current era of media giants. This case also includes a hopeful note with a look at the citizens' media reform movement that has begun to challenge the government's rush toward deregulation of the ownership structure and social responsibility requirements of what may be the most precious public asset: the airwaves.

Chapter 8 concludes the book with a discussion of how politicians, press, and citizens can each act to improve the quality of our public communication. The ninth edition addresses how the journalism crisis and changing citizen information and media habits are pushing toward new models of public information. A new case study explores a variety of new public information models and proposals for supporting them. As in the past, this chapter also discusses how citizens can better "decode" the conventional news that they consume in order to get more useful perspectives from it. This edition retains the discussion of what journalists can do to work more effectively within the constraints of profit-driven news organizations to report news that is more useful to citizens. The chapter also continues to examine ways in which government policies affect the diversity and depth of the political communication that travels over the public airwaves. The case study examines how new communication technologies hold promise for greater citizen engagement. The conclusion returns to take a broader look at the growing social movement for corporate media responsibility in providing communication that addresses citizens and enhances public life.

KEY ORGANIZING THEMES

Several broad themes are woven throughout the book to address important issues in the relations among press, political actors, and the people. New examples are included throughout to illustrate these themes, along with new developments in the field of political communication.

The ninth edition brings the journalism crisis close to home by describing the dramatic decline of the news industry, from the closing of papers, to the firing of the reporters who produce our political information. The crisis is also followed throughout the new edition and woven into new core themes of the ninth edition, such as the loss of press independence and the decline of gatekeeping capacity.

Press independence and accountability. The journalism crisis is also examined in terms of the diminished capacity of the press to hold those in power accountable. Journalists are introduced in their own voices to discuss how an independent press with the capacity to hold government accountable is being replaced by an increasingly passive transmitter of spin. The ninth edition also introduces concerns about rising government corruption due to the power of corporate interests and money in politics. The resulting declines in public trust in government and the press are discussed with examples ranging from current opinion polls to the angry rhetoric of the Tea Party.

The media echo chamber and the loss of gatekeeping. A new integrated theme throughout the book explains the transition from mass media with broadly distributed content to a media echo chamber where viral information spreads from Internet through talk radio to TV news and back again. Examples include:

- The Twitter revolution: how and when news organizations source the Twitter feeds of newsmakers
- Social networks as news sources: how Sarah Palin's foreign policy started out on Facebook and later became a news story on FOX.
- Journalists' resulting loss of perspective and gatekeeping control over news narratives: Includes a new Case Study in Chapter 2 on Obama

losing the battle to control his own narrative, showing how the oil spill of 2010 became a personal test of Obama's capacity to restore order over his narrative.

In addition, a number of classic themes remain from earlier editions:

How strategic communication works (and why it is essential for governing today). Political messages are increasingly defined by communication professionals to shape news images. The book explains political market research techniques that are used to target audiences and design and deliver messages to them. Policy debates within political institutions typically echo the rhetoric of these issue campaigns, making the news more of an echo chamber for partisan information campaigns than a perspective on the underlying issues.

How the press works. To understand why news organizations report so much packaged communication, it is essential to get inside the profession. This book does that by showing why the norms adopted by professional journalists often prevent them from reporting what they know or suspect about the stories behind the stories.

The nature of media effects. It is important to recognize the limits on the degree to which the news shapes public opinion. People may be less swayed by the news when issues become part of daily life experience. Subjects such as sexual morals, abortion, racial discrimination, sexual harassment, environmental crises, and AIDS have all become the subjects of movies, talk shows, and conversations with friends. People with new home mortgages, when the housing crisis hit, may not have needed the news to understand their economic problems, although they may have been reassured that the government was trying to restore stability in the market. Yet the more distant world of politics encompassing issues, such as war, banking, and media regulation may become real and affect opinion largely through the news. Moreover, as shown in Chapter 3, the ways in which news organizations construct and interpret polls on these issues can create misleading images about levels of public attention and concern.

How the news defines citizenship. News images offer implicit definitions of who participates in American politics and who counts in society. This construction of citizenship is crucial for understanding popular attitudes about government and politics today, as well as levels of citizen engagement and information.

Youth civic disengagement and information habits. The book explores new perspectives on why young citizens increasingly reject mainstream news sources and the politics they portray. Chapter 3 examines the problems of young people disconnecting from the information process altogether. It examines how the news fails to address younger audiences, while pointing to positive developments in interactive media that may help with these problems.

The role of political comedy and participatory media. Among the more hopeful developments in the engagement picture is the rise of political comedy such as *The Daily Show* and participatory media networks such as YouTube. Large audiences now participate actively in reacting to news events and sharing their responses via large digital networks.

Political information processing and new information technologies. It is important to recognize that new technologies contain the potential to address some of the problems with citizen disengagement and political disconnection. We need to understand what the information processing capabilities of people are and what motivates them to acquire and apply new ideas and information. While the Internet is clearly attractive to young citizens as a primary information source, the fragmentation of audiences into small communication networks and isolated communities presents challenges to forming larger publics and joining together in broad public action.

Corporate profit pressures in the newsroom. It was hard to imagine that profit pressures could continue to grow and dominate journalistic decisions beyond the levels documented in the last edition. Yet the profit ride of the 1990s has been compounded by the bumpy economy of the new millennium, creating a dynamic that further threatens news quality. This edition continues to trace the effects of this corporate-side profit logic through the news industry and details how the news itself is being redefined by it.

The fragmentation of the news audience. The proliferation of cable and Internet and has changed earlier conceptions of mass communication. The soaring cost of elections is just one indicator of the diminishing capacity of conventional media to engage people with politics. This edition continues the discussion of why this exhilarating time of change in technologies and markets does not automatically result in more meaningful citizen information choices or in much greater diversity of the political content being communicated.

The future of news. Numerous discussions throughout the book examine the responses of journalists and news organizations to the loss of audiences and diminished public confidence in the news itself. Important debates about, and experiments with, civic journalism and other news formats are examined here. The closing case study in Chapter 8 takes an updated look at new interactive news formats that bring citizens, journalists, and politicians into more direct communication about important issues. The recent emergence of a citizen's movement for media reform is an interesting development. And the rising interest in participatory media and audience production of political information content may signal important changes in the way we communicate politically.

ACKNOWLEDGMENTS

Each edition of *News* reminds me that this is still a work in progress. The focus on press, citizens, public officials, and democracy keeps me mindful of historic changes and contemporary events. Each time I do a revision, I also realize that I have learned new things about citizenship, democracy, and the importance of communication in the governing process. I owe much of my continuing engagement with these topics to the many colleagues with whom I have discussed these subjects over the years. Not all of those who have commented and reacted to the ideas in this book agree with my views and interpretations, but their lively engagement has stimulated my thinking and helped me reach new insights about a rich and complex subject.

It is not possible to acknowledge all the people who have influenced my thinking, but I am particularly indebted to Regina Lawrence, Tim Cook, Marie Danziger, B. J. Bullert, Bruce Bimber, William Gamson, Jay Blumler, Steve Livingston, Jerry Manheim, Bruce Williams, Ann Crigler, Marion Just, Michael Delli Carpini, Susan Herbst, Bob McChesney, Valerie Hunt, Bryan Jones, John Zaller, Marvin Kalb, Jerry Baldasty, David Domke, Michael McCann, Bill Haltom, Phil Noble, Bob Entman, Michael Schudson, Dan Hallin, Kathleen Jamieson, David Altheide, Henry Kenski, Lloyd Jansen, Adam Simon, Erik Åsard, Thomas Patterson, Shanto Iyengar, Stephen Coleman, Rod Hart, Scott Althaus, Victor Pickard, Danna Young, and Sabine Lang. A special thanks goes to Doris A. Graber for updating her generous foreword for this edition. Her perspective and insights on this topic have blazed a trail for the entire field. Doris has mentored many scholars, including me, and I shall always be in her debt. I am also grateful to the students who work with me and keep my thinking fresh. The enduring influence of Murray Edelman lives on in these pages.

I also thank the anonymous reviewers who once again struck the right balance between preserving the spirit of the book and suggesting how to keep it current with the rapidly changing worlds of media and politics. Their names, revealed to me only now, are Michael Baranowski, Northern Kentucky University; Paul Freedman, University of Virginia; and Jacqueline N. Mitchell, University of Tennessee. The reviews were both supportive and most helpful.

The continuing relationship with Longman through these many years of corporate mergers, shakeups, and revolving editors that define today's publishing business is nothing short of miraculous. Toni Magyar stepped into the latest editorial breach and has been both supportive and creative in helping to get this edition out.

This edition of *News* is dedicated to my old friends Alan Fowler, John Lind, John Kroeger, and Butch Rager. Also known as The G.R.O.U.P., this longstanding fellowship has been dedicated to sharing our lives and our views over the past four decades. I have learned much about the joys and pains of politics from our discussions of events in the news.

W. Lance Bennett

The News About Democracy

Information Crisis in American Politics

As almost everyone knows, the economic foundation
of the nation's newspapers, long supported by advertising,
is collapsing, and newspapers themselves, which have been
the country's chief source of independent reporting, are
shrinking—literally. Fewer journalists are reporting less news
in fewer pages.
—Leonard Downie Jr. and Michael Schudson

. . . only an overheated 24/7 infotainment culture
that had trivialized the very idea of reality (and with it,
what was once known as "news") could be so easily
manipulated by those in power.
—Frank Rich

The headline for this edition of *News: The Politics of Illusion* cuts to the core of public information in a democracy: "Independent Journalism Is Collapsing. Who Will Tell the People?" One might add: "Will the People Care?" Many observers view the collapse of healthy news organizations as creating an accountability crisis for democracy because there are fewer journalists examining what those in power are doing. Moreover, there are fewer news organizations with the prestige and audience pull to focus public attention on abuses of the public trust, whether they occur in government, business, or other social institutions, such as schools and churches.

1

The most visible cause of this accountability crisis is economic: The commercial underpinnings of the news business are collapsing, as discussed below. Beyond economics, however, there are even deeper challenges to the journalism regime that has served American democracy for the last century. For example, digital technologies now enable individuals to be both producers and consumers of information, to share it across large social networks and to attend to it selectively according to personal tastes. These changes are creating new models of information production, organization, and consumption. Old media formats typically involve packaging generic bundles of heavily edited "authoritative" information about diverse topics into newspapers or TV news programs. Such "department store" information offerings hold less appeal for digital citizens who now have a dazzling array of new technologies to assemble and share a wider, yet more personalized, array of political content, from comedy and blogs to Twitter streams and eyewitness videos of actual events. A notable feature of this emerging public information order is that political content can be transmitted directly to large audiences often without passing through news organizations. For better and for worse, the official sources and independent editorial gatekeepers of the old news order are being challenged by *crowdsourced* information of more diverse origins.

Yet, even as these changes are occurring, the news remains important to politicians and those in power for several reasons:

- Managing the news becomes a measure of who controls the flow of information to high-level audiences—the circles of power—in government, business, and society.
- The contests among viewpoints promoted by various interests in the news constitute the central public arena of democracy. Although these viewpoints are overwhelmingly generated by elites, they are typically represented (by those same elites) as the will of the people.
- Even though coherent audiences and public credibility have eroded, the news remains one of the most important channels for reaching publics. When news messages are repeated often and loudly enough by politicians—and echoed by cable pundits, talk radio personalities, and bloggers—they can shape the polls on important issues in policy arenas and elections.

The rest of this chapter explores the tensions among the key forces that are changing the nature of news and political information in American society: the erosion of accountability journalism, the distraction and disdain of publics, the growing adoption of new information technologies, and the continuing importance of making the news for elite political communication strategies.

THE ECONOMIC COLLAPSE OF THE NEWS BUSINESS

First, let's take a brief look at the surface level of the "accountability journalism" crisis: the collapse of the business model that has long enabled commercial organizations to use the news to lure audiences to advertisers. News organizations in modern America were unusual businesses in the sense that they produced a public good (the news) through commercial transactions involving selling audiences to advertisers.[1] Until fairly recently, the ethics of professional journalism maintained something of a "firewall" between the journalism and the advertising sides of the business, with the result that advertisers had minimal direct control over what the news side did. At the same time, advertisers generally cared little about whether their money helped support a news bureau in Berlin, or paid for reporting a story about the effects of climate change in Bolivia. When the Internet suddenly offered cheaper and more precise means of targeting ads to audiences, both advertisers and audiences began to drift away from conventional media formats, leaving the news itself as an odd piece out in the media picture. Who would pay to produce that story on climate change? Who would pay to consume it? Most other democracies (including America in earlier times) better understood the value of protecting such a valuable public good by figuring out how to support it through public subsidies, much in the way defense, public safety, education, and health care have been variously supported or subsidized as public goods essential for the viability of a democratic society.[2]

Going into this century, news organizations were already suffering extreme pressures from corporate owners and investors who rode the great media profit wave of the 1990s into the ground, forcing cutbacks in reporting staff to sustain inflated profit margins. The economic downturns from 2000 to 2010 left little more to cut, since the profit taking of the 1990s had already closed international bureaus and investigative units, and eaten into core coverage of state and local government.[3] As the maturation of the Internet offered advertisers far cheaper channels for targeting audiences more effectively, many newspapers were simply closed. Others plunged into bankruptcy, looking for buyers. And those that survived cut still more newsroom staff—in many cases by half or more. In the newspaper industry alone, journalism-related jobs shrank from 60,000 in 1992 to around 40,000 in 2009, with the bottom not yet in sight.[4] Most of this decline occurred between 2001 and 2010, when the industry lost roughly 25 percent of its workers.[5]

Many observers see the issue here as gathering and distributing the information that citizens need to monitor powerful leaders in government, business and various social institutions, and hold them accountable.[6] Yet relatively few citizens seem deeply worried worry about this loss of "accountability journalism." Part of the problem here is a longer-term disaffection of Americans from the press system. Even in earlier days, when stronger and more independent news organizations had the capacity to investigate and challenge those who abused power, many Americans sensed that this capacity was not being used regularly or very effectively.[7] In this view, the chase for profits and easy stories (or, in the case of the fragile public broadcasting system, the desire to avoid political reprimand) has left the news watered down to a daily stream of public relations (PR) spun by powerful insiders. To complicate matters, pundits and partisan politicians have fanned public perceptions that the press has somehow taken sides against them, no matter what their side may be. This widespread impression of press bias is discussed in more detail in Chapter 2.

Despite these perceived limitations, a case can still be made that independent journalism is the only hope for regular and reliable information about what those in power are doing.[8] Without it, the lights go out on democracy, meaning that government is left to police itself while illuminating its own activities through the haze of public relations, propaganda, and spin.[9]

Perhaps the imminent death of the old press system does not worry most people because there appear to be so many outlets for information that it is hard to keep up with them. One only needs to enter a topic in a search engine to find hundreds or thousands of sites with information about it. Yet many of these blogs, webzines, and online news organizations are merely recycling the shrinking journalism content produced by increasingly threatened news organizations. Consider a revealing study of one news microcosm: the "news ecosystem" of the city of Baltimore. The Pew Project for Excellence in Journalism conducted a study of where information about politics, government and public life came from in that city.[10] The study looked at various media, from newspaper, radio, and television, to blogs and other online sites. Although this information system seemed rich and diverse, with some 53 different outlets for news, tracking the origins of actual news showed that 95 percent of stories containing original information "came from traditional media—most of them from the newspaper." Even more distressing was a look back in time showing that the sole surviving paper, the *Baltimore Sun*, reported 32 percent fewer stories between 1999 and 2009, and 73 percent fewer than in 1991.

The Baltimore study raises the important question: ". . . if newspapers were to die . . . what would that imply for what citizens would know and not know about where they live?" Media historian Paul Starr has argued that if this trend continues, the growing ignorance of the citizenry and the lack of accountability of officials will surely be accompanied by a great wave of public corruption.[11] Indeed, many citizens already see corruption in government as a major problem. For example, a 2008 poll on the roots of the financial crisis showed that 62 percent strongly agreed with the statement that political corruption played a major role in the crisis, and another 19 percent agreed "somewhat" with that statement.[12] An international survey of perceived government corruption ranks the U.S. just 19th in the world list of clean governments.[13]

Despite evidence that problems with accountability or watchdog journalism had begun long before the business model collapsed, many journalists and news organizations continue to focus on fixing the business model with remedies such as putting up "pay walls" for access to online information. While this solution may work for specialized publications such as *The Wall Street Journal*, it does not seem destined to save journalism in general. The immediate problem is that as long as there are free news outlets, those charging for the same information will not likely attract many paying customers. Whether or not there is truth to the popular Internet mantra that "information wants to be free,"[14] it is also equally true that those who produce quality, independent information want to be paid.

Beyond the economics of the existing model of journalism, there are far larger problems with "saving" the so-called legacy press system. The public, particularly younger citizens, increasingly prefer different forms of information access than engaging with the lumpy collections of content delivered in newspapers or television newscasts. As digital media scholar Clay Shirkey put it, consumers "are not interested in single omnibus publications." Even more challenging, according to Shirkey, is the fact that content flows through social networks according to a very different audience logic than defines the mass media: "the audience for news is now being assembled not by the paper but by other members of the audience."[15]

WHO NEEDS JOURNALISTS WITH FACEBOOK, YOUTUBE AND TWITTER?

For increasing numbers of citizens, information does not reach them through mass distribution processes in which people tune into a scheduled program or subscribe to a newspaper, although some still do. Information increasingly comes from an array of sources not designated by journalists as authoritative, and it travels over social networks that enable access any time, any place, and through many devices. The networks grow or shrink as people share their interests with their friends and friends of friends in loosely structured ways. This means that the sourcing of the information is changing in often very dramatic ways. It is not always necessary for a newsmaker to go through a journalist to reach a large audience.

Consider in this light what at first glance appears to be a normal news story about an accident that happened to performer Pink at a concert in Germany. The *Reuters* article was headlined: **Pink rushed to hospital as stunt fails.** The opening line read: "Pink said she was fine after being rushed to a hospital when the harness supposed to lift her into the air at a gig in Nuremberg instead sent her shooting off stage into a barrier."[16] However, this information was not produced in a press interview with Pink or at a press conference with her publicity agent. Pink tweeted it from the ambulance on her way to the hospital. Thus, Pink's followers likely got the news before journalists did, and they got it directly from the most credible source: Pink herself. Moreover, Pink's 1,765,841 Twitter followers, received far more detailed and timely updates on her condition than likely reached news audiences assembled via the conventional news organizations carrying the story based on her tweets.

Want to know Sarah Palin's foreign policy positions sooner than they appear in the news and in more detail? Just join her nearly 2 million (at the time of this writing) Facebook friends, and the latest on her political thought and activities will arrive in your inbox or on your own Facebook pages.[17] Suggesting new pathways for making the news, the *Huffington Post* wrapped a story around Palin's foreign policy posts on Facebook, proposing that Palin was using social media to shape the Tea Party policy agenda for her 2012 presidential run. In many ways, the story resembled a conventional news report and even included a sound bite from a wonk at the American Enterprise Institute.[18] What differed was that the source of information about Palin's policy positions was her Facebook page, not a direct interview conducted by a journalist. Indeed, Palin's uneven and often parodied encounters with journalists during her 2008 vice presidential candidacy may have left her with the sense that she can better communicate directly to her social networks through Facebook and Twitter.

Journalism seems to be recognizing its uneasy relationship with social media in growing numbers of similar reports, such as a *New York Times Magazine* feature on the "digital diplomacy" of two members of Secretary of State Hillary Clinton's policy staff, Jared Cohen and Alec Ross.[19] Each had several hundred thousand Twitter followers (including, one imagines, many journalists) who learned directly about where they and Secretary Clinton were in the world on a given day. One of their tweets raised eyebrows (and generated news stories) with a remark about "the greatest frappuchino ever" at a university outside Damascus.[20] Whether such incidental information was appropriate for an official pronouncement seemed best judged by their legions of followers who numbered more than for anyone else in government at the time besides President Obama and Senator McCain. Indeed, they had far more followers than their own boss, whose official Twitter stream (@statedept) had less than one-tenth of either of their following. Journalists musing about this trend asked if this was this some sort of new "digital diplomacy," the wanderings of twittering bureaucrats, or a sneaky channel for propaganda masking as news?[21] Perhaps direct communication over social media is all of the above; it is also clearly a growing source of political information that reaches networked publics sooner than conventional journalists can turn it into regular news reports.

One of the most dramatic examples of direct online information distribution online involved the leak (more like a flood) of more than 90,000 classified U.S. government documents on the war in Afghanistan through a site called wikileaks.org.[22] These documents raised questions about the possible double role of U.S. ally Pakistan in supporting U.S. enemies al-Qaeda and Taliban forces while taking billions in American aid to fight those same threats. The documents also described the details of U.S. military attacks that killed civilians. At the same time, the landmark WikiLeaks signaled a continuing role for conventional news media, as the site coordinated the release of the documents with major news organizations in the U.S. (*The New York Times*), Germany (*Der Spiegel*), and the U.K. (*The Guardian*), assuring an amplified impact on international audiences, while enlisting the help of prominent journalistic organizations in sorting through and interpreting a mountain of information that the small staff of WikiLeaks could not do alone.

A sure sign of the changing times occurred when an anonymous personal video posted on YouTube and viewed by millions around the world won the prestigious Polk Award for journalism in 2010. The video was taken during a protest following the Iranian elections and showed the shooting death of a young protester named Neda Ahga-Soltan. Since Western journalists were banned from the country, and the distant events were hazy and chaotic, the highly personal video of a protester who died for the cause of fair elections became the focus of the story in the mainstream media. The spokesperson for the Polk Awards, Robert Darnton pointed to the newsworthy significance of the video that was viewed by millions and became "an iconic image of the Iranian resistance."[23] Darnton also noted that awarding one of the most prestigious journalism prizes to an anonymous citizen who produced important news outside of the usual journalistic processes[24] signaled an historic moment in the history of news: "The award celebrates the fact that, in today's world, a brave bystander with a cell phone camera can use video-sharing and social networking sites to deliver news."

An important question at this critical juncture in news history is how reliably political information—particularly when it is less graphic than the video of Neda's death—will reach audiences as they turn away from everyday engagement with conventional journalism via regularly scheduled news consumption.

WHO FOLLOWS THE NEWS?

As more people follow newsmakers directly on Facebook and Twitter, we may assume that fewer are reading or watching the repackaging of this information in conventional news formats. Consider the findings of a national task force studying the current crisis in the news. Using in-depth surveys, researchers for the Carnegie-Knight task force were able to probe the news habits of teens (12–17), young adults (18–30), and older citizens (over 30). The findings included dramatic evidence that few teenagers or young adults consume news on a daily basis. For example, only 31 percent of both groups say they watch national TV news daily, compared with 57 percent of those over 30. As for young people moving to the Internet, the number who follow the news on a daily basis online were roughly the same for all three age brackets: 20, 22, and 20 percent, respectively. And 65 percent of teens who do get their news online just happen to run across it while they are browsing, compared with 55 percent of those over 30 who purposefully seek it out. This suggests that earlier studies claiming large online populations of young news consumers may be counting those who see a few headlines as they pass through their Internet portals en route to Facebook, fan sites, or games.[25]

Perhaps the attention overload problem is greater for young citizens who are faced with rising education costs, unstable job situations, and a richer media environment than past generations. Casual observers often assume that the news deficit just has to do with being young and that it will change as young people grow up and take on more adult responsibilities, such as starting careers and settling down. Here again, the evidence does not seem optimistic. Martin Wattenberg's careful look at comparable generations of news consumers going back as far as data permit (nearly a century in the case of newspapers) show that each generation of young people over the past 40 years has dropped substantially in news consumption. For example, 70 percent of Americans born in the 1930s read newspapers on a daily basis by the time they turned 20, compared with just 20 percent of those born in the early 1980s. Equally steep declines mark parallel age groups with respect to TV news consumption in later decades. These trends are not unique to America. Most of the advanced democracies report similar declines in news consumption across the age range of their citizens.[26]

Why does this matter? Not surprisingly, it turns out that there is a connection between tuning out the news and not knowing what is going on in the world of politics. Wattenberg also analyzed correlations between age and political information among Americans at different points in time. In the 1940s, 1950s, and 1960s, for example, citizens under 30 were about as well informed as older age groups. After the 1970s, each decade saw younger generations become increasingly less informed and less likely to follow political issues and events (with a few notable exceptions such as 9/11). These trends are also true for most other democracies. He concludes that, ". . . today's young adults are the least politically knowledgeable generation ever in the history of survey research."[27]

SCARE THEM AND THEY MAY PAY ATTENTION: COMMUNICATING WITH ELUSIVE AUDIENCES

Politicians who still seek to reach people through the news seem to have overreacted to their diminished relevance in people's lives by relying on public relations teams to reach people with increasingly shrill messages. The stunning national health care debate of 2009-2010 contained numerous examples of how the communication process has ramped up the PR and hype to reach elusive audiences. One episode began with a press release by House Minority leader John Boehner claiming that a provision in the proposed legislation would lead the country down the road to government-encouraged euthanasia.[28] Soon the talk radio echo chamber, blogosphere, e-mail lists and YouTube videos[29] turned this into chants of how "Obamacare" would "kill your grandma." Talk radio personality Rush Limbaugh likened Obama's plan to Hitler and the Nazis,[30] which provoked Republican columnist David Brooks on NBC's *Meet the Press* to call the attacks "insane."[31] The hyperbole was continuously amped by prominent Republicans, both members of Congress and by Sarah Palin, who talked about "death panels" in her Facebook page, and tweeted: "R death panels back in?"[32] And so the "kill yer granny" messages cycled through the mainstream news media, as they were too tempting too resist for news organizations seeking cheap sensationalism, while covering what prominent politicians were saying.

When the news is consumed with PR, the messages become a mix of absurd sensationalism (the government killing granny) and formula slogans (every politician running as an outsider). Indeed, the desperation to reach audiences who are often running away from this kind of communication has led many politicians to poison the well of politics through negative campaigning and railing against government as the root of most evils. Having warned citizens about people like themselves, politicians who then get into office are forced to hire Madison Avenue–style communication consultants to sell themselves and their ideas back to an evermore wary public. These staged political performances often appear forced and artificial to media savvy audiences— and young citizens are among the most savvy media consumers. Indeed, reality TV and political comedy may seem more authentic than the political performances made for news.[33]

The hallmark of contemporary mediated politics, as Frank Rich noted on the second quote opening this chapter, is that the news has fallen prey to reporting the packaged reality formats produced by political consultants. News that resembles entertainment has earned the name "infotainment" from communication scholars. The difference is that the characters in political programming often seem less sympathetic and emotionally accessible than the young and vulnerable characters starring in reality programs. Yet the economics of the news business (discussed in detail in Chapter 7), like the economics of the entertainment media, makes packaged reality programming attractive to produce and report. News events scripted by communication consultants and spin-doctors are cheap and predictable to cover, thus filling the daily "news hole" more economically than serious investigative reporting. As we will discuss in later chapters, the mayhem that fills much of local TV news is equally formula driven, displacing local political coverage with accidents, shootings, threatening weather, and bizarre happenings. Whether local or national, the dramatic tone of infotainment news aims to get the attention of desirable audience demographics: younger market segments, who, if they watch the news at all, watch it with remote in hand.

The irony of the way the news has evolved is that despite—or perhaps because of—the often shrill and dramatic efforts to attract audiences, many citizens are driven away. Many others are only intermittently attentive. Meanwhile, political insiders watch the same news with great interest. Politicians, lobbyists, public relations professionals, and journalists follow the daily spin with the attention of sports fans to see who is winning and who is losing the daily struggle for image control. The symbiosis between journalists and the communication professionals who spin the messages of their political clients keep the process going, creating what media scholars David Altheide and Robert Snow call a "media logic" that is hard to break out of.[34]

From the standpoint of those on the inside who continue to produce this strange media logic, the shrill voices filling the talk shows and the carefully crafted sound bites in news reports become a substitute for public opinion itself.[35] Not surprisingly, many members of the public express the concern that the news is more for insiders than for them. According to media scholar Robert Entman, this media logic produces a democracy without citizens.[36] As we see in Chapter 3, opinion polls and the occasional public protest bring citizens into the news frame, but generally in cameo roles rather than starring performances. This noisy media echo chamber of clashing images and slogans ends up driving out more thoughtful viewpoints, along with space for deliberation and reflection. Woe to the politician who cannot explain health care in less than 30 seconds (and woe to the citizen who tries to grasp it in 30 seconds). Foreign policies that address the complexities of international relations become vulnerable to charges of weakness and indecision.

Even as people avoid the news, the image machines of government and interest groups keep major issues from the war Afghanistan or climate change spinning in front of the public. Those issues often reach people through entertainment programs such as *E!* or *Access Hollywood* (*Entertainment Tonight* goes on Sarah Palin's campaign plane!), or as they pass through Internet portals (images of car bombings in Baghdad dissolve into celebrity photos of Britney or Paris).[37] The hammering slogans and packaged images become all that most people have to form opinions or make voting decisions.

Those who seek space for more reflection often turn to late-night comedy for perspective and relief from the incessant spin. In the aftermath of the terrible events of 9/11, networks, such as FOX and CNN competed to brand their programming with dramatic infotainment titles, such as *America Strikes Back.* Jon Stewart's *The Daily Show* on Comedy Central offered an antidote to the news melodrama with its own long-running segment titled *America Freaks Out!* And when the war in Iraq began to slip the grasp of administration spin, *Daily Show* coverage was tagged *Mess O'Potamia.* Stewart appeared on the cover of *Newsweek,* and an internal story in that issue described him as changing the presentation of news to appeal to a younger audience that has largely tuned out conventional news.[38] It turns out that audiences for programs, such as *The Daily Show with Jon Stewart* are among the most informed and active members of the public. Despite the worries of many parents and teachers, late-night comedy audiences do not get all their news from the comedians; they bring high levels of news knowledge with them. Otherwise, as Jon Stewart put it, they wouldn't get the jokes.[39] Even if contemporary politics has spawned a comedy boom, the dilemma for citizens remains how to break through such thin and often unsatisfying understandings of politics so that more credible and engaging discussions of public issues might occur.

Despite all the changes outlined above, the communication format that remains most important for political actors to make and for citizens to share is still the mainstream *news.* The core question explored in this book is: *How well does the news, as the core of the national political information system, serve the needs of democracy?* In exploring this question, we examine how various political actors—from presidents and members of Congress to interest organizations and citizen-activists—try to get their messages into the news. Understanding how politics and government work requires understanding who makes the news; who does not; and how that news affects elite positions, public opinion, and the resolution of issues and events. As outlined earlier, a key dilemma facing American democracy is that even as citizens become less central to the news picture, the same old media logic has remained central to the process of governing with the news.

GOVERNING WITH THE NEWS

Political communication scholar Tim Cook described the processes through which politicians and journalists have become so inseparable as "governing with the news."[40] Politicians need to get their positions into the news to establish themselves as movers and shakers in the Washington image game and to signal to their backers and voters that they are visible and active leaders. Observing the rise of news management in governance, CNN pollster and pundit William Schneider described Washington as a town of individual political entrepreneurs whose success and power often depend on their media images. Those images can be boosted when they are associated with the popularity of other visible politicians, like a winning president, or with popular developments, such as economic booms or successful wars.[41] When the president appears to be a loser, other politicians are less eager to be associated with him or his programs. As the news tracks these image games, opinion polls beyond the beltway often reflect (and validate) the spin.

Journalists in this system receive a fresh and economical daily supply of news, along with insider status and professional respect when they land the big interviews and inside scoops. Journalist Marvin Kalb described these perverse developments in "press-politics:"

> . . . there isn't a single major and sometimes minor decision reached at the White House, reached up on the Hill, reached at the State Department or the Pentagon, that does not have the press in mind. The way in which this is going to be sold to the American people is a function of the way in which the press first understands it, and then accepts it, and then is prepared to propagate a certain vision to the American people.[42]

What is ironic in this process is that despite the often-fierce competition for these inside tidbits, the overall results display relatively little variation in stories across the mainstream media. Even organizations with a political point of view, such as FOX *News* or MSNBC start with much the same topics, but favor the spin from one end of the political spectrum over the other. Cook concluded that the similarity of approaches to covering the news and the homogeneity of content across the thousands of mainstream news organizations support the idea that the news media (despite the plurality of the term *media*) operate as a single political institution, covering much the same territory with much the same result. He described this as "the abiding paradox of newsmaking: News professes to be fresh, novel, and unexpected, but is actually remarkably patterned across news outlets and over time. Rather than providing an unpredictable and startling array of happenings, the content of news is similar from day to day, not only in featuring familiar personages and familiar locales, but also in the kinds of stories set forth and the morals these stories are supposed to tell."[43] The mutual dependency of journalists and officials in the production of news means that this institution of the press—even though protected in its freedom and independence by the Constitution—in fact amounts to a fourth, and not so independent, branch of government.

The ability or inability of officials to make and control the news is an important part of the power to govern, as reflected in the capacity of news to (a) shape public opinion among those citizens still paying attention; (b) sway different political factions to join or oppose political initiatives, such as going to war or addressing climate change; (c) hold officials more or less accountable for those initiatives; and (d) simply inform citizens about what the government is doing. At the forefront of information politics is the struggle over influencing or *spinning* journalists and news organizations to report versions of events that favor particular political sides. A case in point is the selling of the Iraq War.

HOW THE NEWS WENT TO WAR IN IRAQ

Few episodes in modern history illustrate the power of spin more than selling the Iraq War to the media and, in turn, to other politicians and the American people. Within a year of the attacks of September 11, 2001, the Bush administration rolled out a well-designed marketing campaign to link 9/11 to Iraq.[44] The United States was already waging a far more credible war with broad international support in Afghanistan. The fight there was against a government that supported al-Qaeda and Osama bin Laden, who were clearly linked to the attacks on America. There was little evidence that Iraq was similarly involved. Nonetheless, the president and other high administration officials began a public relations offensive to create the impression that there was a link between Iraq and that terrible day when airliners full of passengers were hijacked and flown into the World Trade Center towers and the Pentagon.

The news mix was enriched with allegations that Iraq possessed weapons of mass destruction. Officials appeared on Sunday news interview programs and punctuated their arguments with images of mushroom clouds. Those erroneous claims would later become material for late-night comedians, who joked about "weapons of mass deception." Did the Bush administration intentionally deceive the public? Or were the president and his advisors so determined to go to war that they deceived themselves? These questions may never be answered to the satisfaction of the historians who will surely be investigating them. But we can answer the questions of how such dubious claims came to dominate the headlines and how winning the image battle helped win broader support in Washington power circles for the war. The scary images that filled the news dominated the headlines and chilled political opposition. A number of leading Democrats, including presidential aspirants, such as John Kerry (2004) and Hillary Clinton (2008), made strategic decisions to support the war, and then found themselves compromised in their future efforts to oppose it.

Long after the war failed its advertised promise of an easy victory with an open-armed welcome from liberated Iraqi citizens, Americans still had only dim understandings about what happened and why. How was it, for example, that the invasion and occupation of Iraq became part of the war on terror? There were early news reports that the Central Intelligence Agency (CIA) had found no clear link between Saddam Hussein and the al-Qaeda network that orchestrated the events of 9/11. To the contrary, Osama bin Laden had branded Saddam's secular regime a threat to Islamic fundamentalism. Far more evidence linked al-Qaeda with backers in Saudi Arabia.[45] However, the Saudis were official allies of the United States, and their links to 9/11 were displaced in the mainstream news by the single-minded focus on Iraq. With few opposition voices appearing in the news, the war was soon on.

The news was filled with breathless battlefield accounts from reporters embedded in military units. Images of Saddam's statue toppling in Baghdad overshadowed reports that the Bush administration had distorted the case it presented. The few news stories that challenged Saddam's connection to the terrorist attacks of 9/11 or questioned whether he was developing nuclear weapons could not compete for public attention with the daily spin of the administration. On May 1, 2003, President George W. Bush made his dramatic tailhook landing on the aircraft carrier *Abraham Lincoln* to declare "mission accomplished." That "top gun" moment was a media event supreme—designed to capture huge news audiences for the president's ringing sound bite: "The battle of Iraq is one victory in a war on terror that began on September 11, 2001, and still goes on."[46]

Months turned into years, and the battle of Iraq was still going. Triumphal media images became threatened by a civil war that soon took more American lives than the invasion itself, and Iraqi civilian casualties numbered many times the human loss of the 9/11 attacks. Meanwhile, the war in Afghanistan turned ugly, with the resurgence of the Taliban and the growing instability in neighboring Pakistan. In response, the administration stepped up its news management operation, questioning the patriotism of critics and the negativity of the media and continuously hammering home the claim that "Iraq has become the central front on the war against terror."[47]

Beyond the loose facts and the foggy justification for the war, one thing became clear afterward: The battle for control of news images was the most important factor in shaping support both for the war and for the Bush administration's capacity to govern effectively for several more years after the invasion. The first media victory was predictably inside the beltway, among elected officials, where opinion matters most. As the government dominated the media imagery, opponents shrank from challenging the war. The few who spoke out were relegated to the back news pages, if reported at all. From the viewpoint of the mainstream press, they were minority voices on the losing side of a policy decision. The second line of symbolic victory was over the

American public, who grew increasingly attentive to an issue as big as waging war against an alleged terrorist nation.

With so few opposition voices in the news, who and what were the American people to believe? When administration dominance of news was at its peak around the time of the invasion in early 2003, fully 69 percent of the public felt that an Iraq connection to 9/11 was at least somewhat likely. Thanks to continuing administration domination of the news, solid majorities of Americans continued to believe that Iraq had something to do with the events of 9/11 long after facts to the contrary had come to light.[48] And close to a majority (47 percent) substantially overestimated levels of European public support for the U.S. invasion. In fact, popular support among all major U.S. allies was extremely low—even in Britain, which participated in the invasion and occupation.

The misinformation among Americans was considerable, with 24 percent of those polled believing that weapons of mass destruction had been found in Iraq even after U.S. military teams had searched the country to no avail. Although support for the war finally began to decline amid the growing post-invasion chaos and evidence of poor planning on the part of the administration, fully 41 percent continued to believe that Saddam had something to do with al-Qaeda, reflecting the continuing newsmaking power of prominent members of the administration.[49]

When Barack Obama took charge of the wars in Iraq and Afghanistan, he made the fateful choice to escalate the Afghan conflict, much to the dismay of many Americans who began to withdraw support for the costly and lengthy conflicts at a time of economic crisis at home. Following a troop escalation, the unpleasant sacking of the general who engineered it, and discouraging reports from the front, polls showed only 26 percent of Americans thought the U.S. was winning the Afghan conflict.[50] Why does it seem so much easier to manage the news with the aim of selling policies than to use the news to explore the credibility of the policies in the first place? Why is it so often that when critics look back on policy failures, they find that they were so poorly deliberated in public, and based on such incomplete or inaccurate evidence?

WHAT ABOUT EVIDENCE? AN UNCOMFORTABLE TRUTH ABOUT JOURNALISM

Like the reporting on the run up to the Iraq War, many politically heated stories raise troubling questions about what journalists should do when officials say things that are inconsistent with available evidence to the contrary. In the case of selling the war, the question is whether one side of a story should be made so dominant just because other officials in government are afraid or unwilling to challenge it. There are other variations on this dilemma. What if there are two sides to a story being debated within official circles of power, but one is likely not true? For example, many years after the scientific community had reached consensus that global warming was accelerating due to human causes, the Bush administration rejected that consensus and got its doubting views into the headlines. This happened despite statements by administration officials that they had been ordered to change scientific reports commissioned by the government to bring them in line with the administration position.[51]

Should both sides of a story be covered when one is likely not true? Should a story be allowed to become one-sided when there is evidence to challenge it, but powerful officials are simply unwilling to voice that evidence? Either way, American journalism does not have easy answers to these important questions. Finding an answer would require freeing the press from its dependence on government and powerful officials as its reference on reality.

Why has the American press become caught in this curious dependence on what those in power say about reality? I have termed this reporting pattern *indexing*, which refers to the tendency of mainstream news organizations to index or adjust the range of viewpoints in a story to the dominant viewpoints of those in political institutions who are perceived to have enough power to affect the outcome of the situation.[52] This curious reporting system, as explained further in Chapter 5, is a result of the longstanding commitment of the mainstream press to cling to a norm of balance, fairness or objectivity. If the journalists seek to appear objective or balanced, they cannot become involved in interpreting or telling the audience what is going on. Rather, journalists must channel views of reality through external sources, and the safest sources are those who have the power to shape political outcomes. (The advent of more politically explicit news accompanied by the distortion of facts to fit preferred views of reality will be discussed in the next chapter.)

What this reporting system means is that when government is working well, and elected representatives are offering competing alternatives for solving policy problems, the news is filled with competing views that may help engaged citizens think critically about decisions facing the nation. On the other hand, if certain factions in power promote deceptive or untruthful spin in the service of powerful interests, then those ideas also become presented as equally valid alongside more plausible versions of events. Similarly, if political parties decide not to raise doubts about bad ideas—either because they are not easy to explain to inattentive publics, or they might be rejected by emotionally aroused publics—then bad ideas become the dominant news frames. If journalists introduced independent evidence to balance such stories they would be accused of bias or of campaigning for their own agendas. And so, spin rules.

Consider a couple of cases in point. Even though few doubts existed in the scientific community about the seriousness or the clear human causes of global warming, the Republican Party generally adopted a public relations strategy during the early 2000s based on raising doubts about the scientific consensus. The result was that for a critical decade when much of the rest of the world was taking action to combat global warming, the news in the U.S. was indexed in a way that "balanced" those who urged reducing dependence on carbon fuels with another side to the story claiming that the science on the matter was not settled. (This episode is discussed in more detail in the case study in Chapter 4). To return to the example of the war, when the Democratic Party decided not to challenge a then-popular President Bush following 9/11 on the claim that Iraq was implicated in the terrorism attacks, the resulting news was dominated by the administration PR campaign to sell the war. The imbalance in this case again reflected indexing: The mainstream press had no other political power reference point to anchor a sustained challenge to the administration side of the story.

The legacy of the Iraq War raises an uncomfortable truth about the U.S. news system. While many Americans are uninformed because they are inattentive to the news, it may also be the case that paying attention to deceptive news can result in misinformation. In the case of Iraq, some news organizations did a better job than others in helping their audiences critically assess government claims about the war, but most who followed the news from most outlets came away misinformed by the dominant spin. For example, even after claims about weapons of mass destruction and Iraqi links to al-Qaeda had been seriously challenged by sources outside the administration, 80 percent of the viewers of FOX *News* still shared one or more of these factual inaccuracies about the war, while only 23 percent of Public Broadcasting Service (PBS) and National Public Radio (NPR) audiences were similarly mistaken. Other mainstream news sources misinformed people at rates closer to FOX than NPR, with CBS at 71 percent, ABC at 61 percent, NBC at 55 percent, and CNN at 55 percent—the average of print news sources had a reader misperception rate of 47 percent.[53]

Even the best news organizations left large numbers of people misinformed. It also appears that the more mainstream or popular news organizations were least likely to challenge government propaganda. The point here is not that journalists were making up facts but that most news organizations simply emphasized what powerful official sources told them, even though other credible sources were available to challenge those accounts of reality.

These confusions of reality and power may undermine the credibility of news for many citizens. As journalists become spun by officials and join the establishment by sharing often short-lived conventional wisdoms, power becomes the definer of truth. Instead of having a news system that speaks truth to power, the dictates of power produce a news product that comedian Stephen Colbert has referred to as "truthiness."

CASE STUDY

The "Truthiness" About News

Comedian Stephen Colbert coined the term *truthiness* to refer to the many political statements that officials introduce into the news that are not entirely consistent with available evidence—evidence that journalists often have trouble introducing independently unless other officials contest the spurious claims. Thus, the news often conveys mainly the trappings of truth: a sincere sense of conviction and all the authoritativeness that earnest officials and journalists can provide. Yet important elements of reality often seem to be missing. This appearance of truth while important evidence is left out of the picture is "truthiness." The missing reality bits make it possible for political comics like Colbert and Jon Stewart to point out the frequent political follies that officials offer as serious news.

Behind the production of journalistic truthiness is the implicit recognition by powerful figures and their media advisors that what they say in the news generally cannot be challenged effectively by journalists unless they find another Washington source of comparable power or status to do the job. This confusion of power and credibility can lead some politicians to take considerable liberties with the truth in pursuit of strong convictions.

The point here is not that most journalists do not know any better, or do not try to set the record straight. Indeed, many journalists do not take this lying down. As a result, the interplay of press and politicians is often testy and adversarial. The game at press conferences and interviews often becomes one of trying to get officials to reconcile their spin with observable realities. Consider a revealing moment during an interview between Ron Suskind, a prominent journalist, and a senior presidential advisor who grew tired of the cat and mouse game of journalists trying to get him to admit to inconsistencies in the official script. The official suddenly dismissed the journalist as belonging to the "reality-based community." Suskind recalls the revealing moment in these terms:

> The aide said that guys like me were "in what we call the reality-based community," which he defined as people who "believe that solutions emerge from your judicious study of discernible reality." I nodded and murmured something about enlightenment principles and empiricism. He cut me off. "That's not the way the world really works anymore," he continued. "We're an empire now, and when we act, we create our own reality. And while you're studying that reality—judiciously, as you will—we'll act again, creating other new realities, which you can study too, and that's how things will sort out. We're history's actors . . . and you, all of you, will be left to just study what we do."[54]

It is fortunate for democracy that politics still attracts many people of goodwill. But even goodwill may become blinded by strong convictions that block out the reality of other views. In these moments, the press seems unable to make independent corrections for political blindness. Consider an exchange between veteran journalist Ted Koppel and Jon Stewart during an interview on ABC's *Nightline* program. Stewart described a typical news interview format in which journalists preside between two sides that often miss larger realities:

> . . . she throws out her figures from the Heritage Foundation and she throws her figures from the Brookings Institute, and the anchor, who should be the arbiter of the truth says, "Thank you both very much. That was really interesting." No, it wasn't! That was Coke and Pepsi talking about beverage truth. And that game is what has, I think, caused people to go, "I'm not watching this."[55]

As Dannagal Young points out in her analysis of this interview, ". . . Stewart explicitly rejects the premise that the journalist's role is to present opposing sets of facts from

Continued

official sources. Instead, he argues that ignoring the underlying truth-value of those 'facts' denies viewers an important critical analysis of political life, and instead the journalist should act as an 'arbiter of the truth.' "[56] As the interview continued, Koppel seemed a bit wistful about the freedom that comedy gives Stewart to point out deception, or BS as Koppel put it, yet he firmly denied that it was the role of journalists to issue such corrections:

KOPPEL: Those who watch you say at least when I'm watching Jon, he can use humor to say, "BS." You know, "That's a crock."

STEWART: But that's always been the case . . . Satire has always. . . .

KOPPEL: Okay, but I can't do that.

STEWART: No. But you *can* say that's BS. You don't need humor to do it, because you have what I wish I had—which is credibility, and gravitas. This is interesting stuff. And it's all part of the discussion, and I think it's a good discussion to have, but I also think that it's important to take a more critical look. Don't you think?

KOPPEL: No.[57]

Dannagal Young argues that this greater capacity to get at the truth—or at least point out deception and spin—makes comedy "the new journalism." Meanwhile, journalists remain trapped in a system that is largely of their own making. This odd evolution of a mainstream news system that requires official sourcing to sustain critical or challenging points of view was the subject of one of Stephen Colbert's most controversial comedy routines when he addressed the annual dinner of the national press club, an insider affair that had become one of the top A ticket events in Washington due to the attendance of the elite press corps and many powerful politicians, generally including the president. Colbert first took on President Bush, and then the press.

. . . ladies and gentlemen of the press corps, Madame First Lady, Mr. President, my name is Stephen Colbert, and tonight it is my privilege to celebrate this president, 'cause we're not so different, he and I. We both get it. Guys like us, we're not some brainiacs on the nerd patrol. We're not members of the factinista. We go straight from the gut. Right, sir?. . . .

And as excited as I am to be here with the President, I am appalled to be surrounded by the liberal media that is destroying America, with the exception of FOX News. FOX News gives you both sides of every story: the President's side, and the Vice President's side.

But the rest of you, what are you thinking? Reporting on NSA wiretapping or secret prisons in Eastern Europe? Those things are secret for a very important reason: they're super-depressing. . . .

Over the last five years you people were so good, over tax cuts, WMD intelligence, the effect of global warming. We Americans didn't want to know, and you had the courtesy not to try to find out. Those were good times, as far as we knew.

But, listen, let's review the rules. Here's how it works. The President makes decisions. He's the decider. The press secretary announces those decisions, and you people of the press type those decisions down. Make, announce, type. Just put 'em through a spell check and go home. Get to know your family again. Make love to your wife.

Write that novel you got kicking around in your head. You know, the one about the intrepid Washington reporter with the courage to stand up to the administration? You know, fiction![58]

Colbert may have hit the mark too closely, as neither the president nor many reporters in the audience seemed to be laughing as the event was aired on CSPAN. The *Washington Post* later panned the performance, saying that Colbert "fell flat." However, Frank Rich, a former media critic and now a political columnist for the *New York Times*, guessed that Colbert fell flat not because he was rude to the president, but "His real sin was to be rude to the capital press corps, whom he caricatured as stenographers. Though most of the Washington audience failed to find the joke funny, Americans elsewhere, having paid a heavy price for the press's failure to challenge the White House propaganda about Iraq, laughed until it hurt."[59] As Rich noted, even as the national press failed to see its humor, the performance spread virally on the Internet, becoming an overnight sensation on YouTube, and one of the most popular iPod downloads.

Having dismissed this moment of painful insight, the press club vowed not to repeat its embarrassment, and invited comedian Rich Little to do the routine the following year. Little had been popular on television in the 1970s. Frank Rich described Little and his performance as ". . . an apolitical nightclub has-been (who) was a ludicrously tone-deaf flop."[60]

The two-year run of fawning attitude by the national press club toward power led the *New York Times* to decide to stay away from future dinners. However, the more general problem of truthiness remained unaddressed by journalists and managers at most mainstream news organizations. As Frank Rich concluded, ". . . it's far from clear that the entire profession yet understands why it has lost the public's faith."[61]

A DEFINITION OF NEWS

The impact of news on the quality of democracy is always changing. Political communication scholar Bruce Bimber makes a bold assertion about power in American politics: that it is biased toward those with the best command of political information.[62] Bimber follows this claim by tracing the development of American democracy from *The Federalist* to the present day in terms of information regimes. The first great expansion of democratic participation came with the rise of a national mail system that carried many newspapers and publications, perhaps making the U.S. Post Office the most important institution for expanding democracy in the early American republic.[63] If we flash forward to the late twentieth century, American democracy evolved through the information regime of the mass media, which is now in its late stages. Technologies, such as broadcast television and satellite communication enabled Americans to share common experiences that affected the entire nation. Politicians in the mass media age became experts at "going public" by using the media to deliver messages directly to large audiences.[64]

As the mass media information regime begins to erode, many observers worry that multiplying media niches may produce individuals who become informed just about issues and perspectives that suit their personal lifestyles and beliefs. Can a democracy with so many exclusive, personalized media realities have coherent policy discussions, much less, share a common purpose?[65] At the very least, we should bring the news down to earth and recognize that it is continually changing, and that these changes are shaped by a chaotic set of factors that may not engineer an information product with the best interests of democracy in mind.

How do the somewhat chaotic interactions among political actors, publics, and the press affect the way we define the news? As a starting point, it makes sense to adopt a simple definition of political news as:

- What newsmakers (politicians and other political actors) promote as timely, important, or interesting . . .
- from which news organizations select, narrate, and package . . .
- for delivery to people who consume and use it in various ways from entertainment to political action.

Doris Graber suggests that news is not just any information, or even the most important information, about the world; rather, the news tends to contain information that is *timely,* often *sensational* (scandals, violence, and human drama frequently dominate the news), and *familiar* (stories often drawing on familiar people or life experiences that give even distant events a close-to-home feeling).[66] In this view, the news is constructed through the constantly changing interactions of journalists, politicians, and people seeking ends that are sometimes similar and sometimes very different. While journalists are often regarded as "gatekeepers" who screen information according to its truth and importance, it is important to recognize the impact of power and influence on this gatekeeping process. Above all, it helps to notice that the news gates open and close differently depending on how power balances are struck on different issues at different times.

GATEKEEPING: WHO AND WHAT MAKE THE NEWS

Understanding who makes the news begins with recognizing that each news story can contain only a selection of the voices, facts, and organizing ideas that might be involved in understanding a particular issue or event. *Gatekeeping* is a term often used to refer to *whose voices and what messages get into the news.* Journalists and, more important, their news organizations make choices about what to cover and how to report it. Some stories may feature statements by ordinary citizen-activists and interest organizations, whereas most news reports leave most of the talking to government officials. Gatekeeping decisions are made only in part by individual journalists. In a big story, many of these decisions are made directly by editors and executives in news organizations. These organization-level decisions, in turn, are influenced by economic pressures, audience reactions, and a host of other considerations that all go into the construction of the daily news.

In an ideal world, journalists might find the sources representing the most insightful and diverse points of view. These ideal news sources would try to engage their opponents in convincing debate aimed at helping the public decide the best course of action. And the ideal public would want to take the time to learn about different approaches to important social issues. In the real world, many factors work against these ideals of democracy, from business pressures in news organizations to lazy citizens and deceptive politicians.

For all of its flaws, the American information system can produce impressive levels of good information and public deliberation, leading publics and policymakers to helpful understandings of complex social problems.[67] Issues receiving such rich news deliberations most often tend to be personal matters, from moral values to jobs and taxes, over which there is considerable public conflict. Sociologist William Gamson cites abortion as an issue that has attained impressive levels of information quality and diversity of public viewpoints, resulting in sophisticated public opinion responses to complex policy questions.[68] Abortion is also one of those political issues that has spilled outside the bounds of news, becoming the subject of movies and television programs, church sermons, talk shows, and conversations among friends. On many other issues, however, the public is often in the dark. Gamson cites a continuum of other issues that tend to be less citizen-friendly than abortion. In his view, part of what marks the difference between high- and low-citizen involvement is whether the news reports grassroots collective citizen action surrounding issues, a factor that encourages other citizens to get involved by seeing an issue from the standpoint of ordinary people who are concerned about it.[69]

The presence or absence of citizen voices depends largely on whether journalists find powerful government officials or established interests that endorse those grassroots views. As noted earlier, I have coined the term *indexing* to refer to the journalistic practice of opening or closing the news gates to a broad or narrower range of views according to levels of public conflict among the powerful officials and established interests involved in making decisions about an issue. When open conflict breaks out among key decision makers (e.g., Congress vs. the president on energy policy), the news gates will open to broader social voices, from grassroots activists to interest organizations.[70]

Indexing mainly helps us understand how the news organizes the policy world of legislation, executive action, court decisions, and issue debates. When breaking events, crises, or dramatic scandals occur, more fluid news patterns may develop—with the news becoming a national story teller, cultural interpreter, and sometimes even cheerleader for human triumphs over adversity. For example, in the days immediately following 9/11, the news replayed the images of a plane hitting the World Trade Center, the towers collapsing, brave rescue workers trying to save lives, and a nation grieving. In such rare moments, the news becomes a collective screen on which grand images of fear, loss, grief, patriotism, and hope are projected. News organizations produced dramatic stories of a people under siege, responding bravely, and rising from the ashes to deal with the terrorist challenge. Within days, however, the government began to act decisively in waging war and passing new domestic security laws, and the news returned to its familiar focus on government. Indexing comes in at this point to help explain the "truthiness" problem described earlier in the selling of the Iraq war. Because this implicit journalism rule anchors mainstream news coverage around what powerful decision-makers are saying, the result is not always be the most helpful or truthful versions of reality. Indeed, much of what officials say is aimed at creating pre-conceived political realities, reminding us what the role of an independent press might be in a democracy: to expose fateful decisions, such as those surrounding the wars in Iraq and Afghanistan to more enlightening public discussion before they occur.

The centrality of spin in the gatekeeping process opens the news to loss of confidence on the part of citizens along with ridicule by comedians. Stories easily spill beyond the news and into entertainment programming in ways that seem to further diminish the capacity of the press to authoritatively develop perspectives on what is important and why it matters. Communication scholars Michael Delli Carpini and Bruce Williams suggest that for many stories, the news has become a secondary information source behind TV dramas or late-night comedy monologues. They go so far as to suggest that the once-hallowed gatekeeping function of the news may be dissolving as politics spills outside the bounds of news and throughout other media formats that are better suited to telling dramatic and entertaining stories.[71] In a new work, these authors describe the end of the mass media television-centered news regime, and the rise of a much more chaotic public information order. In their view, the new order gives rise to the serious question, "Is there a difference between Tina Fey and Katie Couric?"[72] Despite its increasingly chaotic state, the news remains the core of our political information system. It is important to understand how this system works from the standpoints of its key actors: the press, politicians, and the people.

POLITICIANS, PRESS, AND THE PEOPLE

The three major actors in the news process—politicians, journalists, and the public—occupy quite different positions in both the political system and the communication system. Despite the differences in these actors' political worlds, each set of players contributes important elements to the construction of what we call news. The next sections introduce brief snapshots of the news politics of politicians, journalists, and the public.

Politicians: Spin Rules

From the standpoint of the politicians, businesses, and interest organizations that largely define politics in America, it has long been clear that power and influence depend on the control and strategic use of information. Despite growing public skepticism, newsmaking continues to be the most important way to get issues on the public agenda. The idea of *agenda setting* involves using the news to influence what the public regards as important for them to think about in society and politics.[73] Because of the importance of newsmaking for public relations, politicians from presidents and members of Congress to abortion activists, environmentalists, and antitax groups all have learned to *go public* by finding ways to take their political messages into the news.[74] An irony of mediated politics is that being well informed about the issues on the public agenda often means taking cues from familiar sources using the news to *frame* stories around their partisan viewpoints.[75] When this influence process works, the news not only tells people what to think about, it can also tell them what to think.[76]

The digital age may challenge these familiar governing patterns of mass media because people can more easily avoid common news channels and find personal sources on the issues that matter to them. This makes it more difficult for politicians to reach people with their messages, suggesting both greater information independence and greater difficulties for governing. When political actors have trouble reaching the public with their messages, they typically hire communication professionals, who often drive up the costs of democracy by designing sophisticated strategies for reaching ever-more elusive segments of the public.[77] Democratic theorist Robert Dahl pointed to the growing control of information by elites as the single greatest obstacle to the continued development of democratic citizen participation in the policy process.[78]

The Press: Commercialism and the Fall of Journalism

As noted in the opening of this chapter, news organizations are being driven into the ground by profit pressures from big corporations that now own most of them. Serious political reporting (so-called *hard* news) is being replaced by sensationalism, cheap lifestyle features, and "news you can use" (health, consumer, weather, fashion, and travel information). The tendency is to seek the most convenient and attention-grabbing stories, including the packaged information and news events produced by official spokespersons and communication consultants. These trends are discussed in detail in Chapter 7, but a few examples at this juncture illustrate how the old business model is collapsing around quality journalism.

When billionaire investor Sam Zell bought the Tribune Co. in 2007, he took control of the *Chicago Tribune*, the *Los Angeles Times*, and some 30 other papers and television stations. Making most of his fortune in real estate, Zell cheerfully admitted that he was not a media person, saying "I didn't make this investment for any other reason than economic gain."[79] One of the first targets he announced was to get rid of what he called "journalistic arrogance," which he described as treating readers like students rather than customers.[80] By 2010, the parent company of the *L.A. Times* was operating in bankruptcy, and the paper sold a "fake" front page to Disney for $700,000 to advertise a movie.[81]

This trend toward gutting serious (and more costly) journalism has been in motion for over 20 years, with devastating effects on the reporting of so-called "hard" news. Thomas Patterson defines hard news as news that contains some public policy content or other useful public information:

> Hard news refers to coverage of breaking events involving top leaders, major issues, or significant disruptions in the routines of daily life, such as an earthquake or airline disaster. Information about these events is presumably important to citizens' ability to understand and respond to the world of public affairs.[82]

In his study of more than 5,000 news stories between 1980 and 1999 on television and in newspapers and news magazines, stories without public policy content increased from 35 percent of all news to nearly half of all news. The areas of biggest soft-news increase were sensationalism in general (e.g., scandals), up from just over 20 percent to nearly 40 percent of all news; human interest, which rose from just over 10 percent to over 25 percent; and crime and disaster, which rose from 8 percent to 14 percent of all stories across the local, national, print, and broadcast news media.[83]

The time period between roughly 1980 and the end of the last century is important because it spans the period of greatest corporate media mergers and ownership consolidation in American history. Whether we look at what happened during this period nationally or locally, or in magazines, newspaper, radio, or TV, the information-to-infotainment trends are clear. There is less hard news and more soft news, and there is less reporting about government and politics and more about social chaos and personal drama. Consider just a few of these trends:

- Network TV newscasts between 1990 and 1998 more than doubled the time devoted to entertainment, disasters, accidents, and crime while reducing the coverage of environment, government activities, and international affairs to make the room.[84]
- International news on network TV declined from 45 percent of stories in the 1970s to 13.5 percent of stories in 1995.[85] (The exception to this trend, of course, is for international events that directly affect the personal lives of Americans. Thus, the terrorist acts of 9/11 and the wars in Afghanistan and Iraq have made big news in recent years.)
- Newspapers reduced international news coverage from more than 10 percent of nonadvertising space in the early 1970s to 6 percent in the early 1980s to less than 3 percent in the 1990s.[86]
- In the pages of weekly news magazines between 1985 and 1995, international news declined from 24 percent to 14 percent in *Time,* from 22 percent to 12 percent in *Newsweek,* and from 20 percent to 14 percent in *U.S. News & World Report.*[87] (Entertainment, celebrity stories, recreation, lifestyle, and sports filled the editorial space.)
- Overall, the network news, the cover stories of news magazines, and the front pages of major newspapers saw an increase from 15 percent to 43 percent between 1977 and 1997 in celebrity, scandal, gossip, and human-interest stories.[88]

What did *Time* put on its cover at century's end? Ellen DeGeneres, Steven Spielberg, Jewel, Bill Cosby, "What's Cool This Summer," "How Mood Drugs Work," and "The Most Fascinating People in America." When *Time* and *Newsweek* each ran covers on Princess Diana two weeks in a row following her death, they both had the biggest newsstand sales in their histories.[89] These trends have continued full speed into this century. Even as the 2008 presidential election campaign began to heat up, fully 22 percent of cable news was devoted to the death of celebrity Anna Nicole Smith, compared with 11 percent devoted to election coverage.[90]

Even as media executives like Sam Zell contend that this is what the consumer wants, evidence suggests that infotainment is simply a profitable short-term formula that exploits media corporations for big profits. Indeed, such formulas seem very shortsighted, as they are losing citizen interest in hard news and politics. Patterson concludes that these news trends help explain why the public is tuning out politics. The first step may be tuning out the news itself. When questioned about what kind of news they want, people picked examples of hard news by a margin of 2 to 1.[91] Later on, in Chapter 7, we will hear from news executives who maintain that what people say and what they watch are two different things. The fact remains, however, that news audiences are shrinking.

The People: Seeking Perspective in a Confusing Information Order

As people become bombarded with spin, and encouraged to choose sides in a confusing information system in which the press offers little perspective, it is not surprising that there are different information strategies that people may pursue. Many have simply tuned out. Others are tuning into points of view that agree with their political beliefs and values. And still others have begun to use the direct information channels offered by digital media. No matter the personal strategy, the incessant political spin machines are trying to find ways to get through to people.

As indicated earlier, tuning out the news has become a serious pattern, particularly among younger citizens. However, this does not mean that they are necessarily going without information. As social media now reach large numbers of people directly, political information may increasingly come from Facebook or Twitter. While some may object to the quality of that information, the degradation of the press system may not seem to offer better options. Moreover, as the mass media fragment into smaller niche channels, the news is frequently marketed to the lifestyles and political values of different audience segments. When people seek such self-confirming information, the news does not so much inform or challenge them as it affirms and reinforces what they already want to believe.[92]

Perhaps a more promising strategy for citizens is to join in the production and sharing of quality information using digital media to challenge those in power when the press proves unable to do so. As long as it remains relatively open, the Internet lowers the costs of political communication for many citizens who are learning how to communicate with others in cheap, fast, and effective ways. Communities of environmentalists, pro-choice and pro-life abortion groups, fair labor and fair trade campaigners, human rights workers, and computer privacy groups have mastered communicating with each other and with larger audiences using relatively cheap and available technologies. In the process, many interesting experiments are in progress that may reinvent the news and more generally improve how citizens communicate with each other and with leaders.

Given such diverse forces shaping the future of news and public information, it seems reasonable to ask how we might promote the best possible outcomes for democracy. Many Americans seem to live with the false sense of security that the First Amendment and the Constitution will somehow guarantee a quality press. The chaotic forces outlined in this chapter suggest that there is no overarching plan to keep an ideal democratic information system in order. Even as media owners dismantle news organizations and diminish the quality of journalism, they hide behind the First Amendment to defend against attempts by concerned citizen groups to make them behave more responsibly. The irony of this is that the First Amendment with its protections for press freedom was intended to enable an independent press to stand up to government power. While press freedom remains a crucial protection in democracy, it has also become a shield for corporate media to avoid social responsibility.

THE FIRST AMENDMENT: WHY FREE SPEECH DOES NOT GUARANTEE GOOD INFORMATION

Consider the most shocking example of good news gone bad: local TV news. Paul Klite (who died several years ago) was one of the most prominent critics of the "if it bleeds, it leads" editorial philosophy that guides most local news. Klite was a former radio talk show host and founder of Rocky Mountain Media Watch. The Media Watch, based in Denver, often made news in high-quality outlets with its "mayhem index" that measured the degree to which local news is filled with scary images of crime, accidents, fires, drugs, gangs, child molesting, and other forms of abuse, and the general breakdown of society. The local news mayhem index rose to such an unacceptable level that Media Watch decided to file a petition in 1998 with the Federal Communications Commission (FCC) to deny licenses to four Denver stations on grounds that their local news was "toxic" to citizens. One Denver station (KMGH, the ABC affiliate) scored a stunning 60 percent of its editorial content in the mayhem category. Unfortunately, Denver is fairly typical of national trends. Media Watch asserts that local news across the nation is "severely unbalanced, with excessive coverage of violent topics and trivial events," creating "a public health issue" that "goes beyond bad journalism."[93]

Had local news become toxic to community values and democracy? Here are some trends. You decide:

- A national study of local news by the Center for Media and Public Affairs found that crime dominated most programs and that after removing the combination of crime, weather, accidents, disasters, other soft news, and sports, only 5 minutes and 40 seconds remained out of the 24 minutes and 20 seconds of noncommercial news time for coverage of government, health, foreign affairs, education, science, and the environment.[94] Hard news got less time than commercials.
- Trends in increased violent-crime news cannot be explained as reflections of actual rates of crime in society. On the contrary, the last big wave of crime news went up as actual crime declined. In the period from 1990 through 1998, for example, the number of crime stories broadcast annually on the NBC, CBS, and ABC evening news programs rose from 542 to 1,392, during a time in which the actual levels of most violent crimes dropped significantly in society.[95] If we look just at news about murder on the national networks, the number of murder stories increased by 700 percent between 1993 and 1996, a period in which the murder rate in society actually declined by 20 percent.[96]
- According to a national survey, nearly two-thirds of people get most of their views about crime from television, compared with just 20 percent from newspapers; 7 percent from radio; and less than 10 percent from friends, neighbors, coworkers, or personal experience.[97]

Does any of this matter? People who watch more news and "reality programs" (such as the crime/police shows discussed in Chapter 7) are significantly more likely to misjudge the seriousness of the crime problem and their own chances of being victims.[98] Fewer people felt safe in their neighborhoods (29%) in the late 1990s than in the early 1980s (44%), even though objective crime conditions warrant just the opposite feelings.[99]

Media critic Daniel Lazare summed up this tendency of news to grab the emotions of targeted audiences rather than focus on more genuine problems:

> Consumers grow picky about what they read and watch. Thus, for example, reporting about grim conditions in the inner cities, though perhaps only a few miles away from many readers and viewers, is hard to sell because middle class consumers who pick and choose their reality much as they choose their fashions can't relate to it; because poor people are a turn-off for advertisers and retailers; because a consumerist approach to the news means giving the consumer what he wants, not what he needs.[100]

The Media Watch allegations had touched on embarrassing but financially successful nationwide industry practices. Since the deregulatory bandwagon came to Washington in the 1980s, the FCC had been reluctant to intrude upon programming practices, but the timing of the Media Watch complaint was particularly unlikely to catch the FCC in a regulatory mood. Just prior to the Denver license hearings, media companies had been given the green light by Congress and the president to pursue business interests over social responsibility with passage of the landmark Telecommunications Act of 1996 (stay tuned to find out why this legislation mattered, discussed in Chapter 7). The FCC soundly rejected the Media Watch petition, wrapping itself, its ruling, and the entire broadcast industry in the hallowed language of free speech: "Journalistic or editorial discretion in the presentation of news and public information is the core concept of the First Amendment's free press guarantee."[101] National broadcaster groups and the Denver stations heralded this formulaic pronouncement as an important victory for free speech—a triumph over censorship and the intrusion of government in the newsroom. Many media and law scholars worry about using the Constitution to defend publicly licensed communication content that is produced with little political or social purpose beyond making money.[102] Media Watch argued that such high-minded defenses of bad news are part of the reason that we end up with news that "covers schoolyard shootings but not schools, train wrecks but not transportation, bloopers by local politicians but not local elections, and the latest murder but not dropping crime rates."[103]

The point here is not to weaken the First Amendment, but to identify business practices that may be weakening its spirit. Indeed one of the toughest questions for democracy is how far guarantees of press freedoms should go— particularly in protecting behaviors that may undermine the quality of democracy itself. It is important to acknowledge that the hallowed standing of free speech protects us from the threat of concerted government control of news— and this is a supremely important protection. Other important reasons for keeping constitutional protections strong include protecting a journalist's confidential sources. The lamentable fact is that because there is so little reporting these days that is threatening to the powers that be, news organizations seldom need First Amendment protection.

We may have built a national information fortress with just one wall, protecting the press from formal censorship yet leaving the information system vulnerable to degradation at the hands of poorly controlled business interests. Such interests, as any beginning economics student learns, have no intrinsic reason to embrace social responsibility beyond returning profits to their private investors.

THE FRAGILE LINK BETWEEN NEWS AND DEMOCRACY

Why is something as important as public information left to the current turbulent mix of business profit imperatives, political spin techniques, and consumer tastes? This question would be less compelling if the news was not so important. Yet few things are as much a part of our lives as the news. Although it is tempting to assume that the news is somehow geared to the information needs of citizens, this chapter suggests a more disturbing possibility. There is currently little of an institutional check or monitoring system to guarantee that the news, as it has evolved, will serve the needs of American democracy. To the contrary, substantial evidence indicates that the news is largely a freewheeling entity shaped by a combination of commercial forces in the news business, technologies of communication perfected by politicians and their media consultants, and the tastes and personal entertainment habits of citizens. More than in any other advanced democracy, political information in the United States is manufactured and sold with few of the quality controls that even far less important household products have.

The forces acting on the news operate with little concerted regard for some larger public interest. There is a good deal of complacency about this information system. Consider, for example, the lack of much deliberate public debate and even less governmental inquiry about what kind of information the nation and its citizens need in order to best decide their political course. Despite (or perhaps because of) the faith in the free-press system in the United States, Americans have paid far less attention than other societies to the quality of democracy's most important product: political information.

How can one of the freest press systems in the world produce news that so often misses the political mark? It is hard for most Americans to imagine that freedom and competition do not automatically guarantee the best results. As a result of this deep cultural faith in unrestricted political communication, there is stunningly little public discussion about how to design a news and information system that might better suit the needs of democratic politics and citizen involvement. If we allow ourselves to imagine a different kind of news, there are a number of features that might be desirable from a democratic standpoint:

- Independent-issue agendas developed by each news organization would provide a more diverse information environment.
- Offering diverse voices and viewpoints from credible sources outside of official circles could reduce the "inside the beltway' syndrome—the gap that ordinary people often feel separates them from the politicians and political insiders who dominate news content.
- More explanation of how political decisions are reached, and how to connect with the interest organizations involved, might help people become engaged.
- More historical context would help establish the origins of problems in the news and limit the ability of politicians to reinvent history to suit their purposes.
- More coverage of political citizen-activists would help ordinary people see paths to personal involvement and hear challenging perspectives that might help them evaluate official spin more critically.
- Better use of interactive technologies could link news audiences to each other and to civic organizations to learn more about issues and take effective action.

A goal of this book is to contribute to such a discussion about improving what might emerge from this era of change by explaining how the current news system has evolved: how news is produced and sold, how it is shaped by political actors, how it is reported by journalists and news organizations, and how it is used by citizens. When this larger news picture is considered, problems such as the fabled ideological bias of reporters become the least of the information problems faced by citizens.

NOTES

1. Paul Starr, *The Creation of the Media: Political Origins of Modern Communications* (New York: Basic Books, 2004).
2. See Robert W. McChesney and John Nichols, *The Death and Life of American Journalism: The Media Revolution that Will Begin the World Again* (Philadelphia: First Nation Books-Perseus, 2010).
3. An excellent overview of the crisis is presented in McChesney and Nichols, Chapter 1.
4. Leonard Downie Jr. and Michael Schudson, "The Reconstruction of American Journalism," *Columbia Journalism Review* (November/December 2009): 32.
5. American Society of Newspaper Editors report on its 2010 survey of the industry. April 10, 2010. http://asne.org/annual_conference/conference_news/articleid/763/decline-in-newsroom-jobs-slows.aspx. Accessed July 22, 2010.
6. See, among others: Alex S. Jones, *Losing the News: The Future of the News that Feeds Democracy* (New York: Oxford University Press, 2009); McChesney and Nichols, *The Death and Life of American Journalism*; and Downie Jr. and Schudson, "The Reconstruction of American Journalism."
7. Paul Gronke and Timothy E. Cook, "Disdaining the Media? Americans' Changing Attitudes Toward the News," *Political Communication* 24, no. 3 (2007): 259–281.
8. See McChesney and Nichols, *The Death and Life of American Journalism*; Downie Jr. and Schudson, "The Reconstruction of American Journalism."
9. See W. Lance Bennett, Regina G. Lawrence, and Steven Livingston, *When the Press Fails: Political Power and the News Media from Iraq to Katrina* (Chicago: University of Chicago Press, 2007).
10. Pew Research Center Project for Excellence in Journalism. "How News Happens: A Study of the News Ecosystem of One American City." January 11, 2010. www.journalism.org/analysis_report/how_news_happens. Accessed July 27, 2010.
11. Paul Starr, "Goodbye to the Age of Newspapers (Hello to a New Era of Corruption)," *The New Republic* (March 4, 2009).
12. See the report by Judicial Watch October 21, 2008: www.judicialwatch.org/news/2008/oct/new-judicial-watch-zogby-poll-82-7-american-say-political-corruption-played-major-role. Accessed July 27, 2010.
13. Transparency International, 2009 Corruption Perception Index. www.transparency.org/policy_research/surveys_indices/cpi/2009/cpi_2009_table. Accessed July 27, 2010.
14. Attributed to Stewart Brand at the first hacker's Conference in 1984. http://en.wikipedia.org/wiki/Information_wants_to_be_free. Accessed July 27, 2010.
15. Talk at the Joan Shorenstein Center, Kennedy School of Government, Harvard University. September 22, 2009. www.hks.harvard.edu/presspol/news_events/archive/2009/shirky_09-22-09.html. For a full transcript see: www.niemanlab.org/2009/09/clay-shirky-let-a-thousand-flowers-bloom-to-replace-newspapers-dont-build-a-paywall-around-a-public-good/. Accessed July 27, 2010.

16. Reuters, July 16, 2010. www.reuters.com/article/idUSTRE66F2B820100716. Accessed July 27, 2010.
17. www.facebook.com/notes/sarah-palin/peace-through-strength-and-american-pride-vs-enemy-centric-policy/403777543434. Accessed July 22, 2010.
18. Nick Wing and Erin Booth, "Sarah Palin's Foreign Policy Manifesto: Brought to You by Facebook." July 4, 2010. www.huffingtonpost.com/2010/07/04/sarah-palins-foreign-poli_n_632808.html. Accessed July 22, 2010.
19. Jesse Lichtenstein, "Digital Diplomacy," *The New York Times Magazine*, July 12, 2010. http://twitter.com/JaredCohen/status/16294548702. Accessed July 27, 2010.
20. http://twitter.com/JaredCohen/status/16294548702. Accessed July 27, 2010.
21. Kim Gattas, "Watching Hillary and the State Department by Tweet." *BBC News* July 4, 2010 http://news.bbc.co.uk/2/hi/world/us_and_canada/10502057.stm. Accessed July 22, 2010.
22. http://wikileaks.org/
23. Associated Press report posted in the *Huffington Post*, February 16, 2010. www.huffingtonpost.com/2010/02/16/neda-video-wins-polk-award_n_463378.html. Accessed August 1, 2010.
24. The anonymous person who shot the video gave it to someone else, who sent it via e-mail to several acquaintances outside Iran with the message "please let the world know." One of them, an Iranian expatriate in the Netherlands uploaded it to YouTube. Another in Britain posted it on her Facebook page. Soon there were hundreds of re-uploads of the video on sites around the world, and the process of making news through citizen content sharing on social networks made the story huge and impossible for conventional news organizations to ignore. See the story about the story in Brian Selter, "Honoring Citizen Journalists," *New York Times*, February 21, 2010. www.nytimes.com/2010/02/22/business/media/22polk.html. Accessed August 1, 2010.
25. Thomas E. Patterson, *Young People and News*. A Report from the Joan Shorenstein Center on the Press, Politics, and Public Policy. Kennedy School of Government, Harvard University. Prepared for the Carnegie-Knight Task Force on the Future of Journalism Education. July 2007.
26. See Martin P. Wattenberg, *Is Voting for Young People?* (New York: Pearson/Longman, 2008).
27. Ibid., 5.
28. http://gopleader.gov/News/DocumentSingle.aspx?DocumentID=139131.
29. One of hundreds: www.youtube.com/watch?v=wJb-TrmJl80. Accessed August 1, 2010.
30. http://mediamatters.org/mmtv/200908060023. Accessed August 1, 2010.
31. http://videocafe.crooksandliars.com/david/david-brooks-limbaugh-health-care-rhetoric-i. Accessed August 1, 2010.
32. Jordan Fabian, "Death Panels May Be in Final Healthcare Reform Bill," *The Hill*, December 22, 2009. http://thehill.com/blogs/blog-briefing-room/news/73371-palin-death-panels-may-be-in-final-health-bill. Accessed August 1, 2010.
33. See Stephen Coleman, "From Big Brother to Big Brother: Two Faces of Interactive Engagement," in *Young Citizens and New Media: Learning and Democratic Engagement,* ed. Peter Dahlgren (New York: Routledge, 2008).
34. David Altheide and Robert P. Snow, *Media Worlds in the Post Journalism Era* (Hawthorne, NY: Aldine, 1991).
35. Susan Herbst, *Reading Public Opinion* (Chicago: University of Chicago Press, 1998).
36. Robert M. Entman, *Democracy without Citizens: Media and the Decay of American Politics* (New York: Cambridge University Press, 1989).

37. Matthew Baum, *Soft News Goes to War: Public Opinion and American Foreign Policy in the New Media Age* (Princeton, NJ: Princeton University Press, 2003).
38. Marc Peyser, "Jon Stewart: Seriously Funny," *Newsweek* (January 5, 2004): 70–77.
39. Dannagal G. Young and Russell M. Tisinger, "Dispelling Late Night Myths: News Consumption among Late-Night Comedy Viewers and the Predictors of Exposure to Various Late Night Shows," *Press/Politics* 11 (2006): 113–34.
40. Timothy Cook, *Governing with the News: The News Media as a Political Institution* (Chicago: University of Chicago Press, 1998).
41. William Schneider, remarks delivered at the conference on "The Clinton Presidency: Campaigning, Governing and the Psychology of Leadership," held at the Graduate Center, City University of New York, November 18–19, 1993. (A video of Schneider's talk is available from the university's PhD program in political science; attn: Stanley Renshon.)
42. Marvin Kalb, "Press-Politics and Improving the Public Dialogue," *Political Communication Report* 3 (June 1992): 1.
43. Timothy Cook, "Afterword: Political Values and Production Values," *Political Communication* 13 (October/December 1996): 469.
44. See Bennett, Lawrence, and Livingston, *When the Press Fails*.
45. For investigative reports that were generally not followed up by the mainstream press, see Seymour Hersh, "King's Ransom," *New Yorker* (October 22, 2002): 35–44; and "Selective Intelligence," *New Yorker* (May 12, 2003): 44–51. For an explanation of why, see Robert M. Entman, *Projections of Power: Framing News, Public Opinion, and U.S. Foreign Policy* (Chicago: University of Chicago Press, 2004).
46. For more detailed analysis of this, see the case study in Chapter 5 of this book. Also, W. Lance Bennett, "Operation Perfect Storm: The Press and the Iraq War," *Political Communication Report*, International Communication Association and American Political Science Association 13, no. 3 (Fall 2003).
47. David Stout, "U.S. Ignores Saddam at Its Peril, Cheney Says," *International Herald Tribune*, October 11–12, 2003: 4.
48. Based on national polls of 3,334 respondents taken from June–September 2003 and reported in Steven Kull, "Misperceptions, the Media, and the Iraq War," Report of the Program on International Policy Attitudes, University of Maryland, October 2, 2003.
49. Based on Harris poll of December 29, 2005, www.harrisinteractive.com/harris_poll/index.asp?PID5623.
50. Newsweek Poll (Princeton Survey Research Associates) June 2010. www.newsweek.com/2010/06/25/obama-s-approval-ratings-slump-in-latest-newsweek-poll.html. Accessed July 29, 2010.
51. See Bennett, Lawrence, and Livingston, *When the Press Fails*, ch. 5.
52. See W. Lance Bennett, "Toward a Theory of Press-State Relations in the United States," *Journal of Communication* 40 (Spring 1990): 103–27.
53. Kull, "Misperceptions, the Media, and the Iraq War."
54. Ron Suskind, "Faith, Certainty and the Presidency of George W. Bush," *New York Times*, October 17, 2004. www.nytimes.com/2004/10/17/magazine/17BUSH.html?ex=1255665600&en=890a96189e162076&ei=5090&partner=rssuserland. Accessed August 1, 2010.
55. *Nightline*, ABC, July 28, 2004; from Dannagal Young, "The Daily Show as the New Journalism" (paper presented at the Annual Meeting of the National Communication Association, Boston, November 17–20, 2005).

56. Young, "The Daily Show as the New Journalism."

57. *Nightline, ABC,* July 28, 2004; from Young.

58. Stephen Colbert at the 2006 White House Correspondents' Dinner, http://politicalhumor.about.com/od/stephencolbert/a/colbertbush.htm.

59. Frank Rich, "All the President's Press," *New York Times,* April 29, 2007.

60. Ibid.

61. Ibid.

62. Bruce Bimber, *Information and American Democracy: Technology in the Evolution of Political Power* (New York: Cambridge University Press, 2003).

63. See also, Richard R. John, *Spreading the News: The American Postal System from Franklin to Morse* (Cambridge, MA: Harvard University Press, 1995); and Timothy E. Cook, *Governing with the News: The News Media as a Political Institution* (Chicago: University of Chicago Press, 1998).

64. Samuel Kernell, *Going Public: New Strategies of Presidential Leadership,* 3rd ed. (Washington, DC: Congressional Quarterly Press, 1997).

65. See various perspectives on this in W. Lance Bennett and Robert M. Entman, eds., *Mediated Politics: Communication in the Future of Democracy* (New York: Cambridge University Press, 2001).

66. Doris Graber, *Mass Media and American Politics,* 3rd ed. (Washington, DC: Congressional Quarterly Press, 1989).

67. See Benjamin I. Page, *Who Deliberates?* (Chicago: University of Chicago Press, 1996).

68. William A. Gamson, "Promoting Political Engagement," in *Mediated Politics: Communication in the Future of Democracy,* eds. W. Lance Bennett and Robert M. Entman (New York: Cambridge University Press, 2001), 56–74. See also Myra M. Feree, William A. Gamson, Jurgen Gerhards, and Dieter Rucht, *Shaping Abortion Discourse: Democracy and the Public Sphere in Germany and the United States* (New York: Cambridge University Press, 2002).

69. These issues range from industrial collapse and the dislocation of workers on the low end of citizen-engagement images in news coverage to the controversy over nuclear power on the higher end. See Gamson, "Promoting Political Engagement."

70. See W. Lance Bennett, "Toward a Theory of Press-State Relations in the United States," *Journal of Communication* 40 (Spring 1990): 103–27.

71. Michael X. Delli Carpini and Bruce A. Williams, "Let Us Infotain You: Politics in the New Media Environment," in *Mediated Politics: Communication in the Future of Democracy,* eds. W. Lance Bennett and Robert M. Entman (New York: Cambridge University Press, 2001), 160–81.

72. Bruce A. Williams and Michael X. Delli Carpini, *After the News: Media Regimes and the New Information Environment* (Cambridge University Press, forthcoming).

73. Shanto Iyengar and Donald R. Kinder, *News That Matters* (Chicago: University of Chicago Press, 1987).

74. Kernell, *Going Public.*

75. John Zaller, *Nature and Origins of Mass Opinion* (New York: Cambridge University Press, 1992).

76. Shanto Iyengar, *Is Anyone Responsible?* (Chicago: University of Chicago Press, 1991).

77. For further discussion and illustration of this point, see W. Lance Bennett and Jarol B. Manheim, "The Big Spin: Strategic Communication and the Transformation of Pluralist Democracy," in *Mediated Politics: Communication in the Future of Democracy,* eds. W. Lance Bennett and Robert M. Entman (New York: Cambridge University Press, 2001), 279–98.

78. Robert Dahl, *Democracy and Its Critics* (New Haven, CT: Yale University Press, 1989).
79. Thomas S. Mulligan and James Rainey, "Zell Closes Deal for the Times," *Los Angeles Times,* December 21, 2007: A.27.
80. Ibid.
81. www.editorsweblog.org/newspaper/2010/03/los_angeles_times_runs_front_page_ad_for.php. Accessed July 30, 2010.
82. Thomas E. Patterson, "Doing Well and Doing Good" (Kennedy School of Government Working Paper No. 01-001, December 2000), page 3. Available at SSRN: http://ssrn.com/abstract=257395, doi:10.2139/ssrn.257395.
83. Ibid., 4.
84. Center for Media and Public Affairs study, www.cmpa.com/factoid/prevyrs.htm.
85. James F. Hoge Jr., "Foreign News: Who Gives a Damn?" *Columbia Journalism Review* (November/December 1997): 49.
86. Ibid.
87. Neil Hickey, "Money Lust: How Pressure for Profit Is Perverting Journalism," *Columbia Journalism Review* (July/August 1998): 32.
88. Ibid., 33.
89. Ibid., 32.
90. *Columbia Journalism Review* (May/June 2007): 15.
91. Hickey, "Money Lust," 7.
92. W. Lance Bennett and Shanto Iyengar, "A New Era of Minimal Effects? The Changing Foundations of Political Communication." *Journal of Communication* 58 (2008): 707–731.
93. Lawrence K. Grossman, "Does Local TV News Need a Nanny?" *Columbia Journalism Review* (May/June 1998): 33.
94. Ibid.
95. "Ticker," *Brill's Content* (July/August 1999): 143.
96. Center for Media and Public Affairs study reported in Richard Morin, "An Airwave of Crime: While TV News Coverage of Murders Has Soared—Feeding Public Fears—Crime Is Actually Down," *Washington Post National Weekly Edition* (August 18, 1997): 34.
97. Ibid.
98. See Mark Fishman and Grey Cavender, eds., *Entertaining Crime: Television Reality Programs* (New York: Aldine de Gruyter, 1998).
99. Morin, "An Airwave of Crime," 34.
100. Daniel Lazare, "The Upside to a Downturn," *Columbia Journalism Review* (May/June 1991): 56.
101. Quoted in James Brooke, "The F.C.C. Supports TV News as Free Speech," *New York Times* (May 3, 1998): 27.
102. Robert McChesney, *Rich Media, Poor Democracy: Communication Politics in Dubious Times* (Urbana: University of Illinois Press, 1999).
103. Grossman, "Does Local TV News Need a Nanny?" 33.

News Stories
Four Information Biases That Matter

It is a writer's obligation to impose narrative. Everyone does this. Every time you take a lump of material and turn it into something you are imposing a narrative. It's a writer's obligation to do this. And, by the same token, it is apparently a journalist's obligation to pretend that he never does anything of the sort. The journalist claims to believe that the narrative emerges from the lump of material, rises up and smacks you in the face like marsh gas.

—Nora Ephron

As much as we talk about ideology and competence, our judgment of presidents doesn't hinge on either of these things in isolation. What matters is the perception—or perhaps the illusion—that one is shaping events, rather than being shaped by them. The modern presidency, like the old "Get Smart" series, is about chaos versus control.

—Matt Bai

. . . a year into his presidency, Mr. Obama has lost control of his political narrative, his ability to define the story of his presidency on his own terms.

—Richard Stevenson

The news that Barack Obama won the 2008 presidential election might have come as a surprise to anyone who followed the early campaign coverage closely. Before a single primary vote had been cast, Hillary Clinton had practically been declared the winner by the national press corps—not just winner of the Democratic nomination, but the White House as well. *Saturday Night Live* even ran a skit of a candidate debate in which the host journalist told the other candidates that they could be excused because Hillary had already been declared the winner by the press. The premise for the Clinton victory story was a barrage of early national polling conducted when few voters had formed solid impressions. When Clinton lost the first primary contest in Iowa, her fall from frontrunner status made for the next dramatic story: Clinton campaign in trouble. And so the election news drama goes. . . .

As every American knows, the horse race is the classic election narrative that drives reporters to speculate about winners and losers throughout the campaign (while driving out a lot of other content that might be more useful to voters trying to make up their minds). The horse race story arose well before the modern press system—in the time of Andrew Jackson when election communication was spread along the frontier through song and tall tales.[1] With the advent of scientific polling and the demand for 24/7 news—even when there isn't any—the horse race has turned into a tired journalistic formula that often obscures deeper understanding of the candidate issues and voter concerns. Journalists probably know that it is distracting and frequently misleading, but as National Public Radio analyst Cokie Roberts put it in one of her analyses of the 2008 contest: "Even the pollsters tell you not to focus on the horse-race and look at the other things . . . but the horse-race is irresistible."[2]

If the horse race is the grand campaign narrative, each election displays its own collection of more personal stories about candidates that often seem somehow out of tune with events themselves. Many stories come from campaign operatives working to raise doubts about the patriotism, character, or personal histories of the opponent. The Tea Party movement surrounding the health care battle of 2009–2010 spilled into the 2010 election, echoing claims that supporters of the national legislation were alternately socialists or Nazis who favored death panels that could kill granny (see the case study in this chapter). Even when such stories become heated and extreme, they are so much a part of the news that when campaign press strategists and handlers are not busy feeding the news corps, journalists may take up the slack by refueling old narratives or speculating about new ones.

Elements of drama and playful public theater keep politics from becoming dulled by scripted performances and mind numbing details of policy issues. However, many critics contend that the fragmenting 24/7 media environment that leads media companies to compete desperately for the distracted attention of audiences has resulted in journalism losing control over balance and judgment about what really matters. A blog post by a prominent media critic put it clearly: "Media's Myopic Obsession with Campaign Narratives over Events of Real Significance Does a Disservice to the Public."[3] Another commentator scolded journalists for their role in keeping outlandish narratives in play, while sacrificing their hallowed role as referees and balancers of national political communication: ". . . what I think would really be heroic is if commentators with any pretensions left of journalism spent more energy telling us how a crucial piece of legislation might affect American life and public policy than on how the president might most effectively sell it to the skeptical sheeple. At least that's my narrative, and I'm sticking to it."[4]

In thinking about this, we need to be mindful that there is nothing inherently wrong with telling stories—far from it. Elections may be our most important national storytelling ritual, a time when we remind ourselves, with the help of candidates, what we stand for as a people, what our challenges are, where the next chapter of the national saga is heading, and who may best lead us there. But what happens when journalists, not candidates, do more of the storytelling, or when journalists report the most outlandish things they can find over more centrist and content? One possibility is that the publics who seek rational discussion tune out, while those seeking entertainment and theater—and those promoting extreme positions—tune in.

It is interesting that in this time when they seem to be losing control over creating balance in news narratives, journalists also seem to have become keenly aware of the dominance of narrative in news. Yet they often regard stories as somehow independent of their reporting them (to echo Nora Ephron's words above). As a result, they seem to be chasing their own tales, so to speak. Discussions on journalistic blogs and even in mainstream news reporting often focus on the importance of having a clear narrative for governing. As a result, it becomes very hard to govern after losing control of one's narrative, as *New York Times* reporter Richard Stevenson suggests happened to President Obama (see the last epigram opening this chapter).[5] Following Mr. Obama's first State of the Union address, the news focused on his slipping narrative. A *Washington Post* reporter Jason Horowitz did a news piece on how the news had become obsessed with the president's narrative. The article was aptly titled, "The Obama 'narrative' is overshadowing this presidency's real stories." It opened with several examples, as when the *Washington Post* ". . . characterized Obama's State of the Union address as 'an effort to set the narrative on Obama's first year,' or in April, when the *Huffington Post* set about "Rediscovering the Obama Narrative," or . . . when *New York Times* columnist Maureen Dowd wondered how such a gifted storyteller could 'lose control of his own narrative.' Sing to me, Muse, of the dismay Mark Halperin registered on his blog, the Page, when he wrote 'Pundit/Press Narrative Forms Against Obama.'"[6]

As the examples of health care and other items on the Obama agenda indicate, elections are by no means the only places where journalists participate in telling stories. However, election stories—particularly those involving candidates who are not being held responsible for the mistakes of the past—may be somewhat less constrained by reality, since they are mainly about promising to deliver a better future. There are some differences in covering how institutions engage with policies after elections are over. Routine policy coverage is somewhat more constrained by what we referred to in the last chapter as "indexing":

selecting news sources and viewpoints according to perceived power balances that seem likely to affect the outcome of a policy decision. Even in routine policy coverage, however, journalists still tell stories about the personalities involved in these power struggles, and whether they seem to be winning or losing. The result is that politicians such as Obama in the early years of his administration can become hounded by the press as having lost control of his narrative, and thus become branded as something of a political loser—a symbolic cage from which it becomes increasingly difficult to govern.

And so goes the national communication process in which competing narratives chase each other and often provide poor focus on complex realities. The results are often unpredictable for how elections go, how policies are made, and how well those policies work. An intriguing question, of course, is what is the relationship between having an effective narrative and governing effectively? The analysis in this chapter suggests that it is hard to govern effectively without a clear and appealing narrative about things like strength and vision (or hope and change), but those narratives compete with opponents' efforts to topple them in the media, and journalists search for new stories. However, having a good narrative does not mean that it has much grounding in reality. As a result, good news narratives may not always produce good governance. Journalism mythology has it that it is the job of the press to help sort out the truth and other qualities of the narratives competing for public attention sooner rather than after public stories have proven to be poor accounts of social, political, economic, or environmental realities. Yet the forces favoring sensationalism in the press today are more likely to favor drama over credibility or importance.

Whether the news topic is a policy conflict, such as the great health care debate, a natural disaster such as the oil spill of 2010, or an election that may revolve around such things, the news tends to display certain narrative characteristics. This chapter considers the constructed properties of these common journalistic narrative forms as creating particular kinds of information bias in the news. Recognizing these more fundamental and perhaps more important biases in the news can easily be lost in commonly heard, and often heated, discussions of presumed ideological bias among journalists.

PUTTING JOURNALISTIC BIAS IN PERSPECTIVE

Many people blame the problems with our information system on ideological or partisan biases of journalists themselves. Polls show that growing majorities of people believe that reporters introduce their own political views into the news and generally do not even get the facts straight. According to polls taken by the Pew Research Center for the People & the Press, vast changes occurred in public regard for the press over the last two decades. Even though public confidence in the press began its steep decline by the mid-1980s, a majority (55%) still felt that news organizations at least got their facts straight most of the time. This figure dropped to 37 percent in the late 1990s. Meanwhile perceptions of press fairness—the belief that news organizations generally deal fairly with all sides in news accounts—plunged to a stunning low of 27 percent toward century's end.[7] The patriotic tones of press coverage immediately after 9/11 lowered perceptions of bias below 50 percent for the first time in years. However, the return to normal news was accompanied by the familiar drumbeat of press criticism from politicians and media critics alike, and perceptions of bias hit the 60 percent level by 2005.[8] A 2010 poll revealed that 55 percent of those sampled believed that media bias was a bigger problem than money in politics (and money is commonly regarded as a big problem).[9]

Survey results do show that many journalists are more liberal than the general population.[10] Where conventional wisdom breaks down, however, is with the assumption that the personal politics of reporters translate into the political content of their journalism. In an experimental study in which journalists were asked to imagine how they personally would cover hypothetical stories, the ideology of reporters had only a small effect on their professional judgments.[11] And, in reality, journalists do not work in hypothetical situations in which they have free reign over how to cover a story. The vast majority of individual journalists would have trouble getting consistent ideological slants past editors and owners throughout the news industry who are there to enforce norms of balance and fairness. The few notable exceptions, such as FOX *News*, which slants conservative, and MSNBC, which slants more liberal, are marketing those viewpoints consciously.

For the most part, constructing an attention-grabbing story is more important than introducing political slant in the news. Consider two cases of long-term coverage of prominent politicians that runs counter to the "liberal journalist" thesis. For example, most observers regard news coverage of the Reagan presidency (1981–1988) as generally favorable to Reagan and his "Republican revolution." Even when journalists attempted to take critical stances, they were often diffused by skillful White House press management and by Reagan's media-friendly personal charm—earning Reagan titles, such as "The Great Communicator" and "The Teflon President." By contrast, Bill Clinton's presidency (1993–2000) witnessed some of the most stormy and combative press relations and news coverage of the modern era. As discussed in Chapter 4, Clinton's press relations contrasted sharply with those of the Reagan administration, both in terms of failing to develop daily coordinated communication strategies and in excluding reporters from the everyday work routines and social life of the White House.

George W. Bush ran the whole gamut of news drama. Administration news spin from the aftermath of 9/11 through the early years of the Iraq War was reported faithfully by most of the mainstream press. Such successful news management helped Bush reach the highest recorded levels of public approval. That peak followed the Hollywood-style news coverage of his triumphant "top gun" jet landing on the aircraft carrier *Abraham Lincoln* and his declaration of an end to major combat in Iraq. Yet all that stood between Bush and a shift to more damaging news coverage was his failure to address the human emergency following Hurricane Katrina, followed by rising political opposition among Democrats in Congress pointing out the political instability and chaos in Iraq.

Ideological bias cannot explain these mercurial news patterns. Nor is such bias likely to seep through a code of professional ethics that emphasizes impartiality as a core value. This code may be fraying in some areas due to the economic pressures favoring sensationalism, or in cases such as FOX *News*, where bias has become a financially successful formula. For the most part, however, when reporters lose their perspective, there are editors to correct them. Reporters are small cogs in large business organizations that have a vested interest in producing a marketable, neutral product. As journalism scholar Everette Dennis put it:

> . . . profits are central to the media; the news is more and more driven by market forces and market segmentation. Deliberately or even innocently alienating a portion of the audience through unfair and biased coverage of candidates and causes would be self-destructive. More important, it would be absolutely unacceptable to publishers, broadcast executives, and owners, who, last time I checked, were still running the show.[12]

What accounts, then, for the popular perception that members of the press introduce a liberal bias into the news? Above all, when it comes to politics and its emotional core of values, bias is largely in the eye of the beholder. This generalization is supported by research showing that people in the middle see the press as generally neutral, whereas those on the Left complain that the news is too conservative and those on the Right think the news has a left-leaning bias.[13] Popular perceptions of bias are further swayed because of the long-standing conservative campaign against the so-called liberal media. More than 30 years ago, Richard Nixon charged the press with favoring liberal intellectuals and leftist activists in covering the war in Vietnam and failing to report the views of the great "silent majority" of Americans who favored his policies. In the years since, the right has continued to wage the press bias campaign so effectively that relatively few voices from the Left actually get into the mainstream media. For example, media critics such as Noam Chomsky tend to be heard only in alternative press outlets outside the mainstream.[14] The idea of a "liberal media" has become a household term.

Even though conservatives are more inclined to publicly attack the news, media criticism groups do exist on both the left and the right, and they continue to muster plenty of evidence for dueling charges of political bias. The reader might be interested in comparing the news criticism of the leading conservative organization, Accuracy in Media (AIM), with that of the leading liberal one, Fairness and Accuracy in Reporting (FAIR). The AIM Web address is www.aim.org; the FAIR Web site is located at www.fair.org.

To be sure, fluctuations in the political content of the news do exist, but they tend to reflect journalistic "indexing" of the shifts in political power balances—often between liberal and conservative blocs—on the issues in the news. Such political content fluctuations can almost always be explained by factors outside of the ideological thinking of individual journalists.[15] Everette Dennis has summed up the endless debate over ideological bias in the press as "pointless and repetitive," concluding that "The media, alas, are centrist, determinedly so."[16] To this, I would add that as the political bounds of conflict within government shift, the center may move. Thus, the "center" was more to the Left in the 1960s and has swung to the Right in recent times, and these swings may reflect more the power balances in Washington than any consistent political bias in the American press.

WHAT'S WRONG WITH A PARTISAN PRESS?

Even if perceptions of press bias were somehow true, we might welcome an avowedly partisan press of the sort that thrived before the rise of commercial newspapers in the nineteenth century. Indeed, the role for the press that the founders of this country imagined was far removed from the fantasies of objectivity harbored by many people today. Thomas Jefferson imagined that communities would have many partisan news sources—not that any individual would achieve balance by reading them all. The path to public understanding in a society rich with competing partisan information was described in the famous Hutchins Commission report on the American press more than a half century ago:

> Nor was it supposed that many citizens would subscribe to all the local journals. It was more likely that each would take the one which would reinforce his prejudices. But in each village and town, with its relatively simple social structure and its wealth of social contacts, various opinions might encounter each other in face-to-face meetings; the truth, it was hoped, would be sorted out by competition in the local marketplace.[17]

As the Hutchins report made clear, we no longer live in such a world. Even 50 years ago, it was clear that competing partisan news sources were not commonly available and that people did not live in close-knit communities where they would deliberate until reaching higher understandings of situations. For better or worse, the news has become distilled into highly uniform reports that present themselves as neutral, and from which people are expected to draw their own personal conclusions—generally without confronting fellow citizens with whom they disagree.

The Hutchins Commission also noted that this change from the democratic model of the press on which the nation was founded places important responsibilities on the contemporary press. In particular, news organizations should attempt to challenge dominant points of view that are dominant simply because they are better publicized by government or interests. Those news organizations also need to go out of their way to bring into their reporting the perspectives of diverse voices from communities who have little opportunity for face-to-face deliberation. Unfortunately, the news system fails to live up to these responsibilities much of the time. The result is that citizens lack the perspective and deliberation necessary to reach confident personal understandings, much less public consensus, about many important issues.

The general preoccupation with finding the most dramatic (which is often the best spun) story, rather than the best understanding of a situation, produces little information diversity in mainstream news reporting. For example, a comparative study of journalists in five nations found that American journalists may be the freest in the world—at least they cited fewer limits on their reporting than their counterparts in other democracies. American reporters, however, also made the narrowest range of choices about how they would cover various hypothetical news situations.[18]

A DIFFERENT KIND OF BIAS

The general focus of this chapter is on a deeper but less obvious sort of news bias—one that favors dramatic and personalized aspects of events over more complex underlying political realities. The result of focusing on individual actors and the dramas swirling around them is to make many political situations seem fragmented and confusing. Audiences are often left hanging, waiting for daily story updates about disorder and the restoration of authority, normalcy, and control, rather than installments on news narratives that reveal the politics behind the events.

Consider how one news organization reported that iconic moment when President Bush landed on an aircraft carrier to declare "mission accomplished" shortly after the invasion of Iraq:

> When the *Viking* carrying Bush made its tailhook landing on the aircraft carrier USS *Abraham Lincoln* off California yesterday, the scene brought presidential imagery to a whole new level. Bush emerged from the cockpit in a full olive flight suit and combat boots, his helmet tucked jauntily under his left arm. As he exchanged salutes with the sailors, his ejection harness, hugging him tightly between the legs, gave him the bowlegged swagger of a top gun.[19]

Similar images cycled through the news for weeks afterward. The president's personal popularity soared to record heights. The only trouble with the narrative was that the war was just starting to heat up, and the "mission" was still not accomplished as of this writing.

Consider some of the other choices news organizations had for framing the aircraft carrier landing story. *Framing* involves choosing a broad organizing theme for selecting, emphasizing, and linking the elements of a story. *Frames* also draw attention away from other elements in a situation, much as a picture frame encourages us to look inside it and pay less attention to things on the outside. *Frames* are thematic categories that integrate and give meaning to the scene, the characters, their actions, and supporting documentation.[20]

One possible frame might have pointed out the incongruity of attaching a Hollywood "top gun" image to a president with a checkered military service record. Yet the news tendency is to *personalize* stories along the most dramatic and visually immediate plot lines. Thus, the president appeared as the top gun, and for a brief Hollywood moment, the war seemed over. This frame choice made it difficult to introduce counter-frames showing that fighting continued, even as the president spoke.

These overly simplistic news framing decisions favor *dramatized* narratives filled with personalized drama with exaggerated emotions (melodrama) over more complex realities. Thus the media framing of the "mission accomplished" performance made it difficult to challenge administration claims that the liberation of Iraq had been accomplished, or that the war itself was a sensible strategy to fight terrorism. Such framing choices leave connections between surface events (the carrier landing) and underlying realities of situations (what was happening on the ground in Iraq and the impact on terrorism) *fragmented*.

The news could have focused the framing on the behind-the-scenes Hollywood aspects of the episode, exposing how the government hired television directors and public relations (PR) professionals to influence public perceptions—something that used to be called propaganda. Yet, the path of least resistance was to ignore the backstage context and fill the news frame with a well-staged White House dramatic production starring the president. The Hollywood moment also made for a nice chapter ending in the classic news *authority-disorder narrative*: a promise of return to normalcy—"Mission Accomplished."

As months dragged into years, the framing offered by the administration did not sit comfortably alongside continuing disturbing reports of U.S. battle casualties and civil chaos in Iraq. Yet journalists who tried to shift the framing of the conflict away from White House communication strategies were accused of liberal bias and of being unpatriotic. When reality finally became too much to displace, the administration simply reframed its story in terms of "Saddam Hussein was a very bad guy, and the world is better off without him," or "Would you rather fight the terrorists here or over there?" For their part, the Democrats failed to offer journalists much of an opportunity to open the news gates to bigger questions, apparently fearing public disapproval if they challenged a popular president (who was popular in part because of the absence of news challenges). As a result, only 34 of 414 stories told by ABC, NBC, and CBS on the build-up and rationale for the Iraq War from September 2002 through February 2003 originated outside the White House.[21]

What were people to think? The polls reported at the opening of Chapter 1 show that most citizens accepted what they saw dominating the news and generally supported administration framing even months after the situation in Iraq deteriorated. The increasing chaos in Iraq eventually led opponents in government to surface, which enabled news organizations to introduce more competing frames into the Iraq story. However, the risk with such sudden frame shifts is that people feel deceived and even less sure about what to believe, contributing to a public that is increasingly cynical and disillusioned with politics and government.[22] It is ironic that journalists complain about the scripted and staged events they cover, but they seem unable to find other ways to write stories that might help citizens become more engaged. As a result, large numbers of people actively avoid politics, escaping into ever-more personalized media worlds that one observer has likened to the gated communities and suburban enclaves into which many people have physically migrated in society.[23]

Communication scholar Shanto Iyengar offers a condensed view of news framing biases by saying that most news is episodic rather than thematic. *Episodic news* parachutes the journalist and the audience into the middle of an already developed situation and puts the focus on the people who are in trouble or in conflict. To put it in our terms, such news is personalized, dramatic, and fragmented; it often tells stories about social order and disorder. By contrast, *thematic news* looks beyond the immediate human drama to explore the origins of problems and the larger social, economic, or political contexts in which the immediate news story has developed. Iyengar's research shows that episodic news, which is the most commonly encountered form of reporting, particularly on television, leaves people with shallow understandings of the world around them. For example, viewers of episodic coverage tend to hold the people at the center of news stories responsible for the problems and conflicts that surround them, rather than see more fundamental social, political, or economic causes at work.[24]

Iyengar's work suggests that the news is an important link in a chain of poor reasoning about social problems. If individuals, alone, are held responsible for problems ranging from poverty and crime on the domestic scene to population explosions and wars on the world stage, then politicians and voters are unlikely to find workable solutions to these problems through their public communication process. The key problem with most news, in this view, is that when personal and dramatic elements isolate or fragment a story from larger social, historical, or political context, the news fails to offer a basis for learning and generalizing. It is often in such cases, in fact, that some variation on the authority-disorder plot comes into play as a substitute for a larger point to a story.

Why is there so little innovative coverage that might stimulate citizen engagement with events as they are happening? This chapter takes a close look at news content in terms of the information biases that make news hard to use as a guide to citizen action because they obscure the big picture in which daily events take place. While many Americans are caught up in dead-end debates about ideological news biases that are less dangerous than commonly assumed, few are noticing other information biases that really are worth worrying about. The task for the remainder of this book is to understand the U.S. public information system at a deeper level. Fortunately, most of the pieces to the news puzzle are right in front of us. For all of its defects, the news continues to be largely a public production, with government press offices, media organizations, and popular reactions all available for inspection. The openness of the system may be its saving grace when we turn to questions of reform later in the book.

FOUR INFORMATION BIASES THAT MATTER: AN OVERVIEW

Our expectations about the quality of public information are rather high. Most of us grew up with history books full of journalistic heroism exercised in the name of truth and free speech. We learned that the American Revolution

was inspired by the political rhetoric of the underground press and by print-
ers' effective opposition to the British Stamp Act. The lesson from the trial of
Peter Zenger has endured through time: *the truth is not libelous.* The goal of
the history book journalists was as unswerving as it was noble: to guarantee
for the American people the most accurate, critical, coherent, illuminating,
and independent reporting of political events. Yet Peter Zenger would probably not recognize, much less feel comfortable working in, a modern news
organization.

Like it or not, the news has become a mass-produced consumer product,
bearing little resemblance to history book images. Communication technologies,
beginning with the wire services and progressing to satellite feeds and digital
video, interact with corporate profit motives to create generic, "lowest-common-
denominator" information formats. In particular, four characteristics of news
stand out as reasons that public information in the United States does not always
advance the cause of democracy: *personalization, dramatization, fragmentation,*
and the *authority-disorder bias.*

Personalization

If there is a single most important flaw in the American news style, it is the
overwhelming tendency to downplay the big social, economic, or political picture in favor of the human trials, tragedies, and triumphs that sit at the surface
of events. For example, instead of focusing on power and process, the media
concentrate on the people engaged in political combat over the issues. The reasons for this are numerous—from the journalist's fear that probing analysis
will turn off audiences to the relative ease of telling the human-interest side of
a story as opposed to explaining deeper causes and effects. Whether the focus
is on sympathetic heroes and victims or hateful scoundrels and culprits, the
media preference for personalized human-interest news creates a "can't-see-
the-forest-for-the-trees" information bias that makes it difficult to see the big
(institutional) picture that lies beyond the many actors crowding center stage
who are caught in the eye of the news camera.

The tendency to personalize the news would be less worrisome if human-
interest angles were used to hook audiences into more serious analysis of issues
and problems. Almost all great literature and theater, from the Greek dramas to
the modern day, uses strong characters to promote audience identifications and
reactions in order to draw people into thinking about larger moral and social
issues. American news often stops at the character development stage, however,
and leaves the larger lessons and social significance, if there are any, to the
imagination of the audience. As a result, the main problem with personalized
news is that the focus on personal concerns is seldom linked to more in-depth
analysis. What often passes for analysis are opaque news formulas such as
"he/she was a reflection of us," a line that was used in the media frenzies that
followed the death of Britain's Princess Diana. Even when large portions of the
public reject personalized news formulas, as during the chaotic journalistic and
political preoccupation with President Clinton's personal sexual behavior, the

personalization never stops. This systematic tendency to personalize situations is one of the defining biases of news.

Dramatization

Compounding the information bias of personalization is a second news property in which the aspects of events that are reported tend to be the ones most easily dramatized in simple "stories." As previously noted, American journalism has settled overwhelmingly on the reporting form of stories or narratives, as contrasted, for example, with analytical essays, political polemics, or more scientific-style problem reports. Stories invite dramatization, particularly with sharply drawn actors at their center.

News dramas emphasize crisis over continuity, the present over the past or future, and the personalities at their center. News dramas downplay complex policy information, the workings of government institutions, and the bases of power behind the central characters. Lost in the news drama (*melodrama* is often the more appropriate term) are sustained analyses of persistent problems, such as inequality, hunger, resource depletion, population pressures, environmental collapse, toxic waste, and political oppression. Serious though such human problems are, they just are not dramatic enough on a day-to-day level to make the news until they produce crises that trigger the authority-disorder narrative (discussed later).

Crises are the perfect news material because they fit neatly into the dramatization bias. The "crisis cycle" portrayed in the news is classic dramatic fare, with rising action, falling action, sharply drawn characters, and, of course, plot resolutions. By its very definition, a crisis is something that will reach dramatic closure through cleanup efforts or humanitarian relief operations. Unfortunately, the crisis cycles in the news only reinforce the popular impression that high levels of human difficulty are inevitable and therefore acceptable.[25] Crises in the news are often resolved when situations return to "manageable" levels of difficulty, yet underlying problems often continuing to grow. It is interesting that the great oil spill of 2010 did not serve as a lever to help pass long-delayed environmental legislation to help free the U.S. from oil dependence. On the contrary, the news stayed closely focused on the human drama centering around the impact of the spill on local communities, the responsiveness of BP, the oil company that owned the well, and whether President Obama was in control of the situation.

As with personalization, dramatization is not inherently a bad thing. Drama can help us engage with the great forces of history, science, politics, and human relations. When drama is used to bring analysis to mind, it is a good thing. When drama is employed as a cheap emotional device to focus on human conflict and travail, or farce and frailty, the larger significance of events becomes easily lost in waves of immediate emotion. The potential advantages of drama to enlighten and explain are sacrificed to the lesser tendencies of melodrama to excite, anger, and further personalize events.

One thing that makes the news dramatic—indeed, that may even drive news drama—is the use of visuals: photos, graphics, and live-action video.

These elements of stories not only make the distant world seem more real, but they also make the news more believable. In many ways, particularly for television, the pictures may help editors and reporters decide which stories to tell and how to tell them. Again, there is nothing inherently wrong with emphasizing visuals in news production. In fact, it might be argued that thinking visually is the best way to engage the senses in communicating about society and politics. There is often, however, a tension between not reporting important stories that are hard to picture and reporting possibly unimportant stories simply because they offer great visual images. The discussion in Chapter 7 explains the economics of editorial decisions to start with the pictures and then add the words. The selection of news stories primarily because they offer dramatic images is one of several important reasons the news is often so fragmented or disconnected from larger political or economic contexts that would provide other ways to tell the story.

Fragmentation

As noted, the emphasis on personal and dramatic qualities of events feeds into a third information characteristic of the news: the isolation of stories from each other and from their larger contexts so that information in the news becomes fragmented and hard to assemble into a big picture. The fragmentation of information begins by emphasizing individual actors over the political contexts in which they operate. Fragmentation is then heightened by the use of dramatic formats that turn events into self-contained, isolated happenings. The fragmentation of information is further exaggerated by the severe space limits nearly all media impose for fear of boring readers and viewers with too much information.

As a result, the news generally comes to us in sketchy, dramatic capsules that make it difficult to see the causes of problems, their historical significance, or the connections across issues. It can even be difficult to follow the development of a particular issue over time as stories rise and fall more in response to the actions and reactions of prominent public figures than to independent reporting based on investigation of events. In addition, because it is difficult to bring historical background into the news, the impression is created of a world of chaotic events and crises that seem to appear and disappear because the news picture offers little explanation of their origins.

The Authority-Disorder Bias

Whether the world is returned to a safe, normal place, or whether the very idea of a normal world is called into question, the news is preoccupied with order, along with related questions of whether authorities are capable of establishing or restoring it. It is easy to see why these generic plot elements are so central to news: They are versatile and tireless themes that can be combined endlessly within personalized, dramatized, and fragmented news episodes. When the dramatic restoration of normalcy is not a plausible frame for an event, the news may quickly challenge authority itself, perhaps by publicizing the latest scandal charge against a leader or by opening the news gates to one politician willing to attack another.

In the past, it could be argued (as earlier editions of this book did) that the news more often resolved the authority-order balance in favor of official pronouncements aimed at "normalizing" conflicted situations by creating the appearance of order and control. A classic scenario of politics, according to political scientist Murray Edelman, is for authorities to take center stage to respond to crises (sometimes after having stirred them up in the first place) with emotionally reassuring promises that they will be handled effectively.[26] Today's authorities still play out their parts, but the news increasingly finds ways to challenge the pronouncements of officials and the presumption of order in society. In short, the biggest change in portrayals of authority and order in the news since earlier editions of this book is that the news balance has shifted away from trusted authorities providing reassuring promises to restore chaotic situations to a state of order or normalcy. Normalizing stories continue to appear, of course, but a growing news trend is to portray unsympathetic, scheming politicians who often fail to solve problems, leaving disorder in their wake. Much of this shift may be due to politicians themselves, who have raised the volume of negativity and attack, in part because they make the news and get the (short-term) attention of citizens. Local news has streamlined the authority-disorder formula even further by reporting anything that looks like mayhem.

Whether or not most events fit the authority-disorder plot, it is easy enough to make them fit. The oil spill in the Gulf of Mexico offers an excellent case in point. Even though the spill was not President Obama's fault, he soon became the focus of news attention, focused on the question of whether he was doing enough to control the situation. The authority-disorder plot was so palpable in these stories that the *New York Times* even ran an article with the title "Obama, the Oil Spill and the Chaos Perception." A photo of the president on a beach talking with workers and officials was captioned "IN CONTROL President Obama went to Port Fourchon, La., on May 28, to look at the oil spill and to look in charge."[27] Focusing the enormous crisis on the president sent his popularity even lower, with some polls equating his handling of the crisis with President Bush's lack of command of Hurricane Katrina. We will revisit this episode later in this chapter's case study on how President Obama lost his narrative. Before dissecting the news narrative problems in the Obama presidency, the next sections offer a more detailed look at the four information biases to help bring them into sharper focus.

FOUR INFORMATION BIASES IN THE NEWS: AN IN-DEPTH LOOK

It is important to recognize here that *it is not the stories that create information problems with the news; it is how stories are told.* If personal or emotionally dramatic elements are used to introduce audiences to more insightful ideas or to draw attention to underlying causes of situations, then narratives and drama can be very useful. The conclusion of this book returns to look at how news stories might be told differently and with more positive effect on citizen engagement.

It is important to be able to recognize each of the four types of information biases in action. This section explores more familiar examples of the four biases, with an eye to why news organizations are inclined to pursue stories that fit these information patterns.

Personalized News Revisited

Following the previous overview, *personalized news* can be defined as the journalistic bias that gives preference to individual actors and human-interest angles in events over larger institutional, social, and political contexts. The news is further personalized by creating a brand identity relationship between the consumer and the news product. Television anchors model their delivery styles and even their looks based on the results of market research, and newspapers key in on the lifestyles of readers. This trend toward personalized packaging was pioneered by news consultants, or news doctors, such as Philip McHugh: "There has to be an emphasis on human interest and human beings. You have to have an anchorman who can establish rapport with the audience. . . . It takes a very special kind of personality."[28]

The media (led by television, the major news source for most Americans) have settled on a formula that is profitable, cheap, and easy to produce, but just not terribly helpful to the citizens who consume this news. So important is this private, emotional bias in the news that it is understood as formal policy in most organizations. Here is an excerpt from a memo by an executive producer of ABC *News* to his staff:

> The Evening News, as you know, works on elimination. We can't include everything. As criteria for what we do include, I suggest the following for a satisfied viewer: (1) "Is my world, nation, and city safe?" (2) "Is my home and family safe?" (3) "If they are safe, then what has happened in the past 24 hours to help make that world better?" (4) "What has happened in the past 24 hours to help us cope better?"[29]

One interesting feature of this news maxim is that it has not changed much in the decades since it was written. Consider what Jonathan Wald, producer of NBC's *Today,* said after 9/11: "People want to know when they wake up if their world is safe. They look to us for reassurance that things are OK or not."[30] In today's more sinister news world, the answers to the personalized question of "Is my world safe?" may not be as reassuring, but the personal bias ("my world") remains as dominant as ever.

Examples of personalized news coverage can be found in virtually any newspaper, magazine, or broadcast. Consider, for instance, the personalization of a familiar political issue, welfare reform, followed by the personalization of an important branch of government, the presidency.

Personalizing an Issue: Welfare Reform News coverage of welfare was intensive for more than 20 years. The modern era of welfare politics began with Ronald Reagan's Republican revolution in the early 1980s, a time of fierce political battles over cutting welfare benefits to the poor and chronically unemployed. By the late 1990s, Bill Clinton had stolen the Republican thunder and welcomed sweeping cutbacks of government benefits. A common feature of the news over the two decades of policy change was the focus on personal stories, from Reagan's demonized cheaters and "welfare Cadillac" owners, to the hardships experienced by people whose support was cut, to the later success stories of people leaving the support rolls to take productive jobs in society.

Consider, for example, a *Wall Street Journal* report on an early Reagan-era decision to terminate a large-scale public employment program. Despite the numerous big-picture social, political, and economic themes that could have been used to frame the report, this was the opening paragraph of the story:

> SAN FRANCISCO—As the chill, first light breaks on a Haight-Ashbury curbside, a street sweeper stops to gather the gutter's yield of leaves, litter, and dog waste. "This job's the best thing ever happened to a poor man," he says. "It's feeding babies. When it's over, I'll be putting cardboard in my little girl's shoes, like my mama did me."[31]

Although there is a journalistic convention that stories should be organized with the most important information first and the least important facts last, the article did not mention the large-scale social, political or economic implications of the program cuts until paragraphs eight, nine, and ten. After these brief passages, the article returned to the heart-rending story of the street sweeper's fate.

As Clinton-era reforms of the late 1990s swept through the land, journalists swarmed welfare offices and job-training programs in search of other personal stories to tell. Reflecting the bipartisan consensus behind the reforms, the tone of these stories was positive and authority affirming: The government had done something right for a change. In the process, hundreds if not thousands of poor people got their 15 minutes of media fame. Indeed, the personalization of their stories was so intense that the news often became part of the plot rather than an invisible recorder of personal experiences. When a German film crew asked how a Milwaukee, Wisconsin, training program had helped a young woman, she did not talk about finding a job or getting her degree. Instead, she announced that "It really helped me with the interview for *Dateline NBC*," adding that her social worker had coached her on press interview techniques. Another newly placed job holder had worked out a polished sound bite about welfare from Franklin D. Roosevelt to a new beginning of hope. One woman's story cycled from the *New York Times* to ABC, giving her enough news exposure to generate fan mail. In a later *New York Times* interview, she told a reporter that one of her proudest moments in the transition from welfare to work was when her 11-year-old son declared, "Mama, you're going to be on the news."[32]

Personalizing the Presidency   Personalized treatments are not just reserved for complex policies. Even the coverage of government institutions puts personal themes atop the list of reporting priorities. As a result, we learn more about the powerful and glamorous personalities in government than about how government works. As Paletz and Entman observed, "Prime news generally involves prominent, powerful people in action, or, more desirable from the media's point of view, in conflict."[33]

A textbook case of personalizing the presidency is press coverage of Ronald Reagan's years in office. From the outset of his presidency, Reagan initiated many domestic and foreign policies of great national and international importance. However, the news formula that quickly emerged in most of the stories about those historic actions was the theme of whether Reagan was personally "winning" or "losing" in his battles with Congress, the bureaucracy, business leaders, and foreign governments. This theme reduced momentous political issues to engrossing but trivial questions about Reagan's personal power, his political "scorecard," and his risks of public embarrassment. The personal focus on Reagan so dominated the news that he was able to manipulate and enhance his news coverage simply by emphasizing his personal stake in policy decisions.

Reagan's success was not just due to his personal charm and communication abilities. As the case of George W. Bush's carrier landing demonstrated, on-screen political actors rely on professional communications staff to construct media events and communication strategies to take advantage of the predictable biases of the American reporting style. David Gergen was among the first communication strategists who understood the tendency of the press to personalize Washington politics. Before he worked for Bill Clinton, Gergen was one of the media managers who helped Reagan earn the nickname "the Great Communicator" from the national press corps. As Gergen saw it, politicians live or die depending on whether they appear to be personally weak or powerful in news accounts. His strategy was a media version of "the best defense is a good offense," in which his boss was at the center of events carefully orchestrated by the White House. The goal was to create images of confident control that drove out competing suggestions of presidential failure. (The details of this news management approach are explained in Chapter 4.)

This view of power in the media age has become part of the thinking of Washington insiders. As a result of personal scandals, policy conflicts, and the failure to properly utilize Gergen's talents, Bill Clinton's public approval ratings hovered under 50 percent during many of his major policy initiatives. As a member of his own administration told a reporter: "Any time you have a 48 percent [approval] president, every major vote is a death struggle. You are dealing with members [of Congress] who don't know whether to embrace him or run from him."[34] Shortly after Gergen was shuffled out of the Clinton White House, a major crime bill that Clinton supported was voted down in a procedural maneuver in the House of Representatives. Although a slightly revised version of the bill passed two weeks later, every major news organization played the original vote as a huge personal defeat for Clinton. ABC correspondent and National Public Radio (NPR) analyst Cokie Roberts put it this way in an NPR interview the morning after the defeat: "[For Mr. Clinton, it was] not a good day. I could hear reporters in the [press] gallery hammering out 'Stunning Defeat,' 'Staggering Defeat.' I like your [NPR's] 'Stinging Defeat.'"[35] NPR further personalized its coverage by adding that the president appeared "visibly shaken" as he addressed reporters afterward.[36] Clinton eventually righted his press strategy just in time to help him weather the impeachment storm during his second term in office. So Clinton, like all modern politicians, learned the often painful lesson that the success of his political agenda depended as much on his media image as on the sheer force of his ideas or the strength of his institutional politics.

Few presidents have received more personalized news treatment than Barack Obama. Following the rise of the Tea Party movement, the news and the talk show and online echo chambers were filled with claims that he was a socialist, a Fascist, and other attacks because of his support for the Bank Bailout and health care reforms. Perhaps the most outlandish personal attacks that made the news questioned his American birth. Despite the extremist sources of the so-called "birther" movement, this personal attack on the legitimacy of the president cycled through the news for more than a year, fanned by questions raised by members of Congress in the media. By one count, 17 members of Congress directly or through innuendo questioned the president's citizenship.[37] (Stephen Colbert challenged one of them to prove that he was not the illegitimate grandson of an alligator.) Not only did the president have to produce his birth certificate, but various fact checking organizations also verified that he was born in Hawaii. Even the governor of Hawaii tried to settle the matter as reported by CNN:

> [Gov. Linda] Lingle [R-Hawaii] said, ". . . I had my health director, who is a physician by background, go personally view the birth certificate in the birth records of the Department of Health." Lingle added, " . . . The president was in fact born at Kapi'olani Hospital in Honolulu, Hawaii. And that's just a fact."
>
> "It's been established he was born here," the governor continued. "I can understand why people want to make certain that the constitutional requirement of being a, you know, natural born American citizen . . . but the question has been asked and answered. And I think just we should all move on now."[38]

Unfortunately once such a controversy cycles through the news, people are given viewpoints, which, although false, may seem attractively acceptable to use in forming personal opinions. Thus, a CNN poll released on President Obama's 49th birthday showed that after a year of official demonstrations of the president's American citizenship, fully 27 percent of the public believed that he was "probably" or "definitely" born in another country. Another 29 percent said that he was "probably" born in the United States. Only 42 percent said that he was "definitely" born in the United States.[39]

The Political Costs of Personalized News   The focus on winners and losers and on personalities and their personal conflicts gives the news audience a distorted view of power and its political consequences. As Paletz and Entman have concluded, "Power seems to be understood in a limited sense by the media. . . . Stories emphasize the surface appearances, the furious sounds and fiery sights of battle, the well-known or colorful personalities involved—whatever is dramatic. Underlying causes and actual impacts are little noted nor long remembered."[40] Without a grasp of power structures, it is virtually impossible to understand how the political system really works. As a result, the political world becomes a mystical realm populated by actors who either have the political "force" on their side or do not.

In addition, direct emotional projection onto distant news figures can result in highly egocentric and ethnocentric views of the world. The news gives people a me-first view of the world in which "my" well-being, "my" group, and "my" country are emphasized over social realities that differ from our own. Even the two-sided format used in most reporting provides few intellectual tools for resolving the differences between the sides. On the contrary, the sides are often portrayed as in stark conflict. As a result, the path to easy understanding is to pick the reality that most closely resembles our own beliefs and prejudices. The next best alternative is to remain confused about how to decide who is right or what is really happening.

Dramatized News Revisited

It is no secret that reporters and editors search for events with dramatic properties and then emphasize those properties in their reporting. Consider the conscious emphasis on news drama in the following policy memo from the executive news producer of a major television network to his editors and reporters:

> Every news story should, without any sacrifice of probity or responsibility, display the attributes of fiction, of drama. It should have structure and conflict, problem and denouement, rising action and falling action, a beginning, a middle, and an end. These are not only the essentials of drama; they are the essentials of narrative.[41]

The weight of such evidence led Paletz and Entman to conclude that "drama is a defining characteristic of news. An event is particularly newsworthy if it has some elements of a dramatic narrative. . . . American officials held hostage in the far-off but journalistically accessible land of Iran provide a particularly strident example."[42] Indeed, the hostage crisis that dragged down the Carter presidency offered 444 days of sustained news coverage because it contained so many dramatic angles, almost all of which involved personalized themes and plots: What happened in the story today? How are the hostages? Is the president doing anything to bring them home safely? And, of course, there was the overriding dramatic question that kept people tuning in each day: How will it end?

Dramatized news fits neatly with the personalization bias. Drama, after all, is the quintessential medium for representing human conflict. Promising psychological release and resolution, drama satisfies emotional concerns aroused by the development of characters and plots. Although there are occasional walk-on roles for ordinary people, the majority of news plots revolve around a cast of familiar officials who play standard roles in news dramas. There are also the rich, the famous, the powerful, and the glamorous, along with plenty of bad guys threatening the lives of decent people.

Among the most familiar bad guys are terrorists. Yet who are they? How do they become cast as terrorists in news dramas? There is no universal standard that defines them because our terrorists are almost always someone else's heroes and freedom fighters. A fascinating study by Steven Livingston shows that in nearly all cases, acts of political violence wait for definition in the news until they are labeled (as terrorist, accidental, or heroic) by government officials who have political reasons for designating some groups bad and others good.[43]

In general, the main principle guiding the casting of newsmakers in their nightly roles has more to do with their potential as dramatic actors than with any natural preeminence they may have in the political scheme of things. For example, in the U.S. government, the three branches share equal power, both under the Constitution and, for the most part, in actual practice. Yet the president is the dramatic news actor par excellence: There is only one of him, he is easy to keep track of, he can be typecast (e.g., as a national father figure, as a staunch defender of freedom against an enemy, or as a flawed character who somehow maintains his public support), and he is easy to bring onto the scene for almost any political pretext. It is also helpful that presidents are usually willing to feed journalists as many dramatic "moments" as the latter are willing to broadcast and print.

By contrast, the justices of the Supreme Court make poor dramatic material, largely because they are reluctant to walk on stage and play for the audience. The small number of articulate, often eccentric, justices would otherwise make wonderful dramatic characters. Also, there is no shortage of available information about court proceedings—it is just that the business of the Court, while important, doesn't fit the news bias toward personalized, dramatic coverage. If the media adopted another information format, the Court might share the front pages with the president—a place more in keeping with its constitutional role.

Congress is another political institution with equal standing under the Constitution but with grossly unequal coverage in the media. A handful of glamorous members of the Senate receive the lion's share of coverage, while the House remains largely a jumbled assembly of nameless seat holders. Washington press observer Stephen Hess has noted the following:

> The Senate has the constitutional right to reject a president's treaties and a president's nominees, appealing prospects to a press corps that loves controversy. The Senate is also the incubator of presidential candidates

who are then automatically newsworthy. But most important, there are almost four-and-a-half times as many House members as there are senators. As philosopher David Sidorsky notes, the goal of journalists is to transpose "an inherently ambiguous and complex event into a short narrative that can be simply told, have a central plot, and retain the interest of the reader or viewer." It is easier and faster to build a coherent story with a smaller cast of characters. The House of Representatives is too much like *War and Peace;* the Senate is more on the scale of *Crime and Punishment.*[44]

Because of this news bias, members of Congress have learned to play the media game. As Timothy Cook has shown, members of the once-obscure House increasingly rely on news management to bring attention to legislation and put the spotlight on political careers.[45]

When Journalists Write the Script   Robert Darnton told of his early problems as a journalist before he had learned to parse the dramatic highlights from the dull details of most stories. On one of his early assignments on the city desk of a Newark, New Jersey, paper, he wrote a story of a bicycle stolen from a paperboy. The story was rejected by his editor. A colleague suggested a much more dramatic version involving the boy's love for the bike, his trauma following the theft, and his Horatio Alger–like scheme to pay for a new one. Upon checking this more dramatic new plot against the facts, Darnton decided that reality was close enough to the dramatized version to write the story—a story that was published in his paper.[46]

Lewis Lapham, the editor of *Harper's,* tells of similar experiences in his early days as a reporter. He notes how he marveled at the ease with which the senior reporter in the city room "wrote the accounts of routine catastrophe."[47] Finally, the old reporter's secret came out:

> In the drawer, with a bottle of bourbon and the manuscript of the epic poem he had been writing for twenty years, he kept a looseleaf notebook filled with stock versions of maybe fifty or sixty common newspaper texts. These were arranged in alphabetical order (fires, homicides, ship collisions, etc.) and then further divided into subcategories (fires—one-, two-, and three-alarm; warehouse; apartment building; etc.). The reporter had left blank spaces for the relevant names, deaths, numbers, and street addresses. As follows: "A _____ alarm fire swept through _____ at _____ St. yesterday afternoon, killing _____ people and causing _____ in property damage."[48]

Dramatized news as largely a journalistic creation has progressed to its wildest extremes on local TV. Beyond the focus on mayhem, the delivery and visual formats are painstakingly stylized with the help of news doctors who have developed the so-called action-news format. Nearly all major media markets now have news programs called "Action News" or "Eyewitness News." Action formats set the pace, delivery, scenery, and casting of the program. The action focus also directly affects the story content and presentation. Consider, for example, the multitude of ways in which a routine event like a murder can be covered. At one extreme, a murder can be reported analytically or, in Iyengar's terms, "thematically," in order to show how various aspects of the crime reflect social problems known to be linked with violent crime (e.g., poverty, family violence, unemployment, alcoholism, social instability, or prison system failures). Such reporting angles are seldom used in action-news programs because they contradict the action philosophy of the news doctors. Television and radio stations in competitive media markets tend to follow the costly advice of news consultants like the pioneering Frank Magid, who reportedly endorsed building a murder story around the dramatic effects of the camera retracing the route of the killer as he stalked his victim. Such reporting, according to Magid, has the virtue of making you feel "as if you were really there."[49]

Dramatized news is more melodrama than serious theater, more soap opera than Shakespeare. One does not leave the theater after watching *Hamlet* with the feeling that poor Hamlet was a real loser. If journalists pursued more serious dramatic techniques, the results might be less objectionable. It would not require the talents of a Shakespeare to make big changes in the way the news selects and represents reality. In legitimate drama, including many movies and popular novels, one is made aware of the role played by history, institutions, power, conflict, hidden interests, and accidents in human affairs. These factors are usually missing in news melodrama.

The Political Costs of Dramatized News   The most obvious effect of dramatization is to trivialize news content. In place of unswerving attention to major events and problems, there is an increasing tendency to substitute manufactured drama. Even when the drama may reflect an actual feature of the situation, as in the case of a congressional vote, the preoccupation with drama often distracts attention from any broad or enduring political significance the event may have had. The action imperative feeds on events with some rapidly developing action to report. One result, as Gaye Tuchman has observed so cogently, is that chronic social problems and long-standing political issues often go unreported because they develop too slowly.[50] In these respects, dramatization compounds many of the same effects of personalization.

Its unique blend of emotionalism and dramaturgy sets American journalism apart from other news systems, while setting Americans apart from the world they live in. Fiction writer Don DeLillo has captured these aspects of foreign affairs coverage:

> I think it's only in a crisis that Americans see other people. It has to be an American crisis, of course. If two countries fight that do not supply the Americans with some precious commodity, then the education of the public does not take place. But when the dictator falls, when the oil is threatened, then you turn on the television and they tell you where the country is, what the language is, how to pronounce the names of the

leaders, what the religion is all about, and maybe you can cut out recipes in the newspaper of Persian dishes. I will tell you. The whole world takes an interest in this curious way Americans educate themselves. TV. Look, this is Iran, this is Iraq. Let us pronounce the word correctly. E-ron. E-ronians. This is a Sunni, this is a Shi-ite. Very good. Next year we do the Philippine Islands, okay?[51]

Dramatized news also creates another information dilemma: the temptation for news organizations to look for the most extreme cases rather than the most representative examples of a subject. The preoccupation with drama makes it hard to draw the line between journalists as reporters of fact and as creators of fiction. After noting that drama is a requirement for a major news story, Paletz and Entman observed that some stories deficient in their own "high drama" may "have drama grafted on." "Journalists have been known to highlight if not concoct conflict and to find characters to symbolize its different sides. One reason: to attract an audience that is thought to have little patience for the abstract, the technical, the ambiguous, the uncontroversial."[52]

Because dramas are simple, easy to grasp, and offer a semblance of insight into the individual motives behind an action, they may give people a misguided sense of understanding the politics of a situation. People may think they understand an issue when, in fact, their understanding is based on a mixture of fantasy, fiction, and myth. Under these circumstances, according to Lapham, the political world becomes sheer abstraction, and "we exhaust ourselves in passionate arguments about things that few of us have ever seen. We talk about the third world as if it were a real place rather than a convenient symbol, about the gears of the national economy as if it were as intelligible as the gears on a bicycle."[53] This, ultimately, is what is wrong with the false sense of understanding conveyed by melodramatic news: It leaves people unprepared to deal effectively with serious social problems. The human capacity for planning, compromise, and sensitive analysis dissolve in the face of crisis, confrontation, and simplistic images.

We shall see later on that the public is not as simpleminded as the news experts assume, but this is beside the point. Nowhere in journalism texts is news defined as "whatever the audience wants, no matter how contrived or irrelevant." News, at least in theory, is supposed to inform people, not merely entertain them. The trend toward ever-more dramatic and entertaining news may mean that a new form of communication is emerging. This evolving communication form may still go by the term *news,* but it would be a serious mistake to assume that the traditional meanings of that term still apply. For example, large numbers of people regard cop shows and other dramatized reality programs as news.

In a world where political events are already far removed from the immediate experience of the average person, news dramas may push political consciousness permanently into the realm of fiction. This principle applies equally to coverage of foreign affairs and to issues seemingly much closer to home, such as crime. For example, a big-city television station produced an expensive and much-advertised documentary special on violent crime. The newspaper and television advertisements were dominated by horror-movie use of the word *fear,* which seared the page and dripped from the TV screen. True to its advertising, the program presented numerous examples of particularly violent crimes and showed how local people reacted to them. When the news adopts the images of popular drama and literature, it is little wonder that people begin to confuse reality and fantasy. As the following personal statement of a newspaper columnist indicates, our own lives become dramatized:

> Is it possible for a woman to walk along, footsteps echoing through the night city, without feeling as if she's performing in a Brian DePalma movie? I can't. I've been conditioned into DePalma-style reflexes: twitches and eye rolls, in response to any unlikely sight or sound. What is that shape moving shadowlike in the alley? Is that a garbage bag or a man hunkered down in the service doorway? If I venture out alone after midnight, I enter an atmosphere as different from the everyday world as if I've gone under water. I can hear my own breathing, the hammering of my heart, the clickety-clack of my heels on the pavement. Unescorted, I am accompanied by fear, chaperoned by phantoms of my own imagination. Why has that man changed direction, just as I've turned the corner? Is that he now walking behind me?[54]

There is no doubt that being a victim of a crime is a fearful prospect, but so are things like lung cancer, poverty, hunger, unemployment, homelessness, war, AIDS, and many other social "disasters." As David Altheide has shown so convincingly in his book *Creating Fear,* the news audience is exposed to more fearful images of some of these issues than others—not because they are inherently more or less fearful, but because the conditions conducive to media melodrama come together more coherently around some issues than others.[55] Crime is an issue tailor-made for hyperdramatism. Almost everyone agrees it is a problem and should be eliminated, almost everyone agrees that criminals are bad and have no excuse for their behavior, politicians get a lot of mileage from talking about an issue that is guaranteed to produce a supportive response from a scared public, and the media appear to be performing a useful public service by running cautionary stories on the issue. The result, however, is that the popular fear of crime is way out of proportion to the chances of ever being affected by it, and tax dollars may be thrown at emotionally satisfying solutions that have little real impact on the problem.

Here, then, is the sequence of political effects flowing from dramatized news: (a) distraction from potentially important causes of problems, (b) creation of a false sense of understanding rooted in individualistic explanations, and (c) the political promotion of dramatically satisfying but practically unworkable solutions. As Murray Edelman has argued so persuasively, many of the chronic problems that diminish the quality of life both nationally and on the world stage are surely worsened by the way they are represented in the news. The news has become a means of turning problems into political spectacles that drown out serious debate, while creating an appetite for quick, dramatic resolutions on the part of audiences.[56]

Fragmented News Revisited

Lifting actors out of political context and surrounding their actions with titillating but irrelevant fantasy themes makes it very hard to put together a coherent picture of the world.[57] News fragments exist in self-contained dramatic capsules, isolated from each other in time and space. The impression given by the news is of a jigsaw puzzle that is out of focus and missing many pieces. When focus is provided, it is on the individual pieces, not on how they fit into the overall picture. When information is delivered in such fragments, people are invited all the more to project their own interpretations onto the world. In place of new information about situations, information is either cast adrift or assimilated into old plot formulas. In either case, the world is reduced time and again to myriad encapsulated happenings, each with its own emotional coherence but isolated from the others. The world appears fragmented and confusing, even though each of its parts is coherent and dramatically whole. With respect to information fragmentation, the news defies the old adage that the whole is greater than the sum of its parts. In news reality, the whole is decidedly less than the sum of its parts. Columnist Russell Baker once parodied the typical newscast in the following terms:

> Meanwhile, in Washington, the . . . Administration was reported today as firemen still sifted through the ruins of a six-alarm blaze in Brooklyn that left two Congressmen, who were said to have accepted cash contributions from Korean agents, despite their fifth defeat in a row at the hands of the Boston Celtics. . . .
>
> Seventeen were dead and scores injured by the testimony that two Senators, whom he declined to name, rioted in the streets of Cairo following her son's expulsion from school for shooting a teacher who had referred to him in the easy-going style of the . . . White House, as exemplified by the dispute over the B–1 bomber.[58]

Lacking real guidelines for analysis and criticism, media efforts to be analytical or critical can border on nonsense. Edwin Diamond tells the story of a network news producer who visited a seminar at MIT devoted to television news. The producer proudly showed a videotape of a recent "analytical" report on the economy. Diamond describes the report and his students' reaction:

> There was the anchor wishing us good evening; cut to the Washington reporter with the latest inflation bad news; then quickly three consumer reports from around the country; then a U.S. map with graphics showing cost-of-living rates; back to the anchor and then the Washington reporter, followed by tape and sound "bites"—15-second quotes—from congressional leaders and cabinet officers. Finally, a Wall Street reaction . . . and then break for commercial. In all, no more than three minutes had elapsed.

As the various tape, sound, and graphics parts in the economics package gave way to each other, the producer snapped her fingers and whispered "hit it . . ." right in time with each element. She was proud of the network handiwork, but students in the classroom shot up their hands. What was that all about? What did it mean? What were you trying to tell us about the economy? . . . When we all watched the videotape once again from the point of view of the audience—people who know little about the effort that goes into the smooth mingling of tape and sound videofonts and slides, and care even less—we had to admit that it was difficult to grasp, sort out and understand the news somewhere underneath all the production.[59]

As this example illustrates, action news often tries to imitate analysis by trading in the story format for news collages, called "clusters" in radio and television, which contain many images with few coherent connections.[60] Similar fragmentation effects are achieved in newspapers, which jump back and forth between interviews, actors, scenes, factual information, and plots. Recall, for example, how the newspaper article on the elimination of the government job program required the reader to make the leap from the isolated personal case of a San Francisco street sweeper to the broad economic implications involved.

Long-term trends and historical patterns are seldom made part of the news because it is hard to tell them as simple stories. Events spring full-blown, from out of nowhere, into the headlines. In place of seeing a coherent world anchored in clear historical, economic, and political tendencies, the public is exposed to a world made chaotic by seemingly arbitrary and mysterious forces.

Fragmented news has a life and a reality of its own. Story plots are self-contained and incorporate broader social context only at the peril of overloading the simple melodrama of the moment. A shred of credibility is added to the mix by documenting that at least most of what is reported actually happened. Never mind that much more of what actually happened went unreported.

The Political Costs of Fragmentation There are, of course, numerous "good reasons" for such reporting. Journalism's hallowed prohibitions against commentary and interpretation seem to justify the representation of events as isolated, no matter how interrelated they may be. Moreover, press releases from official news sources seldom take pains to point out inconsistencies, complex relations, or other big-picture aspects of events. These strategies of propagandists are rewarded by the journalistic preoccupation with daily news, which means that the news slate is often wiped clean each day. Update sections are relegated to the backs of newspapers, and analysis pieces are saved for slow news days in radio and television broadcasts.

The imperatives for drama and action further separate stories from one another. Because dramatic formats contain their own plots and resolutions, linkages between these news capsules can reduce their impact and confuse their plots. In fact, connections between news stories can raise the unsettling idea that nothing should be taken at face value and that behind every story there is a still larger story.[61] An unfortunate by-product of using the story as the basic unit of news reporting is that linkages among stories tend to complicate simple, if isolated, realities. By contrast, other forms of presenting information, such as ideologies or theories use connections among issues and events to simplify explanations and enhance meaning.

Consider, for example, how personalization and dramatization also invited fragmentation in the great health care debate of the 1990s, which drew attention to the plight of some 40 million Americans who lacked medical insurance for illness or accident. Instead of putting the focus on how everyone could be accommodated under some new health plan, news reporting generally settled on a more dramatic and personal plot involving the paralyzing issue of whether people already receiving health coverage would have to face change and uncertainty. Doctors, insurance associations, and other opponents of the Clinton plan fed so many fearful images into the media that they quickly drove the story into the fragmentary exchange of scary emotional charges and countercharges. The main casualty of this fearful and fragmented coverage was public understanding of the plan itself. What happened to public understanding of the issues after such intensive news coverage? A disturbing study by the Times Mirror (now Pew) Center for the People & the Press found that fewer Americans understood key aspects of the Clinton administration health care plan after three months of intense news coverage than at the time the plan was first announced.[62]

According to communication scholar Kathleen Jamieson, the coverage quickly strayed from the ways in which a workable policy might be achieved. Audiences were treated, instead, to a mix of fearful threats about loss of existing coverage and a series of personalized battles between the president and Congress. Individual members of Congress became personally identified with a confusing list of alternative proposals as the attacks on the president's plan multiplied. Even Hillary Clinton came under heavy fire for her role in organizing policy groups to work out details of a plan. Above all, the leadership and authority of the president became the focal issue in the news.

The coverage of the health care reforms of 2010 was eerily similar, although dramatized and more personalized with attacks on the president. The news was filled with theatrical protests staged in town hall meetings with members of Congress who had hoped to educate the public about the plan in those disrupted forums. On the eve of the passage of the legislation, a majority had come to oppose it in the polls (despite being strongly in favor of health care reform at the beginning of the process).[63]

In the end, both of those historic efforts to pass health care reform were framed as political games in which the president's authority was a primary issue, and the capacity of the national government to conduct orderly business was implicitly questioned. In the Clinton episode, the president was described as losing his biggest policy battle to date, and doubts were raised about the ability of government to accomplish major national goals. In the Obama case, the reform was passed, and it was equated with saving his presidency. Reporting on the contents of the actual legislation was so sketchy that in one poll taken on the eve of the 2010 vote, only 20 percent of the public felt that members of Congress would understand what they were voting on.[64]

Instead of cutting off connections to surrounding political contexts, the news could have put the focus on many larger questions about the propriety of the health industry's role in defeating (in the Clinton case) or undermining (in the Obama case) health reform, or about the trails of campaign contributions from that industry to members of Congress who suddenly emerged as opponents to reform. These issues were raised but never became dominant frames for the story. Once again, news biases conveniently capsulized events at the expense of broader understandings.

It is no wonder that public opinion studies show that most people have trouble thinking in abstract, logically integrated ways about political issues. An inventory of findings from public opinion research sounds like a list of the effects of news fragmentation: The average person has trouble stating clear positions on issues, most people tend to remember few facts about important issues, the majority of people see few connections between issues, and many people change their opinions easily about issues. John Zaller's research on a number of foreign policy situations from Vietnam to the Gulf War suggests that the more "informed" people are about a situation, the more they simply take their cues from the party leaders and political elites who dominate the news.[65]

Mort Rosenblum, a respected foreign correspondent for the Associated Press, wrote a passionate book about why the world depicted in the American news always seems on the verge of chaos. The book's title is provocative: *Who Stole the News? Why We Can't Keep Up with What Happens in the World and What We Can Do About It*.[66] His comparison of the BBC *News Desk* and the CBS *Evening News* suggests that the difference between British and American coverage patterns and priorities is so vast that they might as well be broadcasting from two different planets! As journalist Mark Hertsgaard concluded about Rosenblum's critical look at American news:

> The unfortunate truth is that, for many Americans, the rest of the world does not really exist. It's more an abstraction than a real place where real people catch the bus to work, read newspapers, raise children, live lives. Our consciousness can be pierced if outsiders start making trouble for us—if swarthy, bearded "fanatics" take Americans hostage or cut off our oil supplies—but by the time we start paying attention, it's often too late; events have taken on their own momentum and there is little choice but to live with the consequences.[67]

The Authority-Disorder Bias Revisited

It is no wonder that details of policy debates often escape the public, even when issues receive considerable news coverage. As several of our examples indicate, intense news coverage can undermine understanding of a situation at the same time that people become more concerned and emotionally involved in it. Part of this disorientation is a result of the biases in many news stories that put disproportionate emphasis on what authorities are doing (taking charge, losing control, winning, losing, or in partisan conflict), and whether the situation in question seems to be moving in a more orderly and reassuring or disorderly and disturbing direction.

Authority plots and order–disorder images provide easy material when larger contexts surrounding events are cut off. Writing dramatic endings for fragmented stories often becomes the highest imperative in the newsroom. Sometimes authorities save the day, and order is restored to some corner of society. Sometimes authorities fight valiantly, but the forces of evil are simply overwhelming, and disorder seems to prevail. In other cases, such as health reform, authorities appear to be weak or deceitful or too preoccupied with their personal squabbles to get anything done, and both authority and order are challenged in the news. The point here is not that news accounts are fictional. Most news stories document aspects of the actual events being reported, but they are often selective in their documentation and tangential in their focus on what is important about a story. The point is that because the biases favoring dramatized, personalized, and fragmented news also favor writing images of authority and order into scripts in the first place, news organizations also have considerable dramatic license as to whether these authorities appear to be solving problems or restoring order in society.

Perhaps the greatest dilemma facing news decision makers is how to resolve this built-in tension between choosing the most dramatic endings for news accounts and the most representative or accurate ones. For reasons discussed in Chapter 7, journalistic misrepresentations find their way into many serious and sensitive areas of social life. For example, Robert Entman shows that news coverage of affirmative action (the policy of providing educational and employment opportunities to minorities) in the 1990s vastly distorted actual public opinion on the subject. Even though polls at the time showed upward of 70 percent of Americans favoring some sort of affirmative action in society, news stories portrayed society as racially divided, hopelessly in conflict, and unable to solve this paralyzing problem. In what Entman calls a process of "manufacturing discord," the media told of a "tide of white anger," "backlash in the white community," and "deep despair among blacks."[68] Entman argues that in reality, the media represented the views of the most extreme politicians and news commentators as typical of the entire society. He suggests that the story could have been told easily and more accurately as one involving broad support among Americans on a difficult issue that a few extremists had attempted (but failed) to make politically disruptive and racially divisive. The only trouble with that sort of news, of course, is that it is not nearly as dramatic. Manufactured disorder is far more dramatic.

Of course, there may also be genuine crises of authority or challenges to social order in the news. It is important to be able to distinguish between the politically genuine and the journalistically contrived. In the modern era, grand news stories such as Vietnam and Watergate are obvious examples of serious challenges to authority and order that were far bigger (e.g., more enduring, triggering more citizen activism, engaging more news makers, and touching on more issues) than could be easily created and contained with dramatically enhanced news writing. Wrenching national experiences, such as Watergate or Vietnam are often regarded by historians and political scientists as exceptional historical events. Many journalists also regard them as exceptional in marking the beginnings of trends toward more critical, watchdog (critics would say scandal-oriented) journalism.[69] For our purposes, there is an important distinction between these landmark conflicts in history and routine journalistic dramatizations of authority and disorder:

- The authority-disorder bias clearly operates by isolating (fragmenting) a particular story from surrounding social or historical trends and dramatizing it in terms of far more one-dimensional plot formulas (e.g., as political game, leadership challenge, sign of social breakdown) than would be warranted by examining it in broader historical, political, or factual context.
- By contrast, grand historic moments generally emerge in the news by breaking down the plot formulas of routine stories and following trails of documentary information into society or institutions. In these cases, issues of authority or order are not used to wall off news episodes from surrounding contexts but to open up questions about the meaning of events and widely shared social experiences.

In the 1960s, for example, with millions of antiwar protesters in the streets and a national civil rights movement in full swing, it could be argued that authority was palpably challenged by large numbers of people and that society was in some disorder. In the case of Watergate, the authority of the presidency was undermined by carrying out and then covering up a long list of illegal activities. The news became a valuable forum for debates about abuses of power and grounds for impeachment. For the most part, however, authority-disorder stories are grafted onto the news by news organizations' application of formulas, not by careful investigation of whether the foundations of public life are shaking. Indeed, the more disturbing or shocking these news formulas become, the more likely they are to score hits as "talker" or "watercooler" stories (what people talk about at work the next day), and the more news directors are likely to press their staffs to create them. For example, it has become common to hear people talking about abuse of the legal system to win large settlements on ridiculous liability claims. A classic story of the 1990s was the McDonald's lawsuit in which a woman won a huge settlement from the fast-food company because she was burned by hot coffee. As political scientists William Haltom and Michael McCann have demonstrated, however, the woman's claim was far more reasonable than it was portrayed in the news. Moreover, the numbers of frivolous lawsuits and extreme settlements have actually decreased, not increased, as implied in the steady stream of disturbing news accounts.[70]

The Political Costs of the Authority-Disorder Bias Among the most common story lines used by journalists is one that goes like this: "Something has gone awry in the world today, but officials are hopeful that the situation will return to normal soon. And now, for a report from the scene, we go to. . . ." The plot thickens when different officials disagree about what measures are appropriate to the restoration of normalcy, or, failing that, when journalists stir up the story by asking an authority-challenging question designed to get a reaction that can be reported as a new development. Two dramatic outcomes or resolutions are generally possible for these authority dramas. One standard ending for the news drama is that some official action wins out, the day is saved, and the story ends with a return to "normal." Alternatively, a course of action fails, or is challenged by another player, and authority and social order are left in doubt. The problem is that either of these dramatic endings is likely to put the focus on pseudo-issues rather than on the underlying politics of the situation. In more routine cases of everyday news, whether the balance is struck on the side of authority and order or on the side of mistrust and disorder, this central news bias displaces other possible ways of representing events. Even worse, with the balance tipping more in the direction of negative and disturbing news, the authority-disorder bias can become distorted to the point of seriously misrepresenting society and politics. We have already discussed coverage of crime and affirmative action as important examples of this problem.

It can be argued that crime and racial equality are, at least, real problems even if they are distorted in the news. Many other stories come dangerously close to being made up, at least in the sense that extreme and unrepresentative cases are offered as though they are typical or commonplace occurrences. As discussed in Chapter 7, for example, news magazines have turned distorted and misleading reporting into a formula: "scare them and they will watch." Grainy hidden-camera videos and dramatic editing and writing create the impression of a sinister world in which a host of threats and dangers lurk behind the orderly facades of the supermarket or the doctor's office.

A prominent journalism review investigated a fairly typical hidden camera exposé on ABC's *PrimeTime* several years after the segment won two journalism awards. The piece was on how medical laboratories often worked too quickly and missed many early warning signs of cancer in women's Pap smears. The show sent producers in disguise into a lab in Arizona and had another producer pose as a new customer who needed a large number of Pap smears read over a weekend (a tactic designed to overwork the lab technicians and create errors in reading the test reports). Sure enough, the lab was reported as having a number of warning signs on the tests. However, according to the journalism review's evaluation of the piece, what the news magazine never reported was that the lab's results were well within normal industry standards for what turns out to be an imperfect and hard-to-read test. Instead, the story created the appearance of sinister lab operators routinely endangering women's health. The overall result was that the lab in the report went out of business, ABC *News* won two awards, and the audience may have been needlessly scared, not to mention selectively misinformed, about a number of aspects of cancer detection.[71] Perhaps information is beside the point with scare TV.

Whether it arbitrarily emphasizes the good or the bad, this sort of daily news falls short of its ideal function of presenting representative accounts of social and political life so that people can draw informed conclusions from them. It is closer to the mark to conclude that the news helps people confirm their favorite political stereotypes because those dramatic distortions fit better with the implicit guidelines for selecting and writing news stories. As one critic observed, both the public and journalists are involved more in a process of creating convenient fictions than discovering convincing facts: "We are all engaged in the same enterprise, all of us caught up in the making of analogies and metaphors, all of us seeking evocations and representations of what we can recognize as appropriately human. Stories move from truths to fact, not the other way around."[72] Few politicians have experienced the loss of control over a political narrative as quickly as Barack Obama after he became president, as described in the case study that follows.

> ► CASE STUDY

How Barack Obama Lost His Narrative

When he ran for president, Barack Obama had a simple and effective narrative: the (relative) outsider who promised hope and change in hard times. The nation was entering a serious economic crisis, and faced two wars and loss of prestige abroad. Obama's main opponents (Hillary Clinton in the primaries and John McCain in the general election) were Washington veterans who had supported the increasingly unpopular wars, and were more easily associated with the failures to regulate the banking industry. Thus he entered office with a strong and emotionally uplifting story—at least for the majority of voters who supported him. As a *Washington Post* article put it:

> Journalists and politicians know that voters, like everyone else, are hard-wired to understand the world through stories. Elections are contests between competing story lines, something Obama, himself an elegant writer, and his team of political image editors were keenly aware of as they crafted the protagonist as a transformative Washington outsider, whose unerringly serious, postpartisan belief in competence, bridge-building and doing the right thing would improve the nation. That sympathetic character won 53 percent of general-election voters. . . . But now his narrative has taken on a life of its own.[73]

Indeed, the transition from campaigning to governing proved rough on the Obama story, as increasingly personal attacks and dramatizations of his legislative initiatives left him seemingly unable to explain and sell his agenda. His tone of civility and reasoned discussion seemed no match for sharp attacks from Tea Party protesters who disrupted health care town halls with signs accusing Obama of being a socialist and a fascist all in the same breath. Images of his iconic "Hope" campaign poster featuring a stenciled image based on a photograph appeared in news and blog coverage of the protests with Hitler mustaches added on. Other images pictured him as a creepy Joker from the Batman movie. As noted earlier, even the legitimacy of his birth as an American citizen was challenged. Yet he continued to reach out to offer discussion and compromise. To many of Obama's own supporters, such overtures seemed pointless when dealing with uncompromising opponents. As a result, the Obama narrative was further undermined by challenges from supporters who wondered in the blogosphere and news editorials about his toughness and ability to stand up for his agenda and his honor.

Whether or not Obama had chosen to respond to the personal attacks in kind, the news narrative would still have been personalized, fragmented and dramatized, with the likelihood of overshadowing the substance of his programs and explanations of how they might help people. The main political focus had become the president himself. In this fragmented political picture, the negative tone from attacks and crises began to erode his popular support. He entered office with an approval rating at a high of 70 percent, but that dipped quickly to barely 50 percent by the time the health care town halls became disrupted with protesters, and slipped to 45 percent as the oil spill dragged on through the summer of 2010.[74]

As the Gulf oil spill dominated the news for months, with images of millions of gallons of oil pouring into waters, contaminating beaches, ruining the fishing and tourism of the gulf coast, the story seemed to be more about the president than the larger questions of how such shoddy operations had been allowed to happen, and how the risks of such accidents might be prevented in the future. As Jason Horowitz put it in a *Washington Post* story about how the Obama narrative was overshadowing the real stories of the time:

> In this particularly meta moment, the overarching Obama story line hovers a level above events, distracting from the disaster in the gulf, glossing over the question of whether the government's concrete actions are sufficient, removing readers and viewers and listeners from reality. The narrative has been constantly updated—Obama's a hero one day, a goat the next—as ravenous news cycles and impatient audiences demand conclusions, and attention-starved media outlets can no longer subsist on the modest first drafts of history.[75]

The speculation about the oil spill turned into a classic news narrative of chaos and control, raising questions of whether the president acted soon enough, whether he treated the BP oil company tough enough, whether he understood the plight of gulf residents and could help them effectively, and whether he was really in charge of the nation's destiny. These are of course tall expectations to place on a single person. Yet they understandably appeal to many people already suffering a longstanding economic crisis that came with high levels of unemployment and economic uncertainty. It is easy to see how the authority—disorder plot may have all the more emotional resonance for a people long suffering challenging levels of personal chaos. As another journalist contemplating the dominance of the chaos narrative over more illuminating accounts of complex events put it:

> On a deeper level, though, we may be reacting to our own lack of control as workers, providers and parents. For about 40 years, since the onset of industrial decline, Americans have been trying to negotiate an increasingly unstable economic and cultural landscape, the effects of which are clear in any community where factories or

Continued

farms (or often both) have withered away—substance abuse, failing schools, higher rates of crime and divorce. The chaos is all around us, and what we ask of a president, increasingly, is to somehow use the instruments of government to rein it in.[76]

It is ironic that the press has ended up channeling more personalized, fragmented and dramatized stories of disorder and authority (or chaos and control) in these times that might call for more perspective from more thematic reporting. Yet, when cued to engage emotionally, publics seem to respond accordingly, for example in their responses to news polls that keep the personalized narratives going when they are not fueled by political spin. Despite securing a $20 billion fund to help victims of the spill and establishing an independent administrator to handle the claims, the media narrative instead focused on whether the president was in control. At the point in the summer of 2010 when the estimates of the volume and potential damages from the spill had grown, and capping the gusher was still a month or more away, a national poll showed that fully 57 percent of Americans regarded Obama's handing of the situation was either the same or worse than President Bush's handling of the Hurricane Katrina disaster in New Orleans five years earlier.[77]

Perhaps it is too much to expect a coherent narrative from a leader faced with two distant wars, an unending economic recession, combative responses to his legislative agenda, highly personalized attacks form a social movement, and topped off by a major crisis that had no immediate solution. On the other hand, even if Mr. Obama had somehow crafted a strong narrative that somehow created the illusion of controlling or rising above all of these disparate forces, would it really help us understand the nature of the issues facing the nation, or promote useful public discussion about them?

BIAS AS PART OF THE POLITICAL INFORMATION SYSTEM

Consider the picture so far: Each day news consumers are bombarded by dozens of compartmentalized, unrelated dramatic capsules. Some emotional satisfaction can be derived from forming strong identifications with or against the actors who star in these melodramas. But what about facts? What about knowledge and practical information? Unless the consumer has an existing interest or perspective on the subject, recalling facts from the news resembles a trivia game played alone. Most people cannot remember three-fourths of the stories in a TV news broadcast immediately after watching it, and information recall about the remembered quarter is sketchy at best.[78]

There is now a sizable literature that reads like an inventory of these problems.[79] The tendencies toward personalization, dramatization, and fragmentation have all been remarkably enduring over time, although they may have become more exaggerated with the economic pressures of the business explained in the last chapter. Although the focus on authority and order is also an enduring defining feature of the news, the shifting balance from order to mayhem and the unreflectively negative tone toward officials has left many observers puzzled and concerned. Indeed, many politicians say they have left government because of the relentlessly negative media scrutiny, while others have surrounded themselves by legions of media consultants and handlers. At the same time that many journalists criticize their own product in these terms, they confess being helpless to change it under the current system of profit- and ratings-driven business values.

NEWS BIAS AND DISCOURAGED CITIZENS

The general perspective developed in this book is that each aspect of the political information system described here is influenced by the others. For example, the weakness of journalism norms and cultural values for educating citizens may result in citizens who are easily discouraged from thinking seriously about serious issues. This, in turn, may encourage political actors to employ superficial and emotional PR techniques in their presentation of partisan political issues and policy choices. Sensing little public interest in hard news and having few resources for investigative reporting, the press passes off these strategically crafted political messages as the substance of the story of the day, perhaps overlaid with cynical commentary about the political games being played by politicians. This core of daily political news is interspersed with scandals and personal dramas justified by ratings reports suggesting that, despite their protests to the contrary, many people really do follow these spectacles.

Whether people follow scandals and mayhem as guilty pleasures or with anger and disgust, the convenient claim by media executives—that this is really what people want—misses at least two important points. First, many people are tuning out political news and homing in on more personal information about health, sports, celebrities, fashion, travel, and lifestyles. As explained in later chapters, these trends are occurring despite the abundance of available news topics and the ease of becoming informed. Perhaps most distressing for the future of political participation is that younger generations are most likely to tune out hard news. Second, according to research by communication scholars Joseph Cappella and Kathleen Hall Jamieson, even the people who consume news often become discouraged about politics and public life by cynical, negative news.[80]

So the public information cycle goes: One element of the press-politician-public news triangle affecting another in a dysfunctional manner until nearly everyone is dissatisfied. However, few citizens possess enough understanding of the overall system to recommend convincing solutions. Rather than thinking about the information system as a rational process in which objectivity is the highest and most desirable outcome, it makes more sense to think of this system as a game in which the different players are not all playing for the same goals or even by the same rules, but in which each uses the others to achieve particular ends:

- Politicians play for public support and favorable insider buzz by using news management and PR techniques intended to put their political bias (or "spin") on news content.

- The press competes for ratings, sales, and "scoops" (being first to break a story) and, perhaps most important, to avoid being "beaten" on a story by other news organizations. Business-driven news formulas dictate manufacturing the most dramatic audience-grabbing stories for the least cost and with a minimum of attention-distracting complexity. At the end of the day, stories often end up looking much the same from one news outlet to another, but the competition for audiences and the aggression toward politicians create the illusion of independence.
- The people occasionally enter the game as voters or as members of organized interests, searching the news for information that helps them decide what to do politically. Sometimes they find useful information, particularly when they are motivated by interest in a particular issue. Often they turn away, confused or discouraged. For the most part, however, they are the spectators. Political scientist Murray Edelman describes the focus of the daily news as political spectacle, attracting attention for its entertainment value even if it often fails to provide much information that is useful to citizens.[81]

REFORM ANYONE?

These trends offer little promise that despite tremendous gains in communication technology and the vast potential of the Internet, the news of the future will come any closer than we are today to meeting the information needs of democracy—unless, that is, people such as the readers of this book begin to understand how this information system works and think about how to fix what is wrong with it. In place of thinking seriously about the problems of information in this information age, many people have simply withdrawn from politics and joined the chorus of those who hurl easy criticisms at politicians and press alike. Public disapproval alone has not produced an improvement in the quality of information on which the health of democracy depends. Although criticisms of the news are rampant, relatively few critics offer much in the way of solid proposals for change. Press reform is the subject of the final chapter in this book, but a brief look at one model of more useful news reporting is in order now.

The most recent attempt to create an information system with more of the qualities just outlined is a now-fading movement for *public* or *civic* journalism. Although there is no single approach to this effort at news reform, it generally involves local news organizations inviting citizen participation in shaping news coverage that "encourages civic engagement—especially in elections—and supports communities in solving problems."[82] This movement grew impressively in the late 1990s. By 1998, the Pew Center for Civic Journalism had funded 62 projects, each involving more than one news organization in coordinating agendas of issue and election coverage through opinion polls and citizen forums in communities.[83]

The irony is that this movement has drawn harsh criticism from prominent journalists and news organizations. For example, editors at the *New York*

Times and the *Washington Post* have condemned the loss of journalistic independence that comes from letting citizens help decide what is important to cover. Many journalists feel that keeping the focus on a set of issues that may not be the ones government is currently addressing risks crossing the line from objective reporting to issue advocacy. A 1997 survey of media executives sponsored by the Associated Press found little in the way of broad support for the civic journalism movement in the industry. For example, only 14 percent of media executives felt that reporting was improved by news organizations listening to input from "citizens' juries" or "citizens' forums." Fully 33 percent felt that establishing such direct communication links between citizens and news organizations was a bad idea. The executives were evenly divided (35% to 34%) on the question of whether crossing the line between reporting and advocacy would further undermine journalism credibility. Perhaps the most damning charge against civic journalism is that it is little more than boosterism, a marketing ploy, or a "gimmick to make publishers feel better about themselves." A plurality of 41 percent of media executives strongly agreed with these charges, while only 33 percent strongly disagreed.[84]

Flash forward to the end of the first decade of the twenty-first century, and the situation has grown dire. As discussed in Chapter 1, those media executives, particularly the print press, are facing extinction. Online information sources churn the spin from government and more citizens receive their news directly from Facebook or Twitter. Yet none of these chaotic shifts has addressed ways in which social institutions and government might try to create more useful public information. The closing chapter of the book examines ways in which citizens and a grassroots media reform movement are trying to discuss and promote various reforms, such as: limiting the corporate influence on journalism, keeping the Internet open and accessible to all, and supporting new news initiatives that introduce diverse high quality information into areas that are losing the illumination of press scrutiny. Along the way, we will examine the promising explosion of blogs and citizen-action Web sites, which stir up a good deal of grassroots opinion and transmit information linked to positive things that citizens can do about issues that concern them. And, as discussed in Chapter 1, the popularity of late-night comedy satire of the daily news offers other channels for citizens to counter the spin and gain perspective. However, the fact remains that the issues and realities of the day for most people are still defined by the conventional news and information system. It is this political information system that continues to shape public opinion in the American democracy, as discussed in the next chapter.

NOTES

1. John William Ward, *Andrew Jackson: Symbol for an Age* (New York: Oxford University Press, 1955).
2. National Public Radio, *Morning Edition,* January 14, 2008, www.npr.org/templates/story/story.php?storyId=18067887.

3. Eric Alterman, in *The Guardian* blog, Blowhards and Windbags, January 11, 2008, http://commentisfree.guardian.co.uk/eric_alterman/2008/01/blowhards_and_wind-bags.html.

4. Matt Welch, "The Obama "Narrative" Narrative: Imagine What the President Could Do If Only He Had A Better Bumper Sticker!" *Reason* (March 18, 2010). http://reason.com/archives/2010/03/18/the-obama-narrative-narrative. Accessed August 8, 2010.

5. Richard W. Stevenson, "The Muddled Selling of the President," *New York Times*, January 29, 2010. www.nytimes.com/2010/01/31/weekinreview/31stevenson.html?scp=7&sq=stevenson&st=nyt. Accessed August 8, 2010.

6. Jason Horowitz, "The Obama 'Narrative' Is Overshadowing This Presidency's Real Stories," *Washington Post,* June 20, 2010. www.washingtonpost.com/wp-dyn/content/article/2010/06/18/AR2010061803052.html. Accessed August 8, 2010.

7. Based on Pew Research Center polls taken in 1985 and 1997, www.people-press.org/97medrpt.htm.

8. Pew Research Center polls, http://people-press.org/reports/display.php3?ReportID5248 (accessed January 7, 2006).

9. *Rasmussen Reports*, April 6, 2010. www.rasmussenreports.com/public_content/politics/general_politics/april_2010/55_say_media_bias_bigger_problem_in_politics_than_big_contributions. Accessed August 9, 2010.

10. This finding is reported, for example, in David Weaver and G. Cleveland Wilhoit, *The American Journalist: U.S. News People at the End of an Era* (Mahwah, NJ: Lawrence Erlbaum, 1996). A 1996 Freedom Forum/Roper survey of 139 Washington news people indicated that those with a left-of-center leaning outnumbered those leaning right-of-center by a margin of 61 percent to 9 percent. See Neil Hickey, "Is Fox News Fair?" *Columbia Journalism Review* (March/April 1998): 31.

11. Thomas Patterson and Wolfgang Donsbach note a slight but significant difference in how liberal and conservative journalists approach hypothetical stories. However, it is not clear whether even such small differences persist when hypothetical stories are replaced by real ones and subjected to editing processes within news organizations. See Thomas E. Patterson and Wolfgang Donsbach, "News Decisions: Journalists as Partisan Actors," *Political Communication* 13 (October/December 1996): 455–68.

12. Everette E. Dennis, "How 'Liberal' Are the Media, Anyway? The Continuing Conflict of Professionalism and Partisanship," *Press/Politics* 2 (Fall 1997): 116.

13. Gallup-Times Mirror, *The People and the Press* (Los Angeles: Times Mirror, 1986): 28–29. See also Robert P. Vallone, Lee Ross, and Mark R. Lepper, "The Hostile Media Phenomenon: Biased Perceptions and Perceptions of Media Bias in Coverage of the Beirut Massacre," *Journal of Personality and Social Psychology* 49, no. 3 (1985): 577–585.

14. Edward S. Herman and Noam Chomsky, *Manufacturing Consent: The Political Economy of the Mass Media* (New York: Pantheon, 1988).

15. See, for example, W. Lance Bennett, "Toward a Theory of Press-State Relations in the United States," *Journal of Communication* 40 (Spring 1990): 103–127.

16. Dennis, "How 'Liberal' Are the Media, Anyway?" 119.

17. From Robert D. Leigh, ed., *A Free and Responsible Press* (Chicago: University of Chicago Press, 1947), 15, Report of the Hutchins Commission on Freedom of the Press.

18. Thomas E. Patterson, "Irony of the Free Press: Professional Journalism and News Diversity" (paper presented at the Annual Meeting of the American Political Science Association, Chicago, September 3–6, 1992, 2).

19. Dana Milbank, "The Military Is the Message: Triumphant President Casts Strong Image for '04 Election," *Washington Post,* May 2, 2003: A24.
20. See Robert Entman, "Framing: Toward Clarification of a Fractured Paradigm," *Journal of Communication* 43, no. 4 (1993): 51–58.
21. Brent Cunningham, "Re-thinking Objectivity," *Columbia Journalism Review* 4 (July/August 2003), http://cjr.org/issues/2003/4/objective_cunningham.asp.
22. See Joseph Cappella and Kathleen Hall Jamieson, *Spiral of Cynicism: The Press and the Public Good* (New York: Oxford University Press, 1997).
23. Joseph Turow, *Breaking Up America: Advertisers and the New Media World* (Chicago: University of Chicago Press, 1997).
24. See Shanto Iyengar, *Is Anyone Responsible? How Television Frames Political Issues* (Chicago: University of Chicago Press, 1992).
25. Murray Edelman, *The Symbolic Uses of Politics* (Urbana, IL: University of Illinois Press, 1964).
26. Ibid.
27. Matt Bai, "Obama, the Oil Spill and Chaos Perception," *New York Times*, June 10, 2010. www.nytimes.com/2010/06/06/weekinreview/06bai.html. Accessed August 9, 2010.
28. Quoted in Edward W. Barrett, "Folksy TV News," *Columbia Journalism Review* (November/December 1973): 19.
29. Reported in David L. Paletz and Robert M. Entman, *Media Power Politics* (New York: Free Press, 1981), 17.
30. Howard Kurtz, "Since September 11 Attacks, TV Morning Shows Rediscover World News," *Seattle Times*, November 25, 2001: A2.
31. *The Wall Street Journal* (June 17, 1981): 1.
32. Jason DeParle, "From the Welfare Rolls to the Starring Roles: TV Offers Recipients Brushes with Fame," *New York Times,* June 25, 1999: A10.
33. Paletz and Entman, *Media Power Politics*, 16–17.
34. Quoted in Ann Devroy and Don Balz, "The White House Wins Again, but Was the Victory Pyrrhic?" *The Washington Post National Weekly Edition,* November 22–28, 1993: 12.
35. National Public Radio, *Morning Edition,* August 12, 1994.
36. Ibid.
37. Gabriel Winant, "The Birthers in Congress," *Salon* (July 28, 2009). www.salon.com/news/feature/2009/07/28/birther_enablers. Accessed August 9, 2010.
38. Eric Zimmermann, "Poll: 27 Percent of Americans Doubt Obama's Birthplace," *The Hill*, August 4, 2010. http://thehill.com/blogs/blog-briefing-room/news/112619-poll-27-of-americans-doubt-obamas-birthplace. Accessed August 9, 2010.
39. CNN/Opinion Research Poll – Obama birth. August 4, 2010. http://politicalticker.blogs.cnn.com/2010/08/04/cnnopinion-research-poll-obama-birth/. Accessed August 9, 2010.
40. Paletz and Entman, *Media Power Politics*, 17.
41. Reported in Edward Jay Epstein, *News from Nowhere* (New York: Random House, 1973), 4–5. Such a conscious statement of a defining characteristic of news is all the more remarkable considering that most journalists have difficulty in clearly defining their professional product.
42. Paletz and Entman, *Media Power Politics*, 17.
43. See Steven Livingston, *The Terrorism Spectacle* (Boulder, CO: Westview Press, 1994).
44. Stephen Hess, "Covering the Senate: Where Power Gets the Play," *Washington Journalism Review* 9, no. 3 (June 1986): 41–42.

45. Timothy E. Cook, *Making News and Making Laws: Media Strategies in the U.S. House of Representatives* (Washington, DC: Brookings Institution, 1989).
46. Robert Darnton, "Writing News and Telling Stories," *Daedalus* 104 (Spring 1975): 190.
47. Lewis H. Lapham, "Gilding the News," *Harper's* (July 1981): 34.
48. Ibid.
49. Reported in Barrett, "Folksy TV News," 19.
50. Gaye Tuchman, *Making News: A Study in the Construction of Reality* (New York: Free Press, 1978).
51. Don DeLillo, *The Names* (New York: Vintage, 1982), 58.
52. Paletz and Entman, *Media Power Politics,* 16.
53. Lapham, "Gilding the News," 35.
54. Opening paragraph of a column by Laura Cunningham, *New York Times,* September 3, 1981: 16, Home section.
55. David Altheide, *Creating Fear: News and the Construction of Crisis* (New York: Aldine de Gruyter, 2002).
56. Murray Edelman, *Constructing the Political Spectacle* (Chicago: University of Chicago Press, 1988).
57. Dan Nimmo and James E. Coombs, *Mediated Political Realities* (New York: Longman, 1983).
58. Russell Baker, "Meanwhile, in Zanzibar," *New York Times Magazine* (February 6, 1977): 12.
59. Edwin Diamond, "Disco News," in *Watching American Politics,* eds. Dan Nimmo and William L. Rivers (New York: Longman, 1981), 250.
60. Paletz and Entman, *Media Power Politics*, 23.
61. See, for example, Edward Jay Epstein's fascinating suggestion that there may have been a much larger scandal behind Watergate than the one revealed in *All the President's Men* by Carl Bernstein and Bob Woodward (New York: Warner Books, 1979). The dramatic plot confined the story to the White House. Moreover, any suggestion of larger conspiracies would have overburdened the already complex plot and undermined the credibility of the neatly contained White House story. See Epstein, "The Grand Coverup," *The Wall Street Journal* (April 19, 1976): 10.
62. Reported in Stuart Schear, "Covering Health Care: Politics or People?" *Columbia Journalism Review* (May/June 1994): 36–37.
63. "Only 20% Say Most in Congress Will Understand Health Care Plan Before They Vote on It," *Rasmussen Reports,* March 19, 2010. http://politicalticker.blogs.cnn.com/2010/08/04/cnnopinion-research-poll-obama-birth/. Accessed August 9, 2010.
64. Ibid.
65. See John Zaller, *The Nature and Origins of Mass Opinion* (New York: Cambridge University Press, 1992). See also, Zaller, "Elite Leadership of Mass Opinion: New Evidence from the Gulf War," in *Taken by Storm,* eds. W. Lance Bennett and David L. Paletz (Chicago: University of Chicago Press, 1994), 186–209.
66. Mort Rosenblum, *Who Stole the News?* (New York: John Wiley, 1993).
67. Mark Hertsgaard, "Isolated by the Media," *Washington Post National Weekly Edition* (November 22–28, 1993): 35.
68. Robert Entman, "Manufacturing Discord: Media in the Affirmative Action Debate," *Press/Politics* 2 (Fall 1997): 32–51.
69. See, for example, Bob Woodward, *Shadow: Five Presidents and the Legacy of Watergate* (New York: Simon and Schuster, 1999).

70. William Haltom and Michael McCann, "Law and Lore: Media Production of Legal Knowledge and Tort Reform" (paper presented at the Annual Meeting of the American Political Science Association, Boston, 1998).

71. D. M. Osborne, "Lab Scam," *Brill's Content* (February 1999): 100–103.

72. Lapham, "Gilding the News," 33.

73. Jason Horowitz, "The Obama 'Narrative' Is Overshadowing This Presidency's Real Stories."

74. "Gallup: Obama Job Approval." www.gallup.com/poll/113980/gallup-daily-obama-job-approval.aspx. Accessed August 10, 2010.

75. *Ibid.*

76. Matt Bai, "Obama, the Oil Spill and the Chaos Perception."

77. Marist Poll, June 10, 2010. http://maristpoll.marist.edu/630-57-say-obamas-handling-of-gulf-spill-no-better-than-bushs-katrina/. Accessed August 10, 2010.

78. David H. Weaver and Judith M. Buddenbaum, *Newspapers and Television: A Review of Research on Uses and Effects* (Washington, DC: American Newspaper Publishers Association Research Center, Report No. 19, 1979); and John Stauffer, Richard Frost, and William Rybolt, "The Attention Factor in Recalling Network Television News," *Journal of Communication* (Winter 1983): 29–37.

79. See, for example, David L. Altheide, *Media Power* (Beverly Hills, CA: Sage, 1985); Michael Parenti, *Inventing Reality: The Politics of the Mass Media* (New York: St. Martin's Press, 1986); Epstein, *News from Nowhere;* Herbert Gans, *Deciding What's News* (New York: Vintage, 1979); Timothy Crouse, *The Boys on the Bus* (New York: Free Press, 1978); Darnton, "Writing News and Telling Stories," 175–197; Mark Fishman, *Manufacturing the News* (Austin: University of Texas Press, 1980); Todd Gitlin, *The Whole World Is Watching* (Berkeley: University of California Press, 1980); Harvey Molotch and Marilyn Lester, "News as Purposive Behavior," *American Sociological Review* 39 (1974): 101–112; Harvey Molotch and Marilyn Lester, "Accidental News: The Great Oil Spill," *American Journal of Sociology* 81 (1975): 235–260; Leon V. Sigal, *Reporters and Officials: The Organization and Politics of Newsmaking* (Lexington, MA: Heath, 1973); Paletz and Entman, *Media Power Politics;* Robert M. Entman, *Democracy Without Citizens: Media and the Decay of American Politics* (New York: Oxford University Press, 1989); and Iyengar, *Is Anyone Responsible?*

80. See Cappella and Hall Jamieson, *Spiral of Cynicism.*

81. For an exploration of the news as popular spectacle, see Edelman, *Constructing the Political Spectacle.*

82. Charlotte Grimes, "Whither the Civic Journalism Bandwagon?" (discussion paper Joan Shorenstein Center, Harvard University, February 1999, 3).

83. Ibid.

84. Ibid.

Citizens and the News

Public Opinion
and Information Processing

Public deliberation is essential to democracy, in order to ensure that the public's policy preferences—upon which democratic decisions are based—are informed, enlightened, and authentic. In modern societies, however, public deliberation is (and probably must be) largely mediated, with professional communicators rather than ordinary citizens talking to each other....

—*Benjamin I. Page*

Media polls today undermine democracy mostly when they don't tell the truth about public opinion or about the public. This is not to say that all media polls suffer this defect. When they focus on people's own experiences and perceptions, the polls can provide useful insights into the culture and values of a population. But most horserace polls, and most polls that claim to measure the public's preferences on policy matters, produce distorted and even false readings of public opinion, which in turn can undermine the democratic process.

—*David Moore*

Public opinion is the engine of democracy. Public engagement can define issues, shape policy debates, and determine the outcomes of elections. Because opinion is important, politicians try both to anticipate and shape it. Some degree of opinion is based on personal experiences and feelings about such intimate concerns as the condition of the economy, health care, abortion, or taxes. Many other issues are more distant and become personally meaning-ful through the appeals of politicians and interest groups. At the dawn of the modern media era in the 1920s, journalist Walter Lippmann lamented that the only experiences most people ever have of the distant realities of politics are those that come through the news.[1] This means that in many areas, opin-ion may be based on news images and other representations of events, people, and problems rather than on direct personal experience. It is important to understand the ways in which such news images are constructed and how they affect our thoughts, feelings, and actions. Consider just three of the many ways in which news content helps people imagine a world they share with others:

1. *Political attention and importance of issues.* News coverage varies in the volume of attention devoted to a few dramatic issues and the scant atten-tion to many others. This emphasis affects the importance that people assign to issues and whether they know enough to even form meaningful opinions about them.

2. *The formation of publics.* In an age in which people may have more in common as talk show or television audiences than as workers, neighbors, or members of political parties and other institutions, they can pick up political cues and public identities through media experiences such as witnessing high-profile news dramas unfold. As a result, individuals may join together as publics and divide into larger or smaller camps of opin-ion through consideration of the cues and images contained in news (and its recycling through talk shows, blogs, and late-night comedy).

3. *Shaping political behavior.* Not all political messages in the news affect individual thinking and behavior, but some do. Marketing research is aimed at finding messages that appeal to popular thinking, and commu-nication consultants are paid to develop strategies to get those messages into the news. Even if only a small percentage of voters or "issue publics" change their feelings about a candidate or an issue, that change can affect the outcome of an election or an issue campaign.

The questions of how much and in what ways people rely on media cues still divide many scholars, but few today are willing to admit—as many did just a few decades ago—that the media have only minimal effects on individuals, a point we will discuss in more detail later in this chapter.[2]

NEWS AND THE BATTLE FOR PUBLIC OPINION

Opinion can be volatile and hard to manage. Thus, the process of polling and refining messages is a continuous element of election campaigns, as well as government and interest-group politics. Marketing research has been adapted to politics to assess the dispositions of various segments of the public. Based on this research, messages are shaped and tested through focus groups and other techniques. Then those messages are sent through many channels, including direct mailings, political advertising, local visits, radio broadcasts, and, of course, the news. Making the news is among the key strategies for persuading publics to support policies.

The opinion management process becomes all the more critical when issues trigger deep and divisive considerations in large numbers of people. Many, and perhaps most issues seem too complex and abstract for many people to follow. When attentive publics for an issue are small, communication often travels through more specialized media such as issue- or industry-oriented magazines or e-mail alerts aimed at people who pay attention to environmental regulations, price supports for farmers, or trade policies that affect currency exchange rates. By contrast, the news only contains a small slice of (usually) the most volatile issues running through society and government.

The news focus on dramatic issues that are personally accessible to large numbers of people is not lost on communication professionals who learn to construct public events to fit with the journalistic biases discussed in the last chapter. Those issues that can be presented most easily in personalized and dramatic terms are the ones that dominate the news, and they also turn out to be the issues that politicians and interest groups battle to define in terms that favor their political goals. Issues, such as abortion, taxes, health care, jobs, terrorism, war, and security are easier to get onto the public radar, and they can be quite volatile when they become news stories.

What is less well understood is that news polls often become completion points in the spin cycle because news organizations that commission polls often phrase poll questions using language similar to the issue frames being promoted by politicians, even when those frames may distort or polarize issues. This means that for many issues, the polls tend to follow the language of political spin, and not other, more neutral or realistic terms that might trigger different, and possibly more reflective, responses. Not surprisingly, when polls asked about invading Iraq because of alleged weapons of mass destruction or al-Qaeda connections (which turned out to be misleading reasons for the war), support for the invasion was higher than in polls that did not mention these things or that balanced war against other political remedies such as continued sanctions against Iraq. However, because polls using Bush administration spin often fit better with news stories on administration justifications for war, levels of public support reported by the media seemed higher than would have been warranted by other polling decisions.

Polls are also driven by news biases at an even deeper level. Because publics are the most important symbol in the grand story of democracy, it is tempting to endow their opinions with greater interest and clarity than actually exists. Thus, news organizations pressure the polling organizations that do their surveys to push respondents to have an opinion even when they do not. As a result, few news polls report high levels of "don't knows." This is because people are pushed to state an opinion even if they may not really have one. David Moore, formerly of the Gallup organization, describes the underlying rationale for this dubious variation on "push polling" in the following terms, using the example of CNN's apparent concern after changing polling organizations that levels of "don't knows" were too high:

> It is my argument that all of the major media organizations have an unwavering commitment to a mythological public that is rational, all-knowing, and fully engaged. CNN's search for a way to reduce even the small percentage of respondents who don't respond to any given question is merely emblematic of the widespread view of all the major media organizations that only a mythological public of that nature can justify their covering the "beat" of public opinion. If a large proportion of the public, sometimes even a majority, has no real opinion on an issue, most media organizations would dismiss the poll results as having no news value. And if that happened on a regular basis, the whole enterprise of media polls would be in serious jeopardy. The media don't want to tell the public the truth about itself.[3]

The combination of poll questions that echo key partisan messages and push people to have opinions on them means that publics in news stories often have far clearer divisions of opinion than actually exist. Even more disturbing is that news polls seldom probe a deeper aspect of opinion: whether people really care if their favored policies happen or their preferred candidates win. A series of sobering studies by David Moore (who ran them while working as an editor at Gallup) showed that if you ask people if they would be upset if their stated preference did not occur, the largest segment of responses on almost every issue indicated they would not be upset if what they appeared to favor did not happen.[4] Yet news reports seldom include such heavily qualified assessments of opinion. They overwhelmingly tend to report much stronger divisions of opinion that suggest a far more involved and a far more conflicted public than usually exists.

David Moore and his colleague Jeffrey Jones asked the "How upset would you be?" question in polling national samples about a variety of issues, including drilling for oil in an Alaskan nature preserve, election campaign finance reform, gay civil unions, missile defense, and human cloning. These were among the most politically contested issues among elites at the time the polls were taken. The surface-level results (typically reported in the news) indicated vigorous public engagement and majority opinions on most issues: campaign finance reform (58% favor, 26% oppose), oil drilling (56% oppose), human cloning ban (53% favor), building missile defense system (64% favor), and gay civil unions (45% favor, 46% oppose). Yet, probing beneath the surface produced majorities or large pluralities that would not have been upset if their preferences did not happen: campaign finance (58% would not be upset no matter how it turned out), oil drilling (44%), gay unions (49%), and missile defense (47%). Of all these issues on which majorities were pushed to have opinions at a surface level (including going to war in Iraq), only human cloning had a majority of supporters and opponents (73%) who actually cared if their preferences did not happen (most opposed human cloning and would be upset if it happened).[5]

These findings raise important questions about the typical characterizations of public opinion in the press. If opinion on many issues is as soft as these findings indicate, then it is most often a misrepresentation to say that publics either support or oppose particular government initiatives. And it is a gross distortion to say that the public is deeply divided on the many issues for which this claim is made in order to spice up news dramas. *It is probably more accurate to say that elites are deeply divided, the news is written in terms of those divisions, and polls reported in the news are constructed to push the public into those same divisions.* As a result, many, and perhaps most, stories that report opinion polls in the news may be distorted on a regular basis. Political scientist Morris Fiorina has also argued that the notion of a polarized America is true only for warring political factions, and not for the public at large.[6]

While exaggerated levels of public engagement and conflict may make for better news, it also inadvertently helps one side or another in a policy or election campaign claim that their side is winning or has far more support than actually exists. This can create a self-fulfilling prophecy triggered by the way polls are reported in the news. For example, voters may decide to back an apparent winner or frontrunner and sacrifice support for a candidate who seems behind in the polls—even though support for the frontrunner is really not as solid as the polls make out. In other cases, citizens may quietly accept policy outcomes or decisions (such as going to war) that actually have far less support than dramatically sharpened news polls suggest. Murray Edelman called this symbolically induced state of public mind *quiescence*.[7]

Consider, here, the issues of race and the continuing conflicts that politicians stir up around them, such as election and legislative battles over immigration. A study by Entman and Rojecki showed that news stories consistently dramatized racial conflict themes and reported poll results that fit the news framing. Thus, the cover of a prominent news magazine blared the headline: "Race and Rage." A more reasonable story could well have been written around points of racial harmony and agreement, depending on how the poll questions were worded. Other observers have noted that the polarizing framing of polls enabled the public to become symbolically drawn into so-called culture wars being waged by small numbers of elites at the most extreme (in this case, conservative) end of the political spectrum.[8] Those elites found news organizations eager to dramatize their polarizing efforts rather than to report more moderate and representative accounts. As Entman and Rojecki have observed:

> Journalists, it seems, built their frame on claims by elite sources with an interest in promoting the impression of White arousal, a goal that meshed nicely with reporters' constant search for conflict and drama. In fact, journalists appeared to confuse *elite rhetoric* with *average citizens' preferences and priorities*.[9]

Such dramatic shaping of public issues by polls can have consequences. One likely result is that this polarizing (or better put, poll-arizing) news may have inhibited moderate and left politicians from publicly supporting affirmative action, or trying to lead a more moderate public consensus on such policies. Entman and Rojecki conclude: "It is clear that some of the most important political leaders who set the media agenda—especially presidential hopefuls— turned more actively hostile to affirmative action. . . . It is far from clear that their views reflected the sentiments of ordinary White Americans."[10] The same could probably be said for the immigration debates swirling in the news in more recent times.

In recent years, immigration politics have introduced hot racial issues into elections and policymaking at all levels of government. In 2010, the state of Arizona passed a law that directed local law enforcement to police the immigration documents of state residents. This was controversial on a number of levels, from directing local law enforcement to police what had traditionally been a federal jurisdiction, to raising the specter of racial profiling, with Hispanic residents feeling more likely to be stopped and screened by police than other racial groups. Extensive polling was conducted by news organizations and other independent survey organizations, with news polling often echoing the dramatized news that filled the 24/7 media. For example, in two national polls taken just a month after the Arizona law was passed, a CNN survey showed that only 6 percent were unsure what to think of the Arizona action, while another random national sample taken at the same time by the survey unit of Quinnipiac University showed fully 18 percent were unsure what to think. The CNN poll evidently created the impression of a much more engaged and clearly opinionated public by pushing as many undecided respondents as possible into the two polar (favor and opposed) camps.[11]

The Arizona immigration conflict also illustrates the powerful effects of question wording on polling results. The highly regarded Pew Research organization asked how respondents felt about the decision of the U.S. Justice Department to challenge the Arizona law. The question they asked was carefully worded to describe the basic facts of the situation: "As you may know, this week the U.S. Justice Department filed a legal challenge to the state of Arizona's recent immigration law. From what you know, do you approve or disapprove of the Justice Department's decision to challenge the Arizona law?" It its version, the Quinnipiac University Poll included the more emotionally loaded terms "Obama" and "strike down" in its question: "The Obama administration has filed a lawsuit to strike down Arizona's immigration law. Do you think this lawsuit is a good idea or a bad idea?" Loading up the question with "Obama" and "strike down" pushed the numbers who disapproved of the action from 45 percent in the Pew poll to a strong majority of 60 percent in the Quinnipiac survey, while the number of undecided respondents dropped from 19 to 12 percent.[12]

In thinking about the polls in news reports that tell us how many people support candidates or policies, it is good to remember how poorly formed such opinions can be. This suggests two things about political efforts to shape opinion: (a) it is doubtful how much the reliance on public relations really produces strong and lasting feelings among large numbers of people and

(b) the way polls are taken and reported in the news most often exaggerates the strength of the effects from PR and persuasion campaigns. Thus, as noted earlier, the news becomes part of completing the spin cycle by constructing images of publics that often exaggerate actual divisions and levels of support or opposition.

REACHING INATTENTIVE PUBLICS

Part of the difficulty facing communicators who seek to mobilize publics is that the attention of audiences is increasingly hard to gain. This is because both the media and society are changing, making audiences hard to reach. In society, people are living ever-more personalized lives, thus sharing fewer group memberships and other experiences in common that help to shape and solidify opinions.[13] The changing media landscape both reflects and reinforces this social fragmentation, with more and more personalized channels of information available to people.[14] These changes make it harder, and often more expensive, to reach individuals. For example, many younger demographics are more likely to be found in gaming environments than watching television, which makes it hard to get conventional messages to them.

It is difficult to shape public opinion and even harder to control it, yet those engaged in politics often put enormous energy into those challenges. For example, the staggering costs of winning the support of relatively small numbers of so-called swing voters in elections suggests that the battle for opinion is difficult, expensive, and seldom a sure thing. Citizens live in a noisy media environment in which politics is generally far down the priority list, behind entertainment, fashion, sports, weather, and shopping. Just getting the attention of distracted and often disinterested citizens requires strong measures—usually involving highly dramatic and personal messages that are repeated time and again. The case study in this chapter explores this national attention deficit disorder.

◢ CASE STUDY

National Attention Deficit Disorder?

In his analysis of the economics of the news, James Hamilton suggests that the conventional "who, what, where, when, and why" of journalism is actually determined by another, more important, set of "five W's": "Who cares about information? What are they willing to pay, or others willing to pay to reach them? Where can media outlets and advertisers reach them? When is this profitable? Why is this profitable?"[15] What he concludes from this is that economic markets do not create conditions favorable to the open exchange of democratic ideas. Markets aim to deliver consumers to sponsors by nearly any means that work. What gets the attention of consumers may not be what matters to citizens. What media organizations do with audience attention once they have it may have little to do with informing and encouraging political involvement. It is hard to decide what comes first: the marketing of soft features and shocking stories that deprive audiences of more serious information, or an overriding general withdrawal from civic life that leaves news producers searching for anything to grab audience attention. Either way, the result is a national spiral of inattentiveness to many of the most monumental issues facing the nation.

Consider just a few of the media attention patterns that Hamilton reports in his survey of the habits of news audiences. Less than 10 percent of men and women aged 18 to 34 regularly view a nightly network news program, compared with 23 percent of men and 32 percent of women over age 50. TV news magazines *(20/20, Dateline, 60 Minutes)* outdraw network news audiences in three of six crucial demographic categories (men and women age 18 to 34 and women age 35 to 49). FOX News beats National Public Radio audiences in five of the six key demographic categories; only women aged 35 to 49 listen to NPR more (16.9 percent) than watch FOX (15.9 percent). Cop programs beat NPR in every demographic category except men over age 50. And more than four times as many people watch talk programs such as *Oprah* and *Dr. Phil* than follow the PBS *News Hour with Jim Lehrer.* Not surprisingly, few Americans claim to follow politics closely.[16] Only one of the six key demographic categories tracked by news marketers (males over age 50) registered a majority claiming to follow politics most of the time.[17]

What passed for "news" for many people is signaled in a search for featured stories on NBC's Dateline program, which produced the Google caption "Dateline NBC: News Stories about Crime, Celebrity and Health." The headline story for the week in which this is being written was titled "TANGLED LIVES: A mother's chilling premonition comes true when she is murdered by a stranger at the door. Another mother knows information that could help catch the killer. Will she risk everything to tell it?"[18]

It is not surprising that the distracted public consuming such infotainment under the guise of news is not well informed about daily political affairs. For example, New York Times columnist Charles Blow noted that President Obama's studious political style resulted only in people not understanding his political agenda. An inattentive public needs sharp and repeated messages to rally them to pay attention even to important issues such as health care. In Blow's analysis, the lack of a focused media campaign by the administration, combined with continuing efforts to engage in reasoned discussions with an entrenched opposition only played into the Republican strategy of just saying no. Far from being hurt by their unyielding opposition, the "party of No" as Obama dubbed the Republicans, barely registered any negative impact on public opinion charts. In part, this may be because public support for both parties in Congress is so low that it would be hard to decline much further. However, Blow cited public inattentiveness as a key reason why the Republican refusal to cooperate or compromise did not seem to hurt them. He pointed to a Pew survey showing that "only 1 person in 4 knew that 60 votes are needed in the Senate to break a filibuster and only 1 in 3 knew that no Senate Republicans voted for the health care bill."[19] Inattentiveness is even more severe among young citizens, as only 16 percent of 18–29 year olds knew how the Republicans voted on health care. Blow's conclusion about such distressing lack of

Continued

engagement with an historic issue was to modify H. L Mencken's famous characterization of the American public:

> H.L. Mencken once famously opined, "No one in this world has ever lost money by underestimating the intelligence of the great masses of the plain people. Nor has anyone ever lost public office thereby." I take exception to that. But if you change "intelligence" to "attention span," I agree wholeheartedly.[20]

Attentiveness is notoriously thin even in national elections – those moments when people allegedly hold the reins to power. In 2000, the World Wrestling Federation's *Smackdown!* drew four times the audience as the first debate among the Democratic candidates (and *Smackdown!* barely made the top hundred in the week's television rating charts).[21] Similar levels of disinterest ran through the entire campaign. A majority of people did not become very interested in the election until after it was over, and Americans woke up to discover that there was no clear winner.[22]

The fragmented media system may explain part of the attention deficit, as attention and interest are reflected in the media sources that people pay attention to.[23] For example, young voters age 18 to 29 are seven times more likely (21% to 3%) to learn about elections from comedy TV shows than voters over age 50. Older voters are twice as likely to pay attention to elections through network news or newspaper coverage. There is some potential for voters and candidates to find each other on the Internet. The percentage of citizens using the Internet to some degree to follow elections increased from 24 to 33 percent between 2000 and 2004, with the greatest gains among young voters. However, polls that asked if respondents regularly used online sources to follow elections found that only 13 percent regularly sought out election information in 2004. These regular Internet users were among the most informed about candidates and their issues. In 2008, a Pew survey fine-tuned these patterns and found that 52 percent said they had found some election-related material on the Internet, but generally while looking for something else. When it came to regularly following the election, only 24 percent often sought out election information online.[24] At the same time, the effective uses of social networking technologies by the Obama campaign, along with the viral spread of many videos produced independently of both campaigns, indicate that there are ways to engage large numbers of people with politics in the new media environment. However, there is no easy formula for making this happen, as during the golden era of broadcast television when a huge "captive" media audience sat down together and watched one of three network news programs that broadcast essentially the same information.[25]

A counterargument to the attention deficit syndrome is that measuring whether people attend to the details of news events is like a trivia test that fails to tap how people actually understand politics. Some political scientists claim that people learn what they need to know from talk shows and entertainment programs—at least they learn enough about key issues to form opinions and participate meaningfully in public life.[26] Yet this view fails to address the quality of the information and reasoning on which such distracted participation rests. Recall the discussion from Chapter 1 on the misperceptions about the Iraq War among different media audiences. Even those who watched news programs varied greatly in their understandings of the basis for going to war. Viewers of FOX *News* were more than twice as likely as viewers of the *News Hour* on PBS to have the basic facts wrong about such key issues as the connections between Iraq and terrorism attacks of 9/11. This raises the question of whether such unfounded or ungrounded opinions fully qualify people to participate in public life. The even more difficult question is whether politicians prey on public inattentiveness to create poorly informed support for policies they promote.

The most important element of the national attention deficit disorder is that politicians and interests may skip efforts to inform or educate publics about issues on grounds that it is nearly impossible to reach them. This may explain why so much highly emotional, repetitive and shallow communication is aimed at short-term opinion mobilization among just enough members of the public to get elected and govern. Perhaps that failure to activate any deeper involvement from most citizens is the greatest problem with the American information system.

Even when the attention of some portion of a targeted public is gained, the message still needs to make sense by creating connections to thoughts, feelings, and, then, actions ranging from voting to protesting. It is no easy task to figure out just what symbols and ideas will make these connections. John Zaller has pointed out that people can bring many often-conflicting considerations into play when they form opinions. This means that any particular message may engage different factors being considered by individuals, and those connections and conflicts may create chain reactions across the millions of individuals who make up a public for an issue.[27] For these reasons, a great deal of polling and focus-group research (probing individual reactions to messages in small-group discussion settings) is done to monitor the words and symbols that activate considerations that in turn produce desired opinions.

The resulting battles for public opinion tend to be won by those who are able to create (a) the simplest messages, (b) that strike the strongest emotional chord, (c) that reach the most people, and (d) that can be repeated often, so that (e) they echo through a fragmented society and media system, with the result of (f) engaging shared considerations (g) that help people convince each other to take particular positions in common.

The news becomes one of several important channels (advertising, talk radio, direct mail, e-mail, and social media are others) for getting this repetition and echo effect going in society.[28] As noted, information biases such as personalization and dramatization turn out to be important both for political communication consultants in their battle for public attention and for news organizations deciding what makes the news. The news biases introduced in the last chapter both arise from and are reinforced by this interplay between the kinds of stories that are easy and economical for news organizations to tell and the kinds of messages that public relations consultants build into the events they try to get into the news. The resulting self-contained stories often end up fragmenting complex situations into isolated media episodes focused on personalized dramas. Once again, this reflects the interplay between journalism and newsmakers, with journalists better able to manage simple, bounded stories than complex ones and public relations managers aiming to keep their messages simple and free of complication.

Often the biggest news stories highlight threats to personal security, playing into the authority-disorder bias of news, and accomplishing the attention-getting needs of politicians. Just as advertisers may create a problem that their product can solve, political communication strategies often suggest a threat to personal security that a policy (or opposition to it) can address.[29] When these information packages reach large numbers of people who share similar considerations (feelings and beliefs), public opinion can be influenced, and those effects may then be magnified by the way polls are used in the news.

SELLING THE IRAQ WAR

With these considerations in mind, let's think about how political communication experts were able to get images into the news that created the impression that there was public support for a large-scale invasion of a country halfway around the world. The Iraq War was sold to the American public based on the repeated and carefully crafted insinuations of a connection between 9/11 and Saddam Hussein, with the added consideration that Saddam was building weapons of mass destruction thrown in for good measure. Saddam was a figure who triggered strong negative considerations among most Americans. He had even been likened to Hitler by communications managers in drumming up support for the first Gulf War in 1991, a war waged to rescue the kingdom of Kuwait following Saddam's invasion of it. But hostility toward Saddam, alone, did not shift opinion in support of another war. Drumming up support for the war required adding other considerations to the communication equation, such as associations with Osama bin Laden and weapons of mass destruction, along with menacing references to mushroom clouds by high-level officials. This practice of highlighting particular issues or features in a complex situation to emphasize the considerations around which opinion forms is called *priming*.[30]

The campaign to sell the second Iraq War began in the fall of 2002. Like most persuasion campaigns, it was timed for a period (in this case, after the summer holidays) when sustained public attention could be secured in the news. As former White House chief of staff Andrew Card put it in an interview that the *New York Times* ran in September 2002, "From a marketing point of view, you don't introduce new products in August."[31]

How were news messages designed so that fearful images could be repeated over and over in the echo chamber of the media and appeal to existing considerations that might shift opinion in favor of going to war? It was clear that hostility toward Saddam Hussein alone was not great enough to push support beyond the existing levels that favored continued monitoring and sanctioning Iraq. The Bush administration introduced a link between Saddam and 9/11, even though there was no evidence that Saddam had been involved in planning the 9/11 attacks. To get around this nagging detail, White House communication strategists set out to suggest a "relationship" between Iraq and al-Qaeda. Every high official of the administration delivered the same message to journalists. Condoleezza Rice, national security advisor, claimed that al-Qaeda "clearly has had links to the Iraqis, not to mention Iraqi links to all kinds of other terrorists." Secretary of Defense Rumsfeld said, "There is no question but that there have been interactions between the Iraqi government, Iraqi officials and al-Qaeda operatives." Vice President Cheney noted that while there was no evidence that Saddam helped plan 9/11, "there is a pattern of relationship going back many years." And President Bush claimed that "We know that Iraq and al-Qaeda have had high level contacts that go back a decade."[32] Even though outside experts tried to point out that there was little or no hard evidence to support these claims, and that there was a good deal of evidence that Saddam was one of the secular Arab regimes that Osama opposed, the high volume of repeated administration messages primed the news for months leading up to the war. This raises the question of whether the press should report dubious claims from officials just because journalistic formulas give official pronouncements the lion's share of space in the news—a question we will consider in Chapter 6.

What were the results of this news campaign? More than 50 percent of Americans soon formed the impression that Saddam had been personally involved in the 9/11 attacks, an opinion formation that peaked around the time of the war and did not begin to correct itself until more than a year later. Furthermore, a majority of Americans believed that they had received generally accurate information from the administration about the al-Qaeda connection and alleged weapons of mass destruction, another opinion formation that did not begin to correct itself until more than a year after the war began.

This example indicates that even though it is not easy to influence opinion, it is possible to do so through dominating the news with simple messages that are personal, dramatic, and fragmented enough to appeal to large numbers of people, particularly when those messages arouse considerations about order and security. This means that the kinds of messages that succeed in shaping opinion are also those that best fit the information biases of news. Television coverage tends to exaggerate these biases, meaning that individuals who get most of their news from TV are less likely to think beyond very personalized considerations when forming opinions. By contrast, those who get most of their news from newspapers tend to reach more complex understandings of problems.[33] Because most people still get their news from television, the incentive is for public relations strategists to create the simplest, most personal, and dramatic made-for-TV events.

Thus, the Bush administration was able to claim strong initial public support for the war and continued to point to that to justify the invasion even as the popularity of the war faded. Yet, before we accept the strength of early public approval for the invasion of Iraq, recall the earlier point about how news polls tend to complete the political spin process. David Moore's study of opinion strength also included asking people who were pushed to have an opinion about the war if they cared whether their preferences came to pass. Suddenly, the alleged popular support began to look rather thin. Only 29 percent favored the war and said they would be upset if it did not occur! Another 30 percent opposed the war and said they would be upset if it did happen.

Fully 41 percent said they would not be upset if the opposite of their opinion happened.[34] This simple question puts a different spin on public support for the war. Yet news reports did not include such analysis. When the goals and values of partisan political campaigns and news reporting become so similar, the public interest may suffer.

NEWS AND PUBLIC OPINION: THE CITIZEN'S DILEMMA

News management is an important part of politics for communication professionals. Even if there is no guarantee of winning the battle for public opinion, failing to have a newsmaking strategy generally ensures losing it. What is less evident is that these mediated communication campaigns may go beyond adding or subtracting points from opinion polls. The way politicians communicate is often noisy and negative. Moreover, as technologies for targeting particular demographic segments of the public become more sophisticated, public communication becomes increasingly exclusionary. Large numbers of people are often not addressed at all, because they are deemed too hard to reach, too difficult to persuade, or simply not necessary for winning an election or generating public pressure on Washington. As a result, increasing numbers of people are tuning out the news and other sources of political information because they find them negative, distressing, discouraging, or simply not speaking to them.

Unfortunately, this escape from the news is too often an escape from politics and civic life as well. Communication scholar Roderick Hart argues that the way we communicate may even make people feel "saintly" about abandoning politics.[35] Like the politicians, pundits, and critics they hear in the news, many citizens adopt the identity of outsiders battling a system run amok. For many, cynicism becomes an angry stance against a political communication process that offers little beyond targeted messages aimed at shaping opinion, shifting votes, or raising and lowering the chorus of public discontent. This does not mean that people necessarily buy all or even most of what the politicians are selling. It does mean, however, that when they enter the political arena, the language and choices they find are products of the communication processes outlined in this book.

Perhaps the most distressing exodus from the news and politics has been among young people, as discussed in Chapter 1. This is becoming a vicious circle, as those who run professional communication campaigns often feel that spending resources to reach young citizens is a waste—they are hard to reach, unlikely to get involved, and best left in their state of inattentiveness (although a massive effort was made by both parties to mobilize young voters in the 2004 and 2008 elections with some positive results). Moreover, younger citizens live in a social world that is less oriented to joining social groups—the clubs and organizations that their parents and grandparents joined and which created important connections to others in society and to public institutions.

As a result of these and other shifts in social and political life, younger citizens participate less in core political activities such as voting, and they have less knowledge of the issues that might engage them in those activities. As Robert Putnam put it:

> The post–baby boom generation—roughly speaking, men and women who were born after 1964 and thus came of age in the 1980s and 1990s—are substantially less knowledgeable about public affairs, despite the proliferation of sources of information. Even in the midst of national election campaigns in the 1980s and 1990s, for example, these young people were about a third less likely than their elders to know, for instance, which party controlled the House of Representatives.[36]

This is not just a matter of young people being distracted while getting their adult lives started, and later becoming more involved citizens. Each generation of young Americans entering society in the last several decades has been less informed, less inclined to follow politics in the news, and less likely to participate in political life than the last. This pattern of generational rejection of politics is unlike anything witnessed in modern times. Here is how Putnam describes it:

> Today's generation gap in political knowledge does not reflect some permanent tendency for the young to be less well informed than their elders but is instead a recent development. From the earliest opinion polls in the 1940s to the mid-1970s, younger people were at least as well informed as their elders were, but that is no longer the case. This news and information gap, affecting not just politics, but even things like airline crashes, terrorism, and financial news, first opened up with the boomers in the 1970s and widened considerably with the advent of the X generation. Daily newspaper readership among young people under 35 dropped from two-thirds in 1965 to one-third in 1990, at the same time that TV news viewership in this same age group fell from 52 percent to 41 percent. Today's under-thirties pay less attention to the news and know less about current events than their elders do today or than people their age did two or three decades ago.[37]

Perhaps the most important aspect of the way we communicate is not that opinion is occasionally influenced but that so many citizens are discouraged and disconnected from politics. Although these trends cannot be traced entirely to communication practices, there are notable failures of both news and politics to engage and motivate people. Even those who continue to try to find meaning in news content are often frustrated with the negativity, sensationalism, and disconnection from their own political concerns and action options. In either case, the news and the larger political communication logic that feeds it frustrate the formation of interested and informed publics on which the quality of democracy depends. On most issues, publics are poorly informed, and those who do follow events are disproportionately older, white, conservative males.[38]

In considering whether to become involved in public life, people confront a dilemma: If they ignore or discount what they hear from the officials and opinion leaders who make the news, they become isolated and unable to contribute to that most precious citizen resource in a democracy—public opinion. By contrast, people who overcome their cynicism and become part of public life often feel pressured to adjust their views to the available media agenda of issues and credible positions. Whether they choose isolation, consensus, or escape, people complain that their opinions are often dashed by government inaction, or by policies that sounded better in the news than when put into action. These experiences may account for the rising tide of political discontent measured in polls and in elections over the past quarter-century.[39] What traps people in this dilemma is that the national political communication process is more often one way than two way, providing little room for grassroots exploration of alternative agendas and programs for public action. Even many citizen revolts—such as the movement to impose term limits on elected politicians—turn out to be organized by interests with ties to traditional politics and big money.

Not surprisingly, this dilemma affects people differently. Some adopt a familiar ideology or party line and embrace it meaningfully, whether or not it seems to be solving real-world problems. Some abandon politics altogether and step behind a shield of isolation and cynicism. Others decide that participating in public life, for all its dilemmas, is better than leading an isolated existence. In general, people are less likely to find issues in the news important when they feel powerless and more likely to engage with challenging stories that explain what average people can do to make a difference. From this we may conclude that the sense of being left out of politics may partly explain why so few people are informed about politics and government.

Most Americans score poorly on basic citizen knowledge tests such as the one developed by Michael Delli Carpini and Scott Keeter.[40] Critics of these tests, such as Doris Graber, argue that they more resemble trivia tests and do not measure the kind of practical understandings that might help people navigate through real political situations.[41] Yet the names of elected officials or the number of votes required in the House or Senate to overturn a presidential veto are not the only things that are vague in the minds of most people. Few people pay close attention to much of what they see in the news. A survey by the Pew Research Center tracked public attention to more than 670 news stories over a ten-year span and found that only 5 percent of the stories attracted close attention from those polled.[42]

PROCESSING THE NEWS

How can we become adequately informed when many political communication strategies are not aimed at broad inclusion and when that information is further filtered by commercial news formulas that add their own narrowing of the communication flow? One thing that seems certain is that the idea of easy mass persuasion through an all-reaching media is farfetched, if for no other reason than this is not how communication strategists or media markets work. Nonetheless, some observers may continue to think that mass persuasion is a regular occurrence. For example, political scientists Russell Neuman, Marion Just, and Ann Crigler argue that some scholars continue to believe that mass media messages hold sway with a large passive citizenry: "The traditional view of the way citizens gain information from the media is dominated by imagery of a vegetative audience, passively absorbing media influence."[43] Because they cite me as holding this view, let me set the record straight: There is considerable evidence that individuals actively select, filter, and personalize the meanings that they draw from the news, and, as noted above, many people actively avoid much of the news altogether.

At the same time, it is not clear that active engagement or avoidance in a highly spun news environment necessarily makes people feel better about society, helps them better relate to others, or act effectively as citizens. Moreover, the failure of news to motivate those who are turned off to the political process means that the escape from public life (particularly among younger citizens) continues to grow. Communication scholars Thomas Patterson and Philip Seib argue that the most important function of the media may not be to directly inform citizens, but to first attract their attention and interest. Once people have developed an interest in politics, they are more likely to seek out information that is often available in the media environment.[44]

Without political interest and curiosity, the information environment can seem overwhelming. One of the pioneers in understanding how people "tame the information tide" is political scientist Doris Graber. Her research on how people process the news reveals that many personal factors shape what people pay attention to and what they think it means: personal interests in the issue or problem; the influence of friends who provide news updates and interpretations; and eventually, the personal frames or models of society that people develop to recognize familiar aspects of news stories. One of her later studies is aimed at how to reconnect young citizens with information that engages and motivates them to act politically. She concludes from research on how the brain processes information that more visual, interactive television and Web-based formats contain the potential to reconnect young citizens.[45]

Most research shows that people develop personal interpretive strategies that help them actively *construct* meanings from the news they choose to engage with. In some cases, these constructions can be quite surprising and removed from the apparently intentional meanings in the news (or entertainment) content itself. For example, communication scholar John Fiske found that homeless people residing in a shelter often produced "oppositional readings" of popular television shows, cheering for the bad guys and rejecting the good guys—mirroring the way that "proper society" had rejected them in real life.[46]

Sociologist William Gamson shows that people explore news issues in often remarkable depth through everyday conversation, applying various interpretations that were not contained in the news stories they consumed. For example, some people overcome the sense of isolation from events by applying "collective action" frames that address issues of justice, common identities, and the possibilities for social action. Gamson acknowledges that breaking out of the sense of isolation often associated with news frames is easier for people with direct personal experience with an issue. People without direct experience are far more influenced by the framing in news stories.[47] Following along these lines, studies by Neuman, Just, and Crigler show that people are less likely to regard even heavily covered issues as important if they feel powerless to do much about them. People are more likely to wade through dense and complex stories if they contain information about "what you can do about the problem."[48]

It also turns out that the medium matters. Contrary to common stereotypes, people actually learn more from television coverage of most issues than from newspaper coverage. It seems hard for most people to decode and organize the greater detail of newspaper coverage unless they already have a personal interest in the issue and unless they have some personal frame of reference to help sort through the dense newspaper format. News magazines are much more accessible than newspapers and nearly as informative as television, perhaps because they offer more of an overview and a thematic perspective in a weekly format than in daily newspaper installments. This research may provide a simple explanation for why the vast majority of people prefer television as their primary news source: They actually learn more from it.[49] However, as noted earlier, when people do have the motivation to dig into print news, they often develop less personal, episodic, and more complex thematic understandings of issues and events.

Why People Prefer TV: Audio and Visual Information

As just noted, people generally learn more from television than from other news media. Not surprisingly, TV is the runaway favorite news source across most demographics. When asked where they go for information on important stories that affect their lives, about half say television, compared with 42 percent for radio, one-third for newspapers, and one-quarter for Internet sites of major news organizations. Only 6 percent turn to blogs and other citizen-based sources. (These figures add to more than 100 because some people rely on multiple sources.) The Internet becomes a more favored source for entertainment news and gossip.[50]

Americans still love TV. Some early surveys claim that people, on average, get more satisfaction from television than from a wide range of other pursuits, including sports, eating, hobbies, and even sex![51] Most people watch TV with the explicit expectation of having a pleasurable or emotionally stimulating experience. Perhaps the most interesting commentary on the centrality of television is from an early study of people (680 households, 1,614 individuals) whose TV sets were either stolen (19%) or broken (81%). In 24 percent of these households, people experienced something like a mourning reaction, and 68 percent reported psychological troubles ranging from anxiety symptoms (39%) to moderate discomfort (29%).[52]

Doris Graber notes these and other studies as indicators that TV (and, one presumes, YouTube) stimulates the human brain in more comprehensive ways than other media do. Graber cites research on human brain functions and information processing to conclude that information is not compartmentalized, but continually integrated across different kinds of sensory input. Television, unlike most other news media, gives us words, sounds, and sights to work with. This enriches the sense of understanding and knowing more about televised situations.[53] The important question, of course, is how those who produce television news approach their responsibility to carefully select the pictures and sounds that go along with the words.

News and Personal Experience: What Gets Through

To reduce information processing to its simplest terms, we can say that after repeated exposure to a mediated issue or problem, some vague attention and recognition may begin to set in. If there is in addition, some active personal interest in the issue, people may categorize, or frame, the issue to help keep it in focus, organize future information, and begin thinking more clearly about it. After people have begun to form categories, they can place finer details and bits of information in the categories and begin to shade their thoughts and opinions. Following the development of attention, interest, and some basic categorization schemes, people may pick up and evaluate news information in the following ways:

- *Cueing:* looking for cues or labels (left, right; Republican, Democrat; hawk, dove; environmentalist, gun lover, terrorist, etc.).
- *Bolstering:* selecting factoids or bits of information that are offered to support positions attached to broad political cues and labels.
- *Weighing:* using emotions attached to cues and information in news reports to direct attention and learning.
- *Personal organizing:* filtering this mediated information into the central organizing principles (values, interests, lifestyle choices) that make up the individual's personal life experiences.

Using these intellectual labor-saving devices, people creatively incorporate the information in various media representations (news, political advertising, editorials, punditry, etc.) into their personal thinking. Each individual develops a strategy for both selecting and tuning out information about politics, and in the process, both draws from and contributes to public opinion. Consider how each of these information processing strategies operates.

Cueing: Taking Broad Interpretive Cues from the News   Most of us simplify busy lives by screening political information through familiar and trusted reference groups. We take (or react against) cues from leaders, political parties, interest groups, and other familiar news sources that interpret (frame) news events and offer opinions that may guide thinking about a confusing world. In addition, stereotypes, slogans, and old-fashioned name calling can provide the basis for simplifying our thinking about otherwise complicated realities. When members of the Tea Party movement denounced the health care reform process of 2009–2010 as fascism, socialism, and Obamacare, among other terms, they invited a larger news audience to identify with them as "Tea Party patriots" who were resisting the evils of government intrusion, while attaching negative sentiments about president Obama to the health legislation. These cues were echoed by Republican leaders in Congress, giving them greater credibility than they might otherwise have had. Then the pundits on conservative talk radio, cable TV and online blogs and discussion forums magnified the audience impact of these simple cues. The result was a steady erosion of public support for the proposed health care reform.

Research by political scientist John Zaller demonstrates that the more closely people follow an issue in the news, the more their opinions follow the cues offered by leaders of the political parties, recognized ideological groups, and other prominent political viewpoints.[54] This means, in effect, that the more informed people are about issues in the news, the more their opinions conform to those expressed by elites, government officials, interest groups, newsworthy movement leaders, and parties.

Perhaps even more startling, these generalizations apply most strongly to more educated people, who tend to pay more attention to the news—the so-called informed public. Although this is an ironic way to think about being informed, it is less surprising when we recall that the information that goes into the news is largely provided by government officials and other prominent elites (or in cases like the Tea Party uprising, reinforced by them).

This does not mean that hearing one statement containing a familiar symbol or information source typically molds understanding of an issue. On the contrary, most people live in a serious state of information overload. They tend not to pay much attention until an issue or event reaches saturation coverage and continues to make the news regularly for an extended period of time with prominent spokespersons taking increasingly clear and simple positions. Once this signal-to-noise ratio (discussed further in Chapter 4) becomes very high, people begin to accept the kinds of broad cues discussed earlier to help organize their thinking. Thus, the ability of the Bush administration to dominate the news leading up to the Iraq War and repeatedly link Iraq to weapons of mass destruction and terrorism led majorities of Americans to conclude that Iraq represented an immediate threat.

Bolstering: Selecting Factoids That Fit the Cues   Even when people are knee-jerk liberals, conservatives, Republicans, Democrats, or Rush Limbaugh "ditto heads," they tend to search for some supporting reasons to accept the cues they get from their favorite political references. This is where *factoids* come in, those bits and pieces of information that fill in emerging understandings of a situation. This is also where news management becomes crucial, with forces on both sides trying to keep a story going and adding elements that reinforce their preferred interpretations while countering those of the other side. For example, in political campaigns where the field of candidates narrows and media scrutiny becomes more intense, there is a daily battle in which each side tries to build up its own message while tearing down the images of the other side.

In the political trenches, the lines between news and advertising, information and propaganda, have become increasingly hard to draw. Media consultants often try to insert news and documentary-type images into TV advertisements while setting up news events with advertising values in mind. The synergy between news and advertising can be important in getting public attention and influencing opinions. When themes from advertising hit the news, they gain an important element of "facticity" (seeming objectivity or legitimacy) that can break down resistance.

During the great health care reform battle of 1994, for example, groups in the health care, insurance, and pharmaceutical industries spent millions of dollars on advertising to create doubts about possible negative effects of the president's call for universal health care. A barrage of commercials sent emotional messages about rising costs, government bureaucracy, diminished quality of care, and long waits for treatment to the politically important middle-class audience (most of whom already had health insurance).

Among the most memorable ad campaigns were the "Harry and Louise" spots produced by the health insurance industry, whose member companies stood to lose a great deal from any plan that regulated their profits or required them to extend coverage to people with expensive health problems, such as cancer or AIDS. The millions of dollars they spent on the slick Madison Avenue spots were minor compared with the billions that the big insurance companies had at stake in the reforms. Harry and Louise were depicted as a sympathetic middle-aged, middle-class couple of the sort that appears in TV series and other commercials. They worried about what they would lose under the proposed reforms, and each ad in the series introduced a new element of doubt about the leading plans, particularly the one championed by Hillary and Bill Clinton.

Meanwhile, behind the scenes, the health care industry was spending widely on lobbying and campaign contributions to key members of Congress to pry their support away from the president's plan. Not surprisingly, the authoritative opposition voices from Congress that were heard in the news echoed the same elements of doubt raised in the advertising.[55] A public opinion one-two punch of cueing and bolstering had been set in motion.

These campaigns took their toll on public support. After more than a year of concerted news and advertising information blitzes, a strong majority of 74 percent still favored the idea of universal coverage, a cornerstone of the Clinton plan.[56] However, only 33 percent backed the Clinton plan, reflecting the 76 percent said they were unwilling to accept less choice in doctors or hospitals, and the 74 percent believed that universal reform would lead to rationing.[57] Perhaps most telling of all was the discovery made by the White House polling team led by Stanley Greenberg that after all the sides had weighed in, the public actually understood less about the Clinton plan than they did at the time it was unveiled.

The health care fight of 2009-2010 produced similar results, with the added introduction of unsavory facts about the president himself, including the claim that he was not born in the U.S., and, thus, was not constitutionally qualified to be the president. While this factoid was not directly related to health care, it emerged from the same general Tea Party movement that filled the media for the year of the health care policy debate, and clouded the thinking of many people about Mr. Obama. Even after the numerous affirmations by officials in Hawaii (the place of his birth) that he was indeed born there, only 42 percent of the public were definitely sure that this was true, while 27 percent felt that it was definitely or probably not true.[58] This case illustrates how getting falsehoods into the media offers people convenient information to use in bolstering their beliefs and prejudices.

The moral of this story is that once the big information cues—such as president and Congress, Republicans and Democrats, big government and small government, popular politicians, or movements recognized by them—have structured the information picture, the fine details added daily in the news and advertising can make a big difference. As Robert Teeter, one of the gurus of the information and opinion management business, put it: "People don't decide based on some great revelation. They form their views based on thousands of little bits of information that shake out from television ads and news stories."[59]

Weighing: Paying Attention to the Positive and Negative Emotions The first two patterns of information processing are seldom enough to account for public reactions to news. In most cases, people would not even attend to stories if there were not some emotional hook or charge in them. It is not surprising in this light that the communication strategies employed by warring political factions can turn downright nasty. This often happens in election campaigns and big national policy battles. The emotions in the long-running national fight over abortion policy come to mind here.

Not only do advocates for a cause challenge factual claims and attack the character of opponents, but they also frequently plant doubts that have little basis in fact. Indeed, when the battle rages for the emotions of the public, the question of what is true or relevant is often the least of considerations. The key concerns of strategic communication become: What gets people's attention? and then, What creates or resolves doubts in their thinking? Although media managers often have more freedom with advertising, they can obtain the greatest effects when the same messages cross over and become part of news stories.

This is not to suggest that emotions are bad or even less relevant than facts in their thinking about politics. On the contrary, research by George Marcus, Russell Neuman, and Michael MacKuen shows that, in many cases, some degree of emotional arousal must occur in order for people to pay attention to other kinds of information in a situation. In some cases, the emotional (or affective) information that people receive may be far more important for their thinking and acting than facts (or cognitions).[60] These important understandings also help explain why TV is more important than other media for most people. Given the emotional satisfactions of social networking sites, and the growing uses by political players to deliver content directly through them, it is easy to see that the future of emotional information processing is online.

Many journalists worry that the loss of quality control through editorial standards may corrupt the communication process and leave it even more vulnerable to manipulation. However, other observers see the current news (and advertising) system as frequently corrupted by spin and political propaganda. The result is that the use of emotion in political communication is often not aimed at enhancing critical thought or judgment, and the reporting tendencies of the press do not always favor the citizen as much as they favor communication strategists bent on winning their immediate political battles. For example, given the tendencies of the press to indulge in feeding frenzies (described in Chapter 5), allegations and charges from one political camp can often turn into news nightmares for another. The failure to counter even the most scurrilous charge planted in the news can begin to gnaw at people and take root in their opinions, even if they try to ignore the dirt and concentrate on substantial information. All this explains one of the great puzzles of political communication: Negativity often works even though a large majority of the public claims that they hate negative communication and that they try to screen it out of their thinking.

An important word of caution is in order here: Negative communication does not always work. A classic case is the difference between the George H. W. Bush election campaigns of 1988 and 1992. Both were extremely negative campaigns, with conservative estimates of the negative message content running at 50 percent or more of Bush's ads and news statements and increasing to as much as 75 to 80 percent in the closing days.[61] Yet Bush won one of those campaigns quite handily and lost the other one quite convincingly. To simplify the reasons greatly, negative campaigning is less successful if the opponent (or the victim, as it were) understands the importance of information bolstering and counters every bit of negative information with bits of information that deflect it, raise doubts about the other side, or refocus public attention on something else. Where Bush's 1988 opponent Michael Dukakis seemed to lack a strategic response to the negative attacks of 1988 (thus allowing them to sink in), Bill Clinton in 1992 developed a "wink and a shrug" that suggested that perhaps President Bush's use of negative tactics meant that he was a bit desperate.

In short, when people encounter negative information that goes uncountered, they tend to incorporate the negativity into their thinking even if, consciously, they try to avoid it. In the view of opinion experts Barbara Farah and Ethel Klein, people make the best sense they can of the information they have available to them, even when that information is negative, of questionable reliability, or generally distasteful.[62]

Personal Organizing: Judging New Information Against Personal Experiences   A popular school of thought about citizen information processing suggests that people are lazy information processors or cognitive misers.[63] Citizens rely mainly on gut feelings, personal experience, and their immediate life circumstances to screen information and reach judgments about politics. In this view, much information from the outer world is discounted simply because it does not dent this shell of personal experience. Thus, people take shortcuts in processing information and arrive at judgments about politics that have been described by political scientist Samuel Popkin as "low information rationality."[64] Such experienced-based reasoning about politics explains why people cannot remember many facts about particular stories in the news, yet draw cues, supporting factoids, and feelings from news coverage as the basis for judgments that often turn out to be fairly stable and meaningful.

Charting the terms of public engagement reminds us that beneath the rough indicators and simple judgments recorded in opinion polls are meanings that people construct in the process of arriving at their opinions on issues. For all that individuals may bring to bear in interpreting the news, there is considerable evidence that well-targeted news content can greatly affect the thinking of the average person. This is particularly true when messages have been shaped to appeal to selected or targeted audiences. The work of Iyengar and Kinder (see Chapter 2) showed that just being in the news makes issues seem more important than issues that are not covered, confirming the hypothesis that the news can tell people what to think about.[65] A follow-up series of experiments by Iyengar found that the personalized or "episodic" *framing* of stories directed audiences to think in short-term, emotional, and personalized ways about issues such as economics and social policy. What is missing in most news coverage, according to Iyengar, are more "thematic" approaches to framing social problems that might encourage people to learn and think about the social, political, and economic forces that affect them.[66] In the process of making judgments that feed into public opinion, people are often shocked, awed, and just plain entertained by news. Indeed, without these elements of human interest, much of the higher political content would be lost on average citizens and of interest only to news junkies.

ENTERTAINMENT AND OTHER REASONS PEOPLE FOLLOW THE NEWS

Thus far we have viewed news information in its most obvious democratic context: People follow the news to gather information that may help them in thinking about politics, forming opinions, and taking more effective political action. However, as noted earlier and illustrated in the case study, there are clearly other reasons people follow the news:

- *Curiosity and surveillance:* scanning for information that may be useful in everyday life (news of airline fare wars, weather forecasts, inflation reports, home mortgage rates).
- *Entertainment and escape:* following the interesting dramas that often develop in politics. People can simply enjoy the spectacle of politics.
- *Social and psychological adjustment:* keeping contact with society and our own places in it (How is my world? Where do I stand in it?).

News organizations also understand that people have such broader uses for the news, and they adjust their content and coverage accordingly. As popular tastes and interests shift, the news generally follows, creating tensions with the democratic ideal of citizen-engagement-oriented news. Critics argue that pandering to public tastes only fuels the spiral of declining news values. Others counter that people will select and convert information to their own uses regardless of the standards that news or entertainment organizations attempt to maintain. For example, studies of popular American television programs in other countries show that viewers often find meanings that American audiences are far less likely to support, including confirmation of some rather nasty beliefs about greed, violence, corruption, and other images of life in the United States.[67]

A great deal of research has been conducted on the so-called uses and gratifications of news and entertainment programming, with a focus on highly personalized decoding of media content.[68] Traditional research on the broader, so-called uses and gratifications associated with the news can be summarized under the three broad categories just listed.[69]

Curiosity and Surveillance

People are blessed with curiosity, which can be a source of sheer pleasure or amusement as well as a means of spotting new information that might be useful in coping with everyday reality. Research has shown that human curiosity is piqued by things (e.g., situations, ideas, scenery, films, art, and news) that contain a mixture of familiar and novel stimuli and features.[70] On the one hand, repeated exposure to completely familiar stimuli results in the formation of subconscious mental "scripts" that make it possible to respond to situations without really thinking about them.[71] Curiosity and attention are minimized in such scripted situations. On the other hand, stimuli that are completely foreign may be so dissonant and hard to assimilate that people tend to ignore, avoid, or misinterpret them.[72]

Even though the political messages in the news are fairly predictable, the events, plots, and characters are constantly changing. Human curiosity is engaged by new events and novel twists on old themes. Moreover, some of the events in the news may have an impact on the people who follow them. Thus, many people find it useful to scan the news just to keep potentially important events under surveillance. News is the perfect blend of the familiar and the novel. There is an intrinsic satisfaction in seeing how a familiar theme will develop in a new plot or whether an old plot will develop a new twist. For example, how will freedom of choice—a theme familiar to every American—be adapted to fit such contexts as abortion, drug use, pornography, health care reform, or the regulation of cigarette smoking in public places? As long as new events keep happening in the world, people will be drawn to the news as a means of applying, testing, and adjusting their understandings about reality.

However, the news may satisfy our curiosity too easily when familiar political scripts confirm popular beliefs and stereotypes that people have scripted into their own thinking. For example, if some people hold racial prejudices against a black person being president, it may be easier to believe that

President Obama is not a "real" American citizen. That belief may become more acceptable when those promoting it are given time in the news. To take another example, if the news persists in portraying the problems of the global south in terms of a long process of development aimed at overcoming the stigma of underdevelopment, the news audience may fail to perceive the problems caused by many the leading models of development. Critics sometimes claim that leading models of development often perpetuate the core problems of underdevelopment by destroying local economies and cultures, fostering export dependence by poor countries on the economies of rich countries, and tolerating the corruption that often accompanies economic growth in repressive regimes. Despite such limitations, magic terms such as "development" and "development aid" are scripted in the news by government officials and reporters.

In efforts to refocus public attention on the false promise of globalization and related development myths, a global justice movement has staged demonstrations in cities around the world where trade and development agencies hold their meetings. Other activists have turned brand images against the corporations that created them by cleverly waging *logo campaigns* against corporations, such as McDonald's, Nike, and Coca-Cola to bring news attention to global problems involving environmental change, labor abuses, and human rights.[73] The news is often the most satisfying when it contains periodic information that is directly relevant to people and contains information that helps them think in action-oriented terms. Thus, putting globalization issues in terms that consumers can understand offers a direct link to political understanding and involvement.

Entertainment and Escape

The news may represent itself as fact, but, as illustrated in Chapter 2, it is communicated to the public with all the trappings of fiction: short, intense scenes; literary rather than analytical treatments; the nearly uniform use of the story format; and the emphasis on drama, emotional conflict, and larger-than-life characters. The news may portray real events, but this portrayal often discourages analytical or instrumental uses for the information it presents. This result is not an inevitable property of narratives, which can, if presented in the right ways, actually provoke thoughtful reflection and action. Indeed, some news narratives appear to have this critical potential, as when people are engaged in sustained and important national deliberations.

Most stories in the news do not go on long enough, however, nor do they contain angles that people identify deeply enough with, to stimulate much thought or critical action. It is, in these cases, easy to become engaged by the sheer drama of news events. The news makes everyday happenings seem larger than life. Most news reports invite us to escape for a minute or two into a world filled with pathos, tragedy, moral lessons, crisis, mystery, danger, and occasional whimsy. The escape into this dramatic world is made all the easier when the happenings involve people like us or people about whom we have strong positive or negative feelings.

Each day's news menu offers a large supply of complete minidramas for our entertainment pleasure. We can step into one fascinating fantasy for a minute or two—experiencing a brief sense of other lives and other worlds—and then move on to the next one. One moment we are a member of a guerilla band on maneuvers in a far-off war, the next we move in with the survivors of an earthquake, and then suddenly we are transported into the nightmare of a bank robbery and murder captured on closed-circuit video system. At last, the string of high-tension episodes is broken by a commercial that gives us a chance to regain our bearings, grab a snack, and get ready for the next install-ment of our evening's journey into real-life adventure.

Vicarious involvement in the news is often even more compelling than more conventional forms of escape via drama and literature. News dramas, after all, are represented as real, serious, important, and worthy of everyone's attention. Fiction, by contrast, does not involve real spies, real robbers, or real earthquakes. Fiction can at times command our attention, but it seldom com-bines intensity, universality of appeal, and realism the way the news does. A best-selling novel about terrorism may sell a million copies during its lengthy run on the best-seller list, whereas hundreds of millions may be riveted by the news on a single day such as 9/11.

The seriousness or realism of the news is, paradoxically, a key to under-standing its power as an escape medium. The general acceptance of the news as factual, important, and objective makes it easy for people to give them-selves over to serious involvement with it. Having done this, the individual is swept away by images and ideas that are often both stranger and more dra-matic than fiction. For example, few novels contain plot twists like the ones in the news story about a band of thieves posing as police officers who were forced by circumstances to try to arrest a group of policemen disguised as a gang of thieves. The real police were—you guessed it—on the trail of the thieves who were posing as police. If a novelist were to submit such a plot to a publisher, it would probably be rejected as incredible or unrealistic. When it becomes news, however, no plot is too incredible to be engrossing. Fictional accounts of political power and intrigue may achieve a measure of credibility, but few can match the daily revelations about power and corruption in the White House that filled the news at the time of the Watergate scandal. The unfolding horrors of 9/11 will forever be etched in the minds of those who witnessed them.

The news is often so dramatic that it supplies the plot material for novels, films, television series, and docudramas. Novels and TV scripts have been written about legal conflicts, murders, robberies, hijackings, and kidnap-pings—subjects that first captured the popular imagination in the news. Jour-nalistic treatments of terrorism, political corruption, military operations, and spy escapades have spawned movies by the score. The people who often arrive at the scene of a news event after the reporters are book agents and movie deal makers. Such a trend only enhances the news as an escape medium. One observer of this trend of life-based reality dramas dominating entertainment media called his book *Life: The Movie.*[74]

As Walter Lippmann pointed out many years ago, the world of politics, as viewed by the public, will always be somewhat dramatized and fictionalized.[75] Politicians who control the flow of information will attempt whenever possible to shape news to their advantage. However, when the media actively seek dramatized reality to feed to a receptive audience, the moderating influence on the representation of political reality is removed. *When politicians, press, and public all judge political performances more in terms of dramatic criteria than moral standards, assessments of truth and balance may become diminished.*

If the dramatization of political reality is a key to understanding the fortunes of public life, it is no less important for understanding the private political worlds of individual citizens. Vicarious political experience may be different from direct participation, but it is nonetheless a valid form of experience. As a result, escape and entertainment are far from being meaningless pursuits. Whatever their other effects may be, political dramas can help people open up their fantasies and subconscious feelings, assisting them in easing psychological tensions and social strains. The escape and entertainment functions of the news thus pave the way for important social and psychological adjustments.

Social and Psychological Adjustment

When people escape into the world of drama found in the news, they do not necessarily leave all their concerns behind them. Although our inclinations for direct action may be inhibited by the one-way communication channels of the mass media, we respond psychologically to the people and issues in news reports. It is, in fact, remarkably easy to identify with actors in the news, respond to them emotionally, and imagine that we are somehow part of their experiences. In a fascinating discussion of the rise of nations, political scientist Benedict Anderson argues that to an important degree, the society of strangers beyond our daily, face-to-face worlds is a product of imagination fueled by the media.[76]

Human beings spend a good deal of both their waking and sleeping time creating imaginary scenarios in which they explore wishes, hopes, fears, and desires. Through fantasies, we can rehearse unfamiliar social roles and anticipate encounters with other people. Fantasies also enable us to contain powerful feelings like anger, sexual desire, or fear when it is inappropriate to express them openly in a particular situation. In other situations, fantasies help in making choices about how best to express those feelings in public.

A healthy fantasy life is essential for adjusting to the conditions and people we encounter in real life. The news, with its powerful images, emotional themes, and colorful characters, is a rich source of fantasy material. We can step into a news plot and imagine what it would be like to be rich, poor, powerful, weak, female, male, sexy, brave, or intelligent. By taking the real world into the privacy of our minds via the news, we can explore feelings and relate to people in ways that might not be comfortable or possible in real life.

The emphasis on drama, emotional themes, powerful images, and strong personalities makes the news a convenient medium for working out psychological tensions and social conflicts. People do not even have to leave their living rooms in order to encounter real people about whom they have strong feelings and issues that seem to affect their well-being. In their encounters with this imaginary society, people can form impressions of their community, their nation, and their places in them. By making connections between personal concerns and events and personalities in the news, people can express feelings and think about their problems in uninhibited and often satisfying ways. This vicarious resolution of social and psychological strains is all the more effective because the realities of news stories are usually too distant for people to experience directly—thus the feelings and understandings people develop in response to the news are seldom subjected to reality testing.

Fantasies require very little anchor in reality to thrive. In fact, because by definition fantasies involve the suspension of ordinary reality, they can spring from the barest of suggestions and the least substantial of images. As far as our fantasy life goes, what does it matter what our favorite newscaster is really like in private life? As long as he or she displays the right style, manner, or looks, we feel comfortable inviting him or her into our home and listening as we would to a trusted friend imparting all the news that has transpired since our last meeting.

Because fantasies feed on such minimal information, and because the news transmits such condensed, ambiguous images, it should not be surprising to learn that people generate very different fantasies from the same story. Who knows what it is really like to be the guerilla fighter dashing through the jungle, locked in a life-or-death struggle for the freedom of her country? Some might imagine that she is a romantic figure, with the virtues of bravery, charisma, morals, and intelligence—the sort of person they would secretly like to be. Others might imagine her as a bloodthirsty heathen—an immoral foe who threatens their values and lifestyles. Same news story, different fantasies.

Part of the fantasy element in the news is caused by the heavy emphasis in politics on fantasy themes of power, community, order, and security.[77] Such concerns are central to the social and emotional well-being of the average person. A political speech without an emphasis on power, community, order, or security would be an atypical and in all likelihood an ineffectual statement. These fantasy themes of politics are transmitted from political performances to the mass audiences by the news. In fact, mass media journalism tends to focus on fantasy themes, which represent the most dramatic and universally appealing components of political performances. Fantasy themes are about the only medium through which a lengthy political performance can be condensed into a meaningful news-length capsule.

Consider, as an example, television news coverage of a presidential inauguration. High rituals of state, such as inaugurations, campaigns, funerals, and State of the Union addresses are good vantage points for viewing fantasy themes in action. These rituals are designed to appeal to the popular imagination with images of strength, community, security, and new beginnings. Inaugurations are always occasions for bringing people together; reminding them that they are one nation with common bonds; and calling for renewed commitment to the goals of prosperity, harmony, peace, and security. Because most people are concerned at some level with prosperity, harmony, peace, and security, it is comforting to have related fantasies evoked time and again by each new leader chosen to preserve and protect these elements of the American fantasy, more commonly referred to as the American dream. Inaugural speeches are open invitations for new presidents to pull out all the symbolic stops in an effort to kindle the deepest fantasies that define the political community.

Ronald Reagan was faced with a challenge when he mounted the platform to address the nation in 1980. The country was plunging into recession, national pride was at an ebb, and people saw a future with little promise. Drawing on the themes that got him elected, Reagan exhorted the country to step back into the past as a means of finding the values and spirit with which to face the future. He chose the perfect setting for such a speech. Standing at the West Front of the Capitol, Reagan pointed to the great gallery of national monuments in Washington, DC. As he mentioned great heroes and episodes from the nation's past, he could evoke their physical presence by indicating those shrines. Mentioning George Washington is one thing, but presenting the dramatic image of the Washington Monument and its stunning reflecting pool is an even more effective way to engage the imagination of the audience.

To realize the full potential of the images in his speech, Reagan needed a little help from the media. He could, of course, talk about the great monuments and symbols of state that surrounded him, but how much more effective it would be if the media incorporated pictures of those things as though they were part of the script for the performance? Reagan and his media advisors must have anticipated what the journalists would do. All the White House needed to do was announce the time and place of the performance and issue an advance copy of the script, and the media could be relied on to do the rest. As the following excerpt from Ernest Bormann's analysis of inaugural coverage by CBS television indicates, journalist and political actor joined forces smoothly to maximize the fantasy potential in the event:

> Toward the close of the speech Reagan noted that this was the first time the ceremony was held on the West Front of the Capitol, then he said, "Standing here, one faces a magnificent vista (The director called up a long shot of the magnificent vista), opening up on this city's special beauty and history. At the end of this open mall (The director had the camera pan up the open mall) are those shrines to the giants on whose shoulders we stand. Directly in front of me, the monument to a monumental man (Cut to a shot of Washington monument): George Washington, father of our country. . . ." After an encomium to Washington, Reagan said, "Off to one side (Cut to a shot of the Jefferson Memorial), the stately memorial to Thomas Jefferson." After some words of praise for Jefferson, Reagan continued, "and then beyond the reflecting pool, the dignified columns of the Lincoln Memorial" (Camera moves to Lincoln Memorial). When Reagan next directed his audience's attention to

the "sloping hills of Arlington National Cemetery with its row upon row of simple white markers bearing crosses or Stars of David . . ." the director had the camera focus on the Cemetery.[78]

With this kind of interplay between political images and news emphasis, it is little wonder that news provides a rich source of fantasy. Two characteristics of such fantasy play are the formation of strong expressions of feeling and opinion (stronger than would ordinarily be acceptable in real-life situations) and the development of vicarious relationships with the actors in news stories. Communication theorists have used the term *parasocial relationship* to refer to the often intimate emotional bonds that people can establish with the distant actors in media relationships.[79] Is Lindsey still in rehab? Did Lady Gaga give up celibacy (or did she ever really practice it)? Will Sarah Palin lead her "mama grizzlies" to power? And what will those Tea Party folks do next?

It is clear that shared lifestyles and persuasions mix with personal fascination with such questions, enabling individual attention to merge into public opinion characterized by distinctive group and demographic differences. For example, the sex scandal involving Bill Clinton and a young intern named Monica Lewinsky engaged people at deeply personal levels, involving not just drama and entertainment but also emotions and social identities. At the same time, the social and emotional dimensions of the scandal produced striking differences in the reactions of lower- and higher-income groups. Pew Center surveys indicated that low-income groups were more likely to approve of Clinton's performance in office and less likely to think he should be impeached. Is this just economic self-interest at work? Perhaps low-income groups believed they had economically benefited from Clinton's policies and supported Clinton while discounting the Lewinsky spectacle. Another related explanation might be that these differences among income groups merely echo the effects of political partisanship. Economic gains and some interaction with party loyalty may well be at work here. For these and other reasons, different social and economic groups behaved very differently in terms of separating their support for the job Clinton was doing as president from their feelings about Clinton as a person. A Pew survey asked respondents to choose among the following statements: "I like Bill Clinton personally and I like his policies"; "I don't like Bill Clinton personally but I like his policies"; and "I don't like Bill Clinton personally and I don't like his policies." Here again, sharp differences were clear among income groups. Whereas only 19 percent of the highest-income group and 24 percent of the next-highest group agreed that they liked Bill Clinton personally and liked his policies, 43 and 47 percent of the two lowest-income groups agreed. In contrast, 76 percent of all respondents earning more than $50,000 said they disliked Clinton personally compared with 53 percent of those earning between $20,000 and $30,000 and 44 percent of those earning less than $20,000.[80]

For many lower-income Americans, Bill Clinton appears to have represented something of a sympathetic character despite the sexual scandal. He is, after all, a child of a lower-class background, and he used that fact quite publicly to build his political image as "The Man from Hope." Clinton's symbolic profile as a poor child who rose to the White House perhaps mattered more to poorer Americans than did his sexual behavior. Poorer Americans, therefore, apparently reacted to the Lewinsky scandal in part based on their symbolic understanding of Clinton-as-a-person, signaling not just policy differences among income groups, different emotional constructions of the narrative itself. Levels of popular support for Clinton actually rose as he was put through an impeachment trial by Republican leaders in Congress who dominated the media with continued negative claims about Clinton's character and leadership.

Such reactions to people and issues in political reporting can be important for emotional adjustment and maintaining a sense of emotional belonging in a vast and often conflicted society. Whereas people often feel pressure not to express their true feelings in real-life settings, they can rail against injustice and political folly through private interactions with the media. A range of clear-cut, simplified, and easily accessible social ties and antagonisms is displayed on a daily basis in the news.

CITIZENS, INFORMATION, AND POLITICS

The ways in which people engage with news suggests a complex picture of political communication. On the one hand, when issues saturate the news and entertainment media—as have topics as disparate as abortion politics, the Clinton scandals, and Barack Obama's birth status—people may engage at deep levels. However, it is not always clear that this engagement translates into positive effects on public policies.

The temptation always exists for political actors to propose magical solutions and fantastic political scenarios through the use of myths, stereotypes, scapegoats, and other symbolic devices. When the media tell such stories because they fit the news values that organizations are looking for, there are few restraints on the fabrication of political reality. Under such circumstances, political actors can manage issues, conflicts, and crises by simply throwing symbols at them—symbols that may be irrelevant to the matters at hand yet provoke powerful emotional responses from the public.

Hope for escaping these political illusions is provided by the research introduced earlier showing that people can be critical and reach their own interpretations. However, in the current news system, critical people may also decide they have been deceived by politicians and government. Still, as William Gamson notes, there is evidence that when people tap into personal experiences with political issues, they can begin to identify with others who have common experiences and think in terms of political actions that might make a difference.[81] Moreover, as noted earlier, news that points to citizen-action alternatives also stimulates greater citizen interest and makes information easier to store and use. Together, these two ideas send a message to journalists to cover more of the experiences that ordinary citizens have with the issues that make the news, while reporting information about the political options available to concerned citizens.

If young people are to become more engaged with politics, it is likely to be through social media that offer richer visual and participatory information formats. It would also help, of course, if political leaders also communicate in ways that are relevant to young citizens. With the notable exception of the Obama campaign in 2008, most electoral and issue campaigns contain little communication with young citizens, either because they are thought to be hard to reach or because they are regarded as so tuned out that their participation will not have much impact, or both. Recent elections suggest that the youth vote is of increasing interest to candidates. In addition, many young people are finding alternative channels of information and action. The global social justice movement of recent years indicates greater interest among young activists than at any time perhaps since the 1960s. Yet without some connection to more traditional political participation such as voting, or to broader information channels such as mass media news, it is unclear how this movement will grow in public support or how it will affect government policies.

Will news organizations change their patterns of coverage voluntarily? Probably not, although shrinking audiences have many news organizations scrambling for new ideas. Because we are talking about an information system, it makes more sense to think about related changes that might occur in all three areas of press, political communication practices, and citizen information habits. The concluding chapter of the book addresses changes that would bring each set of actors in the system closer to constructing the kind of information order that would serve the needs of contemporary democracy. Until such changes come about, the citizen's best defense is to understand how politicians attempt to shape the news and why news organizations end up reporting so much of what is fed to them. These are the subjects of the next three chapters.

NOTES

1. Walter Lippmann, *Public Opinion* (New York: The Free Press, 1922).
2. See, for example, Dan Nimmo and David L. Swanson, "The Field of Political Communication: Beyond the Voter Persuasion Paradigm," in *New Directions in Political Communication: A Resource Book,* eds. Dan Nimmo and David Swanson (Newbury Park, CA: Sage, 1990), 7–47.
3. David Moore, personal communication.
4. David Moore, *The Opinion Makers: When Media Polls Undermine Democracy* (Boston: Beacon, 2008).
5. David W. Moore and Jeffrey M. Jones, "Directive vs. Permissive Public Opinion" (paper presented at the Annual Meeting of the American Association for Public Opinion Research, St. Petersburg, Florida, May 16–19, 2002).
6. Morris P. Fiorina, *Culture War? The Myth of a Polarized America* (New York: Pearson/Longman, 2005).
7. Murray Edelman, *The Symbolic Uses of Politics* (Urbana: University of Illinois Press, 1964).
8. Jennifer L. Hochschild, "Affirmative Action as Culture War," in *The Cultural Territories of Race,* ed. Michele Lamont (Chicago: University of Chicago Press, 1999), 343–370.
9. Robert M. Entman and Andrew Rojecki, *The Black Image in the White Mind: Media and Race in America* (Chicago: University of Chicago Press, 2000), 110.
10. Ibid.

11. www.pollingreport.com/immigration.htm. Accessed August 16, 2010.
12. www.pollingreport.com/immigration.htm. Accessed August 16, 2010.
13. See Robert Putnam, *Bowling Alone: The Collapse and Revival of American Community* (New York: Simon and Schuster, 2000).
14. See Joseph Turow, *Breaking Up America: Advertisers and the New Media World* (Chicago: University of Chicago Press, 1997).
15. Hamilton, *All the News That's Fit to Sell: How the Market Transforms Information Into News* (Princeton: Princeton University Press, 2003), 262.
16. Ibid., 90.
17. Ibid., 85.
18. NBC Dateline, August 13, 2010. www.msnbc.msn.com/id/3032600/. Accessed August 11, 2010.
19. Charles M. Blow, "Lost in Translation," *New York Times*, January 29, 2010. www.nytimes.com/2010/01/30/opinion/30blow.html. Accessed August 11, 2010.
20. Ibid.
21. Thomas E. Patterson, *The Vanishing Voter: Public Involvement in an Age of Uncertainty* (New York: Vintage Books, 2003), 16.
22. Ibid., 18.
23. "Political Information Sources and the Campaign," Pew Internet and American Life Project, www.pewinternet.org/reports/reports.asp?Report=110&Section=ReportLevel1&Field=Level1I&ID=475, Report of January 11, 2004.
24. Pew survey reported at www.electiongeek.com/blog/2008/01/13/new-findings-on-the-internet-election-2008/.
25. Markus Prior, *Post-Broadcast Democracy: How Media Choice Increases Inequality in Political Involvement and Polarizes Elections* (New York: Cambridge University Press, 2007).
26. Matthew Baum, "Sex, Lies, and War: How Soft News Brings Foreign Policy to the Inattentive Public," *American Political Science Review* 96, no. 1 (2002): 91–109.
27. John Zaller, *The Nature and Origins of Mass Opinion* (New York: Cambridge University Press, 1992).
28. See David Domke, *God Willing? Political Fundalmentalism in the White House, the "War on Terror," and the Echoing Press* (London: Pluto Press, 2004).
29. See Edelman, *The Symbolic Uses of Politics*.
30. See Shanto Iyengar and Donald Kinder, *News That Matters: Television and American Opinion* (Chicago: University of Chicago Press, 1987).
31. Barton Gellman and Walter Pincus, "Errors and Exaggerations: Prewar Depictions of Iraq's Nuclear Threat Outweighed the Evidence," *Washington Post National Weekly Edition* (August 18–24, 2003): 6.
32. Tom Zeller, "The Iraq-Qaeda Link: A Short Story," *New York Times*, June 20, 2004: Week in Review, 4.
33. Mira Sotirovic, "How Individuals Explain Social Problems: The Influences of Media Use," *Journal of Communication* 53 (2003): 122–137.
34. See Moore, *The Opinion Makers*, ch. 1.
35. Roderick Hart, *Seducing America: How Television Charms the Modern Voter* (New York: Oxford University Press, 1994), 22.
36. Putnam, *Bowling Alone*, 36.
37. Ibid.
38. See James T. Hamilton, *All the News That's Fit to Sell*, Chapter 3.
39. See the more detailed discussions in W. Lance Bennett, *The Governing Crisis: Media, Money, and Marketing in American Elections* (New York: St. Martin's Press, 1992).

40. See, for example, Michael X. Delli Carpini and Scott Keeter, *What Americans Know About Politics and Why It Matters* (New Haven, CT: Yale University Press, 1996), 21.
41. Doris A. Graber, *Processing Politics: Learning from Television in the Internet Age* (Chicago: University of Chicago Press, 2001).
42. Pew Research Center Database, "Public Attentiveness to Major News Stories, 1986–1998." Updated 2007 http://pewresearch.org/assets/pdf/NewsInterest1986-2007.pdf.
43. W. Russell Neuman, Marion R. Just, and Ann N. Crigler, *Common Knowledge: News and the Construction of Political Meaning* (Chicago: University of Chicago Press, 1992), 8.
44. Thomas Patterson and Philip Seib, "Informing the Public," Report to the Press Commission, Institutions of Democracy Project of the Annenberg Foundation Trust, Commission meeting at Rancho Mirage, California, February 5–8, 2004.
45. Graber, *Processing Politics*; see also, *Processing the News: How People Tame the Information Tide*, 2nd ed. (New York: Longman, 1988).
46. John Fiske, *Television Culture* (London: Methuen, 1987).
47. William Gamson, *Talking Politics* (New York: Cambridge University Press, 1992), 179.
48. Neuman, Just, and Crigler, *Common Knowledge*, ch. 7, especially p. 111.
49. Ibid., ch. 5. See also, Graber, *Processing the News*.
50. Enid Burns, "Blogs Suffer in Poll on Preferred News Sources," ClickZ, October 3, 2006, www.clickz.com/showPage.html?page=3623588; based on LexisNexis survey of 1,500 people aged 25–64.
51. See, for example, Robert Kubey and Mihaly Csikszentmihalyi, *Television and the Quality of Life: How Viewing Shapes the Everyday Experience* (Hillsdale, NJ: Lawrence Erlbaum, 1990).
52. Charles Winick, "The Function of Television: Life Without the Big Box," in *Television as Social Issue*, ed. Stuart Oskamp (Newbury Park, CA: Sage, 1988), 217–237.
53. Graber, *Processing Politics*.
54. Zaller, *The Nature and Origins of Mass Opinion*.
55. For the magnitude of this information campaign, see the report "Well-Heeled," published by the Center for Public Integrity, Washington, DC, 1994.
56. *Newsweek* poll reported in Steven Waldman, Bob Cohn, and Eleanor Clift, "How Clinton Blew It," *Newsweek* (June 27, 1994): 28.
57. Polls reported in Melinda Beck, "Rationing Health Care," *Newsweek* (June 27, 1994): 30.
58. CNN Opinion Research Report, Poll taken July 16-21, 2010.
59. Quoted in Maureen Dowd, "Bush's Top Strategists: Smooth Poll-Taker and Hard Driving Manager," *New York Times*, May 30, 1988: 11.
60. George E. Marcus, W. Russell Neuman, and Michael MacKuen, *Affective Intelligence and Political Judgement* (Chicago: University of Chicago Press, 2000). See also W. Russell Neuman, Michael B. MacKuen, George E. Marcus, and Joanne Miller, "Affective Choice and Rational Choice" (paper presented at the Annual Meeting of the American Political Science Association, Washington, DC, September 1997).
61. See the more detailed discussions in Bennett, *The Governing Crisis*, especially ch. 1 and 4.
62. Barbara G. Farah and Ethel Klein, "Public Opinion Trends," in *The Election of 1988: Reports and Interpretations*, ed. Gerald M. Pomper (Chatham, NJ: Chatham House, 1989), 103.

63. Arthur Lupia and Matthew McCubbins, *The Democratic Dilemma: Can Citizens Learn What They Need to Know?* (New York: Cambridge University Press, 1998).

64. See Samuel Popkin, *The Reasoning Voter: Communication and Persuasion in Presidential Campaigns*, 2nd ed. (Chicago: University of Chicago Press, 1994).

65. Shanto Iyengar and Donald R. Kinder, *News That Matters* (Chicago: University of Chicago Press, 1987).

66. Shanto Iyengar, *Is Anyone Responsible? How Television Frames Political Issues* (Chicago: University of Chicago Press, 1991).

67. See, for example, Tamar Liebes, "Cultural Differences in the Retelling of Television Fiction," *Critical Studies in Mass Communication* 5 (1986): 277–292.

68. For an overview of trends in the field, see Elihu Katz, "Communications Research Since Lazarsfeld," *Public Opinion Quarterly* 51 (1987): 25–45.

69. For an introduction to the "uses and gratification" concept, see Jay G. Blumler and Denis McQuail, *Television in Politics: Its Uses and Influences* (Chicago: University of Chicago Press, 1969). Also, Lee B. Becker, "Two Tests of Media Gratification: Watergate and the 1974 Elections," *Journalism Quarterly* 53 (1976): 26–31.

70. See, for example, Dan Berlyne, *Conflict, Arousal, and Curiosity* (New York: McGraw-Hill, 1960).

71. For an explanation of how such scripts are formed and how they work, see Roger Schank and Robert Abelson, *Scripts, Plans, Goals and Understanding* (Hillsdale, NJ: Lawrence Erlbaum, 1977).

72. For a discussion of how new stimuli become incorporated into a mental picture, see W. Lance Bennett, "Perception and Cognition: An Information-Processing Framework for Politics," in *The Handbook of Political Behavior*, Vol. 1, ed. Samuel Long (New York: Plenum, 1981).

73. See Naomi Klein, *No Logo: Taking Aim at the Brand Bullies* (New York: Picador-St. Martin's, 1999).

74. Neal Gabler, *Life: The Movie: How Entertainment Conquered Reality* (New York: Knopf, 1998).

75. Lippmann, *Public Opinion*.

76. Benedict Anderson, *Imagined Communities* (London: Verso, 1983).

77. "Fantasy theme" is a concept coined by Ernest G. Bormann in his article "The Eagleton Affair: A Fantasy Theme Analysis," *Quarterly Journal of Speech* 59 (1973): 143–159.

78. Ernest G. Bormann, "A Fantasy Theme Analysis of the Television Coverage of the Hostage Release and the Reagan Inaugural," *Quarterly Journal of Speech* 68 (1982): 137–138.

79. See, for example, Donald Horton and R. Richard Wohl, "Mass Communication and Para-Social Interaction," *Psychiatry* 19 (1956): 219–229; see also Mark R. Levy, "Watching TV News as Para-Social Interaction," *Journal of Broadcasting* 23 (Winter 1979): 69–80.

80. These data are presented and analyzed in more detail in W. Lance Bennett and Regina G. Lawrence, "Rethinking Media Politics and Public Opinion: Reactions to the Clinton-Lewinsky Scandal," *Political Science Quarterly* 116 (Fall 2001), 425–446.

81. William Gamson, *Talking Politics* (New York: Cambridge University Press, 1992).

How Politicians Make the News

. . . when information which properly belongs to the public is withheld by those in power, the people soon become ignorant of their own affairs, distrustful of those who manage them, and, eventually, incapable of determining their own destinies.

—*Richard Nixon*

There is literally no such thing as an idea that cannot be expressed well and articulately to today's voters in 30 seconds.

—*Dick Morris*

. . . we have turned into a public relations society. Much of the news Americans get each day was created to serve just that purpose—to be the news of the day. Many of our headlines come from events created by public relations—press conferences, speeches, press releases, canned reports, and worst of all, snappy comments by "spokesmen" or "experts."

—*Walter Pincus*

Few communication professionals have been more effective at changing the way many Americans think about issues, politicians, and parties than Frank Luntz. The Web site of his primary consulting firm "the word doctors" (slogan: It's not what you say, it's what people hear) offers prospective clients a sample of the acclaim from newspapers and magazine articles about Luntz and his political impact:

"It would be hard to name a prominent GOP political operative or member of Congress of the last 20 years who has not been advised by Luntz. . . .

Master of the political message, Luntz's fascination with the use of language has often helped redefine a political debate."

"The maestro of messaging . . . Luntz has forever redefined the way public policy issues will be framed."

"Luntz has a special understanding of the writhing, petulant beast that is the American public. . . . He sees the way the beast responds to political messages."[1]

The Web site of his former firm, Luntz Maslansly Strategic Research included a poke at the Democrats from another glowing news account about his exploits:

"Democrats spoke with awe of Republicans' ability to spin phrases such as "compassionate conservatism," "Clear Skies," "the culture of life," and "the ownership society." The media made a linguistic Svangali out of GOP wordsmith Frank Luntz, who was credited with getting the Republicans to adopt phrases such as . . . "climate change" for global warming. Wherever you went, the Democrats were talking about the importance of "framing" and "remessaging."[2]

Indeed, Luntz opened his book, *Words That Work,* with a story about appearing at a gathering in the home of conservative-turned-liberal pundit (and publisher of *The Huffington Post*) Arianna Huffington. The guests included Hollywood's liberal A-list: Rob Reiner, Warren Beatty, and Larry David, among others. They wanted to know why the Democrats often seemed so inept at communicating, while the Republicans had such powerful images. At the time, the Democrats were out of power, and apparently envious at how Luntz had written the Republican playbook that brought them to power in Congress in the 1990s and the White House for the beginning of the twenty-first century. Luntz told them that his communication principles transcend partisanship, and even politics, offering similar solutions for business and advertising as well. He claimed that his communication techniques work for "every product and politician imaginable."[3] The message for the Hollywood liberal elite was the same he tells clients from *Fortune* 500 companies. Getting what you want involves (a) figuring out who your audience is, (b) learning what they already think about your product or problem, and (c) finding a language that brings your issue into the acceptance zone of their thoughts and feelings.

This simple strategic communication model has been applied to many issues, from taxes to health care. Even when the Democrats regained control of Congress and the White House after 2008, Luntz helped the Republicans develop their strategy of blocking or weakening most every Democratic initiative, including health care, financial reform, and the environment. Equating government action in these areas with the government incompetence that brought on the problems in the first place, Luntz urged using public anger at government to block new government attempts to protect the public. His strategy memo to Republicans said, "The American people are not just saying 'no.'

They are saying 'hell no' to more government agencies, more bureaucrats, and more legislation crafted by special interests."[4] The irony in these words is that it was government actions in the first place—decisions to deregulate industries, to stop enforcing existing regulations, and to appoint former industry insiders to government regulatory posts—that effectively allowed special interests to run amok and create serious crises in the areas of health, energy and the economy. When searching for the strategic goals of a campaign to "stop government," it is useful to look beyond the simple fact that such words feel good to some publics. Getting public support in the short run may serve the larger goal of restoring power to the special interests that Luntz's clients (in this case, the Republicans) preferred to have running these policy areas. Politics is always a question of what interests government serves, not getting the interests out of government. Basing PR campaigns on emotions aroused through longstanding attacks against government has clouded this underlying reality. And so the Republicans became "the party of no," and it did not hurt them appreciably in the polls, nor did Democratic policy gains in the areas of health care, banking regulation, or consumer economic protection seem to help them.

One of the most dramatic examples of how Luntz crafted an effective communication strategy for politicians involved managing public concern (and government action) about the environment at a time when world scientists had reached substantial consensus that global warming was not only happening, but that it also had human causes and seriously harmful effects. Yet the prospect of reducing our dependence on fossil fuels caused alarm among many established business interests. For example, U.S. car companies had positioned themselves in the market against nimble foreign imports by emphasizing (then) hugely profitable gas-guzzlers, such as Hummers, Sierras, and Rams. The legacy of lobbying the government for lax fuel efficiency legislation that favored those dinosaurs ended up in a wholesale government bailout of the auto industry during the financial collapse at the end of the first decade of the twenty-first century. Beyond the automakers, many other industries were dedicated to perpetuating business models based on fossil fuels. At the center of it all were the giant oil companies making great profits as gas and oil prices soared in the face of looming shortages. Many politicians were beholden to the political money that flowed from such interests. These forces converged to stall environmental legislation and clean energy policies even though such policies were supported by scientific evidence of looming global crises, along with even more immediate concerns about the national security implications of continued dependence on fossil fuels.

Luntz had discovered as early as the mid-1990s that public concern about the environment was growing and that Republicans in particular were vulnerable because they appeared to be on the wrong sides of many environmental issues. In 2002, he issued a memo to President George W. Bush stressing the importance of shifting the language used to discuss the whole family of environmental topics from clean air, to water standards, to global warming. He described the Republican image problem in these terms: "A caricature has taken hold in the public imagination: Republicans seemingly in the pockets of corporate fat cats who run their hands together and chuckle manically as they plot to pollute America for fun and profit. And only Democrats and their good-hearted friends from Washington can save America from these sinister companies drooling at the prospect of strip mining every picturesque mountain range, drilling for oil on every white sand beach, and clear cutting every green forest."[5]

The solution was to create a new story to counteract being the bad guy in the prevailing narrative. That story needed to appeal to popular American themes, such as love of nature and preservation of clean and open spaces for all. As he put it, a story that appeals to common experience and emotion opens the audience to listen to messages on specific issues: "A compelling story, even if factually inaccurate, can be more emotionally compelling than a dry recitation of the truth."[6] If more voters sensed that Republicans shared their love of nature, then efforts to shift perceptions on larger issues such as global warming would receive friendlier audiences. Once Republican candidates confirmed their love of nature, they could better address public concerns about clean water, clear air, or global warming with proposals for more balanced and "sensible" policies that preserve our environmental gains without being alarmist or burdening industry and consumers with costly government overreaching.

At every step of the way, from being "sensible" about arsenic levels in drinking water to using the term *climate change* in place of the more alarmist idea of global warming, the common undercurrent of the campaign was to argue that the science wasn't settled on these questions.[7] Challenging science was a brilliant political move, not because the science was, in fact, mostly unsettled, but because news organizations construct political stories around political conflicts, not independent facts. Even though scientific research had reached consensus on most of these issues (e.g., human causes of global warming), the curious way that U.S. journalism thinks about "balance" put the Republican side of the story in the news simply because it came from powerful official sources in government (recall the indexing rule explained in Chapter 1), and was echoed by newly minted experts from dozens of think tanks funded by energy giants like Exxon. These familiar Washington battles made for good news drama, rich with personalities in conflict and formula plots revolving around who would establish an authoritative solution to these unsettled and potentially chaotic issues. Their very isolation from underlying facts left these stories fragmented and confusing. In short, the resulting news coverage achieved a political balance at the cost of a serious imbalance in the facts and scientific conclusions supporting the different sides of the climate change/global warming story. The result was that public concern about the environment dropped over a period when evidence supporting more pressing action mounted.

The case study in this chapter shows how political communication strategies engineered by Frank Luntz, delivered by numerous Republican politicians, and echoed by well-financed think tank experts took advantage of the blind spot in the news created by the "balance" norm discussed further in

Chapter 6. The result was a long running news story that offered scientific facts on one side and doubts about those same facts on the other, with both sides being cued by partisan politicians and ideologies. When the facts become entwined with political battles, citizens are invited to choose the facts that feel best because they fit their political beliefs. The case study in this chapter illustrates how information about climate change became submerged in a partisan news narrative.

CASE STUDY

How Global Warming Became a Partisan News Story

On the eve of an international climate summit in Copenhagen in 2009, the e-mails from a climate research unit at a university in England were hacked. Among the thousands of messages stolen were several mails indicating that scientists were concerned about how to present some sketchy data in the face of the continuous assault they experienced from climate skeptics. This exchange became a big news story implying that climate scientists were faking their data. Although subsequent investigations cleared this charge and affirmed the preponderance of evidence showing human causes for global warming and its damaging effects, the public relations damage had been done. Ongoing public relations campaigns and news making strategies aimed at raising doubts about climate science seized on this bit of drama and magnified it out of context (dramatized, fragmented and personalized it). Between 2008 and 2010 the percentages of Americans who even believed in global warming dropped from 71 to 57 percent, and 41 percent said that they had become much more sure that it was not happening at all. In parallel with these trends, majorities dissolved into minorities around questions of whether global warming had human causes and was serious enough to do something about. Opinion was even split on the question of whether respondents thought that most scientists believed that global warming was happening.[8] Perhaps most telling of all was a Pew national priorities survey showing global warming at the very bottom of a long national priority list (ranked as a top priority by only 28 percent, contrasted with 83 percent for the economy, 65 percent for education, or 44 percent for the environment in general).[9] These trends put the U.S. dramatically out of step with how publics in most other democratic and developing nations regard global warming.[10]

The factors shaping U.S. opinions are far from "natural," as they reflect decades of public relations efforts spearheaded by large energy companies who also support powerful politicians who make the news. Indeed, one reason the U.S. has been out of step with much of the world on this issue is because of the way it has been covered in the news. Global warming has been portrayed largely as a partisan issue rather than as a matter of scientific consensus about the need for action.[11] Indeed, in much of this reporting science

Continued

has been on one side of the story (often cued by Democratic sources), while those raising doubts about science have been on the other side (often cued by Republican officials taking their direction from the Frank Luntz playbook). This partisan filtering of the issue has persisted for more than 20 years, dating to the late 1980s when science began to become clearer on the question of planetary warming, leading to growing public concerns.

In the early days, opponents simply denied that climate change was happening, but public resistance to that idea grew with increasing information from national and UN sponsored scientific communities. Much of this knowledge was brought into focus in the U.S. by a popular film (*An Inconvenient Truth*) starring Al Gore, who won both an Oscar and a Nobel Prize for his efforts to stir attention and action. The growing tide of public concern precipitated the shift in communication strategy noted earlier when conservative opponents stopped denying climate change and simply began raising doubts about how settled the science really was on human causes or the seriousness of the effects. Why has something that may represent a genuine crisis for those who live on Earth (and this includes Americans and their economy) been left largely to politicians to define in the news?

The difficulty of the mainstream news to cover the issue from the standpoint of a growing scientific consensus can be traced to the core press norms of indexing and balance introduced in Chapter 1. The indexing norm means that if powerful political factions in government engage with an issue, their positions will largely determine how it is framed. And if one side takes a position that runs counter to scientific findings, the curious idea of political balance used by the U.S. press makes it difficult to correct the factual imbalance. These press norms explain how political spin can make it into the news and confuse an issue that otherwise seems as clear as global warming.

This is where our earlier story about Frank Luntz comes in. Recall that Luntz warned Republicans that they were at risk of losing the public opinion battle over the environment, particularly on the issue of human causes of global warming. Democratic candidates were exploiting weak Republican positions. As noted earlier, his proposed communication strategy operated at two levels: first, to embrace the environment and nature in personal and emotional terms shared by the audience, and then, to urge reasonable and sensible discussion emphasizing caution due to the lack of scientific proof. In his strategy memo, Luntz argued that science could be moved out of the center of the debate: "The scientific debate is closing [against us] but not yet closed. There is still a window of opportunity to challenge the science."[12]

Luntz's brilliant move reflected important insights about both audiences and the news. Many people do not fully understand or trust science, particularly because scientists themselves typically portray their findings in terms of probabilities and degrees of uncertainty. Given this small opening, doubts about scientific findings can be amplified by experts and think tanks that echo the language of doubt and caution. The newsworthiness of the science challenge is often enhanced by the tendency of scientists to employ poor public communication skills when they are asked for reactions or clarification. Lacking communication consultants, scientists often issue fuzzy pronouncements laden with jargon, or, worse, dismiss their critics as ignorant or not worthy of comment. A popular movie about the ways in which scientists often play into the hands of political opponents was aptly named *A Flock of Dodos.*[13]

Engaging audience doubts about climate science first required establishing a reassuring sense of commitment to the environment that could be shared with the audience. Luntz recommended: "First, assure your audience that you are committed to 'preserving and protecting' the environment, but that it can be done more wisely and effectively."[14] In discussing the issue further, candidates should make sure to use the right reassuring terms: "The three words Americans are looking for in an environmental policy are 'safer,' 'cleaner,' and 'healthier'."[15] Finally, it was important to replace "global warming" (which implies an immediate condition that people get upset about) with "climate change" (which includes the possibility of natural causes that are beyond human intervention). When asked about this framing of the issue, Luntz said: "The public reacts differently to 'climate change' than 'global warming.' Global warming is more frightening to the public. Global warming is something that has a long term consequence to it, whereas climate change, to Americans, is a little bit more benign."[16]

All of this language would be of little use if the news did not privilege political conflict stories centered around powerful factions in government even when one or more of those factions are short on facts. Was the news about the environment really so biased toward such unsupported political spin? Studies of coverage of global warming/climate change suggest that the answer is yes. In contrast to extremely low levels of disagreement on climate change and increasing consensus on human contributions found in leading scientific journals, an analysis of the prestige U.S. press found that more than half the articles were "balanced" to give equal weight to challenges to scientific claims. Maxwell and Jules Boykoff examined a random sample of more than 600 articles that appeared between 1988 and 2002 in the *New York Times,* the *Washington Post,* the *Los Angeles Times,* and *The Wall Street Journal.* They found that 53 percent of the articles were "balanced" by including prominent challenges to scientific claims about human causes of global warming. Another 35 percent favored the human cause viewpoint but mentioned the skeptics. Another 6 percent gave exclusive coverage to the science skeptics. And less than 6 percent gave exclusive coverage to sources claiming human causes of global warming.[17] The conclusion from their study is contained in the title of the article: "Balance as Bias."

Thus, Frank Luntz's communication strategy was shrewd in using political spin both to create, and then point to, the news as confirmation of doubts about climate science. Turning global warming into a partisan issue encouraged the audience to let the facts follow their political beliefs. Polls leading up to the 2008 election showed that popular belief in human sources of climate change were split along party lines: only 23 percent of Republicans believed the human cause thesis, while 75 percent of Democrats accepted the scientific evidence.[18] More Importantly, given the lack of clear leadership on the issue most Americans ranked the environment relatively low on their list of priorities.[19]

In light of these public responses to how the issue was framed, it is not surprising that Frank Luntz answered "no" when asked if the environment would be a central issue in the 2008 election. His reasoning is revealing about the very communication strategies he developed. For the environment to become a top public priority, he said, " . . . you have to create a sense of immediacy." By contrast, he pointed out why the issue of immigration has moved more to the center of national political debate: ". . . when we see illegal immigrants coming across the border every single day . . . every American who's watching this right now says, 'Oh my God, there really is a crisis; we've got to do something about it. . . .' That's the issue with global warming. It may be a crisis, but if it is, it's not right now."[20] Of course, what Luntz failed to add to his analysis is that the reason many Americans

Continued

think of immigration as a major "immediate" problem, yet have trouble getting as worked up about the environment, is that both issues have been systematically spun to those ends by political communication strategists like him.

In his latest incarnation on the issue, Luntz seemed intent on removing his fingerprints from the climate controversy (perhaps to avoid being demonized for killing climate change legislation) by acknowledging that climate science now seems more settled, and perhaps something should be done. In what may be one of the more cynical statements by a person centrally responsible for creating a partisan issue out of the environment, Luntz later said: "People are much more interested in seeing solutions than watching yet another partisan political argument."[21]

THE POLITICS OF ILLUSION

It is hardly surprising that the news is filled with strategically constructed versions of events. Nor is it surprising that with the advent of more sophisticated polling, message development, and marketing technologies, the news often translates the political world into personal terms based on the existing emotions and values of audiences. Indeed, the mark of skill in the political trade is the ability to make the public version of a situation convincing, no matter how actual circumstances may be bent or simplified in the process. As former secretary of state Dean Acheson once said, the task of public officers seeking support for their policies is to make their points "clearer than truth."[22]

As discussed in earlier chapters, much has changed about the news in recent years, but one important pattern holds: most political news still originates from government officials themselves. In many ways, officials seem an obvious and appropriate source of information about politics, which, after all, often involves activities of government. However, letting officials set the news agenda is not just giving them greater voice in what publics think about and how they think about it, it also enables them to deploy the strategic communication technologies that shape the very realities—the issues, situations, and images of citizen involvement—that are portrayed in the news itself. First, we will see how officials dominate political news, then how they construct news realities, and finally, how journalists attempt to combat the impression that they are being manipulated.

THE SOURCES OF POLITICAL NEWS

There are several ways to think about the impact of politicians' continuing efforts to control images in the news. For example, it is useful to know what proportion of the daily news is directly attributable to such official news control efforts. Even a casual look at the daily paper or the nightly TV news suggests that the bulk of important news is devoted to the official actions of the government and elected officials. True, those actions may be portrayed in the cynical tone of political games or against the backdrop of potshots and spin by opponents, but the fact remains that the majority of political stories are simple condensations of what politicians say and do. In short, the news seems to consist mainly of stories in which at least one point of view is an official one. Many stories are framed by two familiar official angles—Republican and Democrat, for example.

How accurate is this impression that the content of the news is dominated by prepared official messages? Leon Sigal addressed this question in his classic study of the news content of two of America's finest newspapers, the *New York Times* and the *Washington Post*. Common sense might suggest that these prestigious organizations would be among the least likely to take their news as it is served up by official newsmakers. The *Times* and *Post* cover a broad range of political stories in depth, and they have large reporting staffs, which should free them from dependence on press releases and wire-service copy as the scripts for news stories. Finally, the *Times* and *Post* have reputations as critical papers that are not afraid of exposing government deception.

As it turns out, these papers are also the leading papers of record for what government officials say and do. How did these leading papers fare against the everyday pressures and temptations to report prepared political information? Among Sigal's findings were the following:

- Government officials (either domestic or foreign) were the sources of nearly three-quarters of all hard news, and only one-sixth of the news could be traced to sources outside the government. The breakdown of news sources looked like this:[23]

Sources	Percent
U.S. officials, agencies	46.5
Foreign, international officials, agencies	27.5
U.S. state, local government officials	4.1
Other news organizations	3.2
Nongovernmental Americans	14.4
Nongovernmental foreigners	2.1
Nonascertainable	2.4

- Less than 1 percent of all news stories were based on the reporter's own analysis, whereas more than *90 percent* were based on the calculated messages of the actors involved in the situation.[24]
- The vast majority of news stories (from 70 to 90%, depending on how they are categorized) were drawn from situations over which newsmakers had either complete or substantial control. Here is the breakdown of the contexts from which the *Times* and *Post* drew their information:[25]

Sources	Percent
Interviews	24.7
Press conferences	24.5
Press releases	17.5
Official proceedings	12.0
Background briefings	7.9
Other nonspontaneous events	4.5

News commentary and editorials	4.0
Leaks	2.3
Nongovernmental proceedings	1.5
Spontaneous events	1.2
Reporter's own analysis	0.9

Research by various scholars since Sigal's pioneering study suggests that much the same patterns persist to this day.[26] Even in this age of live event coverage, officials are quickly introduced into reporting from the scenes of wars or crises to provide framing for stories.[27] The level of official domination tends to be even higher on foreign policy issues, where opposition groups and views from other nations are often pushed to the margins. On domestic matters, such as abortion, health care policy, or taxes, the views of organized interests enter the news with greater frequency. However, the press tends to index the range of diverse viewpoints in a story to the presence of powerful government actors in Washington who also share those views.[28] These patterns are only magnified by the journalism crisis discussed in Chapters 1 and 7. With the firing of journalists and budget cutting for investigative reporting, the news becomes even more open to the prefabricated stories offered up by politicians, businesses and their PR professionals.

By any accounting, the conclusion is inescapable: even the best journalism in the land is extremely dependent on the political messages of a small spectrum of official news sources. This was the moral of the case study on global warming. The *Times* and *Post,* no doubt, include more detailed background information (not to mention more coverage of obscure events) than most news outlets, but the basic messages in their stories still represent official views. Later on we will see that when news organizations run stories counter to government claims about events, they often face pressures to edit, delay, or kill them.

Around this core of official spin there are, of course, other trends worth noting. Recall, for example, that journalists have introduced their own voices into the news in increasing volume, commenting upon and interpreting what their official sources say.[29] Moreover, the increase of scandals and journalistic feeding frenzies indicates that journalists have found ways to assert their control over news content, even if these stories often annoy audiences more than they inform them. The irony is that on stories of greater consequence such as going to war or global warming, journalists are reluctant to insert their own voices or outside sources to challenge official versions of events—even if there is evidence to support the challenge—unless other influential politicians step forward first. A notable exception to this rule was Hurricane Katrina, during which the nation witnessed journalists asking where the government response was, and actually informing clueless officials about the problems on the ground. With Katrina, news organizations had entered the eye of a no-spin zone, a rare moment when government officials and press minders were off the job and literally on vacation, leaving journalists to look directly at events without the usual layer of official spin to shape their reporting.

Why Politicians Work So Hard to Create the Illusions in the News

The economic pressures in the news business mentioned in Chapter 1 and described in detail in Chapter 7 leave less space for serious political news than in earlier times. The political game to get messages and images into the news has become increasingly competitive and often vicious. With the journalistic bias moving increasingly toward stories that are dramatic, personal, and simple (i.e., fragmented) in plot and message, there is not much room for nuance, open deliberation, or background information on issues, policies, and consequences. Getting highly managed communication across in ways that make the desired impact on publics requires strategic communication skills, which makes politicians increasingly reliant on communication professionals like Frank Luntz.

The obligatory contingents of pollsters, image makers, handlers, and spin-doctors advance their clients' political agendas by (a) helping clients craft their political agendas; (b) taking a reading of public concerns; (c) designing messages and the media events to deliver them; (d) keeping their political clients on-message; and, above all, (e) keeping them away from more spontaneous exchanges with press, opponents, and publics; while (f) schmoozing (spinning) reporters with tempting story angles for otherwise planned and predictable events. The irony of this strange dance of newsmaking is that when officials may venture a spontaneous comment, journalists tend to fan it into a major moment, examining its greater implications and inviting opponents to pronounce it rash, ill thought, or dangerous. As a result, politicians learn (the hard way) to stay on-message, and to listen to the professional communication consultants who do the market research that generates those messages. The result is that the public rarely sees politicians up close and spontaneous. The news becomes a sort of scripted reality TV program that may be far less interesting or engaging than *American Idol* or *The Apprentice*.[30]

For these and other reasons, news content may not always be the best mirror on political reality, yet it can have important effects on how—and how well—our national decisions are made, how the public feels about them, and which politicians and groups are perceived as powerful and effective. For these reasons, it is important to understand the manufacture of seemingly naturally occurring news stories by politicians and interests who use publicity to gain recognition, advance policy agendas, and damage political enemies.

The Political Impact of Officialized News

The most obvious political effect of news management is the advantage it gives powerful people in getting their issues on the political agenda. Political activists and groups that are not established players in policy processes have much more difficulty making news. A classic study of grassroots organizations by political scientist Edie Goldenberg showed that it is hard for unofficial actors to develop the credibility, resources, and information control necessary to dominate the news long enough to affect the outcome of issues.[31] When grassroots groups do make the news, it is often in the context of negatively perceived events, such as demonstrations, sit-ins, and other protest activities that may offend the public and draw easy criticism from public officials.

A long-term effect of officially managed news may be to limit the range of problems, solutions, values, and ideas presented to the American people. The political world becomes a predictable terrain of stereotypes, political postures, and superficial images. As Murray Edelman observed, familiar solutions are recycled in melodramatic efforts to solve chronic problems.[32] People come to accept the existence of problems like poverty, crime, delinquency, war, or climate change as facts of life rather than as the tragic results of the concentration of political power, the exploitative nature of economic relations, and the cynical uses of political communication.

The participation of the news media in promoting the official cover stories about these problems—until those stories are attacked or challenged by opponents—further undermines the chances for the kind of public understanding required for effective political action and real political change. As suggested in Chapter 3, audiences can be quite independent in interpreting the news, but people cannot interpret what they don't see. What they don't see or hear in the news is often linked to effective press management.

NEWS IMAGES AS STRATEGIC POLITICAL COMMUNICATION

Walter Lippmann observed more than 60 years ago in his classic work on public opinion, "The only feeling that anyone can have about an event he does not experience is the feeling aroused by his mental image of that event."[33] There is little check on the kinds of images created for political situations when the information received by the masses of people on the outside is controlled by a few people on the inside. As Secretary of State Acheson reminded us, the effective public official does not attempt to educate or convey "objective" images; the official's goal is to represent issues and events in ways that gain support, shape action, and influence outcomes.[34]

If the images contained in official political positions were mere entertainment fare floating about in the electronic ether, there might be less cause for concern. As long as the images in the news are treated as real, however, people may be inclined to respond to them. Even, and perhaps especially, those images with the most dubious links to reality can generate actions in the real world, actions that have real effects: the election of corrupt leaders, the acceptance of oppressive laws or ideas, the labeling of social groups, support for wars such as Iraq, or tolerance of chronic social and economic problems. Thus, news images of the political world can be tragically self-fulfilling. Dominant political images can create a world in their own image—even when such a world did not exist to begin with.

The fact that political actors make a practice of creating images for political situations does not mean that the news is filled with wild, diverse, and highly imaginative political stories. Most political images are, as Murray Edelman noted so perceptively, based on familiar symbols, formulaic plots, standard slogans, and simple rhetoric.[35] The world of political images is built from predictable symbolic transformations: the new into the old, the startling into the familiar, and the self-interested into the public-spirited. Even threats and crises come wrapped in stereotypes of enemy aggression, American firmness, peace through strength, productive and serious discussions, and so on. Political language, in Edelman's view, thrives on banal, predictable, formulaic images that undermine critical thinking in public communication.[36] Both the familiar pronouncements and partisan squabbles of authorities become substitutes for detailed analyses of situations.

There is, therefore, a profound irony in newsmaking. The newsworthiness of a political image often lies not in some independent check on its accuracy or importance but in its past success as a news formula. In this world of media reality, newsworthiness becomes a substitute for validity, and credibility becomes reduced to a formula of *who* applies *what* images to *which* events under *what* circumstances. Ordinary logic tells us that the more standardized an image, the less valid and meaningful is its application to unique, real-world situations. On the other hand, what David Altheide and Robert Snow have termed *media logic* tells us that reality *is* the image constructed for it as long as that image remains dominant and uncontested across different mainstream communication channels.[37] A corollary of this logic is that if other authorities who hold power in a situation challenge the leading official position, the news will dramatize the conflict (generally in personalized terms), leaving the audience to decide what the issues and their merits really are.

These and other aspects of media logic flow from the basic news information biases outlined in Chapter 2. Those biases help explain the evolution of the information and press management strategies used by newsmakers to get their views across in the news.[38] Failure to control the news is often equated with political failure. As the campaign manager for a presidential candidate put it, "the media is the campaign."[39] Or, as a key presidential advisor explained, there is no political reality apart from news reality. That assessment came from one of Ronald Reagan's top aides (and later secretary of state in the Bush administration), James Baker, who was asked by an NBC correspondent why the president seemed so unwilling to compromise on a tough budget proposal he submitted to Congress. Baker said that compromise was undesirable because, in the media, "everything is cast in terms of winning or losing."[40] Thus, the president could not back down, no matter how unrealistic his position. To be seen as unrealistic was preferable to being perceived as a loser because being perceived as a loser would make him a loser.

THE GOALS OF STRATEGIC POLITICAL COMMUNICATION

It is clear that controlling political images in the news is a primary goal of politics, and, as such, it is important to understand what this entails. Most PR experts agree that successful image making involves:

- Being clear about your client's political goals—damaging an opponent, improving the client's leadership image, or representing an environmental regulation as stronger than it will appear to opponents.

- Understanding the client's vulnerabilities so that opponents cannot turn the strategic communication back on its sponsors. For example, taking a moralistic stand against an opponent's sexual indiscretions may be ill advised if there are similar behaviors in the client's own past.
- Identifying the audience(s) most important for accomplishing those goals. Perhaps the main audience is a small demographic group that voted against the client in the last election, or the audience may be the key members of Congress who need to be convinced that there is public support for voting against health care reform.
- Using polling and market research to develop a message and a delivery strategy that reaches those audiences in ways that promote the goals of the campaign.
- Creating news events (often echoing advertising and other direct communication techniques) that dominate public discussion and lend authority to the message.

The core of this strategic communication process involves developing and communicating a message that promotes the political goals of a campaign by appealing to a targeted audience and holding the symbolic high ground if it comes under attack. For example, if your side of a conflict has branded itself around the symbols of patriotism and loyalty to the country, it becomes easier to brand opponents as unpatriotic when they challenge your positions, as happened to Senator John Kerry when he raised questions about President Bush's conduct of the war during the 2004 presidential election. Even though Kerry was a decorated war veteran and Bush had a checkered military record, an advocacy network dubbed Swift Boat Veterans for Truth (referring to Kerry's boat command position in Vietnam) was able to mount a devastating advertising campaign condemning Kerry's war record. Even though the ads themselves were seen by relatively small numbers of voters, they were replayed endlessly on the news and online.

The message construction side of the strategic communication process can be broken down into four important parts:

1. Composing a simple theme or message for the audience to use in thinking about the matter at hand. Call this *message shaping*.
2. Saturating communications channels (that reach your target audience) with this message so that it will become more conspicuous than competing messages. Call this *message salience*.
3. Constructing credibility for the message by finding authoritative settings and recognized sources to deliver it, followed by endorsements from prominent supporters. Call this *message credibility*.
4. Delivering the message with the right scripting (i.e., sound bites) and spin to lead journalists to pick the right story themes to accentuate the message. Call this *message framing*.

Although these four components of political image making work together in actual political communication, it is useful to consider them separately in order to see what each one contributes to the definition of a political situation.

Message Shaping

The content of a political message is usually simple; it is both emotionally and intellectually accessible. One of Frank Luntz's rules for successful communication is "Simplicity: Use Small Words." Another is "Brevity: Use Short Sentences."[41] Political messages generally begin with a key phrase, idea, or theme that creates a convenient way for people to think about a political object, be it an issue, an event, or even a person. For example, Franklin Roosevelt appealed to the hopes of the masses by using the simple term *New Deal* to refer to his complex patchwork of untried economic programs. Borrowing these characteristics of simplicity and idealism, John Kennedy added the power of familiarity when he presented his programs to the people under the title of *New Frontier*. Ronald Reagan used *New Federalism* to label his efforts to dismantle Roosevelt's New Deal, Kennedy's New Frontier, and Johnson's Great Society. When Bill Clinton stole the Republican thunder in his support for welfare reform, he spoke of *New Beginnings*. George W. Bush invoked the concept of an *Axis of Evil* to put the American public and the world on notice that the War on Terrorism would continue after Afghanistan. This example illustrates that simplicity, alone, does not good communication make, as the (lack of) connections between Iran, Iraq, and North Korea—the three Axis members—were challenged by critics.

Effective political themes and slogans invite people to bring their own meanings to a situation. Thus, an image is an impression anchored partly in symbolic suggestion and partly in the feelings and assumptions that people have in response to that suggestion. Research by communication scholars Doris Graber, Marion Just, Russell Neuman, Ann Crigler, Michael Delli Carpini, and Bruce Williams, among others, shows that people actively construct personal meanings from the evocative symbols and images of media coverage.[42] When people begin to supply the facts and feelings necessary to complete an image, the symbolic message component of political communication seems increasingly real and convincing. This explains why some of the most simplistic and insubstantial ideas produce some of the most heartfelt understandings. For example, when Richard Nixon's campaign strategists assessed his presidential prospects in 1968, they concluded that the biggest problem was the widespread perception that he was a loser. In response, the campaign introduced the symbolic suggestion that there was a "new Nixon," borrowing a classic advertising ploy to revive sagging products. The "new Nixon" became a much-discussed term that created for many people a concrete reference for new political actions that otherwise might have seemed ambiguous or deceitful.[43] This is the reasoning behind another of the communication commandments offered by Frank Luntz: "Novelty: Offer Something New." He also suggests creating personal involvement by asking a question such as "Got Milk?"

Message Salience

Lots of catchy messages elude popular imagination because they fail to capture widespread attention. The need for a message to capture attention explains why the second goal of image making is to saturate communication channels with the message and to stay on-message in those communications. The goal of message salience explains why advertisers spend billions of dollars to chant their simple jingles and slogans over and over again in the media. This explains why month after month of the Clinton-Lewinsky scandal involved opponents feeding talk-show pundits and journalists a steady message of SEX, SEX, SEX, while justifying this dubious political information by amplifying the Republican congressional message of CLINTON LIED, CLINTON LIED, CLINTON LIED.

Because the environment is full of competing messages, communication consultants are careful to remind (and script) their political clients that whenever the message *du jour* does go out, it must be "on-point," which means not complicating the idea, not drifting to other topics, and punching the current political theme until the strategic campaign of the moment has run its course. In the Luntz view, "Consistency Matters."

In addition to consistency, message salience can also be enhanced with two other Luntz rules: "Sound and Texture Matter" (make your slogans memorable—even set them to music) and "Visualize" (invite the audience to take away an image). That is why speeches have lines, such as "Imagine, if you will for a moment, a debt free economy strong enough that every American can share in the American Dream" or "Imagine a nation of clean coastlines and safe drinking water."[44]

In view of these patterns, it is easy to understand why politicians are so concerned with their images. In a sense, they are right in thinking that image is everything. Images feed on each other. To the extent that politicians can create appealing leadership images, salience is more likely to be conferred on their specific political pronouncements. To the extent that issues can be made to seem important by calling them "crises," opposing voices are more likely to be drowned out. To the extent that public favor can be won, future messages will receive less criticism, thereby escalating the spiral of popularity, thereby increasing future message salience, and so on.

Message Credibility

Even a public bombarded with salient political messages cannot always be relied on to accept them—even if they hear them often. Salient political messages are more likely to be supported when they are accompanied by some measure of their validity. Most political communication employs some logic, evidence, or authoritative endorsement. Following his advice to keep it simple and keep it short, Frank Luntz offers "Credibility" as another rule. The core of credibility is to find a clear, simple message and to embody it. If this message is "No New Taxes," be prepared to suffer a huge credibility loss if you give in to pressures for raising new revenues (or call them fees, not taxes!).

In addition, politicians often use staged dramatic settings such as the Oval Office or the deck of an aircraft carrier to lend weight to their announcements. Shocking events may be used to push messages, as when killing sprees are followed by renewed appeals for tougher gun control laws or terrorist attacks are followed by renewed efforts to topple Saddam Hussein. However, it is striking how messages that are repeated over and over again by high officials may be believed by large numbers of people even when they are challenged by opponents and experts as dubious. For example, the Bush administration's claimed link between al-Qaeda and Iraq continued to be accepted long after critics pointed out the evidence to the contrary. As we will see in Chapter 6, the news system gives credence to many dubious claims because they continue to be reported as one side of a story simply because they are issued by officials.

Message Framing

Simply creating, repeating, and supporting a message is not enough to ensure a successful communication strategy. The news is not just an information bulletin board; it is, more important, a storytelling process. Stories become pegged to central ideas or categories of meaning that organize, screen, and emphasize information. These meaning organizers, called frames, can distill large amounts of information into very simple capsule summaries—such as sex scandal, government waste, natural disaster, election horse race, terrorism, or weapons of mass destruction, just to name a few.

Framing often involves engagement of many mental activities, emotional, visual, and cognitive. Great political moments have echoed through the fog of daily life with frames such as "I have a dream" that are powerful because they engage emotions that make us aspire to great things, while helping people recognize neglected and perhaps tragic problems. In addition to being good visualizations, such statements also embody another Luntz rule: "Speak Aspirationally." Dreams can evoke our greatest aspirations. Aspirational language often has more impact if it is delivered with the help of this Luntz rule: "Provide Context and Explain Relevance." Martin Luther King Jr. had a particular and timely dream that white and black children would grow up living in the same society with the same opportunities. It was a dream whose time had come, and he helped many Americans frame their thinking about race in America differently as a result. Thus, great frames help people visualize, aspire, and put messages into the contexts of their personal lives.

SYMBOLIC POLITICS AND STRATEGIC COMMUNICATION

The goals of image making are fairly straightforward: Design a theme or message to spark the imagination, make sure that message dominates communication about the matter at hand, surround the message with a context of credibility, and tell or act out a story that offers the best framing for the message. Simple though they may appear, these goals are not easy to attain.

Effective image making requires a sophisticated understanding and use of communication technologies, such as polling, message development in focus groups, market research to see how the message plays, and news management to get the message into the news with the right framing. There is, of course, a good deal of time, energy, resources, and personnel devoted to image making in politics. It has been estimated that anywhere from 30 to 50 percent of the large and well-paid White House staff is involved with media relations in some form.[45] The major preoccupation of the average member of the House of Representatives is running for the next election.[46] The Defense Department spends billions of dollars annually from its huge budget on PR.[47] The U.S. Army even runs a special school to train its corps of PR officers.[48] In view of these efforts, one observer has concluded that "the vast, interlocking federal information machine has one primary purpose: the selling of the government."[49]

In the view of communication scholar Jarol Manheim, the technologies of image making today are so advanced that the term *strategic communication* better expresses this sophistication than does the more traditional term *public relations*.[50] Frank Luntz would seem to agree. What do the political communication experts do? To put it simply, they use symbols in ways calculated to best satisfy the goals of image making.

The Political Uses of Symbols

Symbols are the basic units of most human communication. Words are symbols that stand for objects and ideas. Flags, emblems, and uniforms are symbols of nationalism, group, or authority. Specific people can even symbolize general human attributes, such as heroism, patriotism, beauty, or greed. Because of the existence of symbols, it is possible to communicate about something without having the object of communication immediately present. Thus, the word *tree* is a symbol that permits communication about trees whether or not a tree is present. The term *nuclear war* permits communication about something that does not exist anywhere except in the human imagination. Because a major preoccupation of politicians and interest groups is how to represent actual situations in the most favorable strategic terms, it is obvious why symbols are so important. Through the skillful use of symbols, actual political circumstances can be redefined.

To understand how symbols are used and what makes them effective or ineffective, it is useful to know something about their psychological effects. Every symbol affects us in at least two ways, one *cognitive* and the other *affective*. The cognitive effect refers to the thought and logic engaged by a symbolic message. Affect involves the emotions and feelings triggered by the message. The cognitive associations with a message can be narrow or broad. For example, the term *freedom* has multiple associations for nearly everyone. In contrast, the term *congressional delegation* has a narrow, specific meaning. On the affective side, a symbol may elicit little emotional response or may evoke great outpourings of feeling. For example, the term *freedom* can be used in highly emotional ways, whereas *congressional delegation* provokes relatively little emotion from most people under most circumstances. (However, the term *Congress* can provoke considerable emotional reaction these days.) Symbols that convey narrow meaning with little emotion are called *referential symbols*. Symbols that evoke broad categories of meaning accompanied by strong emotions are called *condensational symbols.*[51] We have even invented symbols to help us talk about symbols!

The kind of image created for a political situation depends on what the key actors want the public to do in the situation. A faction interested in broadening the scope and intensity of public involvement may picture a situation in condensational symbols, whereas a faction seeking to narrow the scope and intensity of public concern can be expected to use referential terms. For example, groups who opposed U. S. involvement in Vietnam represented the bombing of North Vietnam in condensational terms, emphasizing savage destruction, government lying, and dangerous expansion of the war. The government, on the other hand, sought to minimize public concern with the details of the war. Public relations officers in the White House and the Pentagon invented an entire vocabulary of referential symbols to blunt the meanings and feelings attached to military actions. Thus, bombing raids on North Vietnam were referred to as *protective reaction strikes,* a term so narrow and bloodless that only its creators understood precisely what it implied.

In today's high-technology warfare, it is common to hear that enemy positions in Afghanistan were *removed* with *surgical precision* by *smart bombs.* Such terms make the news soothing to home audiences, but they may be of little consolation to the people in the battlefield killed near a target that was being surgically removed. *Collateral damage* and *friendly fire* are political code terms to minimize public outrage at the mistaken targeting of innocent people.

Whether a particular symbol has referential or condensational effects depends partly on the symbol and partly on how it is used. In the right context, even the most innocuous referential term can be transformed into a powerful condensational symbol. For example, in the early days of the Vietnam War, the Pentagon used the term *missing in action (MIA)* to refer to the troops missing and unaccounted for in combat. For years, this symbol was a descriptive term with a specific meaning and little emotional charge. Over the years, however, the number of MIAs grew, and many Americans became increasingly disturbed by the failure of anyone to account for these loved ones. Also during this time, the country became polarized into pro-war and antiwar factions, making for a highly charged emotional atmosphere. Caught in the middle of this situation, Richard Nixon searched for some effective way of justifying his continued war policies despite broad opposition to them. Suddenly Nixon had his issue. He explained to the public that the breakdowns in his peace negotiations had been due largely to the refusal of the North Vietnamese to promise an accounting of prisoners of war and MIAs. He told the public that he could not end the war and turn his back on those brave soldiers. Seemingly from out of nowhere came demonstrations and endorsement of his position. Bumper stickers proclaimed the plight of the MIAs. In the space of a few months, the change of usage transformed MIA from an obscure referential term to a powerful condensational symbol. The lesson is important: Symbols are not static; their effects (both cognitive and affective) depend on how they are used in specific contexts.

Defining the Political Situation

The flexibility of symbols is a great resource for politicians bent on transforming the real world of politics into a world of realistic political images. So great are the possible gaps between symbol and reality that actors sometimes propose truly absurd or transparent definitions of situations. The frequent absence of feedback or commentary in the news can make the ridiculous appear to be acceptable, if not sublime. For example, a local police department's increase in radar patrol activity triggered angry citizen protests against that spine-chilling condensational symbol, the "speed trap." The department launched a PR effort to cool off the citizens, reassuring them that the radar activities were no more than "accident prevention patrols" and that worried motorists could call a special number to find out where these patrols were located each day (presumably so that the motorists would be sure to avoid having accidents in those areas).[52]

In another case, the owners of a nuclear power plant that leaked radioactive gas were determined not to let the incident become a major news story like the one that haunted the nuclear power industry following an earlier leak at Three Mile Island in Pennsylvania. The leak at the Louisa, Virginia, plant was followed by an 11-hour communication blackout during which time press briefings were scripted for simultaneous delivery at the plant site and at the Nuclear Regulatory Commission headquarters in Washington, DC. The announcement stated that the plant "burped" a small amount of radioactive gas into the atmosphere. To clarify, the company spokesperson said, "It wasn't a leak, it was more like a burp."[53] The choice of a ridiculous metaphor worked, as the story died quickly.

There are two morals to these stories. First, if politicians can code complex, ambiguous, or unpopular realities into simple, clear, and pleasing symbols, they probably will do it. Second, grasping what is going on behind the scenes becomes more difficult when the press fails to take issue with the resulting credibility gap. The interplay of politicians' efforts to define political situations and the likelihood of the press to take issue with those definitions largely determines the effectiveness of efforts to manage the news. Political actors try to improve their chances in the news management game by controlling the terms on which they interact with the press.

NEWS MANAGEMENT: THE BASICS

The press displays an odd pattern. In some cases, news organizations seem to be easily seduced by the PR tactics designed to create the grand illusions (historic deceptions) of political news. In other cases, the press turns petulantly critical, putting the news focus on personal scandals, politicians' failures, and partisan attacks. This odd alternation between being spun and providing knowing commentary may mean that news organizations have only a dim sense of their obligations to the public.[54] In crafting stories, members of the press are more likely to pay attention to each other, to the politicians and political insiders they associate with every day, and to the audience research messages that filter through their editors.

As a result of this reference system, journalists are most tuned into the significance of news within insider political circles. Therefore, it is the maneuvering, spinning, and leaking from within these circles that keep the main stories going from day to day. Even though this odd system may undermine public confidence in both press and politicians, it has become central to the conduct of politics, as outlined in earlier chapters. What keeps this illusory news system spinning? The following pages explore various newsmaking situations, from canned new releases and staged events to those less-controlled situations that can sorely test the spin-doctor's art.

Prepackaged News Stories

As it becomes more difficult to get and keep the attention of journalists, newsmakers and their consultants have developed more sophisticated techniques for monitoring public opinion and managing the news flow from the offices of government, business, and interest organizations. The flow of strategic communications puts increasing pressure on understaffed news organizations. Since 1980 the numbers of PR workers have soared from just a bit over a 1:1 ratio with journalists to more than a 3:1 ratio in recent times. As McChesney and Nichols note: ". . . even as journalism shrinks, the 'news' will still exist. It will increasingly be provided by tens of thousands of well-paid and skilled PR specialists ready and determined to explain the world to the citizenry, in a manner that suits their corporate and government employers."[55] Consider just two applications of improved technologies for communicating about politics: prefabricated news and strategic polling.

Video News Releases   One result of the growth of the professional communications industry is that television newsrooms today are deluged with so-called VNRs (video news releases) that tempt understaffed and budget-strapped organizations to run PR materials packaged in news formats. From pharmaceutical companies hawking new wonder drugs to members of Congress trying to remain visible in their home districts, the production of canned news material has become a staple of daily life.

VNRs have been termed the "Hamburger Helper" for news organizations. They generally arrive at newsrooms via satellite feeds similar to the raw feeds that bring the news gathered by actual reporters and wholesale news suppliers. The difference is that VNRs deliver strategic messages wrapped in news packages produced in PR, advertising, political consulting, or corporate communications offices. The VNR generally arrives in two parts: a completed news segment that can either be run as is or used by producers in the newsroom to understand the story, and a so-called B-roll, which contains the raw footage and a script that can be used to build a story at the station.

A study of TV newsroom decision makers by Nielsen Media Research (the ratings people) revealed that all 110 of those surveyed had put VNRs on the air in the last year. Nielsen also tracks the audiences for various VNRs thanks to hidden electronic codes embedded in the footage. Nielsen reported that a Lockheed Martin Corporation story on the first flight of its F-22 fighter jet was watched by 41 million people. The "news story" fashioned for the release of a Nieman Marcus Christmas catalogue was delivered to an audience of 91 million. Perhaps the most successful VNR to date was the one touting Pfizer's wonder drug Viagra, a VNR that was fed to some 800 stations. According to the estimate of the proud PR executive who produced it, it was viewed all or in part by 210 million folks.[56] Advertising as effective as such free and authenticating news coverage cannot be bought at any price. A sample of VNRs that made news in recent years can be found at the PR watch project.[57]

At times, politicians may be tempted to seek even greater control of the news than just producing VNRs, as when the Bush administration paid journalist Armstrong Williams $240,000 to speak out in favor of its education policies on his national TV show and to supportively interview the secretary of education on the program. Williams also produced VNRs designed to look like actual news stories under a larger contract he received from the Education Department's PR firm, Ketchum Communications. The administration had also paid for similar VNRs to promote its Medicare plan as news, complete with a fake reporter signing off like a real one: "In Washington, I'm Karen Ryan reporting."[58] Those government ads were indistinguishable from the pieces that many local stations buy from real Washington-based journalists and news services to provide coverage on national issues that local stations lack the reporting staff to cover.

The Williams episode was followed by an investigation by the Government Accounting Office on the administration use of tax money to produce such propaganda, which resulted in a ruling that it was probably illegal to use taxpayer money for such purposes.[59] Yet, no action was taken beyond Williams's exit from the press corps and a fine for fraudulent billing practices. The administration was not prosecuted for fraudulent communication practices.

Strategic Polls: The Public as Target Polling exemplifies another information area in which advanced communication technology is often not used with regard for the highest interests of democracy. Despite advances in opinion polling and the proliferation of survey organizations, polls are not typically reported in ways that might help people better understand and participate in political situations. Research indicates that neither politicians nor journalists generally use polls to create more enlightened policy dialogues that might engage the general public. In fact, there is evidence that politicians use polls less often than in earlier years to guide their policy thinking. Today, they most often cite polls as helpful for finding the right language to sell already-made decisions to the public.[60]

Even when news organizations conduct independent polls, they often use them to play up extremes and conflicts, along with incessant ratings of politicians. In the words of Jacobs and Shapiro, polling reports resemble "the journalistic equivalent of a drive-by shooting" when only the numbers that support the dramatic focus of a news story tend to be reported.[61] There is also a tendency in news organizations to exaggerate changes in opinion where there are often none at all. Also, in an estimated 40 percent of all references to polls in news stories, no numbers are reported at all.[62] Political actors have learned to play on these journalistic uses of polling to leak their own polls and to commission seemingly independent surveys to suit their political aims.

Controlling Events: From Staging to Damage Control

Many newsmakers have the resources required to produce professional media events: writers, media directors, costume consultants, access to dramatic settings, and an attentive press corps ready to cover official announcements and events. Careful preparation of events enables control over key elements of the news story: the scene (where); the status of the actor (who); the motives, or ends, the political action is to serve (why); the means through which the action will accomplish its ends (how); and the significance of the political action itself (what). However, some situations are too spontaneous, and some actors are too poor in skills or resources to control the news event. Thus, political manipulation of the news runs along a continuum from fully controlled news events at one end to uncontrolled events (the political handler's worst nightmare) at the other extreme.

Pseudo-Events: Fully Controlled News Situations

Fully controlled media presentations are often called *pseudo-events*.[63] Pseudo-events disguise actual political circumstances with realistic representations designed to create politically useful images. A pseudo-event uses careful stage setting, scripting, and acting to create convincing images that often have little to do with the underlying reality of the situation. By incorporating fragments of an actual situation into a dramatized presentation, a pseudo-event tempts the viewer to fill in the blanks and build a complete understanding out of fragmentary facts. According to Daniel Boorstin's definition, a pseudo-event has four characteristics:

1. It is not spontaneous but comes about because someone has planned, planted, or incited it.
2. It is planted primarily for the immediate purpose of being reported.
3. Its relation to the underlying reality of the situation is ambiguous.
4. It is intended to be self-fulfilling.[64]

George W. Bush's aircraft carrier jet landing in full "Top Gun" flight suit, followed by a speech that declared "Mission Accomplished" in Iraq in 2003 was a classic pseudo-event: (1) it was anything but spontaneous—it required practice, costuming, and even holding the carrier off the coast; (2) the event was staged purely for newsmaking purposes; (3) the relationship between the swaggering president and his dubious military record was rendered ambiguous by the self-contained performance; and (4) the images of a confident leader and a victory in war were self-fulfilling in the sense that evidence to the contrary was excluded from the performance. As long as news coverage focused on the staged event, the audience received only the images and messages in the dramatic production. And in the case of the carefully staged Mission Accomplished performance, the press played it to the hilt, even commending the White House communications team for producing such a stunning news event.[65] The only trouble was that in reality the war in Iraq had just begun.

Partially Controlled News Situations

Some political situations are not as easy to control as a presidential landing on an aircraft carrier. Many public settings have an element of spontaneity in them. For example, press conferences can be controlled insofar as choice of time, place, and opening remarks, but they always contain some risk of unexpected or hostile questions from the press. In other cases, an official may be surprised by an issue and asked to comment, even though he or she is unprepared to do so. Perhaps such hard-to-control features explain why modern presidents hold far fewer press conferences than their pre-television-era predecessors.

When the comforting script of a pseudo-event is unavailable, political actors must resort to other means of protecting desired images. A common means of handling partially controlled situations is to anticipate and prevent possible moments of spontaneity in advance. For example, press conferences are often structured tightly to promote desired messages and prevent spontaneous distractions. In a press conference, opening remarks are intended to set the tone and make the headlines, reporters can be called on or ignored, time limits can be imposed, and stage settings can be manipulated. However, even press conferences can become testy and can offer reporters opportunities to challenge official claims and push politicians off message. As a result, presidents have tended to give fewer of them over time, with Ronald Reagan setting a modern era low, as his communications staff preferred media events that communicated his messages over press conferences that enabled the press corps to ask hostile questions. The press conference was revived during the presidencies of George H. W. Bush and Bill Clinton, only to decline again in the administration of George W. Bush, who, by the end of his third year, had offered just 11.[66] Barack Obama set a course that would make him the president with the fewest press conferences, with just 5 in the first 18 months (up to the time of this writing).[67] There are of course different ways to count what constitutes a press conference. Mr. Obama had may press appearances with foreign leaders and at official ceremonies or announcements, and some of these involved taking a few questions from reporters.[68] However, the trend seems to indicate that open question sessions are disappearing. Why have recent presidents been so reluctant to go before the press in this public setting? The reason was simple according to George W. Bush's White House communication director Dan Bartlett: "At press conferences, you can't control your message."[69]

Many officials, including presidents, increasingly prefer interviews with select journalists and television personalities, such as Jay Leno or David Letterman. They often grant those interviews only if ground rules are accepted by the interviewers. In contrast to his press conference behavior, Barack Obama set a record during his first year in office with 158 interviews, including 90 television appearances.[70] In 2010, he even went on ABC's daytime discussion show *The View* in an effort to soften his image and connect directly with women viewers. As media reporter Howard Kurtz put it, while the press grumbled about not having face time with the president:

> In recent weeks, the president has talked to ABC's Diane Sawyer, George Stephanopoulos and Charlie Gibson, Steve Kroft of "60 Minutes" and at Sunday's Super Bowl with CBS's Katie Couric. Each has pressed him on various issues; Obama admitted to Sawyer that he had made a "legitimate mistake" by promising that all health-care negotiations would be televised on C-SPAN. But with strict time limits and a natural effort by the anchors to touch on several subjects, Obama has a built-in advantage.[71]

Sometimes the most effective means of operating in hard-to-control situations is to avoid both press conferences and interviews, and release information through anonymous news leaks. Leaks are useful for delivering messages in many unstable situations. In some cases, an official may favor a policy but not know how the public will react. An anonymous leak describing the policy gives the official a chance to change course if the opposition is too strong. In other cases, the information leaked is privileged or secret, thereby presenting problems for any kind of formal public release. In other cases, a political message is not important enough to be guaranteed coverage if released through normal press channels or presented as a pseudo-event. If the right reporter is given a scoop based on the information, however, the chances are pretty good that the story will receive special attention. Strong emphasis given to a story by one news outlet may prompt others to cover it the next day. This use of leaks was acknowledged humorously when Ronald Reagan opened a press conference by saying that he did not have an opening remark because his planned statement was so important that he had decided to leak it instead.

Leaks also offer control over one of the most important variables in partially controlled situations: timing. The timing of a leak or a press release is crucial. For example, it is common wisdom that bad news is best released on weekends when reporters are off duty, news programs are scarce, and the public is distracted from worldly concerns. In other cases, the issue of timing means getting the jump on opponents who may attempt to plant their own images about a situation. Consider the case of a Reagan administration budget leak. The year was 1983. The proposed budget was a political disaster. There were huge deficits where Reagan had promised a balanced budget. There were painful cuts in already weakened social programs. To top it all off, the country was in serious economic trouble. The news management goal was to soften the blow of more bad news. The Reagan media staff evidently decided that the budget was such a potential news disaster that the budget director leaked the budget on a Friday by "forgetting" his copy in a congressional hearing room following a high-level congressional briefing. In a few hours, the budget had found its way into the hands of news people without the usual embargo. The story that would have dominated the headlines had it been announced on a Monday was, instead, scattered across the less-visible weekend news channels. By Monday, the budget was old news. When asked about the apparent leak, White House communication director David Gergen denied it and explained that the usual "press embargo" stamp had been omitted "accidentally" from the budget books taken to the briefing.[72]

Another advantage of leaks is that the source is often protected by journalists who strike a deal of secrecy to obtain the story. This means that leakers often have an important degree of control over how the story will be told. Because journalists must generally craft the story to make it appear self-contained and removed from its source, leaked stories can often be highly damaging to targeted opponents simply because the whole story and the politics behind it are not told.

Leaks are quite another story when they occur outside of news management strategies, as when reporters were told about a secret government surveillance program on U.S. citizens conducted by the Bush administration. The question of the legality of the program created a long news management battle for the administration. The threat of losing control of such an important issue led the administration to apply pressure on the *New York Times* to hold up the story for a year. The battle over small leaks in the wall of government secrecy was suddenly overshadowed by the torrents of leaks that resulted from the world release of secret government files on WikiLeaks, a new media organization that publishes submissions of inside information deemed credible from anonymous sources. Several bombshell leaks occurred in 2010, including the release of nearly 400,000 military action reports from Iraq. The release of secret Afghanistan War documents and the coordination of the leak with various international newspapers left the Obama administration with little leverage to apply pressure to containing the leak.[73] Even bigger news resulted from the release of over 250,000 U.S. diplomatic cables that filled the world media with inside evidence of corruption in Afghanistan, unflattering profiles of world leaders, and revelations about pressures from Saudi Arabia to stop Iran's nuclear program. Attempts to hack into WikiLeaks sites, and political pressure to stop companies from hosting or supporting the leak torrent only resulted in clones of WikiLeaks appearing across the net, along with retaliation from supportive hackers against companies that had withdrawn services from WikiLeaks. This new phenomenon may well define the nature of uncontrolled news situations in the future.

Uncontrolled News Situations

Few things strike more fear in the heart of a politician than a news story that has gotten out of control. Sometimes control of a story is lost because the underlying reality of a situation is simply too big to hide, as was the case with

Lyndon Johnson's increasingly empty assurances that the United States was winning the war in Vietnam. In some cases, former insiders blow the cover on a story, as happened when John Dean delivered his damaging Watergate testimony against Richard Nixon or when former war strategist Daniel Ellsberg leaked secret government documents about Vietnam. In many instances, a story gets out of control when a politician fails to handle the pressures of a partially controlled situation. A classic case in point was Gerald Ford's blunder during a presidential debate when he claimed there was no Soviet domination in Eastern Europe.

The *damage control* imperative that has grown in response to such politically volatile moments is to contain reality behind a screen of politically advantageous and controlled images. When an oil well off the Louisiana coast spilled vast amounts of oil into the Gulf in 2010, President Obama made numerous trips to the area to walk on beaches, and to confer with affected residents. The president, the first lady and daughter Sasha took a vacation in Panama City, Florida, that included photo opportunities of them swimming in Gulf waters after the spill was finally stopped.[74] Even though the president was not responsible for the spill, his the news narrative of disorder and control undermined his approval ratings as the news repeatedly included reports on what the president was doing about the situation. Creating the image of being closely involved and present on the scene helped mitigate the image damage.

Although there is no magic formula for turning out-of-control situations into fully controlled PR bonanzas, there are important news management techniques that politicians ignore only at their peril. Presidents not only experience more media pressure than most politicians, but they also have more resources to manage the press. Thus it is not surprising that the most sophisticated methods for news control have emerged from presidential press operations. As research by John Anthony Maltese shows, the White House press operation grew phenomenally both in size and sophistication during the half-century from Truman to Clinton.[75] The presidential profiles in the next section illustrate the key ingredients of presidential news management.

NEWS MANAGEMENT STYLES AND THE MODERN PRESIDENCY

When Harry Truman ordered atomic bombs to be dropped on Japan in 1945, he personally broke the news to a White House press corps that numbered 25 reporters. Bill Clinton arrived in Washington to find that more than 1,700 reporters covered the White House, and a total of 2,800 people, including television producers, technicians, and other crew members, were allowed to pass through the press entrance of the president's residence.[76] It is hard to imagine any politician interacting with such a crowd in the absence of considerable staging, planning, and scripting, and so the White House press operations have grown along with, and sometimes ahead of, the press corps. Indeed, press relations may have reached a turning point by 2010, when Barack Obama had not held a press conference in months, and had turned to direct television appearances, bloggers, and his impressive social networking technologies to target messages directly to publics. While these unfiltered communication channels may have offered the president more control over his messages, the loss of mainstream media gatekeeping also enabled the conservative media echo chamber (bloggers, talk radio, Fox TV) to challenge the president with messages of its own, such as whether the president was in fact a closeted Muslim, and not the Christian he professed to be.

A landmark moment in modern era presidential communications came when **Richard Nixon** created the White House Office of Communications with the aim of controlling the flow of information out of the entire executive branch and staging events that would reduce the press to passive transmitters of political messages. This idea of "going over the heads of the press" to communicate directly with the people has been termed *going public* by political scientist Samuel Kernell.[77] These goals were disrupted in Nixon's case when the Watergate affair and a series of congressional investigations aroused a press pack that followed a trail of scandal that led eventually to the Oval Office.

Elected on a promise to restore trust in government, **Jimmy Carter** neglected news management with a possibly foolish determination to run a White House that was open to the press. With plot assists from a struggling economy, opponents in Congress, and an embarrassing 444 days of news about Americans being held hostage in Iran, the media helped the voters send Carter out of Washington with unpopularity levels approaching those suffered by Richard Nixon in the polls. It was not until the Reagan presidency that the White House Office of Communications was fully developed into the well-oiled PR machine that helped turn Reagan into the Great Communicator.

Ronald Reagan

The textbook on how to manage the news was written during the Reagan administration. It is open for others to follow. Few politicians may attempt or even want to manage the press as completely as the Reagan communication staff did, but relations between press and politicians will never be the same again. What does the textbook say about media management for politicians? The first step is to adopt the proper frame of mind. As former White House communication director David Gergen put it: "To govern successfully, the government has to set the agenda; it cannot let the press set the agenda for it."[78] How did Mr. Gergen achieve this goal? According to an analysis by Mark Hertsgaard, here is the step-by-step method:[79]

1. Weekly long-term strategy meetings of policy officers and press handlers to plan the future news agenda and assess the results of ongoing media control efforts.
2. Daily meetings of the White House communication group to decide, as one member put it, "What do we want the press to cover today, and how?"[80] According to Michael Deaver, one of the masterminds of the press operation in the Reagan years: "We would take a theme, which we

usually worked on for six weeks—say, the economy. The President would say the same thing, but we had a different visual for every one of [the regularly scheduled media events]."[81]

3. As the previous step indicates, *repetition* is the key. Feed the press the same message with a new (and therefore newsworthy) visual setting to satisfy the media need for changing video footage and new photo opportunities. As Deaver recalled, "It used to drive the President crazy because the repetition was so important. He'd get on that airplane and look at that speech and say, 'Mike, I'm not going to give this same speech on education again, am I?' I said, 'Yeah, trust me, it's going to work.' And it did."[82]

4. Put out the line of the day to all the other potential newsmakers in the executive branch to "make sure we're all saying the same thing" to the press.[83] During the Reagan years, the line of the day was sent out over a computer network to all administration offices. All that any official had to do was call it up on his or her screen before meeting with reporters.

5. Coordinate the day's news via conference calls to top administration officials to make sure they understand the line of the day and to orchestrate which officials will say something, when they will say it, and who will keep their mouths shut, as in "Look, the President's got a statement tomorrow, so shut up today, goddammit, just shut up, don't preempt the President, [we'll] cut your nuts off if you leak anything out on this one. . . ."[84]

6. Work the press and call reporters and their bosses to see if they understood the story correctly. This has become known as "spin control." During the Reagan years, the White House made it a regular practice to call the national TV network executives just prior to their nightly newscasts to check on what they were running and to offer additional clarification on the stories.

7. Weekly seminars held for the spokespeople of the various federal bureaucracies to educate them on how to present the administration to the press.

8. A heavy volume of opinion polling and market research to see what was on the public's mind and how the president could tap into it through the news. The White House even conducted its own market research on the public images of newspeople to whom they might give interviews and treat more or less deferentially.

There you have it. Follow the eight easy steps, set the media stage, introduce a president who is comfortable with the TV lights and cameras, and you have the Great Communicator—someone whose message is on-point, salient, credible, and effectively framed. The Reagan press management plan was so effective that chief image maker Richard Wirthlin was crowned Advertising Man of the Year in 1989. He did not receive his industry's top award for his creative work for General Foods or Mattel Toys, but for his accomplishments as director of consumer research for Ronald Reagan.[85] In assessing Wirthlin's award-winning performance, one observer concluded that the mapmaker of the public mind "probed just about every aspect of public affairs on a scale unmatched in U.S. history."[86]

Another measure of the success of the Reagan press program is that even when the press attempted to be critical, the efforts seldom produced results that stuck to the so-called Teflon coating that seemed to protect the president from the press. The classic case of news management operating with even a critical press involves CBS *News* correspondent Lesley Stahl, who put together a long report showing the gaps between Ronald Reagan's carefully styled news images and his actual policies in office. Stahl was nervous about the piece because of its critical tone and the practice of the White House Communications Office to call reporters and their employers about negative coverage. The phone rang after the report was aired, and it was "a senior White House official." Stahl prepared herself for the worst. In her own words, here is what happened:

> And the voice said, "Great piece."
> I said, "What?"
> And he said, "Great piece!"
> I said, "Did you listen to what I said?"
> He said, "Lesley when you're showing four-and-a-half minutes of great pictures of Ronald Reagan, no one listens to what you say. Don't you know that the pictures are overriding your message because they conflict with your message? The public sees those pictures and they block your message. They didn't even hear what you said. So, in our minds, it was a four-and-a-half-minute free ad for the Ronald Reagan campaign for reelection."
> I sat there numb. I began to feel dumb 'cause I'd covered him four years and I hadn't figured it out. Somebody had to explain it to me. Well none of us had figured it out. I called the executive producer of the *Evening News* . . . and he went dead on the phone. And he said, "Oh, my God."[87]

There it was. The textbook news management system worked even with uncooperative reporters. Television is the medium through which most people get their news. When politicians and their handlers are careful to stage their public appearances for the right production values (i.e., to convey the right visual images), reporters are denied the video evidence they need to back up a hard-hitting script. As one of the Reagan news wizards put it bluntly, "What are you going to believe, the facts or your eyes?"[88]

George Herbert Walker Bush

It is clear that George Bush's (1989–1992) White House did not set out to manage the media as completely as the communications group did during the Reagan era. Even Lesley Stahl could be heard almost complaining about the "night and day" difference, saying about the Bush administration that "This White House doesn't care if the president gets on the evening news or not."[89] Another reporter responded by saying, "That's not an impeachable offense—yet—but it does raise some interesting questions. Not least for the White House press corps, which seems to be looking back on the slick, well-packaged Reagan presidency with a touch of—can it be?—Nostalgia."[90]

Media criticism of Bush's unwillingness to manipulate the press became too much to tolerate, and the White House soon brought back the media team that got him elected. For example, former PR executive Sig Rogich, who had produced several Bush campaign commercials in 1988, came to the White House as Special Assistant to the President for Activities and Initiatives (i.e., chief image maker).[91] Rogich was rewarded for helping to restore the Bush image by being named ambassador to Iceland. In 1992, Bush once again forgot the lessons of news and image management, and Rogich was recalled from Iceland to produce Bush campaign commercials. However, Rogich and the other image doctors arrived too late; the Bush media management team was far too disorganized during the 1992 campaign to save the president's image or his reelection.

Bill Clinton

Although Clinton displayed little enthusiasm for it, news management became an early preoccupation of the Clinton political operation. Indeed, it had to be, considering the attacks on his draft record and his sex life during the 1992 campaign. Yet, Clinton flirted dangerously with ignoring the press and sometimes trying to circumvent the news altogether. During his first election campaign, when the press became too concerned with Clinton's personal problems, the candidate went directly to the people through appearances on 60 Minutes, MTV, various talk shows, and specially produced electronic town hall programs that created the illusion of intimacy with audiences. When his media image improved, the Clinton news team staged events like the direct-to-the-voter bus tours that sparked considerable positive coverage from the press. However, after the election, Clinton apparently continued to seethe about the personal press attacks he had suffered during the campaign. Convinced that as president Clinton could go over the heads of the news media, the Clinton team closed off the hallway between the press room and the White House press office and kept the presidential press pack at a distance. The results were devastating. Clinton became the object of massive journalistic criticism. As the Washington Post Editorial Page Editor Meg Greenfield put it, she had never seen an administration "pronounced dead" so early.[92]

At last, Clinton brought none other than David Gergen on board to manage his press operations. When Gergen was allowed to implement press management techniques, Clinton's news control visibly improved. However, Clinton's continuing personal frictions with the press corps did not make Gergen's job easy, and he was never given the freedom to run the Clinton press operation that he had been granted under Reagan. This reluctance to give full reign to the "Sultan of Spin" (as Gergen was dubbed by journalists) remains puzzling in light of a report that the communication style that Clinton most admired was that of Ronald Reagan.[93]

Despite the rocky relations with the press that continued through the impeachment ordeal of his second term, Clinton managed to communicate fairly effectively by continuing to "go public." His staff staged numerous controlled events—including ceremonies on the White House lawn, world travels, weekly radio talks, and frequent announcements of policy goals and accomplishments—that gave him opportunities to share his easy media style with audiences who continued to support him with remarkable levels of approval. One of those gatherings on the White House lawn later came back to haunt Clinton: the scene of the president giving a warm hug to Monica Lewinsky later became endlessly replayed as one of the news icons condensing the scandal for television audiences. Yet Clinton's familiar on-screen character of the humble "comeback kid" continued to overcome those damaging images in the eyes of a majority of citizens, even as his resilience astounded political opponents and the press alike.

George W. Bush

For all of its conflicts with the press, and perhaps due to the run of crises and scandals it had to confront, the Clinton administration communication strategy maintained a fairly traditional emphasis on spinning the daily news through direct encounters between communication officers and the national press corps. The George W. Bush administration shifted its press strategy to an event-based newsmaking program that often left the press on the sidelines to transmit well-controlled dramatic images to their audiences. The Bush communication staff of 44 was roughly the size of Clinton's (42), but they were deployed differently. Whereas Clinton had 24 members working in the national press office, the Bush press contact staff was half that size. The majority of the communications staff was employed as "event planners, speech writers, and media affairs specialists whose job it is to reach out to journalists beyond the beltway."[94]

Bush spent much of his early term in office continuing to make quasi-campaign appearances around the country, using events as contexts for messages about policy proposals such as education and tax cuts. The strategic focus was less on briefing and informing the press corps than on offering them controlled events containing political messages that the president had little interest in expanding beyond their sound-bite salience. Presidential communication scholar Martha Kumar explains the Bush shift toward communication and event strategies and away from press office activities: "The difference is that communications operations are about persuasion, while the press office is about information. The Bush people want to develop a message and stay on it. They use the press office to deliver that message and not answer a lot of questions about it."[95] The result was that the administration gave few interviews, and seldom got caught—as the Clinton administration often did—trying to explain differences among statements from different officials. Bush's first Press Secretary Ari Fleischer summed it up by saying, "When the administration has something to announce, it will announce it."[96] Even when reporters succeeded in getting an interview with a top official, such as chief political strategist Karl Rove, they ended up hearing exactly what they heard from the press secretary. The reason is that Rove and his staff have everyone talking the same message. As *Washington Post* reporter Dana Milbank put it, the administration speaks with one voice because everyone has "talking points that they e-mail to friends and everyone says exactly the same thing."[97] The early lessons of the Reagan administration were perfected and extended in the Bush White House. The dual strategy of keeping the Washington press at bay and going directly to local audiences kept approval ratings high until Hurricane Katrina and the war in Iraq both began to take their toll.

Barack Obama

The changing mediascape characterized by the decline of journalism and the rise of digital media and social technologies discussed in Chapter 1 left its imprint on the turbulent news and communication experiences of the Obama administration. As noted earlier, even as it limited the number of open encounters with the press, the Obama communication team found ever more novel ways to communicate directly with audiences. In place of holding press conferences with journalists, the president answered citizen questions on YouTube and streamed the event live on the White House Web site.[98] Many journalists were shocked when news photographers were excluded from a presidential signing ceremony, an event routinely open to press photographers, even if questioning reporters are not invited. Instead, photos were distributed to news organizations from an official White House photographer, raising challenging questions among journalists about whether they should even run them given that they were alarmingly close to the definition of propaganda rather than news.[99]

Press exclusion had become so extreme at an important summit of world leaders on nuclear security that a *Washington Post* reporter wrote a story not about the summit but about the disregard for the press, including this zinger about the president, describing Mr. Obama as: ". . . occupant of an office once informally known as "leader of the free world"—putting on a clinic for some of the world's greatest dictators in how to circumvent a free press."[100]

Explaining the White House communication strategy was Communications Director Dan Pfeiffer: "Not doing press conferences is equated with not taking questions, and that's not true." Noting that it may once have been effective to communicate with the public "through the reporters sitting in the first three rows of the White House pressroom. . . . there's no question that the *Huffington Post, Talking Points Memo* and their conservative counterparts can drive a story as well as the traditional powers at the *New York Times* and *Washington Post*."[101]

Beyond the focus on directed interviews, YouTube, town halls, and talk show appearances, the Obama communications team relied more on social media to get its messages out than any other administration. The importance of digital media had in many ways transformed the campaign communication of 2008, and continued to anchor much of the administration's messaging while in office. An article ominously titled "The Death of the White House Press Corps" in the aptly named webzine *The Daily Beast* pointed out the importance of digital media and direct messaging: "Thirty-one-year-old White House aide Macon Phillips, who directs President Obama's new-media operation, said the White House has 1.7 million followers on Twitter, around 500,000 fans on Facebook, and 70,000 email subscribers. . . ."[102] Followers of one of the administration's social networks often received video messages from the president at the same time they were released to the press, alleviating the need to wait and watch the news. Faced with this kind of competition for audiences, the traditional press began questioning its role, as reflected in these remarks from the veteran television correspondent Bill Plante:

> Technology has made it much easier now for the White House. . . . The availability of all this material means that people have to do their own filtering. The so-called mainstream media, which believes it has the experience to do the filtering, isn't there to do it for them, and for a lot of people that's just fine. They resent the hell out of us anyway.[103]

Plante may rightly sense a turning point in the longstanding relationship between journalists and officials. However, it may be premature to discount the importance of the press in shaping the narratives of power in American politics. Recall here the case study in Chapter 2 about president Obama losing control over his news narrative. The mainstream media continues to play a key role in shaping public perceptions simply because it still sends out the loudest signal. Thus, even as the media echo chamber becomes ever noisier with bloggers, webzines, talking pundits and Facebook news releases, the importance of amplifying clear narrative frames through the mainstream media cannot be underestimated. Television broadcasts and wire service feeds still reach more people than other sources, and they prime the daily agendas of the bloggers and the talk show personalities. As a result, losing control of the mainstream press—whether through poor news management or the belief that they can be ignored—can spell political trouble. History will tell if the Obama strategy of distancing the press in favor of more direct public communication strategies was a turning point or a lesson about the continuing need to feed the beast.

PRESS RELATIONS: FEEDING THE BEAST

Beyond the choice of symbols, the staging of news events, and the development of a news management strategy, the daily working relations between reporters and newsmakers can play a major part in the willingness of reporters to transmit all the news that politicians deem fit to print. As the case of Obama press relations suggests, officials can develop uneasy working relationships with the journalists who cover them. The Clinton administration also felt that the press was hostile to it and took the extreme measure of locking the door between the pressroom and the White House communications staff. Perhaps it was no accident that members of the Clinton press staff referred to the press corps down the hall and past the locked door as "the beast." Indeed, locking that door only made the beast angry, as did the Obama communication staff decision to bar news photographers from a signing ceremony.

Simple courtesies, by contrast, can pay big dividends in terms of controlling the timing, content, and amount of coverage. For example, shortly after Ronald

Reagan became president, he attended a major North–South economic summit conference in Mexico. Reagan's foreign policy prowess was under its first major test, and there were many potentially damaging criticisms of U.S. policies among the Latin American delegates. (At the time, the region suffered under several U.S.-backed wars, dire poverty, and numerous failed economic development initiatives.) Although a huge press entourage accompanied Reagan, few of those reporters ventured beyond the comfortable American compound to find out how other countries viewed such problems in the region. Few negative stories came from a well-fed and carefully handled U.S. press corps. As one observer put it:

> Reagan brought an enormous White House press corps. If the spokesmen for the poorer countries thought that meant access to the American media, which rarely discuss the issues of development, they were in for a surprise. "We'll try to feed you as often as possible," Secretary of State Alexander Haig promised at an early briefing in the makeshift White House press room, situated in the basement of the hotel where most of the American reporters stayed. The Reagan administration did feed the media, and many American journalists' accounts of what happened [at the conference] came straight from that official source. Some members of the White House press spent an entire week without meeting a single foreign delegate.[104]

Cooperation with the media extends beyond the care and feeding of reporters to the scheduling of major news events so they don't conflict with entertainment programming that generates ratings and revenues for the TV networks. Times have changed since the golden days of broadcasting, when a political broadcast gave prestige to a network and saved the production costs of live programs. According to an analysis by Joe Foote,

> During 1934, the year Congress was writing the Federal Communications Act, the two networks managed to find free time for 350 speeches by Congressmen and Senators, an average of nearly one program a day. . . . These political broadcasts substituted in many ways for news programs that were just then coming into their own and demonstrated the networks' commitment to public service.[105]

Now the problem of media access is a much more delicate economic matter resolved for the most part by running political messages during the regularly allocated news slots on the broadcast networks. Politicians' attempts to communicate with the American people at other times can cost a network upward of $200,000 for every 30-second commercial spot it loses when a political broadcast preempts an entertainment program. Failure to cooperate with corporate economic realities can cool political relations with the media, as David Gergen explained about his experiences in the Reagan White House:

> I would never call and say we're going to do a speech on Tuesday night at 8 o'clock without first asking what's on the air that night. Our television guy would look it up and determine how much of a problem it was

going to be with the network. . . . I was aware at all times what our relative standing was with the network—whether we were in good standing,
bad standing. You could take too much. You could go out and try to
gouge them, play them as the enemy, etc. I felt there was a different way
to play. If you do it very professionally, you'll get more out of them.[106]

Intimidation

Even in the most "clubby" of relations between political sources and the journalists who cover them, some exercise of intimidation may come into play. Indeed,
the interplay of intimidation and cooperation strategies can be quite sophisticated, as indicated by another example from the media management lore of the
Reagan years. When the war in El Salvador became dramatic enough in the early
1980s to warrant regular news coverage, the venerable *New York Times* sent a
bright young reporter named Ray Bonner to cover it. Unfortunately, Bonner was
inexperienced in the fine points of press–government cooperation and had the
audacity to develop contacts among rebel leaders fighting the U.S.-backed government. Some of Bonner's early stories suggested that the rebels had considerable
popular support, while the regime proclaimed "democratic" by U.S. officials had
engaged repeatedly in terrorism, torture, intimidation, and massacre of its own
people. Such intrusive realities contradicting the daily line of the White House
became too much for the administration to bear. Bonner was snubbed repeatedly
at the U.S. Embassy in San Salvador (a serious problem for a journalist dependent
on official reactions to all stories). *Times* Executive Editor Abe Rosenthal paid a
visit to San Salvador, where he held a meeting with U.S. Ambassador Deane
Hinton. According to a "well-placed" reporter on the *Times,* Ambassador Hinton
"became hysterical" about Bonner's critical reporting and flagrant disregard for
the daily news images preferred by the administration. Although Rosenthal
denied being influenced by the embassy, he recalled Bonner from El Salvador.[107]

The irony—and the moral—of this story is that more than a decade later,
and long after the wars had ended, much of Bonner's early critical reporting was
backed up with independent evidence. After the war ended, teams of U.N. investigators discovered mass graves in El Mozote, the site of one of the early Sal-
vadoran army massacres of civilians reported by Bonner. Other sources reported
that U.S. officials involved in directing the war knew about such incidents at the
same time they were publicly denying them and discrediting the journalists who
reported them. A front-page *New York Times* article in 1993 finally confirmed
what the *Times* had removed Ray Bonner for reporting a dozen years earlier:

> The Reagan Administration knew more than it publicly disclosed about
> some of the worst human rights abuses in El Salvador's civil war and
> withheld that information from Congress, declassified cables and inter-
> views with former government officials indicate.
>
> Charges that Reagan officials, and to a lesser extent the Carter and
> Bush Administrations, may have covered up evidence of abuses to win
> Congressional approval of about $6 billion in aid were revived with the
> release this week of a United Nations–sponsored report.[108]

After the government and the press finally set the record straight in 1993, a colleague of Bonner's offered the consolation that it took the Roman Catholic Church hundreds of years to reverse its condemnation of Galileo for (among other things) claiming that the sun and stars did not revolve around the earth. He sent a message to Bonner in the form of a headline: "Bonner and Galileo Still Right after All These Years."[109] It is nice to know that the record was finally set straight. However, correcting misinformation 12 years after the fact surely attracted little attention from most Americans. Indeed, that is the great lesson of news management: information is political, and the construction of images that fit political agendas is the object of the news game.

GOVERNMENT AND THE POLITICS OF NEWSMAKING

As explained in the first chapter, the news remains, for all its failings, crucial to governing. At the same time, the relationships among the key players in the American information system—the people, politicians, and the press—have entered a vicious political cycle:

- As the space for serious news shrinks due to the economic crisis facing journalism, political actors must rely even more on communication professionals to capture that precious space for their messages.
- Which means that our public communication is increasingly shaped by using technologies of market research and persuasion to stage, script, and spin news for its most dramatic media effect.
- As a result, the news is made increasingly by and for political insiders, leaving citizens out of the democratic picture.
- All of which feeds the spiral of public disillusionment with both politics and the news.

To make matters worse, the advent of the 24-hour news cycle means that the news never sleeps. There must be developments even when there are none to report. As journalists become more active in keeping stories going, they need reactions and dramatic material from political actors. Failure to "feed the beast" with new installments can result in being on the losing end of a story instead fed by opponents. Those who market ideas for a living learn quickly that dramatized events, spin, rumor, and reaction are helpful to journalists trying to operate within the low-budget, high-hype constraints of the 24-hour news cycle. Reporters are well aware that most of what they cover is heavily managed, but they generally try to maintain the impression that they are on the outside of events looking in. Sometimes these efforts create almost comical results in which the news intrudes upon and shapes the very realities that it appears to represent. A memorable example of this occurred when the United States joined a humanitarian United Nations mission to bring food to Somalia in 1992. The first troops to hit the beaches met with a surrealistic scene. Navy Seals in full camouflage attire and battle gear were startled by journalists, television cameras ablaze, who had already secured the beaches to record the landing for the nightly news back home.[110] Even when journalists attempt to resist the spin, as on the election campaign trail where the same speech is delivered day in and day out, the results often leave journalists awkwardly inserting themselves in stories to the point that they overshadow the politicians they are covering.

This news system does not make many of its players look good. Polls typically show press and politicians competing for last place in the race for public approval. Meanwhile, politicians quietly bemoan the low levels of public understanding of most issues and the selfish attitudes of citizens that hamper solutions for many public problems. This syndrome was summed up by West Virginia Senator Jay Rockefeller, who told a group of reporters:

> Voters . . . are angry with politicians like me. And they're angry with you in the media. Well, let me tell you something. The voters are no bargains, either.[111]

In this age of mediated politics, power is, to an important extent, a communication process that must be monitored and maintained by political actors. As a result of the technologies of strategic communications (polling, market research, news, and image management), the news is not just a record of events, it is an event in and of itself—an integral part of the political process linking politicians and people in the competition for government power.

NOTES

1. www.theworddoctors.com/intheirownwords.html. Accessed August 18, 2010.
2. Luntz Maslansky Strategic Research Web site, www.luntz.com/people.html. Accessed February 15, 2008.
3. Frank Luntz, *Words That Work: It's Not What You Say, It's What People Hear* (New York: Hyperion, 2007), xiii.
4. Sam Stein, "Frank Luntz Pens Memo to Kill Financial Regulatory Reform," *Huffington Post*, February 1, 2010. www.huffingtonpost.com/2010/02/01/frank-luntz-pens-memo-to_n_444332.html. Accessed August 19, 2010.
5. The Luntz Research Companies, "Straight Talk: The Environment: A Cleaner, Safer, Healthier America." www.ewg.org/files/LuntzResearch_environment.pdf, page 132. Accessed August 18, 2010.
6. Ibid.
7. I am indebted to Leah Ceccarelli, a colleague in the Department of Communication at the University of Washington, for her helpful analysis of how the political attack on science has been so effective.
8. Poll commissioned by the Yale Project on Climate Change. http://environment.yale.edu/climate/publications/americans-global-warming-beliefs-and-attitudes-2010/. Accessed August 19, 2010.
9. Pew Research Center for the People and the Press. "Public's Priorities for 2010." January 25, 2010. http://people-press.org/report/584/policy-priorities-2010. Accessed August 19, 2010.
10. See for example, the results of international polls commissioned by the World Bank showing the U.S. population rating the seriousness of global warming at levels comparable to Russia and China, and about half the international averages: http://blogs.worldbank.org/climatechange/who-earth-cares-about-climate-change. Accessed August 19, 2010.

11. Maxwell T. Boykoff and Jules M. Boykoff, "Balance vs. Bias: Global Warming and the US Prestige Press," *Global Environmental Change* 14 (2004): 125–136.
12. The Luntz Research Companies, "Straight Talk: The Environment: A Cleaner, Safer, Healthier America," page 138.
13. Leah Ceccarelli suggests that scientists should engage more positively with political challenges to their work in order to gain the attention of audiences and show them in direct language why the challenges are not credible.
14. The Luntz Research Companies, "Straight Talk," page 131.
15. Ibid.
16. Frank Luntz interview, PBS *Frontline*, November 13, 2006, www.pbs.org/wgbh/pages/frontline/hotpolitics/interviews/luntz.html. Accessed August 18, 2010.
17. Boykoff and Boykoff, "Balance vs. Bias."
18. Pew Center for the People & the Press (2007). http://pewresearch.org/pubs/282/global-warming-a-divide-on-causes-and-solutions. Accessed December 10, 2010.
19. Matthew C. Nisbet and Chris Mooney, "Framing Science," *Science* 316 (April 6, 2007): 56.
20. Luntz interview, PBS *Frontline*.
21. "Frank Luntz," *Wikipedia*. http://en.wikipedia.org/wiki/Frank_Luntz. Accessed August 19, 2010.
22. Dean Acheson, *Present at the Creation: My Years in the State Department* (New York: Norton, 1969), 375.
23. Leon V. Sigal, *Reporters and Officials: The Organization and Politics of News Reporting* (Lexington, MA: Heath, 1973), 124. (Percentages total slightly over 100 due to rounding.)
24. Ibid., 122.
25. Ibid., 122.
26. See, for example, Daniel C. Hallin, Robert Karl Manoff, and Judy K. Weddle, "Sourcing Patterns of National Security Reporters" (paper presented at the Annual Meeting of the American Political Science Association, San Francisco, August 30–September 2, 1990); and Jane Delano Brown, Carl R. Bybee, Stanley T. Wearden, and Dulcie Murdock, "Invisible Power: Newspaper Sources and the Limits of Diversity," *Journalism Quarterly* 64 (1987): 45–54. More recently, see W. Lance Bennett, Regina G. Lawrence, and Steven Livingston, *When the Press Fails: Political Power and the News Media from Iraq to Katrina* (Chicago: University of Chicago Press, 2007).
27. Steven Livingston and W. Lance Bennett, "Gatekeeping, Indexing, and Live Event News: Is Technology Altering the Construction of News?" *Political Communication* 20, no. 4 (October/December 2003): 363–380.
28. W. Lance Bennett, "Toward a Theory of Press–State Relations in the United States," *Journal of Communication* 40, no. 2 (1990): 103–127.
29. Thomas E. Patterson, "Doing Well and Doing Good: How Soft News and Critical Journalism Are Shrinking the News Audience and Weakening Democracy—and What News Outlets Can Do About It." Joan Shorenstein Center on Press, Politics, and Public Policy, Harvard University, December 2000.
30. For further discussion of this point, see these articles by the author: "News as Reality TV: Election Coverage and the Democratization of Truth," *Critical Studies in Media Communication* 22 (2005): 171–177; and "Beyond Pseudoevents: Election News as Reality TV," *American Behavioral Scientist* 49, no. 3 (2005): 1–15.
31. Edie Goldenberg, *Making the Papers* (Lexington, MA: Heath-Lexington Books, 1975).

32. Murray Edelman, *Constructing the Political Spectacle* (Chicago: University of Chicago Press, 1988).

33. Walter Lippmann, *Public Opinion* (New York: Free Press, 1922), 9.

34. Acheson, *Present at the Creation.*

35. See Murray Edelman, *Political Language: Words That Succeed, Policies That Fail* (New York: Academic Press, 1977).

36. Edelman, *Political Language.*

37. See David L. Altheide and Robert P. Snow, *Media Logic* (Beverly Hills, CA: Sage, 1979).

38. See, for example, Mark Hertsgaard, *On Bended Knee: The Press and the Reagan Presidency* (New York: Shocken, 1989); also, Jarol B. Manheim, *All of the People, All the Time: Strategic Communication and American Politics* (Armonk, NY: M. E. Sharpe, 1991).

39. Quoted by F. Christopher Arterton, "Campaign Organizations Face the Mass Media in the 1976 Presidential Nomination Process" (paper presented at the Annual Meeting of the American Political Science Association, Washington, DC, September 1977), 4.

40. NBC *News*, "White Paper on the Reagan Presidency," December 30, 1981.

41. Luntz, *Words That Work*, 4–5.

42. See Doris Graber, *Processing the News: How People Tame the Information Tide*, 2nd ed. (New York: Longman, 1988); Russell Neuman, Marion Just, and Ann Crigler, *Common Knowledge* (Chicago: University of Chicago Press, 1993); and Michael Delli Carpini and Bruce Williams, "Television in Political Discourse" (paper presented at the Annual Meeting of the American Political Science Association, Washington, DC, September 1991).

43. For a detailed discussion of how this worked, see Joe McGinniss, *The Selling of the President* (New York: Pocket Books, 1969).

44. Luntz, *Words That Work*, 22.

45. David Wise, *The Politics of Lying* (New York: Vintage, 1973).

46. David R. Mayhew, *Congress: The Electoral Connection* (New Haven, CT: Yale University Press, 1974).

47. See J. William Fulbright, *The Pentagon Propaganda Machine* (New York: Vintage, 1970); also Richard Barnet, *Roots of War* (Baltimore: Penguin, 1973).

48. Wise, *The Politics of Lying.*

49. Ibid., 273.

50. Manheim, *All of the People, All the Time.*

51. For the classic discussion of symbols in politics, see Murray Edelman, *The Symbolic Uses of Politics* (Urbana: University of Illinois Press, 1964).

52. This incident involved the Bellevue, Washington, police department and was reported on KIRO News Radio, Seattle, February 16, 1982.

53. United Press International (UPI) wire story, reported in the *Seattle Post-Intelligencer* (September 26, 1979): A2.

54. See Susan Herbst, *Reading Public Opinion: How Political Actors View the Democratic Process* (Chicago: University of Chicago Press, 1998) and Robert M. Entman, *Democracy Without Citizens* (New York: Oxford University Press, 1989).

55. Robert W. McChesney and John Nichols, *The Death and Life of American Journalism: The Media Revolution that Will Begin the World Again* (New York: Nation Books, 2010), 49.

56. Jeff Pooley, "Tricks of the Trade: Hamburger Helper for Newscasters," *Brill's Content* (December 1998/January 1999): 46.

57. www.prwatch.org/fakenews/findings/vnrs. Accessed August 22, 2010.

58. Robert Love, "Before Jon Stewart: The Truth About Fake News. Believe it," *Columbia Journalism Review* (March/April 2007): 33.
59. Greg Toppa, "Education Dept. Paid Commentator to Promote Law," *USA Today,* January 7, 2005. www.usatoday.com/news/washington/2005-01-06-williams-whitehouse_x.htm.
60. See Richard Morin, "Public Policy Surveys: Lite and Less Filling," *Washington Post National Weekly Edition* (November 10, 1997): 35.
61. Lawrence R. Jacobs and Robert Y. Shapiro, *Myths and Misunderstanding about Public Opinion Toward Social Security* (New York: The Century Foundation, 1999), 23. See also Jacobs and Shapiro, *Politicians Don't Pander* (Chicago: University of Chicago Press, 2000).
62. See Richard Morin, "Which Comes First, The Politician or the Poll?" *Washington Post National Weekly Edition* (February 10, 1997): 35.
63. Daniel Boorstin, *The Image: A Guide to Pseudo-Events in America* (New York: Atheneum, 1961).
64. Ibid. , 11–12.
65. See W. Lance Bennett, Regina G. Lawrence, and Steven Livingston, *When the Press Fails: Political Power and the News Media from Iraq to Katrina* (Chicago: University of Chicago Press, 2007).
66. Ken Auletta, "Fortress Bush," *The New Yorker* (January 19, 2004): 60.
67. http://seminal.firedoglake.com/diary/48094. Accessed August 22, 2010.
68. http://mediamatters.org/research/201005210052. Accessed August 22, 2010.
69. Ken Auletta. "Fortress Bush," 60.
70. www.cbsnews.com/8301-503544_162-6119525-503544.html. Accessed August 22, 2010.
71. Howard Kurtz, "White House press corps feels bypassed by Obama in favor of TV shows, YouTube," *The Washington Post*, February 8, 2010. www.washingtonpost.com/wp-dyn/content/article/2010/02/07/AR2010020702693.html Accessed August 22, 2010.
72. AP wire story, *Seattle Times*, February 8, 1982: A3.
73. http://wikileaks.org/wiki/Afghan_War_Diary,_2004-2010. Accessed August 22, 2010. (Note that this site was later shut down and others appeared under new URLs. The reader will have to search for WikiLeaks to find where it is operating more recently.)
74. www.cnn.com/2010/POLITICS/08/14/obama.gulf.swim/index.html. Accessed August 22, 2010.
75. John Anthony Maltese, *Spin Control: The White House Office of Communications and the Management of Presidential News* (Chapel Hill: University of North Carolina Press, 1992).
76. Source: Office of the Press Secretary for the President, 1992.
77. Samuel Kernell, *Going Public*, 3rd ed. (Washington, DC: CQ Press, 1997).
78. Quoted in Hertsgaard, *On Bended Knee*, 33.
79. The following overview of Hertsgaard's analysis, ibid., is organized along the lines suggested by Steven Livingston of George Washington University.
80. Hertsgaard, *On Bended Knee,* 35.
81. Ibid., 48.
82. Ibid., 49.
83. Ibid., 36.
84. Ibid., 36.
85. From Jack Honomichl, "Richard Wirthlin, Advertising Man of the Year," *Advertising Age* (January 23, 1989).

86. Source: Hedrick Smith, *The Power Game: How Washington Works* (New York: Ballantine, 1988).
87. From Smith, *The Power Game*, 409.
88. Ibid., 407.
89. Quoted in David Ignatius, "The Press and the President," *Seattle Times* (from the *Washington Post*) (May 28, 1989): A16.
90. Ibid.
91. See Honomichl, "Richard Wirthlin."
92. Quoted in David Shaw, "Dire Judgment on Clinton Started Just Days into Term," *Los Angeles Times* (September 16, 1993): A1.
93. Ann Devroy and Ruth Marcus, "Guess Who Clinton's Picked to Be His Presidential Role Model," *Washington Post National Weekly Edition* (November 23–29, 1992): 14.
94. Ryan Lizza, "The White House Doesn't Need the Press," *New York Times Magazine* (December 9, 2001): 108.
95. Ibid.
96. Ibid.
97. Auletta, "Fortress Bush," 55.
98. Nicholas Johnson and Edwin Chen, "Obama Answers Questions on YouTube in Voter Outreach," *Bloomberg Businessweek* (February 1, 2010). www.businessweek.com/news/2010-02-01/obama-hits-youtube-to-answer-questions-in-outreach-to-voters.html. Accessed August 22, 2010.
99. Kendra Marr, "White House Photos Irk Press Corps," Politico, March 24, 2010. www.politico.com/news/stories/0310/34972.html. Accessed August 22, 2010.
100. Dana Milbank, "Obama's Disregard for Media Reaches New Heights at Nuclear Summit," *The Washington Post*, April 14, 2010. www.washingtonpost.com/wp-dyn/content/article/2010/04/13/AR2010041303067.html. Accessed August 22, 2010.
101. Howard Kurtz, "White House Press Corps Feels Bypassed by Obama in Favor of TV Shows, YouTube," *The Washington Post*, February 8, 2010. www.washingtonpost.com/wp-dyn/content/article/2010/02/07/AR2010020702693.html. Accessed August 22, 2010.
102. Lloyd Grove, "The Death of the White House Press Corps," *The Daily Beast*, April 3, 2010. www.thedailybeast.com/blogs-and-stories/2010-04-03/death-of-the-white-house-press-corps/2/. Accessed August 22, 2010.
103. Lloyd Grove, "The Death of the White House Press Corps."
104. Sanford J. Ungar, "North and South at the Summit," *Atlantic* (January 1982): 7.
105. Joe Foote, "The Network Economic Imperative and Political Access," *Political Communication Review* 10 (1985): 2.
106. Ibid., 9.
107. Reported by Michael Massing, "About-Face on El Salvador," *Columbia Journalism Review* (November/December 1983): 42–49. Quotes from p. 45.
108. Clifford Krauss, "How U.S. Actions Helped Hide Human Rights Abuses," *New York Times*, March 21, 1993: 1.
109. Ibid., 34.
110. Although the Pentagon had authorized this publicity spectacle in advance, the unruly press pack tailing the Seals created such chaos that camera crews were finally ordered to shut down the lights and cease the coverage.
111. Richard Morin, "Budget Czars for a Day," *Washington Post National Weekly Edition* (November 23–29, 1992): 36.

How Journalists Report the News

Journalists today find fault with most everything that politicians say and do. The press no longer even has much respect for public officials' private lives—even their bedroom behavior is fair game for news stories.

—Thomas Patterson

. . . People may expect too much of journalism. Not only do they expect it to be entertaining, they expect it to be true.

—Lewis Lapham

Online information sources from blogs to WikiLeaks are pumping political information into the news stream in ways that are changing the gatekeeping control and editorial policies of mainstream news organizations. Further transforming news standards are the economic pressures introduced in Chapter 1 and explored in more detail in Chapter 7. One sign of the new economic reality is the trend toward delivering content to draw valued demographic audiences. When marketing research and cheap production considerations drive the news, the result is generally a decline of hard news about politics and the rise of more soft stories about celebrities, lifestyles, and political scandals. All of these factors come clearly into play in a rapidly fragmenting media sphere in which cable channels pick up spin from dubious blog and online sources and market news and commentary to the political viewpoints of increasingly partisan audiences.

For example, FOX News has found its viewers responsive to conservative slants, and to highly dramatized framing of many stories. The combined impact of poorly checked information from the blogosphere and the dramatic impact of charging the Obama administration with being "racist" led to a scandalous accusation that an administration official named Shirley Sherrod gave a racist speech at the 2010 Freedom Fund Banquet of the National Association for the Advancement of Colored People (NAACP). It later turned out that the charge was based on a short clip from the speech that was taken out of context from a much longer long speech talking about how Ms. Sherrod had overcome feelings of racial prejudice. The clip was distributed online and to FOX by a conservative blogger and political operative named Andrew Breitbart who had a history of politically slanted attacks on Democrats.[1] The clip was from the opening of a story about how Sherrod and her family had suffered from racism, and that she was initially reluctant to go out of her way to help a poor white farmer who came to her agency for help. Had anyone involved in publicizing the out of context clip listened to the whole speech, they would have heard Sherrod go on to say that she realized this was wrong, and then went out of her way to help the farmer and his family. The farmer later supported Ms. Sherrod's account.

Fueled by the prospects of a media scandal and press feeding frenzy, the following events unfolded rapidly in the hours following Breitbart's blog post on Monday morning July 19, 2010. Despite the lack of fact checking, Breitbart's intentionally scandalous accusations appeared within a few hours on FOX Nation, the social networking site of the news organization, under the headline: "Caught on Tape: Obama Official Discriminates Against White Farmer." The video clip also appeared on the FOX Web site, along with charges of racism against Sherrod, the Obama administration, and the NAACP. After learning that the episode would be taken up as a cause célèbre on FOX TV later that day, the head of the Agriculture Department asked for Ms. Sherrod's resignation.[2] Indeed, in his show taped just ahead of news of Sherrod's firing and aired a few hours later, Bill O'Reilly called for her immediate resignation, later creating the appearance that his program alone had made it happen.

Although intended to head off the news scandal, the forced resignation only made matters worse by appearing to validate the charges and touching off a major frenzy on FOX TV the next day. Anchors and commentators called for a response from the NAACP and from the U.S. Department of Agriculture. Sean Hannity referred to the speech as "just the latest in a series of racial incidents" coming from the Obama administration. And Newt Gingrich described her speech as "viciously racist."[3]

The speed at which misinformation turned into news in this case was breathtaking: Breitbart posted the misleading clip of the speech on his Web site on a Monday morning, and Bill O'Reilly used his top rated program to call for Sherrod's removal that evening (by which time she had already been fired). The only problem was that nobody bothered to look at the rest of her speech to discover that the moral of the story was overcoming racism and recognizing that poor black and white people had been at odds for generations, while failing to recognize that their mutual condition centered around poverty, not racial difference. But telling the whole story would have robbed the news of its scandal value and its political slant, and thus, would have been of little interest to FOX News (or presumably much of its audience). Although Sherrod later received an apology and an offer of a new job at the Agriculture Department, the lasting image as the scandal swept through the media was one of racism in the Obama administration and the NAACP, an image suffered by Ms. Sherrod.

Later in the same week, FOX artfully dodged its role in promoting the scandal and denied any responsibility for Ms. Sherrod's firing. Sunday news anchor Chris Wallace engaged in a heated debate with former Democratic National Committee chair Howard Dean in which Wallace blamed the government for firing Sherrod before checking the facts.[4] As for Andrew Breitbart, the blogger/operative who spun the story, he later did both FOX and CNN interviews in which he boldly claimed that the excerpt from the speech was fair because it demonstrated racism at the NAACP, which again magnified the media impact of the intended political spin from the story.[5] Breitbart implied that turnabout was fair play, admitting that his spin campaign was payback for the earlier NAACP challenge to the Tea Party to get racists out of its ranks. And so, an essentially false story raced through the new media landscape, becoming a spin vehicle for the strategic political message that the Obama administration and the NAACP are racist.[6]

HOW SPIN WORKS

While the above example may take the battle between spin and facts to a new extreme, it illustrates a growing concern in the news system. The moral of the story seems to be that facts should not get in the way of good spin. It may be obvious why politicians attempt to control the news, but the journalistic response to news control is more complicated. When news management operations by officials are competent and journalists are heavily spun, the mainstream press often has trouble reporting independently on stories, with the result that the news sounds much the same no matter which mainstream outlet one consults. True, the *New York Times* may have more stories on more subjects, and contain more detail than *USA Today*, but neither strays far beyond official messages and spin. Even FOX News, with its distinctive political flair, merely samples more from one side of the official spectrum than the other. This curiously American form of journalism becomes all the more confining as shrinking news budgets restrict investigative reporting and squeeze the space for hard news in favor of more entertaining soft news and features. The spiral of managed news intensifies as newsmakers compete to get their messages into that shrinking hard-news environment. As a result, today little room is afforded either by news organizations or politicians' communication strategists for candor, complexity, dialogue, or risk in public life.

The communication offices of government and political interests may set the tone and the boundaries of hard news so effectively that spin from established sources may be reported to balance a story even when there is little evidence to support it. As noted in the case study in Chapter 4, this can result in years of strategic political diversion of national attention from pressing issues, such as global warming and other environmental issues. The quest for balance can be so ritualized that news organizations may impose it even when investigative reporters reveal situations that seem to have the evidence clearly stacked on one side. For example, Ken Silverstein, an investigative reporter for the *Los Angeles Times*, told of his experience doing a solid piece of investigative reporting on Republican efforts to use influence in St. Louis to disqualify African American voters in the 2004 presidential election. He found that the Republican abuses in Missouri might have been significant enough to affect the outcome of the election, while alleged transgressions by the Democrats were comparatively minor. Despite this finding, his editors chose to run a more "balanced" story about the parties charging each other with dirty practices. In Silverstein's view, creating artificial balance out of political spin rather than reporting the actual independent findings was anything but balanced. He went public with his frustrations, saying: "I am completely exasperated by this approach to the news. The idea seems to be that we go out to report but when it comes time to write we turn our brains off and repeat the spin from both sides. God forbid we should . . . attempt to fairly assess what we see with our own eyes. 'Balanced' is not fair, it's just an easy way to avoid real reporting and shirking our responsibility to readers."[7]

The greatest irony of this system is that considerable competition exists among journalists for what generally amounts to a pretty homogeneous result—with the notable exception of the recent trend to market political content to partisan audiences on FOX and MSNBC. Perhaps the next greatest irony is that so much antagonism between journalists and politicians also exists, even though they frequently end up serving each other's mutual interests. Journalists often resent the canned news they end up serving to audiences, and so look for moments of spontaneity or poorly staged news events. And the drift toward sensationalism magnifies the tendency of journalists to turn against politicians at the hint of a slip, a rumor, or an accusation from an opponent. Thus, politicians may suddenly find reporters biting the hand that feeds them (recall "feeding the beast" from the last chapter) if they slip or indulge in a spontaneous moment that can be interpreted as a problem. As a result, the press is often kept at a distance from the officials they cover, particularly the president. As noted in the last chapter, even presidential news conferences have declined sharply over the past several decades. The result is that the journalists who cover the most storied political office seldom have much to distinguish their stories from one another. Former White House correspondent for CNN, Charles Bierbauer, has described the intense scramble for some nugget or nuance that makes a report different, something that leads someone else's editor to call and say "Bierbauer's got the story. Where's yours?"[8]

This strange American news pattern alternates between publicizing patent political spin and trying to trap politicians in slips and scandals. Far from enhancing public respect, the press politics game conveys an air of smug insiders often struggling over little of substance while ignoring gaping realities. When the press pack attacks, the adversarial behavior appears largely ritualistic. This "gotcha" journalism often comes across to audiences as posturing—as a game that journalists play to make themselves appear independent and adversarial.

The press also played "gotcha" with Democratic presidential candidate Al Gore during the 2000 election. Leading news organizations, such as the *Washington Post* and the *New York Times* ran incorrect and out-of-context versions of Gore's remarks on his involvement with facilitating access to the Internet and helping establish a program to clean up toxic waste sites. He soon became branded in the national press as a "serial exaggerator" (a term supplied by the Bush communication team). Late-night comedians made him a national laughingstock. Between February and June of 2000, a sample of 2,400 national news articles showed that 76 percent of the stories contained charges that Gore lied, exaggerated, or was somehow involved in scandal. The students and teachers at the New Hampshire high school where the most damaging press misquote originated tried in vain for months to fix the inaccuracy and came away discouraged. A media literacy class at the school compared their tape of the Gore visit with national coverage and issued a press release titled "Top Ten Reasons Why Many Concord High Students Feel Betrayed by Some of the Media Coverage of Al Gore's Visit to Their School."[9]

In the 2004 presidential race, the press anointed former Vermont governor Howard Dean as the early frontrunner, and then just as quickly changed the narrative in response to Democratic insiders who pronounced him unelectable. Dean suddenly became a candidate who was too angry and hotheaded for voters and who could not challenge President Bush on Iraq (even though Dean's rise to the top in the first place was based largely on his opposition to the war). Dean suffered a surprising defeat in the Iowa caucuses, and the press had new frontrunners to take to the next primary, creating new plot material for the familiar horse race story that journalists tell in every election.

In the 2008 race, it was not long after Arizona Senator John McCain appeared to have the Republican nomination sewn up that stories began to surface about his legendary anger, suggesting that many moments in which he smiled through intense debate exchanges or heated interviews with journalists were forced efforts on his part to mask his inner rage.

This chapter explores why so much journalism falls into the two broad categories of (a) reporting the official lines of the day and (b) then playing personal "gotcha" games, often with the same officials and newsmakers. This dynamic is at the core of the authority-disorder syndrome discussed in Chapter 2, and it contributes in various ways to the other news biases as well. Both of these reporting tendencies present serious problems for citizens and their relation to government. The tendency of the press to open the gates to officials and their carefully managed messages is hard to reconcile with the common assumption that the media are (or at least have the potential to be) objective, independent, professional, and even adversarial in their relations with news sources. The problem of a free press relying so heavily on what officials (and, more important, their handlers and their opponents' handlers) feed it is so perplexing that the reasons have been explored by a number of researchers in the fields of communication (e.g., Jay Blumler, Michael Gurevitch),[10] sociology (e.g., Herbert Gans, Gaye Tuchman),[11] and political science (e.g., Bernard Cohen, Timothy Cook).[12]

The second tendency of the press to bite the hand that feeds it is in many ways equally puzzling because the resulting adversarialism is more often personal than substantive. As Thomas Patterson has pointed out in the larger analysis from which the epigram that opens this chapter was drawn, the resulting news content is an odd mix: a narrow range of political ideas, interspersed with cranky criticisms of politicians and the games they play. Patterson describes the rising levels of journalistic negativity as follows:

> . . . negative coverage of politics has risen dramatically in recent decades. Negative coverage of presidential candidates, for example, now exceeds their positive coverage. . . . By 1990, negative coverage of Congress and its members was over 80%. Each president since 1976—Carter, Reagan, Bush, and Clinton—has received more negative coverage than his predecessor. Federal agencies have fared no better; in the 1990–1995 period, for example, not a single cabinet-level agency received more positive than negative coverage. As portrayed by the press, America's public leadership is universally inept and self-serving.[13]

Although different researchers propose different specific reasons for why the news comes out in this odd way, all seem to agree that the general answer is a combination of four factors: (a) the economics of the news business, (b) the dependence of journalists on sources who control the information that journalists need, (c) the routine news-gathering practices of reporters and their news organizations, and (d) the professional norms and codes of conduct that grow up around those organizational routines. Because two of these factors (the political economy of the news and the information management strategies of news sources) are discussed extensively in other chapters, this chapter and the next look inside journalism itself, beginning with the organizational news-gathering routines that keep reporters and officials locked into their strange dance.

WORK ROUTINES AND PROFESSIONAL NORMS

Organizational routines are the basic rules and practices that journalism schools and news organizations train reporters and editors to follow in deciding what to cover, how to cover it, and how to present the results of their work. Journalistic routines give the news its reassuring familiarity and create a steady supply of news product in a competitive marketplace. *Professional norms* are those moral standards, codes of ethics, and guidelines about inserting one's voice and viewpoint into a story that enable journalists to make personal decisions. In addition, these codes of the profession enable news organizations to justify what they produce. Both of these factors are shaped strongly by the business pressures explained in Chapter 7. The recent wave of economic change sweeping the news industry not only introduced changes into reporting practices, but also created serious strains in important journalistic norms, such as objectivity, as discussed in Chapter 6.

It is increasingly clear that the everyday work routines inside news organizations bias the news without necessarily intending to do so. Our first order of business (and the focus of this chapter) is to show how the everyday practices of journalists and their news organizations contribute to the authority-disorder bias, as well as to personalized, dramatized, and fragmented news. In addition to explaining how reporting practices bias the news, it is important to understand why these habits persist and why neither the press nor the public seems to grasp their true political significance. For example, many members of the press continue to defend their reporting habits as being largely consistent with the professional journalism norms of *independence* and *objectivity*. These standards may go by different names, such as *accurate, fair, unbiased*, or *nonpartisan*, but the point is that a surprising number of American journalists continue to espouse some notion of objectivity. The peculiar nature of objectivity is so important to understand that the next chapter is devoted primarily to its origins and its defining consequences for American news. In the discussions of professional norms and work routines in this chapter and the next, the critical focus is on how they contribute to the news biases outlined in Chapter 2 and to the capacity of politicians to make the news as described in Chapter 4.

A word of clarification is in order about the intent of this critical discussion. In many instances, the practices and professional standards of American journalism have been commendable. In a few celebrated cases, for example, reporters and editors have even gone to jail to protect the confidentiality of sources or to defend the principle of free speech. Moreover, routine news coverage of some political issues and situations is rich and full of diverse viewpoints. For example, both reporting and entertainment media treatments of the divisive national issue of abortion have been as full of information, as rich in competing viewpoints, and as diverse in the social voices represented as we can expect a democratic communication system to be.

In other respects, however, the professional norms of independence and objectivity have backfired. In fact, American journalism may have become trapped within an unworkable set of professional standards, with the result that the more objective or fair reporters try to be, the more official bias they introduce into the news.[14] A five-nation study of political journalists by Thomas Patterson and a group of international colleagues produced a startling finding: Although the American press is arguably the most free or politically independent in the world, U.S. journalists display the least diversity in their decisions about whom to interview for different hypothetical stories and in what visuals they chose for those stories. Patterson concluded that the strong norms of political neutrality or independence among American journalists actually homogenize the political content of their reporting. By contrast, reporters in countries such as Italy, Britain, Sweden, and Germany (the other nations studied) are more likely to regard political perspectives as desirable in covering events. As a result, journalists in other nations tend to cover the same events differently—that is, by interviewing a broader range of political sources and using different visual illustrations.[15]

EXPLAINING DIFFERENCES IN THE QUALITY OF REPORTING

It is important to remember that different news organizations occasionally report original investigations. These moments of independence from spin remind us of how important the press can be for engaging publics in a democracy. For example, in 2010, the *New York Times* ran a series of investigative reports on the somewhat mysterious military outsourcing firm Blackwater (which changed its name to the even more mysterious Xe, following the criminal prosecution of five employees for shooting unarmed civilians in Iraq).[16] However, most routine news most of the time looks much the same, because most news organizations direct their journalists to use similar news-gathering methods. The resulting quality of the reports (factual correctness and richness, points of view included and excluded) can vary widely depending on various factors, such as how powerful sources are spinning stories, and the economic incentives to look beyond the spin (or not).

When is high quality—more information-rich, diverse, and broadly based—news coverage likely to emerge in the U.S. system? News content is most diverse, detailed, and open to competing views when public officials are willing to debate issues openly for extended periods. This is what the indexing theory introduced in earlier chapters predicts about the quality of news. When powerful newsmakers engage in open public debate, news organizations are more likely to cover issues in depth and follow the political process through the halls and hearing rooms of government, and citizen comprehension often increases. We find such relatively open and detailed coverage in a handful of historic cases, such as Vietnam or the Watergate investigations, and more often in coverage of the moral issues that rage through American politics. Abortion, civil rights, gun control, the role of religion in public schools and other places, and other enduring moral controversies often pit politicians and parties against each other, expand the range of political viewpoints, and take the public on extended tours of government at work. In these cases, the news may show citizens how issues move from elections to legislatures, to executive offices, to courts, to regulatory agencies, and at times spill over into the streets in sustained political conflicts.

By contrast, officials are often more guarded about going public on economic issues such as business subsidies or the political influence of banks and energy companies, or on foreign policy issues such as war and covert operations. Thus, the discovery that the CIA and military had engaged in illegal activities involving torturing prisoners in the war against terror became a rather tortured story in the press.[17] As a result, many issues that are important to America's future are apt to be reported in the fragmented and officialized language that keeps people guessing about what is going on and why. Many important events receive detailed media attention only after poorly understood policies have already become facts of life.

An important case in point is the war in Iraq. Even years later, most citizens were unsure about its origins and rationale. When President Obama delivered a speech in September of 2010 announcing the end of U.S. combat operations, he received a 57 percent approval rating on handling the war—one of the few positive areas in his presidency at the time.[18] Yet the speech was no declaration of victory. Obama even remarked beforehand that his speech would be no "victory lap."[19] Indeed, the fighting was not over, the Iraqi government was in disarray, and the promises to rebuild the country seemed empty to many Iraqis. All that seemed clear to most Americans is that they wanted to get out. Yet few understood why we were there in the first place.

Among the factors contributing to public confusion and disillusionment with the war were the successful spin efforts by the Bush administration to sell the war to the public in 2002-2003.[20] The result was a stunning absence of uncritical reporting in the mainstream media, effectively making the press an important player in the sales effort. That lack of another side to the story can be attributed, in part, to the absence of organized Democratic opposition for the simple reason that the party did not want to oppose a then popular president who had stirred up a national patriotic (media) rally in support of war. (It is ironic that the depth of public support may not have been all that great, as discussed in Chapter 3). As a result, the majority of Washington elites quickly joined the national rally.

With elites lined up in favor of the war, critical voices seldom passed through the news gates. For example, in February 2003 on the eve of the invasion of Iraq, some 15 to 20 million people around the world took to the streets to protest the impending war and to urge their governments not to support it. These were the largest organized protests in human history. Although large demonstrations took place in many American cities, including hundreds of thousands who turned out in New York, relatively little attention was given to this expression of public opinion in the news. When the president was asked to comment, he said that they were entitled to their opinion, but that he would not be swayed by a "focus group." The press continued its march to war guided by spin from the administration, reporting few perspectives from outside high official circles.[21]

The full story behind one of the most successful (and perhaps misguided) spin campaigns in history involves more than just the Democrats and indexing. Indeed, selling the Iraq War to the press and, in turn, to the American public resulted from something of a perfect storm of political factors that favored the communication strategies of the Bush White House. The case study in this chapter provides an analysis of why the press overwhelmingly reported Bush administration spin during the time when public opinion on that war mattered most.

Top Ten Reasons the Press Took a Pass on the Iraq War

"Weapons of Mass Deception" was the headline on Jon Stewart's *The Daily Show* after the U.S. military had finished months of unproductive searching for weapons of mass destruction (WMD) in Iraq. The administration's case for the war had been built on fearful WMD scenarios, capped by Saddam Hussein seeking nuclear weapons that might be used against nations in the Middle East and even in attacks on American cities. The case for war was also built on claims that Iraq had connections to al-Qaeda and to the events of 9/11. As the Iraq invasion turned into a messy occupation, it became clear that many of the claims used to convince the public and quiet the opposition had little supporting evidence and a good deal of intelligence information that contradicted them. It even seemed likely that key players in the Bush administration promoted these fearful images to sell a war that they had sought even before 9/11 happened. Enough of this was known to the press in time to generate a healthy public debate before the invasion took place. Few news organizations, however, offered any serious challenge to administration news management efforts.

It was even clear beforehand that the administration was marketing the war as a partisan political product. In a good piece of investigative reporting (lamentably not followed up by the *Post* or other news organizations), two journalists for the *Washington Post* described a systematic media campaign that began in August 2002 with the formation of the White House Iraq Group (WHIG) aimed at rolling out communication strategy for the coming war. WHIG's "strategic communications" task force planned publicity and news events for a campaign that would start in September, after most Americans (and Congress) had returned from their summer vacations. As former White House chief of staff Andrew Card put it in an interview that the *New York Times* ran in September 2002, "From a marketing point of view, you don't introduce new products in August."[22]

The selling of the war went according to plan. The nation's talk shows on the weekend after Labor Day 2002 were filled with administration officials staying on-message and reading from a script that turned out to be more scary fiction than fact.[23] On NBC's *Meet the Press,* Vice President Cheney raised the specter that Saddam's nuclear, chemical, and biological weapons presented an immediate danger to the United States. National Security Advisor (later Secretary of State) Condoleezza Rice acknowledged on CNN's *Late Edition* that solid evidence was scarce, but that waiting only increased the risk. Her punch line was: "We don't want the smoking gun to be a mushroom cloud." Defense Secretary Donald Rumsfeld warned the audience on CBS's *Face the Nation,* "Imagine a September 11 with weapons of mass destruction. It's not 3,000, it's tens of thousands of innocent men, women, and children."[24] Like many of the emotional images in the campaign to sell the war, this one was based on little evidence beyond administration claims themselves. Why did this campaign pass through the press so easily, being reported just as it was scripted?

At least 10 factors converged in Perfect Storm fashion to push the press pack to write stories that seldom challenged administration framing even though gaps in the credibility of that framing were available to knowledgeable reporters at the time.[25] Here are the ten factors that created this perfect propaganda storm:

1. *9/11 happened.* The national public was softened by those horrific events to accept almost anything that might produce closure, leading to restrictions of civil liberties on the domestic front and the rise of empire discourse from administration officials such as Paul Wolfowitz, Richard Perle, Dick Cheney, and Donald Rumsfeld, who had long harbored fantasies of a militarist reassertion of American power. Where was the press after 9/11? Apparently too wrapped in its cultural-patriotic storytelling to find credible sources to challenge that vision. Thus, the administration was able to push a weak case for war based on fantastic assertions of an al-Qaeda–Iraq link, and the even stealthier innuendos that Saddam Hussein was somehow involved in the 9/11 attacks—a connection that 71 percent of the public attributed to the administration as late as the summer of 2003.[26]

The capacity of the administration to successfully push deceptions and misrepresentations through a docile press to an emotionally volatile public may stand as the most ruthless press control operation in history—an operation that achieved such sophistication that the next three factors involve separate forms of press management.

2. *Master scripting and directing by Karl Rove.* Often called "Bush's Brain," Karl Rove had managed Bush's rise to Governor of Texas, and then on to the White House, where he was chief communication and policy advisor until he stepped down on the heels of a scandal in his boss's second term. The Rove White House communication operation made Reagan press management under Deaver and Gergen seem modest by comparison. No news management opportunity was missed, from the Top Gun carrier landing described in Chapter 2, to edgy assertions that Iraq was a key front in the War on Terror. Even the president's deer-in-the-headlights media presence was countered, as described in the case study in Chapter 2, with the relentless spin that he in fact had a natural "swagger."

3. *Beyond spin: Outright intimidation.* Intimidation of journalists and news organizations began within hours of the 9/11 catastrophe. The censorship campaign involved a chorus of conservative talk and news media that shouted down any news organization that deviated from patriotic support of the administration. Key moments of punctuation were provided when administration officials called out reporters and other media personalities who dared to question the administration. This intimidation campaign continued through the aftermath of the war in Iraq. When whistleblowers came forward—from former Ambassador Wilson who investigated claims of the alleged Iraq–uranium connection, to former Treasury Secretary O'Neill and security advisor Richard Clarke who reported rapid efforts inside the administration immediately after 9/11 to link the terrorist attacks to Iraq in an effort to set up an invasion—they were swiftly shouted down in public and intimidated with personal reprisals.[27]

4. *The press was embed(ded) with the military.* A good journalist is likely to be a vicarious adventurer who seeks to be at the scene of the action, telling a "big story." Apparently, one could not be closer to the Iraq War story than inside a tank hurtling across the desert toward Baghdad. Nearly every respected journalist (including those too old to go into action themselves) initially hailed the military embedding as a ringside ticket to great journalism, a perspective that would bring the uncensored reality of war to the American people. Only later did some journalists admit what they might have seen beforehand: that

Continued

the "big story" was dictated from Washington, and the scenes from inside the tanks were little more than B-roll filler that authenticated a story told by the government. If the embedding operation was as telling about the dramaturgy of the press as about the press-control proclivities of the administration, the next factor moves us even farther into the realm of press responsibility.

5. *Telling the story that promises maximum drama and most likely plot advancement.* When journalists make story choices, they favor narrative elements that are most likely to advance a coherent, dramatic story into the future. In some cases, those choices produce stories that ignore potentially damning evidence to the contrary. Such cases typically involve looking away from sources less likely to deliver future installments and favoring (usually official) sources more prepared to deliver regular updates. Consider the reporting decisions to downplay the volume of doubt linking al-Qaeda—and, more generally, 9/11—to Iraq. Consider, too, the volume of doubt about Saddam's weapons of mass destruction. Although doubts were reported, they were pegged largely to foreign sources and domestic protesters and were dismissed insultingly by Rumsfeld and company.

At the same time, few mainstream news organizations even noted the strong al-Qaeda links to Saudi Arabia, a friend of the Bush administration. Few stories followed up a postinvasion revelation by Saudi officials that al-Qaeda operatives had continued to conduct training operations as late as July 2003 on Saudi farms. And few reports challenged the Bush administration's refusal to release an intelligence report allegedly linking al-Qaeda to prominent members of the Saudi political elite. One exception was independent journalist Seymour Hersh, who published an early investigative report in *The New Yorker* presenting evidence against the Iraq connection to al-Qaeda, while pointing something of a smoking gun at Saudi Arabia.[28] Such rare acts of investigative journalism were virtually ignored by the larger press community because standard Washington official sources would offer nothing to advance those stories. They served up, instead, daily installments on Saddam and terrorism. What would it have taken for the press to turn those potential blockbuster alternatives into serious frame challenges to the administration? Did I mention the Democrats?

6. *Where were the Democrats?* Apparently, the defeated Democrats had been advised to offend no one and to take no political risks. Although this advice might be questioned as making them seem even more defeated by looking weak and indecisive, they apparently paid enough for their professional communication counsel to follow it. Thus, the party left criticism to a few isolated representatives and to a pack of 2004 presidential candidates who criticized each other more often than they criticized the president. News organizations are so dependent on prominent official sources to advance challenges to a leading news frame that the strategic silence of the Democrats all but killed media deliberation about the war.

Why were the concerns of 2004 presidential primary candidates such as Howard Dean or Dennis Kucinich not enough to reframe the story? Because the U.S. press is taken with reporting only who and what the Washington consensus anoints with *gravitas.* Without major figures weighing in, strong antiwar sentiment among the public went largely unreported. Consider a small case in point. In January 2003, I was called by a *Newsweek* reporter who asked the stunning question (as I paraphrase it): "We in the press have become aware of a substantial antiwar movement. Why do you think we are not reporting it?" Why, indeed, did the press fail to report organized large-scale opposition? I explained that the failure to report on the antiwar movement was due to the dependence of the press on official opposition, and the Democrats largely took a pass. And so, on February 15, 2003, when between 15 and 20 million people across the globe raised their voices in what may well be the largest coordinated public demonstrations in world history, the American press allowed the president to dismiss it as the ramblings of a "focus group" to which he would not respond.

7. *The absence of credible progressive think tanks.* News stories are often advanced through reactions from experts at think tanks who promote the political policy objectives of those who fund these high-level opinion-making operations. The conservative right has enjoyed considerable media success through a combination of aggressive news management (see point 2), dense networking of radio and TV talk pundits, and rapid-response networks to create a public "echo chamber" to support policy initiatives and attack opponents (see point 3)—all supported by the timely delivery of think-tank reports and experts to journalists. Perhaps it is because of funding disparities between the Left and the Right—or simply because of the dim capacities of the Left to understand how the press works—that there was virtually no coordinated expertise to counter the Bush administration's war frames.

8. *Press construction of a spectator public.* It is some consolation that publics form their opinions only in part through cueing from the news. In their lives beyond the media, people look elsewhere for clues about what to think. Perhaps the most impressive thing about public opinion as measured by polls up to the eve of the invasion was that clear majorities favored war only if the administration could build an international coalition (one suspects that a "coalition of the willing" that included Palau and Tonga over France and Germany was not what they had in mind). However, as the news narrative built toward inevitable war, opposition levels in the polls were reported only as footnotes for the record. It seems that polls and protests were not enough for the press to turn the public into players in the media spectacle. As often happens, journalists forgot that publics can take active roles in the news story of democracy. Yet, when the public predictably rallied their support at the outbreak of the war, it would have been easy to conclude that the public supported the rationale for the war all along. Moreover, reports of public support in the polls failed to note that the majority in favor of the war was really rather weak, as many did not really care if the war did not happen. Such weakness of the poll support was not reported in the news, as discussed in Chapter 3.

9. *Press ethnocentrism.* More than any other Western democratic press system, the U.S. press is remarkably closed to world opinion. Perhaps this reflects the press's implicit mirroring of the confusing popular cultural impulses of isolationism and patriotic intervention. The inward turn of American journalism may also reflect the unwillingness of most politicians (a.k.a. leading news sources) to risk their patriotic credentials either by questioning the values and motives behind government decisions to use force or by crediting outsiders when they do so. In any event, international reactions of outrage to the administration's "you're either with us or against us" stand on Iraq were duly noted for the news record and then easily spun away by administration news sources and journalists alike. While news features reported on boycotts of French wine and the renaming of french fries as *freedom fries,* many commentators adopted a condescending tone for discussing the din of international criticism. No national news organization was more aggressive in its

Continued

patriotic support for the Iraq War—or its vitriolic condemnation of administration critics, foreign and domestic—than FOX.

10. *The FOX effect.* This is the last, and, I think, the least important factor explaining why the press faithfully reported so many administration claims that could have been challenged. Because of the levels of patriotic cant from FOX reporters, anchors, and talk-show hosts alike, many observers felt that FOX exercised a chilling effect on a competition that was worried about ratings losses among audiences allegedly swept with patriotic fervor. It is true that new standards of jingo-journalism may have been set by the FOX anchor who described antiwar protesters in Switzerland as "hundreds of knuck-leheads," or by the decision to run a crawl at the bottom of the screen branding nations that refused to join the "coalition of the willing" as the "axis of weasels."[29] FOX's hyperbolic reporting notwithstanding, we should not forget the stiff competition among television news organizations during the first Gulf War to display their patriotism—long before FOX News was a gleam in the eyes of Roger Ailes and Rupert Murdoch.[30] If FOX's competition took a pass on critical journalism, I would argue that the effects of factors 1 through 9 were considerably more important than looking over their journalistic shoulders at the FOX effect.

The emerging conclusion about mass-mediated democracy is that news debates tend to be more open and informative when the government itself is already functioning ideally—that is, when government officials are openly debating and investigating public policies in front of the news cameras. On the other hand, when elites are not debating policy options in public, journalism routines close the news gates on stories that might be quite important to the public interest. The weakness in the American information system appears to be those crucial and all-too-common cases where government officials do not confront difficult issues or choices. Should information be shaped so thoroughly by what elites and elected officials are doing in public? In the remainder of this chapter we examine how the daily work routines of journalists keep them so focused on the inner circles of power.

HOW ROUTINE REPORTING PRACTICES CONTRIBUTE TO NEWS BIAS

Much like any job, reporting the news consists largely of a set of routine, standardized activities. Despite some obvious differences involving the nature of assignments and personal writing styles, American reporters (as noted earlier) tend to cover news events in remarkably similar ways. A fascinating example of how these work routines affect news content was discovered by Timothy Cook in a study of international crisis coverage in the United States and France. In the months after the Iraqi invasion of Kuwait, crucial international diplomatic efforts attempted to prevent the looming war. When news of these efforts broke, television networks in both countries assigned their reporters to get reactions from key sources. American newscasts flipped through the "golden triangle" of Washington news beats: the White House, State Department, and Pentagon. Even though there was no official U.S. reaction to be had, the reporters were pressured to say something, and they effectively invented the kinds of vague pronouncements that one might expect from officials in sensitive political posts at the early stage of a world crisis. By contrast, French reporters (who do not operate with a U.S.-style beat system) interviewed various political party leaders and generated a comparatively broad range of political views about the meanings and implications of the diplomatic talks.[31]

The existence of standardized reporting behaviors and story formulas is not surprising when one considers the strong patterns that operate in the news environment. For example, the events staged by political actors tend to reflect the predictable political communication goals outlined in Chapter 4. Moreover, most mass media news organizations tend to impose fairly similar constraints on reporters in terms of acceptable story angles, deadlines, and newsgathering resources. Also, reporters are subject to the standardizing influence of working in close quarters with one another, covering the same sorts of events under the same kinds of pressures.

In short, reporters confront three separate sources of incentives to standardize their reporting habits:

- Routine cooperation with (and pressures from) news sources
- The work routines of (and pressures within) news organizations
- Daily information sharing and working relations with fellow reporters

Each of these forces contributes to the development of standardized reporting formulas that favor the incorporation of official political messages in the news, interspersed with the feeding frenzies that may undermine the officials themselves. These reporting patterns also lead reporters to write personalized, dramatized, and fragmented news stories. We will now explore each source of everyday pressure on journalists.

REPORTERS AND OFFICIALS: COOPERATION AND CONTROL

Most political events are so predictably scripted that reporters can condense them easily into formulaic plot outlines: who (which official) did what (official action), where (in what official setting), for what (officially stated) purpose, and with what (officially proclaimed) result. For example:

> President _____ met at the White House today with President _____ from _____ to discuss mutual concerns about _____. Both leaders called the talks productive and said that important matters were resolved.

It does not take a careful reading to see that such a formula is virtually devoid of substance. The pseudo-events that provide the scripts for such news stories are generally designed to create useful political images, not to transmit substantive information about real political issues. Because such events are routine political occurrences, reporters quickly develop formulas for converting them into news whenever they occur. Compounding the temptation to report official versions of political events is the fact that reporters live in a world where the "divide and conquer" mentality is ever present. Careers are advanced by receiving scoops and leaks and are damaged by being left out in the cold, excluded from official contact. Like it or not, reporters must depend on the sources they cover. When those sources are powerful officials surrounded by an entourage of eager reporters clamoring for news, it is always possible that those who report what officials want them to will be rewarded, whereas those who fail to convert key political messages into news will be punished.

In view of the patterned nature of political events combined with the press tactics of politicians, it is not surprising that the news seems to emerge from formulas that virtually write themselves.[32] Of course, knowing the formulas does not mean that reporters will always use them. However, in a workday world filled with short deadlines, demanding editors, and persuasive news sources, the formulas become the course of least resistance. Even when a formula is abandoned, there is seldom enough other information available in a typical political setting to construct another story.

In the illusory world of political news, formulas describe official actions, and the seal of official approval becomes a substitute for truth and authenticity, which in turn makes the formulas seem legitimate.[33] Robert Scholes developed these ideas a bit further when he said:

> Perhaps the credulous believe that a reporter reports facts and that newspapers print all of them that are fit to print. But actually, newspapers print all of the "facts" that fit, period—that fit the journalistic conventions of what "a story" is (those tired formulas) and that fit the editorial policy of the paper. . . .[34]

Anyone for changing that famous slogan to "All the News That Fits, We Print"? The formulas used to select and arrange facts in the news are produced largely through the mutual cooperation of reporters and newsmakers. These partners may not share exactly the same goals or objectives, but together they create information that satisfies each other's needs. It is all in a day's work.

The Insider Syndrome

In addition to developing work habits that favor official views, reporters are also human beings. Behind the occupational roles are people who sometimes identify with the newsmakers they cover. Because reporters have regular contact with officials under stressful conditions, it becomes easy for them to see these officials as sympathetic characters. Of course, when officials go out of their way to antagonize the press, as the Nixon administration did during the early 1970s and as the Clinton administration did for most of its first term, it is more difficult for reporters to identify with the officials. When officials court the favor and understanding of reporters, they are often paid back with sympathetic coverage that sticks close to the officials' political lines.[35] Such coverage is easily justified as an objective account of the officials' public actions.

Yet another aspect of the subtle working relations between reporters and officials is that journalists who cooperate with powerful officials often receive recognition and flattery and are taken into the confidence of those officials. In the intensely political environments in which most of our news occurs, nothing is valued as much as power. If one cannot possess power (and there always seems to be a shortage), then the next best thing is to be on the inside with the powerful—to be seen with them, to be consulted by them, to socialize with them, and perhaps even to have them as friends. As Tom Bethell puts it:

> To be on close terms with elite news sources is to be an "insider," which is what almost everyone in Washington wants to be. It is interesting to note how often this word appears on the dust jackets of memoirs by Washington journalists. But Nixon—his great weakness!—didn't like journalists and wouldn't let them be insiders. . . . Kissinger, on the other hand, was astute enough to cultivate the press, and he survived—not merely that, was lionized as "the wizard of shuttle diplomacy." (Is it not possible that the most awesome "lesson of Watergate" . . . will be a social lesson?)[36]

The perils of being a Washington insider were summarized by Tony Snow, a Detroit news columnist and former speechwriter for George H. W. Bush: "We spend a lot of time hanging out with the high and mighty. It's intoxicating. In Washington, access to people in power is important, if nothing else for social reasons, for name dropping."[37] Snow went on to become press secretary for George W. Bush. As the distinguished reporter Murray Kempton put it: "It is a fundamental fact about journalism, and might even be a rule if it had the attention it deserves, that it is next to impossible to judge any public figure with the proper detachment once you begin calling him by his first name."[38]

Ellen Hume, a journalist and scholar of the press, says that she has come to feel that journalists can be "more powerful than any elected official" and that something "urgently" needs to be done to "dynamite" the insiders out of their privileged positions.[39] Steve Goldstein, Washington correspondent for the *Philadelphia Inquirer,* suggested term limits for Washington journalists. If news organizations would agree to rotate their stars out of Washington, the power of the "unelected media elite" might be diminished. Even more important, says Goldstein, media term limits:

> . . . might counteract the potential for disconnection, whereby the correspondent suffers a loss of understanding of issues that Americans really care about. Federal policy-making and the impact on the folks at home is supplanted by the view from Washington. There is a difference between Here and There. In Sodom-on-the-Potomac the political culture is secular, while most of America is religious. Here the character issue is often framed as: Did he/she sleep with her/him/it? Out there, the issue is often one of fairness, justice, integrity. All the sleaze we print doesn't fit.[40]

In a lighter vein, Goldstein suggests the following "self-test" for Washington reporters. Offering apologies to David Letterman, he lists the "top 10 telltale signs that a journalist has been in Washington too long":

1. You cannot recall the area code of your hometown.
2. Your best sources are at other news organizations.
3. You go to Duke Ziebert's a second time [a restaurant notorious as a meeting spot and watering hole for the power elite].
4. You think a regional story refers to Upper Northwest [a district in Washington, DC].
5. The conductor of the Marine Band salutes you.
6. You reject an interview with the mayor of your hometown because it conflicts with Gridiron rehearsal [a Washington journalist's club that puts on an annual show in which press and politicians satirize each other].
7. *The Capitol Gang* [a TV pundit gathering] offers honorary membership.
8. Larry King calls you by your first name.
9. You cover the story by watching CNN.
10. You become eligible for Redskins' season tickets.[41]

However, before thinking that journalists and the officials they cover are too cozy, or that they are any cozier than in earlier eras, it is important to remember that "cozy" is hardly the way most of them would describe their relationship. Many politicians today describe their relations with the press as regrettably antagonistic and, therefore, necessarily guarded. Reporters often complain that they never get close to officials and must fight through the "spin patrol" of handlers, consultants, and flaks. It is surely the case that today's political scene is, in many ways, far less cozy and more filled with "gotcha" journalism than in the years before Vietnam and Watergate. In those bygone days of greater direct contact between reporters and officials, many prominent journalists and officials were more likely to socialize, be friends, drink and party together, and go off the record after 5 p.m. However, the greater personal distance in press-source relations today does not mean that reporting is less dependent on official spin. Far from it.

REPORTERS AS MEMBERS OF NEWS ORGANIZATIONS: PRESSURES TO STANDARDIZE

If reporters' relations with officials breathe new life into old news formulas, their own news organizations reinforce the use of those formulas. Novice journalists experience constant pressures (subtle and otherwise) from editors about how to cover stories.[42] These pressures are effective because editors hold sway over what becomes news and which reporters advance in the organization. Over time, reporters tend to adjust their styles to fit harmoniously with the expectations of their organizations.

In many cases, these organizational expectations are defended by journalists as simply preserving the "house style" of the news organization—the tone, editorial voice, and format that makes one news outlet distinguishable from another.

This level of formula reporting is as unobjectionable as it is inevitable in any kind of organization that has standard operating procedures. However, there are deeper levels at which organizational preferences for story formulas do matter. To an important extent, there are industry-wide norms about story values that define what news is and that, in turn, open the news to the kinds of biases outlined in Chapter 2. For example, one young reporter serving an apprenticeship with a major big-city newspaper talked about the somewhat mysterious process of having some stories accepted and others rejected without really knowing the basis for many of the decisions. Equally mysterious were the conversations with assignment editors in which the editor seemed to know what the story was before it had been covered. Over time, the socialization process works its effects, and young reporters learn to quickly sense what the story is and how to write it.

Beyond the style of this or that news organization, the whole media system begins to emulate particular formats, themes, and news values. Bending news genres to fit commercial values and socializing reporters to recognize how potential stories fit the familiar formulas are the roots of the news biases discussed in Chapter 2. In all of their variations, however, organizational pressures result in news that typically fits a formula.

Why Formulas Work

Standardized news is safe. Managers in news organizations must constantly compare their product with that of their competition and defend risky departures from the reporting norm. As Epstein observed in his classic study of television network news, even TV news assignment editors look to the conservative wire services for leads on stories and angles for reporting them.[43] The wires cover the highest portion of planned official events and stick closest to official political scripts. Following the daily lead of the wires becomes the most efficient way to fill the news hole.

Other organizational arrangements also strongly influence standardized reporting. Among the most powerful standardizing forces are daily news production routines. Newspapers and news programs require a minimum supply of news every day, whether or not anything significant happens in the world. Perhaps you have seen a television news program on a slow news day. In place of international crises, press conferences, congressional hearings, and proclamations by the mayor, the news may consist of a trip to the zoo to visit a new "baby," a canned report on acupuncture in China, a follow-up story on the survivor of an air crash, or a spoof on the opening of baseball spring training in Florida. Slow news days occur during weekends or vacation periods when governments are closed down. News organizations run fluff on slow days because their daily routines report official happenings from the news centers of government.

The News Hole

For a news organization to function, it must fill a minimum "news hole" every day. Producing a large amount of cheap, predictable news normally means assigning reporters to events and beats that are sure to produce enough acceptable stories to fill the news hole by the day's deadline. During normal business periods, the public relations (PR) machinery of government and business fills these organizational needs by producing events that are cheap, easy to report, numerous, and predictable.

With the advent of 24-hour news channels and Web sites linked to papers and broadcast organizations, the news hole has become a gorge. Pressures increase to update stories many times a day, in contrast to once or twice a day in the old era of morning and evening news. The journalistic credo of "advancing" a story has become an obsession for many organizations. Reporters learn to ask leading or challenging questions, often based on little more than trying to elicit a reaction from a newsmaker in an effort to generate new material to report. "President Obama denied rumors today . . ." becomes a familiar lead in a news age with an ever-larger news hole to fill.

Beats

Filling the daily news hole on time means that news organizations must figure out how to make the spontaneous predictable. The obvious solution to this problem is to anticipate when and where the required amount of news will happen every day. Because this task is made difficult by the size of the world and the smallness of reporting staffs, the solution is to implicitly adjust the definition of news so that things that are known to happen on a regular basis become news. Reporters can be assigned to cover those things and be assured (by definition) of gathering news every day. As a result, the backbone of the news organization is the network of beats, ranging from the police station and the city council at the local level, to Congress, the Supreme Court, and the presidency at the national level. Beats produce each day's familiar run of murders, accidents, public hearings, press conferences, and presidents entering helicopters and leaving planes.

Special Assignments

To break the daily routine, some reporters are given special assignments to cover big stories, such as elections or spontaneous events like assassinations and floods. However, the expense of special-coverage assignments dictates that even the truly spontaneous must be translated into familiar formulas. If an event is important enough to justify special coverage, then it must be represented in dramatic terms. Even assassinations, invasions, and floods quickly become scripted. For example, when it became clear that the United States was planning an invasion of Haiti in the summer of 1994, television news organizations readied large libraries of canned material on the island nation and extensively scripted their coverage well in advance.

Because special coverage is costly and must be kept going, even no news often becomes news. Frank Cesno, a former Washington Bureau chief for CNN, told of his week of special coverage when John F. Kennedy Jr.'s airplane was missing in July 1999. He personally anchored much of the coverage and spent a good bit of it announcing that there was not much news from the search-and-rescue teams. However, making the decision to go live and assigning the story the top priority for the network required being on the air and keeping the news flowing.[44]

Bureaus

In addition to beats and special-coverage assignments, many large news organizations have developed a third news-gathering unit, the geographically assigned crew. For example, television networks have news crews (a correspondent and video and sound technicians) stationed in large cities, such as Chicago, New York, Houston, Los Angeles, and Miami. The assumption is that enough news will be generated from these areas to warrant assigning personnel to them. The use of geographical assignments reflects another way in which organizational routines have shaped the definition of news into a convenient formula. Because national news cannot all come from Washington, reporters must be assigned to other locations. But what other locations? Any location chosen suddenly becomes a defining center for national news. As Epstein discovered in his study of television network news, almost all non-Washington news originates from the handful of cities where the networks station their crews.[45]

To an important extent, the reliance on bureaus has decreased in recent years due to budget cuts that eliminated many of these branch offices. As the profit imperative has been felt at both print and broadcast organizations, expensive bureaus are often the first things to be cut. Among American television news operations, only CNN has retained a substantial network of worldwide information-gathering outposts—in large part because CNN also runs an international channel that demands serious world coverage. However, all major news organizations have dropped bureaus and reporting staff. The result is that ABC, CBS, and NBC have increasingly settled for buying their raw product secondhand from a variety of world TV wholesale news suppliers. In the newspaper business, pressures to cut luxuries such as remote bureaus have been equally intense. Many big-city papers have been purchased by large conglomerates, which feed all the papers in the chain the same material from centralized bureaus. The few remaining independent big-city papers increasingly rely on secondhand suppliers, such as the Associated Press, the *New York Times,* and the *Washington Post,* which continue to maintain extensive bureaus and sell their stories to smaller organizations. The overall trend is an increasing consolidation of the information channels on which media organizations rely for their daily supply of news.

Public Relations and News

As noted in earlier chapters, the PR industry has grown in size and technological sophistication in recent decades. The goal of many PR and communications campaigns is to place news stories that advance the images and political goals of clients. As news organizations reduce staff, shrink bureaus, and become more conscious of budgets, the supply of PR events and news releases becomes more attractive as news material. Indeed, PR wires run into most newsrooms, and PR workers (who often have experience as journalists) work up contacts with journalists and supply them with story ideas and sources. As a result, packaged pieces on personalities, movies, entertainers, and, more generally, staged events in communication campaigns become featured in the news. Good news organizations with reasonable reporting budgets avoid packaged PR fare, but small-market TV stations and low-budget papers may succumb to the temptations of using these news helpers.

REPORTERS AS A PACK: PRESSURES TO AGREE

As a result of the increasingly routine nature of news gathering, reporters tend to move in packs. They are assigned together to the same events and the same beats. More than most workers, they share close social experiences on the job. Together they eat, sleep, travel, drink, and wait, and wait, and wait. They also share that indescribable adrenaline rush of "crashing" a story—hurtling through those precious minutes between the release of key information and the deadline for filing the story. As a result of such intimate social contact, reporters tend to develop a sense of solidarity. They learn to cope with shared pressures from news organizations and news sources. They come to accept news formulas as inevitable, even though they may cynically complain about them in between mad scrambles to meet deadlines. They respect one another as independent professionals but engage in the social courtesies of comparing notes and corroborating story angles.

In his insightful description of press coverage during the 1972 election, Timothy Crouse called the reporter's social world "pack journalism."[46] He concluded that reporters come into such close contact while under such sympathetic conditions while covering such controlled events that they do not have to collaborate formally in order to end up reporting things the same way. Once a reporter has been assigned to a routine event for which news formulas are well known, there is a strong temptation to produce a formula story. Added to this are a tight deadline and an editor who will question significant departures from the formula used by other reporters; as a result, the temptation to standardize becomes even stronger. Finally, put the reporter in a group of sympathetic human beings faced with the same temptations, and the use of formulas becomes easily rationalized and accepted with the social support of the group.

So strong are the pressures of the pack that they have been felt even by a trained sociologist who posed as a reporter in order to study news gathering from an insider's perspective. While working as a reporter for a small daily paper, Mark Fishman was assigned to the city council beat. He quickly fit into the routine of writing formula stories that mirrored the council's careful efforts to create an image of democracy in action—complete with elaborate hearings, citizen input, serious deliberations, and formal votes. In a rare case when an issue before the council got out of control and turned into a hot political argument, the reporters at the press table reacted strangely. Ignoring a bit of news that did not fit the mold took some social prompting from various members of the pack. As Fishman described it:

> The four members of the press [including Fishman] were showing increasing signs of impatience with the controversy. At first the reporters stopped taking notes; then they began showing their disapproval to each other; finally, they were making jokes about the foolishness of the debate. No evidence could be found in their comments that they considered the controversy anything other than a stupid debate over a trivial matter unworthy of the time and energy the council put into it.[47]

Fishman noted the strength of group pressure operating against independent news judgment: "Even though at the time of the incident I was sitting at the press table [as a reporter] making derisive comments about the foolishness of the council along with other journalists, it occurred to me later how this controversy could be seen as an important event in city hall."[48]

Just as Fishman succumbed to the pressures of the pack while still recognizing them at a conscious level, most reporters are aware of group pressure but seem unable to escape it. In a study of the Washington journalism corps, the nation's reporting elite, Stephen Hess found that reporters regarded pack journalism as their most serious problem.[49] As Hess noted, however, pack journalism will persist as long as news organizations establish their routines around the predictable actions of officials.

Although the pack generally feeds on the handouts offered by spin-doctors and political handlers, it can also turn on the unprepared or vulnerable politician. Cases of the pack devouring its political prey are legendary: Lyndon Johnson fell to a feeding frenzy over the Vietnam War; Richard Nixon lost control of the press during the Watergate crisis; Jimmy Carter was himself held hostage in the Oval Office by the press for 444 days during the Iranian hostage crisis of 1979–1980; Gary Hart withdrew his presidential candidacy in 1984, when the press pack took up his challenge to prove that he was having an extramarital affair; the first George Bush plummeted from his standing as the most popular president in the history of modern polling as the press pack followed the Democrats in attacking him for an economic recession; and Bill Clinton saw the customary presidential honeymoon period curtailed prematurely by a feeding frenzy. The growing chaos and criticism surrounding the Iraq crisis provided openings for the press pack to turn on George W. Bush, but those openings were balanced against the somber fact that the country was at war. And, as discussed in Chapter 2, the press pack reached consensus early in the Obama administration that the president had lost control of his "narrative." Whether the members of the press pack accept their daily news handouts with equanimity or bite the hand that feeds them, the problem remains much the same: The resulting news becomes standardized and distorted.

Feeding Frenzy: When the Pack Attacks

Although the political content of the mainstream press may be remarkably uniform, it does not always follow the scripts of politicians. What is often mistaken for a critical, independent press is a phenomenon popularly known as the "feeding frenzy."[50] When politicians become caught up in personal crises, scandals, or power struggles, the news media may descend like a pack of hungry dogs to devour the political prey. Add the hint of a sex scandal or produce the proverbial smoking gun of political corruption, and the frenzy can bring down the high and mighty.

Few politicians have felt the sting of the feeding frenzy as repeatedly as Bill Clinton. The news was spiced during the 1992 election by charges of Clinton's extramarital affairs, pot smoking, draft dodging, and other personal issues. Clinton's character became a major preoccupation of the press during the campaign.[51] The resulting challenge for the Clinton communication team was to reassure voters about the character defects raised in the news and reinforced by opponents during the primaries and the general election. The fact that Clinton survived the nearly nonstop negative news and then won the election struck one Republican media consultant as something close to a miracle. He likened Clinton to the crash test dummy of American politics: "I've never seen anybody come back from being attacked in that fashion. It's like going through a car crash with no seat belts and then going through the window and hitting a wall and walking away. It's absolutely astounding."[52]

After the election, Clinton and his staff remained bitter about their treatment by the press during the campaign. When they came to Washington, it seemed as if they felt that they could govern much as they had won the election, by going over the heads of the press through electronic town halls, controlled news events, and heavy polling and image construction. The daily world of Washington politics proved different than the campaign trail, where paid advertising and controlled events stand a better chance of countering press attacks. The now-famous decision to close the corridor between the press room and the White House communication office amounted to a declaration of war on journalism's elite corps. The icy relations left the press pack surly and ready to pounce at the hint of a scandal or personal failing. Clinton's run of personal incidents continued after the inauguration, and the press pounced on such items as Clinton's expensive haircut aboard an idling Air Force One on a Los Angeles International Airport taxiway and a scandal in the management of the White House travel office that was quickly dubbed "Travelgate" in the media.

One analysis of this nonstop feeding frenzy opened with the observation that "Twelve days after President Clinton took office—with *only* 1,448 days left in his term—Sam Donaldson of ABC *News* was on a weekend talk show saying "This week we can all talk about, Is the presidency over?"[53] Another reflective piece was titled "The White House Beast" after the derisive nickname given the press corps by George Stephanopoulous, who was Clinton's early (and disastrous) communication director, and now serves as a pundit for ABC *News*. As *Washington Post* correspondent Ruth Marcus put it in that article, "The White House press corps is like this large, dysfunctional family. It's weird. It's not normal. Half the time I'm at the White House, my attitude is: No one would believe this."[54]

There are at least three reasons for the series of feeding frenzies that plagued the Clinton presidency from the start. As these factors often contribute to other feeding frenzies, they are stated here in more general terms:

- Cooperative relations between the president's communication staff and the press had broken down. (See the discussions of press–politician cooperation earlier in this chapter and in Chapter 4.)
- The communication staff seemed to think it unnecessary (or beneath the dignity of the office) to follow the basic rules of news management in response to the initial outbreaks of negative coverage, as outlined in Chapter 4. They provided few packaged stories to interrupt the negative news, and they had no apparent game plan to spin the incidents that kept the feeding frenzies going.
- The charged and actual offenses involving the president resulted in numerous uncontrolled news situations.

With the exception of the stories that David Gergen was allowed to manage during his brief stay in the Clinton White House (recall the earlier discussions of Gergen's news management style in Chapter 4), press relations for much of the Clinton first term remained rocky. For example, influential *New York Times* correspondent (now an influential columnist) Maureen Dowd listed the numerous instances of poor press handling on the part of the press office staff during a European trip commemorating the 50-year anniversary of D-Day. She recounted a reflective moment at a British pub after a missed deadline: "Sipping champagne ordered by the *Paris Match* reporter, I fantasized about replacing the corner dartboard with the head of one of Clinton's prepubescent press-minders."[55]

Relations between press and president may have hit an even lower point in the George W. Bush administration. Traveling extensively in order to get messages directly into local news markets, relying on tightly crafted news events, and using a national conservative talk-radio echo chamber to spread its messages, the Bush communication team often bypassed the national press corps, which it seemed to hold in disdain. The feeling soon became mutual and bubbled into frequent squabbles between reporters and administration communication staff. For example, when Vice President Cheney accidentally shot a friend on a hunting trip in 2006, the press feeding frenzy lasted more than a week. When did the president know? Why did Cheney wait hours to tell the press? Why was the story given to a small Texas local paper and not the national press? The questions went on, indicating that the press is sometimes capable of sustaining a story without the cooperation of the officials at its center. It is unfortunate for the democratic role of the press that such independence seldom appears in stories of greater importance.

As President Obama lost his narrative, the opposing Republicans were ever ready to supply theirs to the press. The Republican minority managed to capture a substantial portion of the news by threatening to filibuster Obama initiatives in the Senate, and echoing the Tea Party activities in the streets. Meanwhile the administration seemed unable to generate or stay on messages of its own, preferring to continue to communicate directly with its supporters through social media networks, which worked far better to mobilize public support during the election campaign than in the governing process.

THE PARADOX OF ORGANIZATIONAL ROUTINES

The problem with routine news gathering is that most of the news on most of the channels starts looking pretty much the same. The paradox is that because there are many papers, radio programs, and television broadcasts from which audiences can receive the daily news, it is hard for competing organizations to establish a competitive edge in the news market. In short, routine reporting of news may be efficient, but it limits the share of the market that any media source can capture. For example, if all the news on television is pretty much the same, each network should capture an equal share of the audience, all other things being equal. Thus, efficiency may impose an unintended ceiling on audience share, which limits the growth of profits in the news organization—and news is, after all, a business. The ways around this dilemma involve marketing strategies, budget cutting, and the various other business moves described in Chapter 7—none of which improve the quality of news.

Breaking out of the news routine toward more independent, less sensational news has not been attractive to news organizations because it is not clear what the alternative would look like even if it were profitable enough to worry about. For example, television executives may point to the *News Hour* on the Public Broadcasting Service (PBS) as an example of how more in-depth reporting only drives audiences away. Some critics argue, however, that PBS news, while more detailed and more likely to broadcast hard news over soft, is otherwise very similar in content to that available on the commercial networks. Why should audiences seek a bigger dose of the same product?

Because news is largely the result of convenient conventions between politicians and journalists, it is not clear where to look for guidance in reforming the product. Any new format would surely draw criticism from politicians and other news organizations, and it might startle the public, risking the possible loss of audience share. As a result, the media do not like to think too much about tampering with the standard news-gathering routines. Instead, the competition in most news markets tends to be waged in terms of marketing strategies, brand images, and other matters of style over substance.

Should the Market Rule the News?

After receiving a survey of audience reading habits, the management of one major daily paper reportedly issued a memo to reporters calling for more "fine examples" of rapes, robberies, and auto accidents on page 1.[56] Whether the marketing strategy involves more human-interest stories or more stereotyped coverage of political heroes in action, the result is the same as far as political information goes: The news trends are toward replacing coverage of government and civic affairs with sex, personality, lifestyle, entertainment, sports, weather, and mayhem.

The contribution of the news doctors to standardized news raises a number of important questions, including the following:

- Should news be based on market considerations, or should it be based on some independent criteria of importance and newsworthiness?
- Because some people (i.e., enough to turn a profit) watch or read news about fires, murders, accidents, and political scandals, does this necessarily mean that (a) they want more of it, (b) they think these things are important, (c) they think these things belong in the news, (d) they do not want alternatives to formula news, and (e) they would not be engaged by news that actually *explains* more about politics and society?

Such questions are dodged by news doctors and media executives, who reply simplistically that they are only interested in making the news more relevant to people. It is doubtful that current marketing surveys really measure popular demand at all.[57] For example, most media surveys are designed with the assumption that formula news is a given. Audiences are not asked if they would prefer alternatives to news formulas; they are simply asked which news formulas they like best. Thus, the standard excuse that the news reflects what the people want might be stated more properly as "the news reflects what people prefer among those choices that we find profitable and convenient to offer them." This is not the same thing as saying that the news is responsive to popular demand.

WHEN JOURNALISM WORKS

Within the limits of business pressures and journalistic routines, there are clearly some news organizations that seem to make greater commitments to news content that displays more diversity, detail, and coherence. Journalists turn out to be among the most self-critical of professionals. Perhaps because they receive such volumes of criticism from all sides (public opinion, politicians, other journalists, and media scholars), they sometimes experiment with news formats in an effort to try to improve the quality of their product. Although these changes are often modest in their impact, they are worth noting.

Fighting the Mayhem? A Hopeful Trend in Local TV News

In Austin, Texas, the news looked pretty much the same on all the channels: more mayhem than at least some local journalists felt accurately reflected life in the increasingly cosmopolitan Texas capital. Then, ratings leader KVUE-TV broke from the pack. News executives decided that they would screen the mayhem stories for their social or political significance before making an automatic story assignment based on the "if it bleeds, it leads" principle. For example, before a crime story would be shown on KVUE, it had to meet at least one of five significant criteria:

1. Does action need to be taken?
2. Is there an immediate threat to safety?
3. Is there a threat to children?
4. Does the crime have significant community impact?
5. Does the story lend itself to a crime prevention effort?[58]

Soon after these standards were developed, they were put to a test by a Saturday night brawl in a local town that resulted in a triple shooting and murder. KVUE investigated the incident and judged that none of its significance criteria was engaged. The station held its ground and did not report the story, while its competitors gave it the prominent play generally assigned to such a good example of local mayhem. As the news director at Austin's K-EYE put it simply, "When somebody's killed, that's news."[59] Perhaps it was easier for KVUE to try a new kind of journalism in Austin because it was already the ratings leader. However, the ratings for the new format made for happy news executives. The ratings for the first full month of the experiment were the best ever for the station's 10 p.m. newscast, and over time, the station became the ratings leader for all of its evening newscasts.[60]

A more general look at national trends shows that KVUE is not alone in its efforts to improve the quality of local TV news. For example, KARE in Minneapolis features a lengthy report on an important issue of the day, and its ratings have risen. KAKE in Wichita has twice the national average in issue coverage and is also doing well in the ratings. WCTV in Tallahassee goes where others have closed operations (such as reporting on state government) and leads its market. These examples are from a larger study of 61 stations in 20 cities conducted by Columbia University's Project for Excellence in Journalism.[61]

The most interesting finding from the study is that serious news tends to be compatible with good ratings primarily when a station makes a commitment to breaking completely with the mayhem format. In other words, stations that incorporate a mix of serious issues and mayhem are not as likely to be rising in the ratings as stations that either make serious news their dominant format or that continue to go with "more mayhem most of the time." This interesting finding was summarized and interpreted this way:

> The stations least likely to be rising in the ratings were those in the middle, which were often hybrids—part tabloid and part serious. This suggests that audiences are not schizophrenic—they are segmenting. There is a group that embraces news full of revelation, scandal, and celebrity. There is another group that prefers a more sober, information-based approach.[62]

With the exception of five out of the eight stations in the high-quality group that were experiencing rating gains, the rest of the picture was decidedly mixed. Indeed, the overall profile of the 8,500 stories from the 600 broadcasts monitored on the 61 stations in the study was not an optimistic portrait of a revolution sweeping local TV:

> Despite the good news, the study found that most local newscasts are far from excellent. The general picture of local TV news is superficial and reactive—journalism on the run. Almost half (46%) of all stories were about commonplace events. Less than 10 percent originated from ideas in the newsroom. Of stories involving controversy, many (43%) gave only one side.[63]

Although this study found a somewhat more reassuring crime volume (28%) than other research (using different samples) has found, the substantive problems with local news still seemed large. The Project for Excellence team cited major failings on the local scene with "sourcing, getting both sides of the story, thinking ahead."[64]

Reforms on the National Scene

The economic crisis in journalism discussed in Chapter 1 is producing a wave of innovation and experimentation in small online news organizations, blogs, and hybrid organizations such as the *Daily Beast* and *Huffington Post*. Yet most so-called legacy or mainstream news organizations seem incapable of much innovation, and continue to deal with the crisis through budget cuts that further undermine the quality of their product. The power of organizational routines and the inability to rethink the definition of journalism, itself, seem to hold these organizations in place even as they face their own demise.

Even when news organizations vow to improve the quality of coverage, other pressures in the information system often intrude. For example, CBS announced a policy in the 1992 presidential campaign to reverse the trend toward shrinking "sound bites" (those direct statements by candidates and politicians that are sandwiched in television news packages). According to a study by Daniel Hallin, the length of the average sound bite hit an all-time low of under 10 seconds during the 1988 campaign.[65] The CBS goal of running at least 30 seconds of direct statement from the candidate in each story was soon abandoned, however, as it became clear that the media managers who run campaigns had learned to script their candidates' performances with those ten-second political marketing jingles in mind.[66] As a result, the length of the sound bite shrank even further in 1992 to 8.4 seconds. Although it seems impossible to shrink candidate statements much farther, they weighed in at a puny 7.2 seconds in the 1996 election, according to a study conducted midway through the campaign by the Center for Media and Public Affairs.[67] The 2000 election held firm at 7.3 seconds, with candidates getting only 11 percent of campaign news time.[68] Election night TV coverage has reduced the role of reporters familiar with campaigns and candidates in favor of greater face time for star anchors and pundits who now talk in clipped, rapid-fire exchanges.[69]

The shrinking sound bite and rapid pace of TV talking heads are signs that it is hard to change news formats in the direction of more information-rich fare. The sound-bite trend reminds us that not all of the inhibitions to change arise from inside news organizations. Candidates hire communication consultants who are also quite comfortable shrinking ideas to fit media formats. Critics argue that the now-standard 30-second ad spots used in election and issue campaigns permit candidates to skip over the details of their proposals and aim at often volatile public emotions.[70] Yet many media consultants like former Clinton advisor Dick Morris see no such problem. According to Morris, "There is literally no such thing as an idea that cannot be expressed well and articulately to today's voters in 30 seconds."[71]

DEMOCRACY WITH OR WITHOUT CITIZENS?

Recall from Chapter 1 that political communication scholar Robert Entman has argued that our mass-mediated democracy is in danger of becoming a *democracy without citizens*. This is in part because most news coverage is driven by forces that involve people more as passive consumers than active citizens.[72] For both politicians and journalists, the public has become more of a market to be tested, persuaded, and sold than an equal partner in communication and government. The reality of much opinion and participation is anchored in electronic images that move people psychologically in private worlds that may be detached from society and face-to-face politics.[73]

The irony in this is that the technology exists to communicate more information—farther, faster, from more sources, and to more people than ever before. At the same time, the political and business pressures operating behind the news may create just the opposite results. Perhaps the electronic age would not be so worrisome if politicians and the press used the potential of today's electronic technology to communicate critical ideas to people. The question is how to move politicians and journalism away from the paths of least political and economic resistance in their communication strategies.

In short, it is not hard to imagine how the news could be more citizen-oriented than it is. For example, the press could keep more citizen voices in reporting on important issues—even when public officials attempt to manage, downplay, or ignore those voices. News organizations could require their reporters and editors to run more direct statements from newsmakers and less commentary from journalists. News organizations also could minimize the writing of rapid "meta-narratives"—such as the campaign horse race or the authority-disorder plot—that can be applied to almost any generic political situation.

Above all, citizens and their activities should be covered in the news even when officials are not engaged with the issues or viewpoints in question. News organizations could include citizens in their reports and create paths from the broadcast or the news page to Web sites where audiences can learn more about what they can do to make a difference. There are signs of movement in this direction as journalists laid off from news corporations begin to explore how digital technologies may attract more active audience involvement. Recent years have seen the rise of blogs, discussion forums, instant polls, YouTube channels, social networking sites, and invitations for citizens to report stories they have documented on cell phones and digital cameras. What do you think? What kind of news would best fill the needs of a *democracy with citizens?*

NOTES

1. See his news online service: www.breitbart.com/. Accessed September 8, 2010.
2. The timeline of these events is documented by the liberal media site Media Matters: http://mediamatters.org/research/201007220004. Accessed September 9, 2010. Another interpretation of the same event is available on the conservative site: www.rightpundits.com/?p=6778. Accessed December 11, 2010. A more detailed account can be found in Wikipedia: http://en.wikipedia.org/wiki/Resignation_of_Shirley_Sherrod. Accessed December 11, 2010.
3. An account of the FOX coverage is offered by Media Matters: http://mediamatters.org/blog/201007200060. Accessed September 8, 2010. The key issue in FOX spinning the incident is the claim that Sherrod was fired before Bill O'Reilly's program aired, and that therefore FOX did not cause the firing. This begs the fact that the story had already appeared in FOX online before the firing, and in firing Sherrod the secretary of agriculture clearly anticipated the full scandal coverage from FOX, which in fact occurred. At the same time, the firing was conducted in response to the anticipated media scandal, and without consulting the facts of the situation, either. All of which suggests that media scandals take on their own realities, often independent of underlying facts.
4. Hal Boeodeker, "Shirley Sherrod: Fox News Becomes an Issue on "Fox News Sunday," July 25, 2010. http://blogs.orlandosentinel.com/entertainment_tv_tvblog/2010/07/shirley-sherrod-fox-news-becomes-an-issue-on-fox-news-sunday.html. Accessed September 8, 2010.
5. See Breitbart's own account on his blog: http://biggovernment.com/publius/2010/07/21/breitbart-its-not-about-shirley-sherrod-its-about-naacp-attacking-tea-party/. Accessed December 11, 2010.
6. For an account of the sequence of events, see Howard Hurtz, "Finger-pointing at Fox in Shirley Sherrod Firing," *The Washington Post, July 22, 2010.* www.washingtonpost.com/wp-dyn/content/article/2010/07/22/AR2010072201265.html. Accessed September 8, 2010.
7. Quoted in Michael Massing, "The Press: The Enemy Within," *The New York Review of Books* 52, no. 20 (December 15, 2005).
8. Remarks at the conference "Politics and the Media in the New Millennium," hosted by the Annette Strauss Institute, University of Texas, Austin (held at Belo Mansion, Dallas, Texas, February 18, 2006).
9. "Al Gore and the 'Embellishment' Issue: Press Coverage of the Gore Presidential Campaign." Kennedy School of Government Case Program, C15-02-1679.0.
10. See, for example, Jay G. Blumler and Michael Gurevitch, "Politicians and the Press: An Essay in Role Relationships," in *Handbook of Political Communication,* eds. Dan Nimmo and Keith Sanders (Newbury Park, CA: Sage, 1981), 467–493.
11. Herbert J. Gans, *Deciding What's News* (New York: Pantheon, 1979); and Gaye Tuchman, *Making News* (New York: Free Press, 1978).
12. Bernard C. Cohen, *The Press and Foreign Policy* (Princeton, NJ: Princeton University Press, 1963); and Timothy Cook, *Governing with the News* (Chicago: University of Chicago Press, 1998).

13. Thomas E. Patterson, "Doing Well and Doing Good: How Soft News and Critical Journalism Are Shrinking the News Audience and Weakening Democracy—And What News Outlets Can Do About It," Joan Shorenstein Center on the Press, Politics, and Public Policy, Harvard University, December 2000, 10.

14. See the argument in Robert W. McChesney, *The Problem of the Media: U.S. Communication Politics in the Twenty-First Century* (New York: Monthly Review Press, 2004).

15. Thomas E. Patterson, "Irony of a Free Press: Professional Journalism and News Diversity" (paper prepared for the Annual Meeting of the American Political Science Association, Chicago, September 3–6, 1992). See also Patterson's *Out of Order* (New York: Knopf, 1993).

16. An archive of these reports can be found here: http://topics.nytimes.com/top/news/business/companies/blackwater_usa/index.html. Accessed September 9, 2010.

17. See W. Lance Bennett, Regina G. Lawrence, and Steven Livingston, *When the Press Fails: Political Power and the News Media from Iraq to Katrina* (Chicago: University of Chicago Press, 2007).

18. CNN poll reported in CNN's Politicalticker: http://politicalticker.blogs.cnn.com/2010/09/03/cnn-poll-obama-approval-up-after-iraq-speech/. Accessed September 9, 2010.

19. Sam Youngman, "Obama Promises No 'Victory Lap' During Address on Iraq," *The Hill*, August 31, 2010. http://thehill.com/homenews/administration/116621-obama-promises-no-victory-lap-during-iraq-address

20. See Frank Rich, *The Greatest Story Ever Sold: The Decline and Fall of Truth in Bush's America* (New York: Penguin, 2006).

21. For a more detailed analysis of press coverage of the Iraq War, see Bennett, Lawrence, and Livingston, *When the Press Fails: Political Power and the News Media from Iraq to Katrina.*

22. Barton Gellman and Walter Pincus, "Errors and Exaggerations: Prewar Depictions of Iraq's Nuclear Threat Outweighed the Evidence," *Washington Post National Weekly Edition* (August 18–24, 2003): 6.

23. "With Few Variations, Top Administration Advisors Present Their Case," *New York Times*, September 9, 2002:.A8.

24. Todd S. Purdham, "Bush Officials Say Time Has Come for Action in Iraq," *New York Times*, September 9, 2002: A1..

25. See Bennett, Lawrence, and Livingston, *When the Press Fails*. Also see Robert M. Entman, *Projections of Power* (Chicago: University of Chicago Press, 2004).

26. Paul Krugman, "Bush and Blair, So Far, Face Different Fates," *International Herald Tribune*, July 30, 2003: 7.

27. See, Bennett, Lawrence, and Livingston, *When the Press Fails.*

28. See Entman, *Projections of Power* (Chicago: University of Chicago Press, 2004).

29. Ken Auletta, "Vox Fox," *New Yorker* (May 26, 2003): 64.

30. See Daniel C. Hallin and Todd Gitlin, "The Gulf War as Popular Culture and Television Drama," in *Taken by Storm: The Media, Public Opinion, and U.S. Foreign Policy in the Gulf War*, eds. W. Lance Bennett and David L. Paletz (Chicago: University of Chicago Press, 1994), 149–166.

31. Timothy Cook, "Domesticating a Crisis: Washington Newsbeats and Network News After the Iraq Invasion of Kuwait," in *Taken by Storm: The Media, Public Opinion, and U.S. Foreign Policy in the Gulf War*, eds. W. Lance Bennett and David L. Paletz (Chicago: University of Chicago Press, 1994), 105–130.

32. See, for example, the numerous accounts of reporters, including Lou Cannon, *Reporting: An Inside View* (Sacramento: California Journal Press, 1977); Robert

Darnton, "Writing News and Telling Stories," *Daedalus* 104 (Spring 1975): 175–194; and Lewis Lapham, "Gilding the News," *Harper's* (July 1981): 31–39.

33. For an excellent discussion of this syndrome, see Tuchman, *Making News.*
34. Robert Scholes, "Double Perspective on Hysteria," *Saturday Review* (August 24, 1968): 37.
35. For a detailed analysis of how this pattern occurs, see Leon Sigal, *Reporters and Officials* (Lexington, MA: Heath, 1973).
36. Tom Bethell, "The Myth of an Adversary Press," *Harper's* (January 1977): 36.
37. Ibid., 31.
38. Quoted in David Owen, "The Best Kept Secret in American Journalism Is Murray Kempton," *Esquire* (March 1982): 50.
39. Steve Goldstein, "How About Term Limits for the Unelected Elite," *Columbia Journalism Review* (May/June 1994): 35.
40. Ibid.
41. Ibid., 36.
42. See, for example, Warren Breed's classic study, "Social Control in the Newsroom," *Social Forces* 33 (May 1955): 326–335.
43. Edward Jay Epstein, *News from Nowhere* (New York: Vintage, 1973).
44. Frank Cesno, "The New News Environment," Brown-bag Lunch, Joan Shorenstein Center, Kennedy School of Government, Harvard University, September 21, 1999.
45. Epstein, *News from Nowhere.*
46. See Timothy Crouse, *The Boys on the Bus* (New York: Ballantine, 1973).
47. Mark Fishman, *Manufacturing the News* (Austin: University of Texas Press, 1980), 80–81.
48. Ibid., 81.
49. Stephen Hess, *The Washington Reporters* (Washington, DC: Brookings Institution, 1981), 130.
50. See Larry Sabato, *Feeding Frenzy* (New York: Free Press, 1991).
51. See W. Lance Bennett, "The Cueless Public: Bill Clinton Meets the New American Voter in Campaign '92," in *The Clinton Presidency*, ed. Stanley Renshon (Boulder, CO: Westview Press, 1995).
52. Quoted in Maureen Dowd, "How a Battered Clinton Has Stayed Alive," *New York Times,* March 16, 1992: 1.
53. David Shaw, "Dire Judgments on Clinton Started Just Days into Term," *Los Angeles Times,* September 16, 1993: A1.
54. Jacob Weisberg, "The White House Beast," *Vanity Fair* (September 1993): 169.
55. Maureen Dowd, "Beached," *New York Times Magazine* (June 19, 1994): 18.
56. Fergus M. Bordewich, "Supermarketing the Newspaper," *Columbia Journalism Review* (September/October 1977): 27.
57. See, for example, Philip Meyer's criticism of market research and defense of more reliable social science investigations in his article, "In Defense of the Marketing Approach," *Columbia Journalism Review* (January/February 1978): 61.
58. Reported in Joe Halley, "Should the Coverage Fit the Crime? A Texas TV Station Tries to Resist the Allure of Mayhem," *Columbia Journalism Review* (May/June 1996): 27–32.
59. Ibid., 28.
60. See: www.austin360.com/television/new-keye-formats-slip-some-kvue-leads-news-712979.html. Accessed September 9, 2010.
61. Based on studies by the Project for Excellence in Journalism at Columbia University, as reported in Tom Rosenstiel, Carl Gottlieb, and Lee Ann Brady, "Local TV

News: What Works, What Flops, and Why," *Columbia Journalism Review* 37, no. 5 (January/February 1999):. 65–70.

62. Ibid.
63. Ibid.
64. Ibid.
65. Daniel C. Hallin, "Sound Bite News: Television Coverage of Elections, 1968–1988," Woodrow Wilson Center Paper, 1991.
66. See John Tierney, "Sound Bites Become Smaller Mouthfuls," *New York Times*, January 23, 1992: 1; and Richard L. Berke, "Mixed Results for CBS Rule on Sound Bite," *New York Times*, July 11, 1992: 7.
67. Mitchell Stephens, "On Shrinking Sound Bites," *Columbia Journalism Review* (September/October 1996): 22.
68. Center for Media & Public Affairs, September 28, 2000. www.cmpa.com/pressrel/electpr5.htm.
69. Thomas E. Patterson, "Diminishing Returns: A Comparison of 1968 and 2000 Election Night Broadcasts," Shorenstein Center on Press, Politics, & Public Policy, December 2003. www.shorensteincenter.org.
70. See, for example, Kathleen Hall Jamieson, *Dirty Politics* (New York: Oxford University Press, 1992).
71. The statement is from Morris's memoir *The New Prince,* quoted in a review by Andrew Sullivan, "As the Focus Group Goes, So Goes the Nation," *New York Times Book Review* (June 13, 1999): 8.
72. Robert M. Entman, *Democracy Without Citizens: Media and the Decay of American Politics* (New York: Oxford University Press, 1989).
73. Dan Nimmo and James E. Coombs, *Mediated Political Realities,* 2nd ed. (New York: Longman, 1989).

Inside the Profession

Objectivity and the Political Authority Bias

"Objectivity" demanded more discipline of reporters and editors because it expected every item to be attributed to some authority. No traffic accident could be reported without quoting a police sergeant. No wartime incident was recounted without confirmation from government officials.

"Objectivity" placed overwhelming emphasis on established, official voices and tended to leave unreported large areas of genuine relevance that authorities chose not to talk about. . . . It widened the chasm that is a constant threat to democracy— the difference between the realities of private power and the illusions of public imagery.

—Ben Bagdikian

C an the news be objective? Should it be? These questions fuel much public debate and offer instant topics for pundits on 24/7 cable channels. At the time of this writing, a Google search on "journalism bias" produced a healthy 2,260,000 hits. Among the more reflective entries in this list is an NPR *Talk of the Nation* program that asked: "Does the ideal of balance distort the news? What if there are more than two sides to the story—or the sides aren't equal?"[1] Yet if you ask most people what's wrong with the press, the concerns are seldom this deep. The most common complaint is that journalists fail in their obligation to be fair or objective.

You may recall from discussion in Chapter 2 that the issue of ideological bias is confounded because most people view the world through their own political biases and think that perspectives deviating from their views are unbalanced. Because there are so many different views operating in the public on almost any issue, the quest for news coverage that strikes a majority as fair, balanced, or objective appears to be an impossible dream. The paradox of converting something as value-driven as politics into generic news does not keep people from demanding it. As explained in Chapter 2, it is commonly assumed that news bias involves journalists abandoning their professional norms about balance and objectivity to insert their personal prejudices into their reporting. In this chapter, we will consider the disturbing possibility that the most serious biases in the news occur not when journalists abandon their professional standards, but when they cling most closely to the ideal of objectivity.

The weak link in the idea of trying to be balanced or objective is that, in practice, news organizations default to authorities and officials as surrogates for objectivity. If democracy works perfectly to represent all citizens, then this is probably a reasonable working standard. However, if there are any biases in politics (see Bagdikian's opening comments) that distort what officials say or do, then giving authorities the main role in defining the news also builds these general and situational biases right into the news. Because authorities of all political stripes often filter what they say and do through political calculations, this makes the news more a window on power and political strategy inside government than a platform that examines politics critically in some broader democratic context.

What kinds of political calculations do officials make when thinking about how to spin the news? The case study in Chapter 4 illustrates one sort of political calculation that introduces distortion into news coverage: corporations dependent on a carbon fuel economy spending huge amounts of resources on think tanks and political candidates willing to discredit climate science in order to delay action on global warming. In cases like this, the efforts of news organizations to achieve balance can turn stories that have just one dominant side into two-sided reports that confuse or weaken our understanding of an issue. To cite another example of this, a good investigative report on election improprieties by one of the political parties may make a nervous editor ask the reporter to develop the possibility that the other party is doing the same thing. This may "balance" the story with an accusation by the guilty party that it has been wrongly accused (never mind the evidence) and that the other party is actually trying to rig elections. Such reports only reinforce popular perceptions that everyone in politics is crooked and that the story can be dismissed as politics as usual.

In contrast to one sided stories that somehow develop other sides, there are also two sided stories that somehow lose the other side simply because the kinds of official sources that journalists seek are silent, or occupy weak power positions in a conflict, or both. This happened as described in the case study in Chapter 5, when the Democrats were helpless to do much about the invasion of Iraq. They did not organize an opposition to a then popular president, which, in turn, deprived the press of a strong counter voice to a war that turned out to be ill considered and eventually unpopular. Meanwhile, the doubts raised by potentially credible sources such as United Nations weapons inspection officials (who could not find any weapons of mass destruction) did not qualify for much sustained coverage because they were not engaged directly in political conflict with powerful U.S. officials.

Beyond the one-sided stories that arguably have more sides, and two-sided stories that arguably have only one credible side, there are stories that are essentially made up for political purposes. Scandals, rumors, and viral innuendo are often released into the digital mediascape where they gain traction among bloggers and partisan networks, and eventually surface as attractive audience-building topics for radio and TV talk show personalities. True or not, these inventions may also be attractive for some politicians who see them as low cost opportunities to appeal to angry voters and to attack political opponents in the mainstream media. For example, Barack Obama was haunted throughout his term as president by charges that he was a Muslim and that he was not born in America (the latter charge challenging his constitutional eligibility to be president).

Rather than dismiss these charges as untrue (and fueling prejudice and intolerance), the mainstream media often reported them as serious political issues. How did this work? Start with the vast networks of unfiltered information in cyberspace. Even several years after these rumors surfaced in the 2008 election, a Google search on the term "birthers" (the name for the movement that continued to raise doubts about the political legitimacy of the president's birth) produced 2,130,000 hits. A news search (also at the time of this writing) showed that the term was still actively circulating in the news. What was the bridge from cheap Internet rumor to serious news? Many conservative political officials (e.g., Republican Senators, Representatives, state and national party officials) echoed these rumors to stir up negativity in news reports and punditry. An analysis in a *Washington Post* blog showed more than 20 Republican politicians validating these charges one way or another in the news.[2] Not only was the president helpless to make these pseudo issues go away, but they continued to erode his political credibility: fully 20 percent of the public believed he was Muslim, and less than half were certain about his birth status.

Mr. Obama understood both the impossibility of countering such news fantasies, and the insidious online networks that feed the news system with them. In an interview in 2010, he seemed frustrated that these invented charges had been dogging him for years, saying: "I can't spend all of my time with my birth certificate plastered on my forehead." He also noted the difficulty of keeping these stories out of the contemporary news system: "The facts are the facts. We went through some of this during the campaign—there is a mechanism, a network of misinformation that in a new media era can get churned out there constantly."[3]

Thus, the formulaic application of balance, fairness and objectivity can produce results that seem anything but balanced, fair, or objective. In an acerbic look at how so many competing news organizations manage to converge on such an unhelpful information format, Joan Didion describes the code of Washington reporting:

> The genuflection toward "fairness" is a familiar newsroom piety. In practice the excuse for a good deal of autopilot reporting and lazy thinking but in theory a benign ideal. In Washington, however, a community in which the management of the news has become the single overriding preoccupation of the core industry, what "fairness" has often come to mean is a scrupulous passivity, an agreement to cover the story not as it is occurring but as it is presented, which is to say, as it is manufactured.[4]

These simple reporting codes explain a great deal about the information system that the American people live with. Cut into this system where you will, each player—whether political actor, journalist, or citizen—has a different view of it. As noted in the last chapter, the system produced by this core reporting code is competitive, adversarial, and fully captivating for those insiders (politicians and the press) who are caught up in it. Yet the result is a remarkably standardized information system that displays the clearly recognizable biases that we explored in Chapter 2. Perhaps equally important for democracy, this system is held in substantial disapproval by majorities of the public, who often see themselves as outsiders.

JOURNALISTS AND THEIR PROFESSION

Some things have changed and other things have stayed much the same in the ways journalists view their jobs. For example, the speed of communication has increased greatly in the past quarter-century, and journalists correspondingly sense the importance of getting the news out quickly. In the early 1970s, 56 percent of journalists surveyed regarded getting information to the public quickly as extremely important. By the 1990s, 69 percent felt that news speed was a top priority. Perhaps due to the pressures to produce news quickly, the perceived need to provide analysis of complex problems in the news dropped from 61 to 48 percent. The avoidance of complex stories may, in turn, account for a somewhat diminished sense of the importance of investigating government claims—long the hallmark of journalism's contribution to democracy. The perceived importance of investigative reporting dropped from 76 to 67 percent between the 1970s and the beginning of the 1990s.[5] Indeed, the latest edition of the classic study *The American Journalist in the 21st Century* shows a sharp drop in the number of journalists covering the news, yet the same basic standards of reporting persist.[6] All of this comes at a time when the amount of political information passing as news through more communication channels is increasing.

Despite the rapidly changing business and audience contexts, one feature of the profession that has remained nearly constant since the rise of a professional press in the 1920s to the present day is the overriding commitment to objectivity, neutrality, or balance. Because journalists do not have a scientific method through which to deploy these professional values, they quickly resolve into the idea that political situations involve some essential facts that can be reported and that they should be reported through the words and facts offered by authoritative sources.[7] The irony is that this notion of objectivity is not easy to defend: Officials are known to have biases, facts are easily disputed, and the news can never include all the viewpoints that may be important to understanding events.

As charges of press bias have become more intense in recent years, many journalists backed away from the term *objectivity* and used words such as *balance* and *fairness*. Whatever its name, there is a broad, exceptionally American, cultural ideal to cast politics in generic public interest terms and essential procedures that are free of, well, "politics." Journalists are both the carriers of this ideal and its major casualties.

Despite opening journalism to charges of bias from all sides, the commitment to objectivity or neutrality also provides a defense mechanism in a difficult job: If everyone is mad at us, we must have gotten it right. Sociologist Gaye Tuchman called objectivity a "strategic ritual" that offers a defense against career-threatening moments in which a risky report might receive the brunt of official or other public condemnation.[8] The curious result of seeking a common reality is perhaps the most standardized reporting system in the free world—a system that blurs the lines between objectivity and political authority, and between fact and political spin. Indeed, when questions of truth are raised, journalists often seem unable to engage with them, as illustrated in the Case Study in this chapter.

CASE STUDY

Why Mainstream Professional Journalism Favors Spin over Truth

The case study in Chapter 1 talked about the concept of "truthiness" made popular by comedian Stephen Colbert. This is a way of thinking about how much distortion and spin becomes news, and how little news organizations seem able to do about it (indeed, how much they assist in promoting it). The continuing assault on reason in the news has made this concept part of the national vocabulary. Even after Colbert had stopped using it as a comedy schtick, fans lobbied to bring it back with an online movement that made "restoring truthiness" one of the top Google trends of 2010.[9]

Seeking the truth can be an elusive goal, particularly in the value-laden and disputed world of politics. However, journalistic practices that end up giving a select set of often-partisan actors the main say in defining political situations are highly unlikely to offer publics the kind of information they need to deliberate or to reach sound opinions. A small proportion of attentive citizens who roam widely for their information and engage in open

Continued

exchanges may reach independent understandings, but the news makes it difficult for ordinary citizens to assess political situations beyond the shrill, competing, and often incomplete claims of the partisan officials who are given the power to define stories. In particular, the journalistic practices that support the ideal of objectivity or balance result in several common information gaps that may actually undermine clear understandings of news events: *omissions* of story elements that are not sanctioned by officials, *artificial balance* even when clear evidence suggests one side is more correct, and *deception and lies* entering the news through unchallenged official pronouncements.

Omissions

News stories often oversimplify larger and more complex realities. In many ways, this is good. People want heuristics to use to simplify distant and complex situations. However, the news may radically simplify realities to the point of distortion or omission of important information for various reasons: some situations are just too complex for editors to want to present to audiences thought too distracted to pay attention; officials deny certain aspects of stories and thereby remove the easiest basis for continuing to report them; or pressures are applied by officials or political groups to stop reporting those elements and return to being "fair and objective." Thus, pressures from politicians and conservative media personalities pushed reports of civilian casualties in the war in Afghanistan out of the U.S. news. By contrast, the foreign editor of the British paper *The Independent* noted that his reporter covered an American strike against an area where Osama bin Laden was suspected of hiding, but instead of hitting Osama or his troops, the strike missed the target and killed 115 innocent men, women, and children in a nearby village. Such elements of stories might be useful for the American people to know about, yet a CNN correspondent stood atop the same pile of rubble witnessed by the British reporter and reported the Pentagon line that the strike targeted Osama and that civilians were not involved.[10]

Similarly, in the coverage of the Abu Ghraib prison scandal, the fact that many innocent civilians had been rounded up and subjected to mistreatment was seldom discussed in the news, although it was widely known and reported in the region. Whatever one may think of torturing terrorists, it might have been relevant to consider if interrogation policies were applied with any more precision than the air strikes just noted. As for civilian casualties of the lengthy war in Iraq, the vast numbers of dead and displaced were barely noted in U.S. news. At the same time, many world relief organizations and news reports termed Iraq a vast humanitarian disaster. On the fifth anniversary of the war in 2008, U.S. headlines were filled with a speech by President Bush proclaiming conditions to be vastly improved and the Iraqi people supporting the continuing American liberation effort. And in 2010 when President Obama announced the end of the war (during a slow news period just ahead of the Labor Day holiday), there was little news analysis of the levels of chaos, political corruption, escalating violence or impending insurgency. Vice President Biden visited Baghdad as part of the ceremonies to end U.S. combat operations. He was asked about the violence throughout the country, and he replied simply, "It is much safer."[11] Meanwhile, reporters accompanying him wore helmets and body armor, and the delegation seldom left the heavily fortified Green Zone. The war was simply not a political issue in Washington any longer, and the press and public seemed happy to look the other way from a painful episode in history.

Artificial Balance

The editor of *The Independent,* Leonard Doyle, said regarding pressures to tone stories up or down that "the loudest demands for objectivity are made by groups or lobbies who want to ensure that they get equal time in any story."[12] Recall, for example, the story from Chapter 5 involving a reporter who investigated voting abuses in St. Louis and concluded that the Republicans appeared to be involved with disenfranchising far more voters than the Democrats, yet his editor insisted on playing the story as a more balanced look at the "charges" that each side lodged against the other. It is easy, of course, to make empty charges in politics; indeed, politics is full of such occurrences. The question is whether journalists should pass them along to the public as though they hold equal weight.

In another example, pressures on editors to be fair and balanced drove a second side to the story of global warming long after the vast majority of scientific experts felt that there was very little support for another side to that story. Similar stories can be told about a number of scientific areas (such as evolution and stem cell research) that were part of heated political battles and became two-sided science stories in the news. The point here is that political challenges may be lodged against almost anything, but reporting the claims from both sides in balanced fashion as though they have equal weight factually may leave audiences confused and unable to distinguish the credibility of any side. This not only undermines faith in science and knowable realities, but it signals that it is acceptable to challenge almost anything just for political gain. The result is that political partisans learn to subordinate facts to their ideologies, while those in the middle often become confused and disillusioned.[13]

The tendency to let politics define social realities is perhaps most pronounced in coverage of political campaigns. For example, in campaign 2004, the Bush team put out a press fact sheet proclaiming that "109 million American taxpayers will see their taxes decline by an average of $1,544." The implication was that most people would get this size cut. In reality, a small portion of wealthy taxpayers received huge cuts, jacking up the average, and leaving the majority to get far less than this figure. Rather than doing the math, most news stories simply ran the Democratic challenge to the claim, making it a partisan but balanced story, where it could have been sorted out easily in newsrooms on factual grounds. Quick to recognize this tendency in the press, the Kerry campaign invented its own special economic measure by cherry-picking economic indicators that looked bad for Bush, and naming the result the "misery index." Many news stories ran Kerry claims about Bush economic failure and Bush rebuttals without investigating the dubious origins and credibility of the index itself.[14]

Lies and Deception

It is a small step from adopting a forced balance in reporting to simply letting untruths and deceptions go unchallenged. An interesting moment that revealed how difficult it is for journalists to independently write stories about the truthfulness of official claims also occurred in the 2004 election following the vice presidential debates between Dick Cheney and John Edwards. Chris Matthews, host of MSNBC's *Hardball* pundit program, asked CBS correspondent Bob Schieffer about getting the facts right in campaign debates and other news settings. While Matthews felt that Cheney had won the vice presidential debates, he

Continued

was disturbed by a couple of glaring factual errors that Cheney made without being challenged by the press, either at the time or in subsequent coverage. One was Cheney's continuing assertion of a connection between Iraq and 9/11 long after repeated efforts to establish one had failed, and the other was Cheney's claim that he had never met Edwards while they had appeared sitting side by side at a major event earlier. Here is a portion of the exchange:

MATTHEWS: What do you think is more important? The drama of the hour and a half we watched together as a country. . . . Or the analysis later. . . . I'm talking about who was right on the facts. Do the facts . . . ever catch up to what these guys say in these major prime-time performances?

SCHIEFFER: Probably they don't. Substance is important. Content is important. But you know, Chris, as well as I do, the vote for president is much different than any other vote that we cast. . . . We vote for a president, it's a gut vote. It's a vote from the heart. It's who we feel most comfortable with in the time of a crisis. And so I think that's why manner, if a person appears in control, if he appears cool, collected, I think that's a big thing for people in deciding who they're going to vote for for president.[15]

Matthews came back on the point that Cheney seemed to be spreading an important misconception about the Iraq War, and in the end, Schieffer had no answer for what journalists can do independently when politicians are simply not telling the truth. What journalists do, of course, is let other political elites say that their opponents are lying, but this reduces the situation to the usual political finger pointing and shouting, while conveying the impression that it is acceptable to make the truth subject to political dispute without offering citizens anything beyond choosing the truth they prefer to believe.[16]

THE PARADOX OF OBJECTIVE REPORTING

"If only the press would be more objective. . . ." Every embattled politician since George Washington has accused the press of adversarial coverage, and most members of the public seem convinced that the news, at worst, has a liberal, rather than an establishment, slant.[17] Nowhere in this popular view is there much room for the idea that the news follows the lead of powerful elites and well-organized interest groups, while underreporting the interests of large numbers of silent Americans. Consider a *Newsweek* report on a new plan for improving the lives of poor people in Chicago. The article featured the mayor of the city who proclaimed: "What people want is education, jobs, and job training." Lines like this are repeated so often by politicians that they ring true by sheer force of familiarity. Yet an unreported survey by a community organization found that people actually wanted better health care, more things for children to do, and more cultural activities in their communities.[18]

This chapter confronts the paradox of objective journalism by showing that the news is biased not in spite of, but precisely because of, the professional journalism standards intended to prevent bias. The central idea is that the professional practices embodying journalism norms of independence and objectivity also create conditions that systematically favor the reporting of official perspectives. At the same time, the postures of independence and objectivity created by the use of these professional practices give the impression that the resulting news is the best available representation of reality. In short, professional journalism standards introduce a distorted political perspective into the news yet legitimize that perspective as broad and realistic.

DEFINING OBJECTIVITY: FAIRNESS, BALANCE, AND TRUTH

Journalists sometimes substitute terms, such as *accuracy, fairness, balance,* or *truth* in place of *objectivity* to describe the prime goal that guides their reporting. Objectivity is a tough standard to achieve, particularly with so many critics and citizens charging that journalists today do not even come close to achieving it. *Accuracy, balance,* and *fairness* are softer terms. They seem to be more reasonable reporting goals in light of all the obstacles to objectivity:

- The values inherent in political events
- The deceptions of newsmakers
- The difficulty of achieving a wholly neutral point of view
- The impossibility of covering all the sides and gathering all the facts
- The rush to meet unreasonably short deadlines
- The pressures of breaking information online and the 24/7 news cycle

Because of these difficulties, the press is sure to come under fire no matter how hard it tries to present the facts. To many embattled journalists, accuracy, balance, or fairness sound like more defensible goals. One sign of the times is that the Society of Professional Journalists' code of ethics dropped the word *objectivity* in 1996 after many years of featuring it as the core principle. However, journalist and historian David Mindich notes that *objectivity* was replaced in the code with terms, such as *truth, accuracy,* and *comprehensiveness.* In his view, the decision to replace *objectivity* with these synonyms signals that many journalists are tired of defending an embattled word, yet remain committed to its meaning and guiding spirit.[19] There is strong evidence that no matter which name it goes by, the vast majority of journalists subscribe to an ideal of objectivity. For example, in a national survey conducted by the Pew Research Center for the People and the Press, three-quarters of journalists polled agreed that their ideal standard is to report the "true, accurate, and widely agreed upon account of an event."[20]

Changing the names of reporting ideals might be more laudable if there were also changes in the actual practices that create the news information biases discussed in Chapter 2. The new terms, however, refer to much the same journalistic practices that once passed under the lofty claim of objectivity. Moreover, fairness, accuracy, or balance may be even more misleading than objectivity as a description of news content. At least objectivity stands in sharp contrast to the reality of personalized, dramatized, fragmented, and authority-oriented (whether normalized or chaotic) news. *Fairness* or *accuracy* are fuzzier terms that invite rationalizing these information biases as the best we can hope for given the limits within which well-meaning journalists operate.

Consider, for example, the case for the term *fairness*. One may say, isn't presenting the facts offered by both sides and giving them equal time about as close to accuracy as we can get? Isn't *fair* a better description of this approach than *objective*? Consider the number of dubious assumptions on which the term *fairness* rests. First, there is the problem of limiting complex, multisided issues to two sides. Second, there is the question of which two sides to admit through the news gate. The two sides that appear in most stories are anything but a broad sample of possible viewpoints. For example, fairness in reporting presidential addresses means that the opposition party will be given an opportunity to reply. Fair enough, right? But this definition is based on the poorly examined, commonsense notion that the two political parties are the two most legitimate other sides in American politics. This assumption is reinforced every time journalists build a story upon it, yet the gradual weakening of ties to parties by both voters and candidates in recent years raises serious doubts about this premise.

A second hallmark of fairness is equal time (as in allowing both sides to present their positions). Given equal time, the information edge goes to the most predictable, stereotypical, official pronouncements in almost every case. New ideas take more time and effort to communicate intelligibly than old, familiar ideas. The press could devote extra time to make new ideas accessible to people, but that would seem unfair to the dominant actors and their supporters. It is safer to stick with an easy idea of fairness that involves granting equal time to the statements of the two most vocal—and often most stereotypical—sides.

All this raises the possibility that seemingly simple ideas such as balance and equal time are not as simple as they may appear. To raise just one more troublesome issue, should balance be achieved in every news story or over a period of time? That is easy, you say. Indeed, most people look for balance in every story, meaning that they cry foul if a report emphasizes one point of view over another. However, as noted earlier, what if one point of view is seldom heard, and it is more complicated than the already established positions? Why not give new perspectives more time, without interruption from a perspective that is heard every day?

When people encounter new ideas alongside familiar ones, the psychological tendency is to discount the new and embrace the old. When we look at fairness this way, the attempt to achieve balance within every story between new ideas and familiar political formulas hardly seems fair at all. If the goal of the news is to present information so that new perspectives can be grasped along with the old, then a new conception of information balance over time might replace the currently popular assumption that balance within each story is the ideal.

These reporting standards are so familiar and sensible that they seem to have been put there to serve obvious and laudable purposes. Indeed, it is difficult to imagine any other function for adversarial roles or documentary reporting or standards of good taste than improving the quality and objectivity of the news. Yet, the following discussion suggests that the evolution of norms such as objectivity, fairness, and balance had more to do with the somewhat haphazard course of the developing news business than with the rational or determined pursuit of truth. In short, practices were dictated more by historical, technological, or business circumstances than by rational human design. The resulting reporting practices later became rationalized as good and even noble things.

The historical story of these modern reporting standards involves a radical shift over the course of the nineteenth century from a press supported largely by political parties to one supported by business models based on the sale of advertising. Journalism historian Gerald Baldasty describes this transformation in these terms: "In the early nineteenth century, editors defined news as a political instrument intended to promote party interests. By century's end, editors defined news within a business context to ensure or increase revenues. News had become commercialized."[21] This commercialization, and its continuing evolution to this day, resulted in what we now understand to be sensible and proper ways to report on the world we live in.

THE CURIOUS ORIGINS OF OBJECTIVE JOURNALISM

It is tempting to think that modern journalism practices derive logically from the norm of objective journalism. However, there is considerable evidence that the practices preceded the norm. The first modern journalism practices can be traced to mid-nineteenth-century economic and social conditions surrounding the rise of mass-market news.[22] According to David Mindich's historical analysis, various components of objective journalism emerged at very different points in time and often under odd circumstances. For example, the "inverted pyramid" style may have originated with a nonjournalist, secretary of war Edwin Stanton, who wrote a series of important communiqués about the Civil War.[23]

Mindich claims that the foundations for all the practices that go into objective reporting were established, one at a time, by the end of the 1800s.[24] However, the idea that what many reporters were already doing might be called "objective journalism" did not appear until after the turn of the century. In many ways, this retrospective ideal of objectivity can be viewed as both an ennobling claim on the part of a journalism trade looking to become a profession, and as a rhetorical appeal to an increasingly educated middle-class news audience who responded favorably to those claims about professionalism.

In the early days of the American republic, the news was anything but objective. Most newspapers were either funded by or otherwise sympathetic to particular political parties, interests, or ideologies. Reporting involved the political interpretation of events. People bought a newspaper knowing what its political perspective was and knowing that political events would be filtered through that perspective. In many respects, this is a sensible way to approach the news about politics. If one knows the biases of a reporter, it is possible to control for them in interpreting the account of events. Moreover, if reporting is explicitly politically oriented, different reporters can look at the same event from different points of view. The idea was that people would encounter different points of view and bring them into face-to-face debates about what the best course of action might be—an idea that came directly from some of the nation's founders, such as Jefferson.

The commitment to political analysis in news reporting began to fade as the nature of politics itself changed after the age of Jackson from the late 1830s on. As Baldasty notes, politicians became less dependent on party papers to communicate with voters as, among other things, strict norms against candidates campaigning directly in public began to change.[25] With these changes, party financial support for papers began to dry up. The early papers were modest operations with small, local readerships. These small and increasingly impoverished newspapers could not compete for large audiences as the nation and its communication system grew.

As the country grew, the economics of the news business changed. For example, the population began to move to the cities, creating mass audiences for the news. Also, the expansion of the American territory during the nineteenth century created a need for the rapid and large-scale distribution of national news. Breakthroughs in printing and communication technologies made possible the production of cheap mass media news that could be gathered in the morning on the East Coast and distributed by evening on the West Coast.

These and other patterns in the development of the nation produced dramatic changes in the news. By 1848, a group of newspapers made the first great step toward standardized news by forming the Associated Press (AP).[26] Pooling reporters and selling the same story to hundreds, and eventually thousands, of subscribing newspapers meant that the news had become a profitable mass-market commodity. Of course, the broad marketability of the news meant that it had to be stripped of its overt political messages so that it would be appealing to news organizations of all political persuasions. An early prototype of objective reporting was born. Moreover, the need to send short messages through an overloaded mail system was followed by the transmission of national news over telegraph wires that also dictated a simplified, standardized reporting format. The *who, what, where, when,* and *why* of an event could be transmitted economically and reconstructed and embellished easily on the other end.

As the market for mass media news grew, the demand for reporters grew along with it. Whereas writing a persuasive political essay required skill in argumentation and political analysis, it was far easier to compose stories, which are the basic media for communicating about everyday events. The use of stories also guaranteed that the news would be intelligible to the growing mass-news audience.

In this manner, the overlapping effects of communication technology, economic development, and social change gave rise to large-scale news-gathering and news-marketing organizations. Along with these organizations came a standardized set of reporting practices. As mentioned previously, news services like the AP ushered in the *documentary report*. The use of wire transmission, along with untrained reporters, promoted the shift to the *story form*. The discovery that drama sold newspapers promoted the first *adversarial reporting*. Early reporters were rather like provocateurs stirring up controversy and conflict in order to generate dramatic material for their stories.

As news bureaucracies grew in response to the papers' economic success, editorial review practices became expedient means of processing the huge flow of news. *Standards of good taste* guaranteed that a news product would be inoffensive to the mass market. Much of today's news format in the mainstream establishment press evolved at the turn of the century with the growth of a large, educated middle class of affluent consumers who wanted serious reporting and bought the household products that were advertised along with the news. There was initially stiff competition between this highbrow press and the tabloids or "scandal sheets" (also known as the yellow press) at the turn of the twentieth century. These highly sensationalized versions of news were marketed to a less-educated, working-class population seeking escape as much as information from the media.

By the 1920s, urban life and local politics became dominated by an affluent middle class of business and professional people with formal education. Representing the news as objective, nonpartisan, and tasteful was an effective marketing ploy geared to the lifestyle of this group. Consider, for example, the early slogans of the *New York Times*, "All the News That's Fit to Print" and "It Will Not Soil the Breakfast Cloth."[27] This professional image dressed existing practices in a new style. This image also became a convenient means to discredit the muckrakers on the journalistic left and the sensationalistic scandal sheets on the political right.[28]

Finally, there was a growing expectation among intellectuals following World War I that democracy was in trouble and could be saved by a professional press dedicated to the mission of providing objective information to the public.[29] This noble purpose helped define a movement for a professional press and a code of objective journalism. Led by persuasive spokesmen like Walter Lippmann,[30] journalists began to regard objective reporting as both a description of their existing work practices and as a high moral imperative.

In these ways, journalism, like most professions, developed a set of business practices first and then endowed those practices with an impressive professional rationale. Successive generations of reporters began to regard their work as a skilled occupation that should demand higher status and better wages. The move toward a professional status both enhanced the social image of reporting and paved the way for higher wages by restricting the entry of newcomers off the street into the journalism ranks. Professionalism meant that formal training and screening could be required for skills that had been acquired formerly on the job.[31] As a result, journalism programs emerged at universities and began to formalize and refine the received practices as professional standards. Perhaps the best capsule summary of this curious transition of journalism from a business into a profession is Lou Cannon's observation that what began "as a technique became a value."[32]

PROFESSIONAL JOURNALISM IN PRACTICE

Because the ideas of accuracy, balance, truth, and fairness have their roots in what was originally called *objective reporting*, the following discussion will use the term *objectivity* to preserve historical continuity. If the reader prefers the alternate terms, feel free to substitute them; bear in mind, though, that the words may change, but the underlying practices remain much the same.

A review of journalism texts by David Mindich finds a common set of perspectives and practices that reporters are taught and that bring objectivity into their daily work. These defining ingredients of objectivity include *detachment, nonpartisanship, reliance on "facts," balance,* and the use of the *inverted pyramid* writing style (which puts the most important facts in the lead paragraph).[33] The following discussion shows how the ideal of objectivity is embedded in these and other defining journalistic methods; it thus remains a key to understanding the general workings of news organizations. Drawing from the review by Mindich and other sources, the standards and practices that embody objective journalism include the following:[34]

1. The professional journalist assumes *the role of a politically neutral adversary,* critically examining both sides of an issue and thereby ensuring impartial coverage. Journalists see adversarialism as an important counterpoint to becoming too close to their sources, ensuring detachment and balance in their reporting. As discussed in the last chapter, the adversarial role has been corrupted by "gotcha" journalism in recent years, but many journalists and scholars continue to think of this as adversarialism.
2. The journalist resists the temptation to discuss the seamy, sensationalistic side of the news by *observing prevailing social standards of decency and good taste.* Standards of taste establish boundaries as a story makes its way toward becoming "objectified." Like adversarialism, this norm has also become strained with the increase of sex scandals and tabloid coverage in the mainstream press. Many critics wonder if news organizations are losing their commitment to sticking to important issues and avoiding rumor and gossip.
3. The truthfulness and factuality of the news is guaranteed by *the use of documentary reporting practices* that permit reporters to transmit to the public "just the facts" that can be observed or supported with credible sources.
4. News objectivity is also established by *the use of a standardized format for reporting the news: the story.* Stories serve as implicit checks on news content by requiring reporters to gather all the facts (who, what, when, where, how, etc.) needed to construct a consistent and plausible account of an incident. Because stories are also the most common means of everyday communication about events, they enable the public to judge the consistency and plausibility of news accounts. Within the story format, journalists use other conventions, such as writing in an inverted pyramid style, meaning, as noted earlier, that the most important elements of the story appear in the lead paragraph.

5. Because they share the methods just listed, news organizations often favor the idea that reporters should be generalists, not specialists. The use of standardized reporting formats enables any reporter to cover any kind of story, further separating reporters from personal bias vis-à-vis the subject matter of the news. The *practice of training reporters as generalists,* as opposed to specialists, also helps minimize undesirable interpretive tendencies in news reporting.[35] In recent years, specialization has appeared in areas such as the environment, health, science, and technology, but many key areas such as business and politics still favor generalists.

6. Practices 1 through 5 are regulated and enforced by the important practice of *editorial review,* which is a check against violations of the practices and norms of the profession.

Each of the defining elements of objective journalism just listed makes a direct contribution to news bias by creating or reinforcing conditions favorable to the reporting of news filtered by Washington officialdom. This should not be surprising in light of the previous capsule history of the news profession. The basic practices that later became known as professional journalism were developed to sell mainstream social and political values to a mass audience. As diverse political perspectives gradually disappeared from the news or became discredited as not objective, it became easier to convince people that the officiated political perspective that remained was somehow objective. The logic of such a claim is simple: As one reality comes to dominate all others, that dominant reality begins to seem objective. The absence of credible competition supports the illusion of objectivity. The following discussion shows how each element of objective journalism actively promotes narrow political messages in the news.

The Adversarial Role of the Press

If the media were always adversarial in their dealings with politicians, they would face a serious dilemma: The news could end up discrediting the institutions and values on which it depends for credibility. To a remarkable degree, then, maintaining the illusion of news objectivity depends on the general reliance on and acceptance of official views to certify reports as credible and valid. As sociologist Gaye Tuchman put it:

> Challenging the legitimacy of offices holding centralized information dismantles the news net. If all of officialdom is corrupt, all its facts and occurrences must be viewed as alleged facts and alleged occurrences. Accordingly, to fill the news columns and air time of the news product, news organizations would have to find an alternative and economical method of locating occurrences and constituent facts acceptable as news. For example, if the institutions of everyday life are delegitimated, the facts tendered by the Bureau of Marriage Licenses would be suspect. One could no longer call the bureau to learn whether Robert Jones and Fay

Smith had married. In sum, amassing mutually self-validating facts simultaneously accomplishes the doing of newswork and reconstitutes the everyday world of offices and factories, of politics and bureaucrats, of bus schedules and class rosters as historically given.[36]

It is equally true, of course, that the news would also lose its image of objectivity if reporters openly catered to the propaganda interests of public officials and government institutions. If neither extreme adversarialism nor its polar opposite support the illusion of news objectivity, then there is an obvious implication: most adversarial behavior on the part of the press should reveal itself as ritualistic, and in keeping within the cooperative interests of reporters and officials. A ritualistic posture of antagonism between press and government creates the appearance of mutual independence while keeping most news content to political perspectives certified by authorities. Such ritualistic posturing dramatizes the myths of a free press and an open government that have long defined American democracy. It is the nature of rituals to evoke such myths and beliefs without challenging them.[37]

Adversarialism as Ritual   If the adversarial relationship is a ritual that both mystifies and legitimizes the reporting of narrow political messages, then the following characteristics should be observed: (a) the incidence of criticism and confrontation should occur regularly, as a matter of everyday reporting orientation, as opposed to just when there is a serious political issue at stake; (b) challenges and charges will aim to provoke personal mistakes or political confrontations between politicians rather than deeper investigations of issues; (c) charges against officials will be restricted to them personally and generally separated from their institutions and offices; and finally, (d) these characteristics should pertain equally to routine news coverage (e.g., reporters' beats) and nonroutine coverage (e.g., crises and scandals).

As illustration of these points, consider C. Jack Orr's study of earlier presidential press conferences.[38] Analyzing data from a sample of Kennedy, Johnson, and Nixon press conferences, Orr found that the proportion of hostile or critical questions was virtually constant across presidents, conferences, issue categories, and political contexts.[39] Not only did the incidence of confrontational questions fall into a routine pattern, but nearly all hostile questions were personal in nature. Yet many of those personal questions also signaled clear deference to office and institution. Moreover, questions that could have held the line on an issue contained open invitations to the president to redefine the issue or dismiss the entire question. Based on these patterns, Orr concluded that the adversarial postures of press and president create a dramatic image of journalistic aggressiveness while communicating a subtle message of institutional deference.

In an age in which personal image and public approval are key elements of political power, politicians increasingly avoid even ritualistic skirmishes with the press pack. As a result, fewer press conferences have been held in recent decades, indicating that presidents prefer to deliver their messages to the public in more controlled settings. With news organizations increasingly keying on the most personal and dramatic aspects of politicians' lives, stepping in front of the pack can prove challenging to a president. For example, George H. W. Bush stepped to the podium with a world leader to announce the results of important talks (part of the politician's ritual) only to be asked about whether he had had a love affair a few years earlier. When Bill Clinton introduced Supreme Court nominee Ruth Bader Ginsberg to the press, she told a moving story about her difficulties as a woman in a male-dominated world. After her statement, the opening question from the press pack challenged the president's political motives for her appointment and so angered Clinton that he lectured the journalists on their common decency.

Broad ritualistic elements have also been observed in the reporting of less routine events such as scandals and crises—to the extent that a number of observers have argued that crises and scandals are becoming routine news events, complete with standard reporting formulas.[40] For example, Altheide and Snow showed how a scandal involving an aide to Jimmy Carter was cast quickly into a standard reporting formula that emphasized political damage to the president while offering little measure of the importance of the issue itself.[41] Similar patterns ran through the Whitewater scandal involving Bill and Hillary Clinton, as they were subjected to guilt by association with a number of shady real estate dealings. Despite saturation coverage implying the possibility of serious wrongdoing, few members of the public ever understood what the scandal was about. Yet these scandals and rumors leave residues of image damage and doubt, as illustrated by Barack Obama's continuous engagement with questions about his birth and religious beliefs.

Tag-Team Journalism   The format of virtually every news interview and talk program is designed to promote adversarial displays, from the stage settings that place press and politicians in confrontational poses to the tag-team question-and-answer formats to tone of voice and terms of address. Cable personalities, such as Glen Beck, Bill O'Reilly, or Keith Olberman are examples of frenzied adversarialism. The journalists and other guests on their shows not only display little respect for politicians, but they seem to delight in being rude to each other as well. Yet, the rituals have limits, as illustrated by Jon Stewart's famous 2004 appearance on CNN's former dueling-pundit program *Crossfire*. Stewart asked the hosts why they didn't become a real news program rather than an entertainment theater for political spinmeisters who were ruining American politics. The response from conservative host Tucker Carlson resembled the talk-show equivalent of a cafeteria food fight. Carlson soon left the program under fire, and the whole program was later canceled—perhaps because this revealing moment reached a larger Internet audience than the program ever attracted on cable.[42]

For their part, politicians contribute to the enduring antagonism ritual by routinely attacking the press as liberal, biased, or hostile. Such attacks frequently appear in elite publications and occupy the agendas of business, government, and journalism symposia.[43] Occasionally, such charges are dramatized through formal political attacks, such as the ones during the McCarthy era and the Nixon administration. One analyst found the Nixon-Agnew attacks on the press so ritualized that he interpreted them in terms of ethological concepts of animal aggression and territorial defense.[44]

None of this means that politicians or the press take their often-antagonistic relations lightly. Indeed, the mark of a good ritual is that those involved are deeply moved by it. For example, Bill Clinton raged in a *Rolling Stone* interview with William Greider that he was the most poorly treated and misrepresented of presidents.[45] Clinton was hardly alone. The list of presidents claiming this distinction is a long one, dating from George Washington and Thomas Jefferson to Lyndon Johnson and Richard Nixon. Few have taken their press treatment as personally as Nixon, who kept a personal enemies list, which included a good number of journalists who were singled out for wiretaps, IRS audits, and other special punishments.[46] Although the press ritual can be quite animated and engrossing, both for those who play it and for the audiences who watch it, this should not distract us from understanding what this ritual accomplishes: narrowing the focus of human attention to convincingly exclude large categories of experience from public discourse.

The Uneasy Partnership Between Reporters and Officials For all of the structure and routine that define the news, there are still times when the press provides a fairly wide range of critical information to the American people. As explained in Chapter 1, some information diversity enters the news through journalistic routines such as indexing content to the degree of conflict among actors whom journalists regard as having potential impact on the course of a story. All the same, narrating the state of society and politics is a delicate business, and journalists have considerable choice over how to build up and how to end these stories. This means that press–government rituals still have an edge to them. Indeed, both sides have enough to gain and lose to make the displays of aggression genuine.[47]

The ritual works as long as neither side undermines its credibility by raising questions about the system that legitimizes their roles. Even Watergate, long regarded as the model of modern investigative reporting, stopped short of challenging the authority of government or pushing too far into institutional failings, such as flaws in the secrecy and espionage systems that may have contributed to presidential abuses of power. For the most part, the press pack settled for the limits established by congressional investigations. The press ultimately pronounced the normalizing conclusion that "the system worked."

Despite the rich possibilities for a story that might go well beyond the personal failings of one flawed president, the press avoided them all in favor of reporting the steady stream of leaks from a fabled inside source nicknamed Deep Throat (later revealed to be the second in command at the FBI), along with the activities of various congressional investigations at work on the case. This brand of investigative reporting ignored questions about institutional problems or abnormalities in favor of dramatizing the personal culpability of the most publicly visible actors involved.[48] Whereas all the institutional paths for the story led to questions of change and reform (questions the press chose largely to avoid), the personal drama held out the promise of returning the political system to normal as soon as the individuals were accused, charged, and removed from office. True to the chosen normalizing plot, when Nixon resigned from office under threat of impeachment, NBC correspondent Roger Mudd led the nation in the cheer "The System Worked!"

The melodramatic resolution—a tearful Nixon saying goodbye to the White House staff and an upbeat ending of good news for the system—seemed to make sense at the time. In retrospect, however, it seems that the news exonerated a system containing the institutional weaknesses that permitted the abuses of power to occur in the first place. Even at the level of personal melodrama, "The System Works" seems an ironic ending. After all, the system pardoned the worst offender, gave light sentences to most of the others, and turned many criminals into millionaires and media celebrities in the process.

The more recent (2005–2006) coverage of domestic spying by the Bush administration follows a similar path. The press broke the investigative story (although the *New York Times* withheld publication for over a year after being lobbied by the government), and then let government sources define its importance and outcomes. Rather than rely on the available volume of independent evidence and sources to advance one side of the story on whether the president broke the law, coverage soon reverted to a battle between the president's assertion that he had the power to do it and a weak congressional response led from within his own party suggesting that existing procedures should be followed more carefully.

From Watergate to the Bush spying episode, a delicate balance between deference to authority and adversarialism continues to exist, but it seems increasingly challenged by a loss of perspective on how to strike that balance. With the increase in "gotcha" journalism, authorities are routinely challenged on personal grounds involving their morality, their gamesmanship, or their credibility. It is ironic that journalists seem able to advance stories on the basis of scandal and innuendo but unable to sustain independent questions about corruption of national institutions or the democratic process. Whether this is more a cause or a consequence of lowered public trust in government is a good question. What is clear is that news audiences see journalists as less objective than at any point since polling has tracked this issue. Popular objections to journalists advancing stories with sensationalism and negativity also challenge another tenet of the modern-day journalism profession: the commitment to standards of decency and good taste.

Standards of Decency and Good Taste

Standards of decency and taste seem designed to keep the focus of news on important issues and away from the seamy, sensationalistic aspects of political life. These standards have clearly changed in recent years. The sex-drenched coverage of the Clinton-Lewinsky affair suggests a tabloid trend in the press. During that scandal, audiences learned of oral sex in the Oval Office, presidential semen stains on a blue dress, and graphic sexual accounts published in the report of special prosecutor Kenneth Starr. Such a media spectacle would be hard to imagine even ten years earlier.

While an earlier era of media morality would have avoided such things, current moral standards seem to involve publicizing them with expressions of shock and disapproval. Even as they drag up seamy details, journalists are also quick to pronounce moralistic judgments. It would have been useful during the Lewinsky affair to do a count of the number of raised eyebrows on the Sunday morning news shows or the numbers of shocked and disdainful expressions uttered by the cast of journalists turned shouting pundits. Whereas an earlier generation of journalistic morality police may not have published such material in the first place, a later generation driven to sensationalism will publish first and then decry its sorry content.

Although the media seem to have become obsessed with the private lives of politicians and other public figures, there are other areas that are avoided with great consistency. For example, graphic images of gruesome death, profane language, erotic art, or depictions of the human anatomy seldom appear in the news. Even as standards of news taste evolve, there remains a curious strain of middle-American morality that the mainstream press long ago adopted as part of its professional code. Even coverage of scandals generally carries the moral message of family values and the enduring obligation of politicians to uphold them. As for the collection of things regarded as too tasteless, offensive, or obscene to include in the news, excluding them legitimizes the middle-class values that may often be at odds with the actual events that reporters witness. To put it bluntly, reporters and editors may censor their coverage to bring news images in line with social values and sensitivities. The practical application of standards of good taste creates two paradoxes for news content. Standards of taste have a bias in favor of precisely those status quo values that the bulk of political propaganda promotes.[49] Moreover, the avoidance of offensive ideas removes from public awareness many undesirable but true aspects of the real world. As a result, the definitions of and the solutions for the problems represented in the news, however artificial, may appeal to the ideals of the middle-class, church-going public.

The Morality Police   Censoring news according to standards of taste runs counter to a key feature of politics. Politics is the primary social activity through which widely divergent values and morals come together in struggles for dominance and legitimacy. The selective attention to preferred morals not only passively promotes the work of propagandists, as mentioned previously, but it actively distorts the values and issues at stake in many situations. In this latter role, standards of taste may lead to overt censorship of some aspects of news events, thereby making journalists active agents in shaping the definitions of political situations. Should journalists join forces with society's morality police? Consider the following cases and decide for yourself.

A classic example of how standards of taste can affect the definition of political events is illustrated by the news coverage of a statement made by agriculture secretary Earl Butz during the 1976 presidential campaign. While flying between campaign appearances, Butz made a blatantly racist remark to a group of reporters. This remark was not only significant on its own merits due to its appalling racist content, but it was also pertinent to the campaign because it was offered in response to a question about Republican election strategies. Although the statement contains offensive language of the sort not often found in scholarly writing (not to mention news stories), its political magnitude can be conveyed only by quoting it directly. When asked about the efforts of the Republican Party to mobilize the black vote, Butz remarked that it was pointless to worry about the black vote because blacks were unconcerned about politics. He then summarized his view of the concerns of blacks as follows: "I'll tell you what coloreds want. It's three things: first, a tight pussy; second, loose shoes; and third, a warm place to shit."[50]

It is arguably in the public interest to publicize a racist remark uttered by a U.S. cabinet officer while campaigning for the president who appointed him. However, the professional press regarded Butz's offense to good taste as a higher consideration than his offense to political sensibilities. The pervasive commitment to the decency code was reflected in a simple fact: not one major news outlet ran the Butz remark at the time it was made. Only when the statement was quoted later, at the end of a rambling article on the campaign in the (then) underground magazine *Rolling Stone*, did the respectable press have to acknowledge that the incident had in fact happened. Even when major press and broadcast outlets ran the story, only one major daily paper (the Madison, Wisconsin, *Capitol Times*) used the verbatim language. In defense of their use of inoffensive euphemisms in place of the real language, editors and news producers pronounced the litany of the decency code. An editor at the *New York Times* put it this way: ". . . we recognized that if we used this series of filthy obscenities then we'll probably use the next." The editor of the *Des Moines Register* said he found the remark so offensive and so atrocious that "I couldn't bring myself to give it to people with their breakfast." The editor of the *Washington Post* produced a tortured chain of logic leading to the conclusion that only if the president himself had uttered the remarks would he have printed them, but lesser officials did not merit such a violation of the journalism code.[51]

The impact of the statement was lost when euphemisms were substituted for the actual language. As a result, the Ford campaign was spared the painful embarrassment of this rare lapse from its agenda of carefully staged and scripted performances. When the national press finally acknowledged the incident, Ford had little choice but to fire Butz. However, one suspects that Butz's desire to exit the situation gracefully and Ford's wish to minimize his political losses could not have been satisfied any better than through the delicate treatment accorded to the episode by the journalistic community.

Changes in some of these news standards have been created by online media that offer audiences direct information about actual events. For example, in 2002 Senate Republican leader Trent Lott issued some remarks applauding retired colleague Strom Thurmond at a birthday celebration for his crusading presidential campaign in 1948. The campaign was based on a blatantly racist platform. Reporters on the scene reported the grand celebration, but not the remarks. Soon, however, the Internet was ablaze as bloggers (led by Republicans who did not want their party associated with such reactionary ideas) soon brought the remarks to public attention and facilitated the leap of the story into the headlines. YouTube videos have led to the downfall of political candidates. The age of crowdsourced reporting has added pressures to conventional journalism standards, yet most mainstream news organizations continue to try to hold the line on those standards.

Sex, Death, and Censorship   The decency code is so entrenched that it even applies to coverage of important health and biological issues. For example, it took more than two years for the mainstream media to explain that one way in which the dreaded disease AIDS (acquired immune deficiency syndrome) is spread is through anal intercourse. The threat posed by a large-scale, life-threatening AIDS epidemic would seem to call for rapid delivery of as much explicit information as possible to the public. Yet in the early, panicky years of the disease, the decency code governed information content about AIDS. Early stories suggested that the disease was transmitted "not through casual contact," and through the "exchange of bodily fluids." As one editor put it, "We would make the reader guess what was going on rather than use the term 'anal intercourse' . . . We wouldn't spell it out." A television reporter recalls receiving pressure from her producer to refrain from using explicit language in response to a few phone calls from morally offended viewers. It took years for consensus to emerge in the media that informing the public about health risks was more important than censoring offensive language from the news.[52]

What is the obligation of the press to communicate information that people may not want to hear, read, or see? Imagine, for a moment, that you were an editor for a news organization covering the Gulf War in 1991. The United States just routed the Iraqi army from Kuwait City, and the fleeing army has been attacked by American airpower, creating a scene that was widely described as "the highway of death." The carnage was so distressing that some of the American pilots involved asked the commanders to stop it. Behind the scenes, a high-level debate was raging about whether to go on with the war, knowing that it would produce a massacre of the enemy's disorganized army, or whether to stop it and leave the enemy with a substantial portion of its fighting force intact for the future. A photojournalist visited the highway of death and took a terrifying picture of the remains of an Iraqi soldier burned alive with a hideous expression on his face, his arms raised in the macabre position in which he died while trying to climb out of his flaming vehicle. It was an image right out of a horror movie.

Would you run the picture? Why not run a picture in the news that is no worse than an image that millions of people might pay money to see in a horror movie? More to the point, why not run a photo that appeared in leading English and French newspapers on the grounds that it brought home the fact that at least 100,000 Iraqis died in the war, and people should be forced to consider the human consequences of decisions to go to war? However, the newspaper and magazine editors of America never even had the chance to struggle with these issues because the leading photo wire service that had the option to buy and distribute the picture censored it at the source. The picture never even went out over the wires.

The AP editor explained that he did not buy and distribute the photo because he already knew what the reaction of newspaper editors would be: "Newspapers will tell us, 'We can't present pictures like that for people to look at over breakfast.'"[53] The picture editor at *Time* magazine later said this about the picture: "It's dramatic. It's horrific. It says it all about war." However, he admitted that even if he had seen it in time, *Time* probably would not have printed it because, "Whenever we run a picture like that, we're heavily criticized. We get a lot of reader mail."[54]

Should such images be part of the news? Are they worse than images commonly shown in movies? How should the news limit its representations of reality? The case of the photo of the Iraqi soldier and many similar episodes from the Gulf War raise the troublesome question of whether people in a country at war should see comforting images of war as they prefer to think about it or whether they should be stimulated, even shocked, into thinking about the consequences of the political decision to go to war.

Notice that the decisions of both the wire service editor and the picture editor at *Time* magazine hint at the economic costs of running the photo. The wire editor in effect said that nobody would buy it anyway, so there was no point in wasting the money to acquire and distribute it. The *Time* editor noted that subscribers would object to it. Their reasoning suggests that, as with the grand principle of objectivity, the moralism of the press also has economic roots. A key part of the market strategy of the turn-of-the-nineteenth-century press was to appeal to the moral sensibilities of the most affluent, rapidly growing, and untapped mass news market: the middle class. Since that time, the news has continued to present a restricted picture of American society in two ways: First, by representing the world through middle-class values, the news became an implicit model for social propriety; second, by introducing selective moral perspectives into news coverage, the press tacitly became the legitimator of the same values it helped to promote.

The strength of middle-class moralism in the news business is formidable. For example, even a tabloid paper like the *New York Daily News* did not print the word *syphilis* until 1931, long after it had become a major social problem. Similarly, the prototype of the highbrow family newspaper, the *New York Times*, refused to review Kinsey's landmark study of sexual behavior until years later when it had been certified by the academic community as a serious scholarly work. One also suspects that human sexual behavior was a significant and widely practiced phenomenon long before the *Times* endorsed it as a subject worthy of discussion.[55]

The frenzied coverage of the Clinton-Lewinsky sexual affair, and the more recent coverage of the use of prostitute services by New York Governor Eliot

Spitzer (who quickly resigned), suggest that the standards for reporting on the private lives of public figures are changing. Yet many other areas of moral standard-bearing are still protected by mainstream journalism. As with other reporting codes and practices discussed in this chapter, filtering the real world through the value lenses of middle America lends the news a familiar, safe quality. This morality filter contributes to the illusion of objectivity not because the resulting news content mirrors the diversity of the social world, but because it reflects the values of the news audience.

Documentary Reporting Practices

Objective reporting assumes that journalists do not embellish their stories, advocate particular interpretations of ambiguous events, or otherwise make up the news. These principles define the practice of documentary reporting. Reporters trained in the documentary method report only the information that they have witnessed and only the facts that credible sources have confirmed. Although the goals of documentary reporting are hard to fault, in practice the method creates a trap for journalists confronted with staged political performances. Only in rare cases when performances are flawed or when behind-the-scenes staging is revealed can reporters document in good professional fashion what they know otherwise to be the case: the news event in question was staged for propaganda purposes. The problem, as Daniel Boorstin has pointed out, is that manufactured news events, or pseudo-events, contain their own self-supporting and self-fulfilling documentation. Thus the documentary method highlights the very aspects of events that were designed to be reported, blurring the underlying reality of the situation.[56] The paradox of the documentary method is clear: the more perfectly an event is staged, the more documentable and hence reportable it becomes.

In response to this dilemma, news organizations have begun to expose some of these planned media events.[57] However, the proportion of stories exposing media events is minuscule in relation to those based on media events. This imbalance between reported and actual occurrences of staged events has a distorting effect similar to adversarialism. However, by exposing even a fraction of the political manipulation in the news, journalists may reassure the public that they are monitoring such manipulation and alerting the public when it occurs.

A more common practice reflecting the "new cynicism" that seems to characterize the press in recent times is to frame political situations as games between manipulative actors. This tendency has been described by various scholars, including Kathleen Jamieson and Thomas Patterson, as noted in Chapter 1. The focus on political motives and maneuvers may or may not capture the essence of contemporary politics, but it conveys an essence of politics that seems to ring true for many disillusioned citizens, who, perhaps correctly, see the press as part of the game. As a result, the documentary method has bent in ways that reflect the odd changes that have resulted in "gotcha" adversarialism and steamy moralism. Reporting the political game, rather than the institutional safeguards or social values at stake in it, may continue to look like objective reporting to journalists, but it may undermine the sense of news authority on the part of audiences.

The Use of Stories as Standardized News Formats

Although adopting the story as the basic news unit also had economic roots, stories quickly became justified under the norm of objective journalism. Stories can be defended as standardized and mechanical means of communicating information. This representation gives journalists a claim to a universal methodology of objective reporting. The problem with this definition is that it is a very selective rendition of what storytelling is all about. Telling a story requires choices about what information to include, what words to assign to the included information, and how to tie together all the chosen symbols into a coherent whole. These choices in turn depend on assessing the audience, deciding what point to make to that audience, and choosing what plot techniques (flashbacks, sequencing, character development, climax, etc.) will best make that point. In short, stories are not mirrors of events.[58]

A well-constructed story may be plausible, but plausibility and truth in the world of storytelling have little necessary connection.[59] An obvious implication of these features of storytelling is that they give reporters room to emphasize dramatic and narrative aspects of events.[60] Epstein suggests that the use of artistic (i.e., literary and dramatic) forms in news construction is encouraged by editors, one of whom even issued a memo containing formal instructions about how to incorporate dramatic structure into stories.[61] Gans notes the frequency with which reporters "restage" aspects of stories to heighten their dramatic qualities.[62]

The dramatic license in storytelling creates a tension: The wholesale invention of news plots would place enormous strains on the norm of objective reporting. This tension between the value of dramatic news and the commitment to documentary reporting helps explain the receptivity of news organizations to events that are staged dramatically by news sources. Staged events are designed to be documented, and their dramatic features are built in. So important is the dramatic element in political performances that they are often judged for newsworthiness on this criterion. Gans observed that:

> an exciting story boosts morale; and when there is a long drought of exciting stories, they [reporters] become restless. . . . Some magazine writers, left "crabby" by a drought of dramatic domestic news, joked about their readiness to be more critical of the President and other public officials for their failure to supply news that would "make adrenalin flow."[63]

The Limited Stock of News Plots   The use of stories further constrains news content by promoting the use of standardized plots in news reporting. Any communication network based on stories will become biased toward particular themes. For example, criminal trials are dominated by such familiar plots as mistaken identity, victim of circumstances, and others relevant to the legal judgment of cases.[64] The national obsession with the O. J. Simpson murder case in 1994 and 1995 can be explained in part by the rich set of plots and subplots that ran through the developing story: celebrity, murder, circumstantial evidence, allegations of framing, the fallen hero, the abusive relationship, sex, and shady characters. Add to these dramatic ingredients the element of race, and an already big human-interest story became even richer with political plot possibilities. One newspaper headline even proclaimed: "Modern Shakespearean Tragedy Rivets Nation."[65]

When a unique event engages familiar dramatic themes, the stage is set for an interesting story. This principle of communication holds true whether in a conversation between friends or in a journalistic account about lofty national issues. Storytelling between friends frequently centers on recurring themes that define the relationship and express the identities that the individuals have created in it. In politics, consensus and legitimacy can be promoted through the frequent use of dominant values, beliefs, and myths of the political culture.[66] Gans has noted the news is dominated by a remarkably small number of recurring themes. These plot devices include ethnocentrism (America first, America-the-generous, America-the-embattled, etc.), altruistic democracy, responsible capitalism, and individualism, among others.[67]

Political performances scripted around routine themes legitimize the status quo at the price of severely limiting the range of political discourse.[68] The formula-story syndrome enables reporters to use plots to screen and organize facts so that few details are left dangling, and the resulting story can be viewed as an exhaustive representation of reality. This naive approach to objectivity gives news writing a mystical quality described by Robert Darnton:

> Big stories develop in special patterns and have an archaic flavor, as if they were metamorphoses or *Ur*-stories that have been lost in the depths of time. . . . News writing is heavily influenced by stereotypes and by preconceptions of what "the story" should be. Without preestablished categories of what constitutes "news," it is impossible to sort out experience.[69]

Just as stories lock in the narrow political messages of routine news events, they can introduce distortions into investigative reporting. Stories, by definition, encapsulate events, making them seem self-contained and independent of external forces. Yet the tips provided by inside sources to investigative reporters are often (usually, one suspects) motivated by the source's own political considerations. These motives are seldom included in the stories fashioned by reporters. Recall, for example, the earlier discussion that the Watergate story based on the investigative reporting of Woodward and Bernstein may have been only part of a much larger political scandal (see Chapter 2). The source of the inside information necessary to keep the story unfolding seemed to provide only information that would turn the story toward the Oval Office. Epstein noted that there might have been other political actors, who could have been caught up in the Watergate scandal had the reporters not encapsulated the issues in a story centered on the president and his men.[70]

It took 30 years to find out who provided the information that trapped Nixon within the damaging Watergate story. It is ironic that the reporting practices involved so delayed finding out who did it or why. The obvious need to protect the confidentiality of sources is not the only or even the most important reason the political contexts of news stories are seldom disclosed. The elevation of the story form to a professional practice places an even more subtle prohibition on revealing the politics behind political news. It would be devastating to the simple view of news reality to show that behind every story lies another story that comes much closer to revealing the true politics of the situation. As Epstein explained, the story-behind-the-story approach to news reporting would blow the cover off the normative claim that objective reality can be encapsulated somehow in stories.

Reporters as Generalists

Stories play another role in journalism as a universal reporting methodology employed by all reporters, whether of politics, sports, or business. Reporters are trained as generalists who are able to write stories on any subject. Although a small percentage end up reporting in a specialized area such as science or fashion, the majority change beats periodically and pride themselves on their ability to cover any news story.[71]

The emphasis in the profession on training reporters as generalists has obvious origins and payoffs. As Gans noted,

> . . . the news is still gathered mostly by generalists. One reason is economic, for general reporters earn less and are more productive. Beat reporters can rarely produce more than one story per television program or magazine issue, while general reporters can be asked, when necessary, to complete two or more assignments within the same period.[72]

Despite these obvious economic advantages, generalism is justified almost exclusively in normative terms. A key element of the journalism code is informing the average citizen. The use of generalists who tell simple stories is justified as the best means of presenting comprehensible information to the average person.

Keeping It Simple If a reporter has any special expertise on a topic, he or she may run the risk of complicating a story or violating the story form altogether by lapsing into technical analysis. Editors and news producers seem to widely believe that the general public cannot follow news produced by specialized reporters. For example, Epstein reported this response by an NBC *News* executive to a Justice Department suggestion that the TV networks use correspondents with special knowledge of ghetto problems to cover urban riots: "Any good journalist should be able to cover a riot in an unfamiliar setting. . . . A veneer of knowledgeability in a situation like this could be less than useless."[73] In another case, Gans reported a comment by an executive producer to his economics reporter following a good story on a complicated subject. "You scare me with your information; I think we'll put you on another beat."[74] Gans also noted that many specialists shared a general anxiety that they were becoming too knowledgeable for the tastes of their audiences or their superiors.

Although generalism is justified normatively as a necessary concession to a mass audience, the audience may pay a high political price in exchange for the alleged gains in news comprehension. Generalist reporters are often at the mercy of the news source. In technical areas, they are seldom qualified to ask critical questions.[75] As a result, reporters may have to ask news sources for guidelines about appropriate questions. Even when generalists are assigned to fairly straightforward political stories, they may have to fashion their stories almost entirely from official pronouncements and the story angles pursued by other reporters.[76] Because generalists are more dependent on their sources than are specialists, the odds are even greater that they will report fabricated events. Moreover, generalists may be less likely than specialists to spot flaws in performances that would make it possible to expose the contrived nature of an event. For example, Gans noted of generalists:

> Not knowing their sources well enough to discount self-serving information, they may report an opinion or a hopeful guess—for example, the size of an organization's membership—as a statistical fact. In this way, enterprising politicians sometimes get inflated estimates of their support into the news. . . . Occasionally, general reporters may cover only one side of a story without ever knowing that there are other sides.[77]

This generalization about generalism applies even to areas in which we might expect more perspective and sophistication. For example, business reporting reflects news values that seriously neglect the political or social impacts (or the inner politics) of corporations in modern life. Instead, business news tends to be a mix of shallow reports of mergers and profit analyses, alongside personality profiles of corporate celebrities such as Donald Trump or Bill Gates. As noted by Diana Henriques of the *New York Times,* one of the relatively few investigative business reporters in the mainstream news business, even business editors at prestigious news organizations often have little sense of big business as a social or political force. Indeed, because these editors often parachute into the business desks as generalists with little understanding of economics or the inner workings of corporations, their news assignments and decisions about what to run reinforce the tendency to report a shallow mix of profit and loss and profiles of companies and executives. Lacking much depth or perspective, such business news implicitly promotes the myths of business virtue and the superior rationality of free markets.[78]

When the giant Enron Corporation went bankrupt in 2001 and the unbelievable story of its shady pyramid schemes and corrupt accounting practices came to light, there was little in the business press to prepare the public for the spectacle. Even *The Wall Street Journal* investigation of Enron the year before stopped short of blowing the whistle on the company because the journalist assigned to the story could not understand how the company actually worked. Similarly, the political story of Enron's involvement in shaping Bush administration energy policy was not even hinted at until after the collapse of the company in a cloud of deception and corruption.

The Practice of Editorial Review

It is hard to imagine that the practice of editors' reviewing, checking, and approving reporters' preliminary accounts of events could be criticized. The review policies of most news organizations are represented as ensuring that the professional practices discussed earlier will be used in reporting the news. In a sense, editorial review does serve this function, thereby also ensuring the news distortion produced by these journalistic practices. Editorial review exerts its own influence on the political content of the news as well. Editors are not just the overseers of news production; they are accountable to management for the competitive position of their news product in the marketplace. As a result, editors and owners (or managers) typically develop guidelines that their reporters must follow in order to be successful and professionally respectable in their eyes. Studies of the internal workings of news organizations make it clear that these often subtle editorial pressures are major influences on reporters and on the political content of news.[79]

These editorial pressures would not be so worrisome if they were idiosyncratic, giving each news organization its own perspective and encouraging reporters to be different. However, the safest editorial course is often to cover the same stories in the same ways as other organizations but to package them differently, using concerned anchors, catchy theme music, or bold headlines to attract the audience. It is no secret that most editors take their leads from the wire services and the prestige papers, such as the *New York Times*, the *Washington Post*, and, increasingly, *The Wall Street Journal*. The reliance on the wire services and the prestige papers as implicit standardizing mechanisms applies to both print and broadcast media.[80] In addition, editors tend to standardize their product further by comparing it with the competition. It is easier for them to justify similarities in the coverage of stories than to account for differences between organizations. To put it simply, the transparency of the objectivity or fairness claim becomes most evident when the coverage of one organization differs from the others and, as a result, journalists must defend it against queries by publishers, politicians, and the public. The best defense of objectivity is contained in the implicit standardization of editorial review practices.

The obvious political consequence of standardized editorial policies was captured nicely by Edwin Diamond, who noted that editorial practices reinforce the worst tendency in the news business to stereotype stories. News stereotypes conform to the major plot outlines of fabricated news performances and give the news its obvious status quo bias. As Diamond notes, none of this bias can be attributed directly to political motives on the part of reporters. On the contrary, the professional standards of journalists cleanse the news of such motives; yet, somehow, the resulting product does seem to display a particular slant:

> The press isn't "racist," though as the skins of the participants become darker, the lengths of the stories shrink. The press isn't "pro-Israeli," though it is very sensitive to Jewish-American feelings. The press isn't afraid of the "vested interests," though it makes sure Mobil's or Senator Scott's denials appear right along with the charges. The paranoids are wrong: there is no news conspiracy. Instead there are a lot of editors and executives making decisions about what is "the news" while constrained by lack of time, space, money, talent, and understanding, from doing the difficult and/or hidden stories.[81]

In short, the editorial review standards pointed to as the fail-safe mechanism for preventing news distortion are, paradoxically, the very things that guarantee it.

OBJECTIVITY RECONSIDERED

A number of observers (including many journalists when they are not being pressured by critical academics) have argued persuasively that whatever the news is, it is not a spontaneous and objective mirror of the world. Nevertheless, it would be a mistake to leap from this to the conclusion that both the ideal of objectivity and professional reporting practices do not matter. Professional standards still work in several ways that are worth noting. For example, high-minded norms such as objectivity, even if they are not clear themselves, hide the connection between the news and its economic, organizational, and political contexts. Above all, the objectivity norm gives the press the look of an independent social institution. Moreover, even though actual reporting practices distort the political content of the news, they can be rationalized and defended conveniently under the objectivity code, thereby obscuring their political effects. In this fashion, journalistic norms and reporting practices operate together to create the aforementioned information biases in the news—biases that are well hidden behind the facade of independent journalism. Indeed, the cluster of practices with objectivity or fairness at their center may have the ironic result of often replacing the pursuit of truth with the best available political spin, as discussed in the following case study.

As explained earlier, claims about "objective" (or even fair and balanced) reporting rest on shaky foundations. For every source included, another is excluded. With each tightening of the plot line, meaningful connections to other issues and events become weakened. Every familiar theme or metaphor used in writing about an event obscures a potentially unique feature of the event. Above all, when officials are allowed to script the news, journalists give up their most important democratic function: to assess and critically examine public officials and business elites on behalf of the public interest. Although these and other factors make it impossible for the news to be objective, it is important that it seem objective or, in the terms of the trade, "believable." Perhaps most important of all, the practices and perspectives that go into creating the appearance of objectivity or believability depend heavily on striking the right balance between adversarialism and deference toward official sources. It is this balance that seems most in danger of tipping in ways that damage the credibility of news. Not only do reporters and officials seem to vacillate wildly between cooperation and antagonistic posturing, but these displays clearly leave most of the public cold toward both sides of the news process.

"Gotcha" Journalism and the Crisis of Credibility

As explained in Chapter 2, even though representations of authority and social order appear to have tipped toward the negative in recent years, the reason may have little to do with whether officials are really more venal, government is more corrupt, or levels of social disorder are objectively higher. Instead, the increasingly negative images of public authorities and social disorder can be traced at least partly to commercial news pressures for more sensationalism, emotion, and drama and to generate new story developments to feed the 24-hour news cycle. This trend toward sensationalism is also supported by politicians whose use of negative rhetoric and public attacks on opponents also feeds the news formulas. Both news producers and politicians seem to have bought the formula of "scare them and they will watch." The trouble is that after watching for a moment, people often change the channel.

Recall the argument by sociologist Gaye Tuchman from earlier in this chapter: The illusion of news objectivity depends on journalists treating the world of officialdom as authoritative.[82] If this is true, then "gotcha" journalism may have the effect of undermining the very essence of news objectivity. No matter how much journalists dedicate themselves to the professional ideal (by whatever name it goes), the legitimacy of the news may suffer under the burden of "gotcha" adversarialism. *This is not to imply that achieving credibility by blindly reporting the pronouncements of officials is a good idea either. It is simply to say that the ideal of objectivity may be flawed, no matter how journalists try to pursue it in a given era.* What matters is not debunking objectivity but understanding that the endless debate about it may keep people from seeing that the underlying biases in the news are created by the very efforts of journalists to achieve it.

It is also important to understand that just as the basic practices that define objectivity evolved over the course of the nineteenth century, and just as the idea of objectivity became a solid foundation of American journalism in the twentieth century, the pace of change in the news business will surely continue to affect both the ideal and the practice of objective journalism in the twenty-first century. Changes such as the 24-hour news cycle, the viral flows of the Internet, or the introduction of marketing people into the editorial offices of news organizations (discussed in the next chapter) are characteristic of the kinds of changes that have spurred the historical evolution of reporting practices and news values discussed throughout this chapter. In short, what accounts for any particular change in the news may be a combination of economic, technological, and social conditions. The results of such change may appear far from rational or coherent.

Yet journalism, as much as any profession, continues to try to make sense of its practices and even glorify them with such sobriquets as fair and balanced (formerly known as objective) reporting.

When journalists and their audiences grow as far apart in their perceptions of whether a defining concept such as objectivity is really being practiced properly, we know that serious tensions exist among the different elements of the news system. Those who produce news and those who consume it appear to have different understandings of what they are doing. In the process, they may have lost an important measure of respect and understanding for each other. Is objectivity possible, or even desirable? That is a question for the reader now to decide. One thing, however, is sure: We live in a time where there is little consensus on just what good reporting might be.

NOTES

1. *Talk of the Nation,* National Public Radio, April 17, 2006. www.npr.org/templates/story/story.php?storyId=5346256. Accessed December 15, 2010.
2. *Washington Post,* "Lawmakers and the 'birther'/Muslim myths (updated). Politics 44 Blog: Politics and Policy in Obama's Washington. August 30, 2010. http://voices.washingtonpost.com/44/2010/08/lawmakers-who-push-the-birther.html. Accessed September 15, 2010.
3. Alex Spillius, "President Barack Obama Hits Back at Birthers and Rumor Mongers," *The Telegraph,* August 30, 2010. www.telegraph.co.uk/news/worldnews/northamerica/usa/barackobama/7971928/President-Barack-Obama-hits-back-at-birthers-and-rumour-mongers.html. Accessed September 15, 2010.
4. Joan Didion, *Political Fictions* (New York: Alfred A. Knopf, 2001). The quote is from Joseph Lelyveld, "Another Country," *New York Review of Books* (December 20, 2001): 10.
5. Trends of surveys of American journalists taken in 1971, 1982–1983, and 1992, reported in David H. Weaver and G. Cleveland Wilhoit, *The American Journalist in the 1990s* (Mahwah, NJ: Lawrence Erlbaum, 1996).
6. David H. Weaver, et al., *The American Journalist in the 21st Century* (Hillsdale, NJ: Lawrence Erlbaum, 2006).
7. John W. C. Johnstone, Edward J. Slawski, and William W. Bowman, *The News People: A Sociological Portrait of American Journalists and Their Work* (Urbana: University of Illinois Press, 1976); see also, Charles J. Brown, Trevor R. Brown, and William L. Rivers, *The Media and People* (New York: Holt, Rinehart and Winston, 1978); and Stephen Hess, *The Washington Reporters* (Washington, DC: Brookings Institution, 1981).
8. Gaye Tuchman, "Objectivity as Strategic Ritual: An Examination of Newsmen's Notions of Objectivity," *American Journal of Sociology* 77 (1972): 660–679.
9. Meena Hartenstein, "Fans Lobby Stephen Colbert to Host 'Restoring Truthiness' Rally in D.C. to Rival Glen Beck's Event," *New York Daily News,* September 7, 2010. www.nydailynews.com/entertainment/tv/2010/09/07/2010-09-07_fans_lobby_stephen_colbert_to_host_restoring_truthiness_rally_in_dc_to_rival_gle.html. Accessed September 15, 2010.
10. "Brits vs. Yanks: Who Does Journalism Right?" *Columbia Journalism Review* (May/June 2004): 44. Anonymous article.

11. Leila Fadel, "As Obama Declares Iraq War Over, Iraqis Brace for Uncertainty," *Washington Post*, August 31, 2010. www.washingtonpost.com/wp-dyn/content/article/2010/08/31/AR2010083105193.html. Accessed September 15, 2010.

12. Ibid.

13. See Chris Mooney, *The Republican War on Science* (New York: Perseus, 2005).

14. Bryan Keefer, "Tsunami: The Campaign '04 Information War Is Fast, Deep, and Fraught with Lies. The Press Must Rethink Coverage or Drown in a Toxic Tidal Wave," *Columbia Journalism Review* (July/August 2004): 20.

15. *MSNBC Hardball with Chris Matthews,* October 11, 2004. MSNBC. http://msnbc.msn.com/id/6232178/. Accessed January 13, 2005.

16. For a more detailed analysis of this example, see W. Lance Bennett, "Beyond Pseudo Events: Election News as Reality TV," *American Behavioral Scientist* 49, no. 3 (November 2005): 1–15.

17. See, for example, Edith Efron, *The News Twisters* (Los Angeles: Nash, 1971); and Doris Graber, *Mass Media and American Politics* (Washington, DC: Congressional Quarterly Press, 1980), Chapter 10.

18. Brent Cunningham, "Across the Great Class Divide: Today's Journalists Are More Isolated Than Ever from the Lives of Poor and Working-Class Americans. So What?" *Columbia Journalism Review* (May/June 2004): 35.

19. David T. Z. Mindich, *Just the Facts: How "Objectivity" Came to Define American Journalism* (New York: New York University Press, 1998), 5–6.

20. Pew Research Center for the People and the Press survey, March 1999, www.people-press.org/press99sec1.htm.

21. Gerald J. Baldasty, *The Commercialization of News in the Nineteenth Century* (Madison, WI: University of Wisconsin Press, 1992).

22. For supporting evidence for this claim, see, among others, Meyer Berger, *The Story of the New York Times* (New York: Simon & Schuster, 1951); Frank L. Mott, *The News in America* (Cambridge, MA: Harvard University Press, 1952); Edwin Emery and Henry Ladd Smith, *The Press in America* (New York: Prentice-Hall, 1954); John Tebbell, *The Media in America* (New York: Mentor, 1974); and Michael Schudson, *Discovering the News*: *A Social History of American Newspapers* (New York: Basic Books, 1978).

23. See Mindich, *Just the Facts.*

24. Ibid.

25. See Baldasty, *The Commercialization of News in the Nineteenth Century,* Chapter 2.

26. For discussions of the origins and impact of the wire services, see Bernard Roscho, *Newsmaking* (Chicago: University of Chicago Press, 1975); Mott, *The News in America;* and Emery and Smith, *The Press in America.*

27. Schudson, *Discovering the News,* Chapter 3.

28. Upton Sinclair, *The Brass Check* (Pasadena, CA: Author, 1920); see also, Berger, *The Story of the New York Times;* and Tebbell, *The Media in America.*

29. For a history of this period and its ideas, see, among others, Harold J. Laski, "The Present Position of Representative Democracy," *American Political Science Review* 26 (August 1932): 629–641; John Diggins, *Mussolini and Fascism: The View from America* (Princeton, NJ: Princeton University Press, 1972); and Schudson, *Discovering the News.*

30. See the following books by Walter Lippmann: *Drift and Mastery* (New York: Kennerly, 1914); *Liberty and the News* (New York: Harcourt Brace, 1920); *Public Opinion* (New York: Free Press, 1922); and *The Phantom Public* (New York: Harcourt Brace, 1925).

31. Tebbell, *The Media in America*, Chapter 12.
32. Lou Cannon, *Reporting: An Inside View* (Sacramento, CA: California Journal Press, 1977), 35.
33. Mindich, *Just the Facts*, 8.
34. For a review of these professional norms, see Tebbell, *The Media in America*; Johnstone, Slawski, and Bowman, *The News People*; Gaye Tuchman, *Making News: A Study in the Construction of Reality* (New York: Free Press, 1978); and Schudson, *Discovering the News*.
35. In recent years, the much-touted specialist has entered the reporting ranks. However, the use of specialists continues to be restricted to a few subject areas, such as science and economics. Also, specialists are employed by a relatively small number of big news organizations. Because the bulk of political reporting continues to be done by generalists who rotate assignments periodically and who refrain from introducing technical or theoretical perspectives in their reports, the practice of generalism merits inclusion here.
36. Tuchman, *Making News*, 87.
37. See, for example, Murray Edelman, *The Symbolic Uses of Politics* (Urbana: University of Illinois Press, 1964); Peter L. Berger and Thomas Luckmann, *The Social Construction of Reality* (New York: Anchor, 1966); and W. Lance Bennett, *Public Opinion in American Politics* (New York: Harcourt Brace Jovanovich, 1980), chapters 13 and 14.
38. C. Jack Orr, "Reporters Confront the President: Sustaining a Counterpoised Situation," *Quarterly Journal of Speech* 66 (February 1980): 17–32.
39. Ibid., 22.
40. See, for example, Harvey Molotch and Marilyn Lester, "Accidents, Scandals, and Routines: Resources for Insurgent Methodology," *Insurgent Sociologist* 3 (1973): 1–12; Harvey Molotch and Marilyn Lester, "News as Purposive Behavior: On the Strategic Use of Routine Events, Accidents, and Scandals," *American Sociological Review* 39 (February 1974): 101–112; Murray Edelman, *Political Language* (New York: Academic Press, 1977), Chapter 3; Todd Gitlin, *The Whole World Is Watching* (Berkeley: University of California Press, 1980), chapters 2 and 7; and Graber, *Mass Media and American Politics*, Chapter 8.
41. David L. Altheide and Robert P. Snow, *Media Logic* (Beverly Hills, CA: Sage, 1979), chapters 3 and 4.
42. The Web site iFilm.com alone claims that nearly 3.5 million viewers watched its posting of the Stewart *Crossfire* appearance at www.ifilm.com/ifilmdetail/2652831?htv=12.
43. See, for example, Howard Simmons and Joseph A. Califano Jr., eds., *The Media and Business* (New York: Vintage, 1979).
44. Henry Beck, "Attentional Struggles and Silencing Strategies in a Human Political Conflict: The Case of the Vietnam Moratoria," in M. R. A. Chanu and R. R. Larson, eds., *The Structure of Social Attention: Ethological Studies* (New York: Wiley, 1976).
45. Jan S. Wenner and William Greider, "The Rolling Stone Interview: Bill Clinton," *Rolling Stone* (December 9, 1993): 40–45.
46. For a fascinating look at Richard Nixon's ins and outs with the press, see Marvin Kalb, *The Nixon Memo* (Chicago: University of Chicago Press, 1995).
47. It is not hard to understand why politicians often become personally embittered over their treatment by the press. Although it often seems that politicians adopt a sour-grapes attitude about the adversarial norm itself, the politicians' typical complaints

that news coverage is arbitrary, gratuitous, and unpredictable may be reasonable and valid perceptions of journalists' ritualistic behaviors.

48. For a more detailed analysis of the spoon-fed aspects of Watergate investigative reporting, see Gladys Engel Lang and Kurt Lang, *The Battle for Public Opinion: The President, the Press, and the Polls During Watergate* (New York: Columbia University Press, 1983). The Langs also provide extensive documentation on the overwhelming emphasis, both in the White House and among the press, on Nixon's personal image and popularity during the Watergate saga.
49. See Jacques Ellul, *Propaganda* (New York: Vintage, 1973).
50. Quoted in *Rolling Stone* (October 7, 1976): 57.
51. For these and other editors' responses, see Priscilla S. Meyer, "Hello, Rolling Stone? What Did Butz Say?" *The Wall Street Journal* (October 7, 1976): 18.
52. "AIDS and the Family Paper," *Columbia Journalism Review* (March/April 1986): 11. Anonymous article.
53. Quoted in David Walker, "The War Photo That Nobody Wanted to See," *Photo District News* (August 1991): 16.
54. Ibid.
55. Tebbell, *The Media in America*, 141.
56. Daniel Boorstin, *The Image* (New York: Atheneum, 1961).
57. See Edwin Diamond, *Good News, Bad News* (Cambridge, MA: MIT Press, 1978).
58. See W. Lance Bennett, "Storytelling in Criminal Trials: A Model of Social Judgment," *Quarterly Journal of Speech* 64 (February 1978): 1–22; and W. Lance Bennett and Martha S. Feldman, *Reconstructing Reality in the Courtroom* (New Brunswick, NJ: Rutgers University Press, 1981).
59. Bennett and Feldman, *Reconstructing Reality in the Courtroom*, Chapter 4.
60. James David Barber, "Characters in the Campaign: The Literary Problem," in *Race for the Presidency: The Media and the Nominating Process*, ed. John Barber (Englewood Cliffs, NJ: Prentice-Hall, 1978).
61. Edward Jay Epstein, *News from Nowhere* (New York: Vintage, 1973), 4–5.
62. Herbert Gans, *Deciding What's News* (New York: Vintage, 1979), 173.
63. Ibid., 171.
64. Bennett, "Storytelling in Criminal Trials"; and Bennett and Feldman, *Reconstructing Reality in the Courtroom*.
65. *Atlanta Journal and Constitution* (June 18, 1994): 1.
66. See Murray Edelman, *Political Language* (New York: Academic Press, 1977); and Bennett, *Public Opinion in American Politics*.
67. Gans, *Deciding What's News*, Chapter 2.
68. See Tuchman, *Making News;* and Mark Fishman, *Manufacturing the News* (Austin: University of Texas Press, 1980).
69. Robert Darnton, "Writing News and Telling Stories," *Daedalus* 104 (Spring 1975): 189.
70. Edward Jay Epstein, "The Grand Cover-Up," *The Wall Street Journal* (April 19, 1976): 10.
71. Johnstone, Slawski, and Bowman, *The News People*.
72. Gans, *Deciding What's News*, 143.
73. Epstein, *News from Nowhere*, 137.
74. Gans, *Deciding What's News*, 143.
75. Ibid.
76. Ibid.; also Timothy Crouse, *Boys on the Bus* (New York: Ballantine, 1973).
77. Gans, *Deciding What's News*, 142.

78. A summary of remarks by Diana Henriques at a seminar on "Corporate Power: You Can Run, but You Can't Hide," Shorenstein Center, Kennedy School of Government, Harvard University, October 12, 1999.

79. See, for example, Warren L. Breed, "Social Control in the Newsroom," *Social Forces* 33 (May 1955): 326–335; Walter Geiber, "Across the Desk: A Study of 16 Telegraph Editors," *Journalism Quarterly* 33 (Fall 1956): 423–432; Epstein, *News from Nowhere;* Crouse, *Boys on the Bus;* and Gans, *Deciding What's News.*

80. For discussion of the impact of wire services on newspaper coverage, see Crouse, *Boys on the Bus;* and Leon Sigal, *Reporters and Officials* (Lexington, MA: D.C. Heath, 1975). The impact of the "wires" on television news is discussed extensively in Epstein, *News from Nowhere;* and Gans, *Deciding What's News.*

81. Diamond, *Good News, Bad News,* 228.

82. Tuchman, *Making News.*

The Political Economy of News and the End of a Journalism Era

It's one thing to be marched to the gallows by an uncaring
and unappreciative public, sentenced by shifting technological
and cultural habits and a few bonehead moves of your own.
But it's quite another having to go to your death stripped
naked as a jaybird.

— Phil Bronstein

. . . think about the implications of the do-more-with-less
meme that is sweeping the news business. I call it the Hamster
Wheel. . . . it's motion for motion's sake. The Hamster Wheel is
volume without thought. It is news panic. . . . It is copy
produced to meet arbitrary productivity metrics. . . .
Journalists will tell you that where once newsroom incentives
rewarded more deeply reported stories, now incentives skew
toward work that can be turned around quickly and generate a
bump in web traffic. . . . The Hamster Wheel, really, is the
mainstream media's undoing in real time, and they're doing it
to themselves.

— Dean Starkman

Most of the buzz about the journalism crisis is focused on the death of newspapers. There are many reasons for this, not the least of which is that print news organizations produce most of the journalism content that recycles through the rest of the media system, as discussed in Chapter 1. The production of quality news cannot occur with the business is in freefall. Newsrooms lost 25 percent of their workers between 2001–2010.[1] Compounding these concerns is the panic response of a dying industry that has led to the breakdown of the once important firewall between the marketing side and the editorial side of the news business. The above epigram from Phil Bronstein (editor-at-large for the *San Francisco Chronicle*) was a somewhat mocking reference to members of the *L.A. Times* newsroom who protested the paper's decision to start selling the front page for ads for movies and television programs made to appear as realistic news mockups. Like so many other once independent news organizations, the *Times* was sold to a larger chain, which encountered financial trouble when the business model for news went bust, and was eventually bought and taken into bankruptcy by an investor named Sam Zell (introduced in Chapter 1). Zell famously announced to shocked employees: "It's very obvious that the newspaper model in its current form does not work and the sooner we all acknowledge that, the better."[2] Bronstein added insult to injury by adding that: "For people who still love print, who like to hold it, feel it, rustle it, tear stuff out, do their I. F. Stone thing, it's important to remember that people are living longer. . . . That's the most hopeful thing you can say about print journalism, that old people are living longer."[3] Add to these concerns the understandable nostalgia for the rich history surrounding that revolutionary invention, the printing press, and the focus on the death of journalism becomes deep and passionate.

THE NEWS BUSINESS IN FREEFALL

As the business collapses, the above-defined Hamster Wheel becomes the new model for getting more productivity from fewer workers. Reporters are being replaced by content assemblers who refashion wire stories or celebrity Twitter feeds and then blog about them to keep content flowing across multiple and rapidly changing media platforms. As serious investigation and time-consuming news analysis fall away, stories are based on the easiest sources, and content updates grow to keep online sites buzzing. When Lady Gaga tells her Little Monster fans on Facebook to press for gay rights in the military, the story is refashioned as news with a comment from a politician thrown in for authenticity, and then discussed in blogs, with hyperlinks flowing far and wide. This new news is aimed at grabbing people when they check in briefly at work or on the commute home. Pablo Boczkowski has found this cycle of more numerous and less substantial content proliferation to be something of a global media trend, occurring in Argentina as well as the United States.[4]

The trend is driven in part by doing more with less, and in part by the assumption that keeping the online version of a news organization refreshed and full of short, attention-getting features is the future of the business. Starkman's analysis of the Hamster Wheel indicates that distant corporate owners of failing businesses believe that more and shorter content bits are what busy people want. News on the go is like fast food—momentarily satisfying but ultimately unhealthy. Later in this chapter, we will see that what media executives think people want is generally severely limited by what they decide their organizations can afford to feed them at lowest cost.

This new information content model is rapidly replacing what was formerly known as journalism across the industry. Even organizations that are still profitable see the Hamster Wheel as a means of becoming even more profitable. For example, Starkman studied the *Wall Street Journal (WSJ)*, which is generally regarded as one of the two best papers in America. The journal is interesting on several counts: It is still profitable because it feeds information to a special interest audience of high income investors and firms; it was purchased by media baron Rupert Murdoch's giant News Corp and put through a profit ratcheting reorganization; and, so it stands out as a profitable exception that nonetheless reflects industry trends toward more shallow and less analytical stories. Between 2000 and 2008, the number of *WSJ* stories increased from 22,000 to 38,000 per year as the staff shrank at least 13 percent.[5]

Many other former high-quality news organizations, from the *L.A. Times* to the *Washington Post*, have been pushed to go even faster on the Hamster Wheel. The irony of all this, according to Starkman, is that there is no evidence that this trend is even leading to a successful stabilization of the business. He notes, for example, that the measures for Web ratings and site traffic are woefully unreliable, and, in any event, few online news operations are turning a profit. Moreover, as we will discuss in Chapter 8, there are now so many competing information models for people to choose from that the current effort to do more with less in the news business may well be bypassed by publics who discover more satisfying media formats beyond the news that offer deeper information about the topics they care about. This is what Starkman means by the real time undoing of the mainstream media.

THE LOSS OF NEWS AS A PUBLIC GOOD

Meanwhile, what is being lost is serious reporting. At the height of the mass media era, news organizations were more independent and less likely to be driven by sheer goals of maximizing profits. Journalism was once thought to be valuable in itself, because it was an important good or resource for the public in a democracy. The government once helped media organizations maintain commitments to these values by holding them to some public service standards as a requirement for license renewal. Newspapers were often run by people committed to journalism and who made a commitment to balance their profits with the value of political reporting as a public good. The rest of this chapter tells the story of what happened to these values, and sets up the discussion in Chapter 8 about the future of news.

The bottom line in the present system is that the American news system is on the brink of losing its capacity to produce information that is independent and that serves the public interest. The economic collapse has produced a double blow to the public interest. First, the amount of serious political information is shrinking in favor of rumor, scandal, and increasing focus on entertainment and lifestyle news. Second, what political news remains comes through newsroom doors that open ever wider to public relations stories and political spin. Thus, the mainstream news media are ever more tied to officialdom, even as they cling to the norms of objectivity discussed in Chapter 6. The result according to Starkman's analysis is this: "The Paradox of the Wheel is that, for all the activity it generates, the Wheel renders news organizations deeply passive. The greater the need for copy, the more dependent reporters are on sources for scoops and pitiful scraps of news."[6] How did all this happen?

HOW WE GOT HERE: PROFITS VS. THE PUBLIC INTEREST

The single greatest contributor to the collapse of journalism was the political pressure from large media corporations to buy and squeeze ever-greater profits from smaller media organizations during the heyday of market deregulation in the 1990s, which is a story that we will explore in the Case Study and in much of the rest of this chapter. The second major factor leading to the fall of journalism is the dramatic change in audience preferences for receiving and sharing information. Some of these changes no doubt were driven by the cheapening of the profit-driven news product to the point that it lost its value for many citizens. Another part of the changing audience story reflects the dramatic changes in citizen information preferences centered on social media, which are changing the relationship between journalism and its audience (discussed in Chapter 8).

The experience of journalists today is one of losing the battle for maintaining public interest standards against corporate managers who think of news as just another product. Quality news in the television industry is in many ways just as endangered as in print journalism. One case in point is the resignation in 2010 of David Westin as president of ABC News. Westin reportedly gave up fighting with Disney executives over what profit level the news division should be expected to deliver. A very good investigative report in the *New York Times* (which is still striving to remain a high-quality news organization) noted:

> The ABC News staff member informed of the decision said that Disney and ABC managers had pressed Mr. Westin for years to make the division more profitable, but had been unhappy with his efforts to accomplish that goal. ABC announced in February that it would reduce its staff by up to 400 employees, about 25 percent of its work force.
> . . . Another senior ABC News executive said the division had been consistently profitable, but ABC had sought to increase its profit margin to 15 percent, from 5 percent.[7]

Since government deregulation of the media industries beginning in the 1980s, journalists have been under increasing pressure from corporate executives promoting cheap news to generate higher profits. The loss of advertising to online sites in the early 2000s, magnified by the Great Recession of the end of the decade, led to wholesale collapse of any remaining balance between profits and the public interest value of the news product.

Rank-and-file reporters in newsrooms across the land have long been forced to accept the "lite" news and features that turned newspapers and television stations into highly profitable businesses by the 1990s.[8] The story here is not that audiences really demanded lite news. On the contrary, in most markets, TV news audiences and newspaper readership began shrinking, particularly in the audience demographics that advertisers pay more to reach: people under 35. So the cheapening of the product came at the expense of the long-term viability and public appeal of the industry.

If audiences were running away, why did the downgrading of news content continue? The simple reason is that most media calculate their business model in terms of delivering prime demographics to advertisers, and using as cheap a product as possible to attract those demographics. Thus, the loss of absolute audience numbers was initially not as serious a blow to some organizations, as long as they were able to produce a product that still appealed to target audiences of high value to sponsors. For example, newspapers turned out to be highly profitable in the early days of profit-driven media consolidation. Many of them actually saved money on production and distribution as they lost non-critical readers, and they added lifestyle (e.g., fashion, food, and travel) features that continued to draw key demographics (e.g., 30–50 age brackets with disposable income) that drove the heyday of consumer spending in the prosperous 1990s. Later in the 2000s newspapers suffered the double blows of Internet advertising and the Great Recession. Television network news, by contrast has been in relatively steady decline as a result of shrinking audiences that left generally older demographics not as attractive to advertisers.

The bottom line throughout the industry during the corporate buyout era of the 1990s and 2000s was to cheapen the news product itself. Serious political news costs more to report because it often requires the time and initiative of experienced journalists who know who to call, what to ask, and where to follow the leads. Soft news often requires no reporters at all, save perhaps sending a camera crew to shoot fires, floods, accidents, and other disasters that can be scripted back at the studio. Much of the other content circulates through generic news feeds and wires, requiring only repackaging for putting on the front page or for the anchor to report on the air. Saving the costs of reporters, remote news bureaus, and other aspects of quality journalism produced such a boost in the profits that the corporate consolidation reached unprecedented levels, as more and more news organizations were bought up solely for their investment potential. Profits of 25 percent a year were not uncommon, and soon became demanded by distant corporate owners. During this time, the government gave the green light to media concentration (see the Case Study in this chapter), with virtually no consideration about the impact on the quality of public information. It is perhaps unreasonable to ask most politicians to worry about independent journalism, considering their reliance on spin and strategic communications as discussed in Chapter 4.

The purchase of these cash machines by larger media companies and investment conglomerates made the demand for high profits a requirement. This set up a collision course with Internet sites that siphoned advertising revenues online, along with news and entertainment fare, which drove more of the audience away as well. What were news organizations to do to keep the profits high? The answer, of course: cut reporting staff even more and shore up the content with more "news lite." While local TV was an early adopter of the lite news formula, many cities still had quality newspapers for those who wanted to stay in touch with politics and community affairs. Yet, fueled by government deregulation that enabled more concentrated ownership of media outlets (as discussed in the case study in this chapter), high-quality papers were bought and stripped by big corporations beholden to distant investors rather than to the public. The story is the same in Chicago, Los Angeles, Philadelphia, Atlanta, San Jose, Dallas, and many other cities: Papers and television and radio stations that once reported serious news became milked by investors concerned about short-term gains rather than long-term stability or community responsibilities. Indeed, some venerable institutions, such as the *Philadelphia Inquirer* were simply cast adrift by new owners seeking steep profits and left to struggle under unstable ownership or simply fade away.

Consider just one example here. At the turn of the twenty-first century, *The Dallas Morning News* was rated in a national survey of newspaper editors as the nation's fifth best daily paper.[9] However, the large company that owned it, Belo, had made a number of bad investments and decided to raise profits where it could. Rather than seeing the Dallas paper as a gem of good journalism and an asset to the brand, it was viewed as a place to make cuts and reap short-term gains. Between 2004 and 2006, 200 newsroom staff members were laid off, amounting to about one-third of the news workers. The paper soon led the country in declining circulation (with a whopping 14.3% decline in one six-month period in 2007), and reader satisfaction plummeted from 79 to 60 percent.[10] Gone were bureaus in Europe, Asia, the Middle East, Cuba, South America, Houston, and Oklahoma City. The Washington bureau was cut from a staff of 11 to 2 reporters and a columnist.[11] More of the news was simply ripped from wire feeds. Even though Belo profit margins (still showing profits in the hundreds of millions) continued to slide due to various problems, the CEO was given a 50 percent raise. Journalism scholar Philip Meyer surveyed the damage: "It seems to me that papers that do what Dallas did have decided to liquidate the business and get as much money out of it as they can. That's not crazy. That's a rational strategy if you only care about what happens on your watch as a manager because it takes a long time for a newspaper to die, and while it's in its death throes, it can still be a pretty good cash cow. But it's really bad for the community and for the business in the long run."[12]

And so it went, with the business pages filled with glowing tales of profits in the media sector (and few stories in the mainstream media about the loss of content quality). The 1990s dawned brightly: The average profit margin was a healthy 14.8 percent for companies in the newspaper industry. The prospects of even greater profits stimulated an even larger wave of mergers and buyouts in the 1990s. The megamedia companies squeezed a whopping 21.5 percent average profit from their expanding newspaper holdings by the end of the decade.[13] Such stunning profit margins were achieved through the three-step industry formula: (a) cheapening the content, (b) marketing content directly to the audiences that were most attractive to advertisers, and (c) allowing the less profitable audiences to wither away, producing a net savings of printing and distribution costs. Indeed, within the shortsighted economic logic of the time, dwindling audiences did not set off as many alarm bells as one might think, since cheap content could be thrown at them to keep the balance sheets in line.

REPLACING QUALITY NEWS WITH INFOTAINMENT

Moving away from quality information made everything seem economically viable for a time. Putting the political news focus on personalities at the center of dramatic conflicts may have accentuated the fragmentation bias discussed in Chapter 2, but it made stories easier to report in terms of generic plots of authority and disorder. Echoing some of our themes about news biases from Chapter 2, here is how Matthew Baum describes the trend:

> The net effect is that traditional news programming has been supplemented, and in some respects supplanted, by a variety of new types of entertainment-oriented informational programs, which I have collectively termed soft news media. Relative to traditional news programs, soft news outlets place a greater emphasis on episodic human-interest-oriented stories with highly accessible themes—themes that are particularly suitable for cheap framing. Conversely, the soft news media are far less likely than their traditional news counterparts to employ *thematic* frames, which provide broader context for understanding the causes and consequences of a given issue or event, but which also tend to be more complex, and, hence, less accessible for politically uninterested individuals.[14]

Baum also notes, however, that many disconnected citizens might never hear of important world issues at all unless they appear in news magazines or on entertainment programs such as *E!, MTV News,* or their Internet portal. The good news seems to be that infotainment gets information about a select few big issues to people who are otherwise walled off from politics. The bad news is that the information may be so fragmented and personality driven that it offers little useful understanding.

THE ECONOMIC TRANSFORMATION OF THE AMERICAN MEDIA

The conventional wisdom among the chieftans of giant media corporations during the heyday of the 1990s was *bigger is better,* as expressed in the mantra of *synergy.* The common goals were (a) to become large enough to own the production, marketing, and distribution of media content; (b) to have enough channels and publications to dominate advertising markets, while using free internal advertising to draw audiences from one channel or publication to others in the media empire; and (c) to recycle both talent and old prime-time programming within the system to reduce the costs of filling the schedules of multiplying cable and broadcast outlets. However, the model did not anticipate various changes in the media environment that affected the profitability of both print and broadcast news.

What Happened to Print Media?

Just when the new economic formulas seemed to be working smoothly, the dot-com boom shook newspapers with the migration of audiences to online information sites that offered free features (movie reviews, weather, sports, fashion, and even political news), drawing precious advertising dollars away from papers. Web services, such as craigslist (**www.craigslist.org**) appear to have permanently undermined certain newspaper revenue engines, such as employment, personals, and housing listings.

Beyond the shifting economic foundations of print media was a far more worrisome trend: Young people had stopped reading newspapers in anything close to the numbers of earlier generations. What could be done to attract young readers who really are flocking to the Web, or even beyond the Web into the world of videogames? This was not the first great upheaval in the life of newspapers, and like those that had gone before, it surely will result in new ways to communicate about society.[15]

What will the newspaper of tomorrow look like? Not like that of today. Papers have scrambled to get into the Web business, building often impressive, but seldom profitable, sites that channel more readers online. Some of these sites are rich and interactive: the *Washington Post* (**www.washingtonpost. com**), Public Broadcasting Service (**www.pbs.org**), National Public Radio (**www.npr.org**) are some great examples. NPR has developed novel apps for iPad and iPhone and computers, which enable access to most news and features, anytime, anywhere. One of the pioneers in creating online audiences for conventional media is the British Broadcasting Corporation (**www.bbc.co.uk**). Most online editions, however, soon became known as "shovelware" in the industry, referring to the practice of simply shoveling the print paper into Web pages, perhaps adding more wire-service filler and greater reader input than was possible to include in the print version.[16] Few of the commercial electronic ventures proved profitable, still raising the question of how to reinvent a viable news form that serves the public interest.

What Happened to TV?

Meanwhile, the television news picture became similarly turbulent as viewers had more choices in cable channels and the Internet, and the average age of TV news consumers continues to rise (meaning that the young audiences in the 18-to-35 demographic prized by advertisers are eluding most news programming).

Compounding these pressures are corporate owners who demand more profitability from their media investments and who see news as little different from sports or game shows in terms of its product status. In the heyday of television news, the majority of the nation's households tuned to one of the three network nightly news shows. The companies that owned those networks regarded news as part of the prestige associated with their brand images and, therefore, allowed greater spending and less income from news divisions than they required from sports or entertainment units. By century's end, TV news audiences were not just shrinking and aging—they were also scattering across multiplying broadcast and cable channels. In the midst of this changing picture, all three pioneering networks were devoured by giant corporations.[17]

For example, at the turn of the century, NBC was owned primarily by General Electric, which later spun off a corporate entity called NBC Universal that was 20 percent owned by the French media group Vivendi. More recently the cable giant Comcast bought a controlling interest, signaling a potential conflict of interest as cable and Internet providers may seek to give preferential treatment to their own content channels. ABC is owned by Disney, which also owns many other media organizations from ESPN to the Disney Channel. CBS, which had been bought in 1999 by cable giant Viacom (www.viacom.com), was spun off into a separate broadcast company— a sign that the economic synergies promised by the merger mania were difficult to achieve. Similarly, Belo (of the Dallas story earlier the chapter) spun its newspapers off into a separate division to attract investors to its still more profitable television holdings.

Looking beyond the ownership of the original TV networks, we see Time Warner, the largest media conglomerate on the planet and owner of CNN, HBO, TBS, TNT, Warner Bros., and more than 150 magazines (including *Time, Fortune,* and *Sports Illustrated*).[18] The new media giant on the block is Google, which bought YouTube for $1.65 billion, and was promptly sued for $1 billion by Viacom, which claimed that more than 1.5 billion viewings of its program content (such as *The Daily Show*) had been offered illegally on YouTube without copyright compensation. Things are getting interesting in the media environment once dominated by television, but increasingly converging with online content streams.

CORPORATE PROFIT LOGIC AND NEWS CONTENT

Let's take a look at life on "Planet Viacom"[19] at the time of the original megamerger—before a later decision to pursue the prime younger demographic on cable and online led to spinning off the CBS broadcast system into its own company. At the time it swallowed CBS and its holdings, Viacom's media empire included 39 wholly owned TV stations reaching more than half of all American households and more than 200 affiliates reaching nearly all the rest; ownership of the UPN network with its 189 affiliates; ownership of five radio networks, including Infinity Broadcasting Corporation, which alone ran 165 radio stations, including six out of the top-ten highest-grossing channels; a healthy cable collection that included MTV, VH1, Nickelodeon, Showtime, and Comedy Central; several movie companies including Paramount; dozens of commercial Web sites; a publishing empire that included Simon & Schuster, the Free Press, and Pocket Books; and theme parks, movie theaters, advertising companies, product promotion and licensing companies, and on and on.[20]

At the height of this empire, when the belief in synergy reached almost religious proportions, one observer likened Viacom to a giant media mall with CBS as its anchor store: "Viacom sees the CBS network as the anchor store of a huge mall—one in which Viacom owns all the stores. With its still-popular shows, CBS will draw in many people who can then be directed to Viacom's many smaller outlets—MTV, Nickelodeon, VH1, and so on. The process should work in reverse, too."[21] The problem with this logic is that advertisers pay more for the prized 18-to-34 demographic that spends most of its disposable income on the entertainment and consumer goods that fill up most ad content: clothes, beverages, food, electronics, movies, music, and cars. The miscalculation was that those young consumers did not pass through the aging world of CBS programming on the way into its vast media mall. Even with programming makeovers such as the successful *Survivor* reality TV series, young consumers were more easily (and more cheaply) enticed to enter Viacom's world directly through cable portals such as MTV. The original music video channel had mastered a brilliant format: low-cost programming of virtually wall-to-wall commercials: advertising the songs and artists in the videos produced and given to MTV free by music companies, running endless ads for MTV itself, and still finding room for conventional product ads in between.

But What About the News?

On the way through this bumpy process, CBS—like most media companies that went through similar experiences—lost sight of the news as anything special. As a former chairman of General Electric (GE), the company that bought NBC put it so bluntly: "Network news isn't the strategic center of what happens here. . . . News is not the core of the asset."[22] News simply became a tiny piece of the corporate profit and synergy picture. When CBS was an independent company, profits were not as important for the news division, which was regarded more as an asset that added prestige to the CBS brand image. Legend has it that founding owner William S. Paley once told his news division to concentrate on the best reporting possible, and he would make profits from sports and entertainment. That idea of using the news quality brand as something of a corporate loss leader was stimulated by far stronger government requirements that broadcasters had to produce some public responsibility programming in exchange for getting free licenses to use the public airwaves for profit. Most of those responsibility requirements have been dropped or diminished as advocates of deregulation point to profits as the number-one public value that government should encourage.

The Viacom merger thus accelerated the fall of the once-pioneering CBS news operation (the home of Edward R. Murrow and Walter Cronkite) from corporate flagship to corporate profit problem. Among other things, this meant adjusting news content and delivery formats to fit the lifestyle interests of the audiences already tuning in to entertainment programs. When CBS decided to lower the median age of its audience with programs like *Survivor,* the move set in motion a reformatting of other network programming, including news. The trouble is that with news in general being less interesting for young people, the network news programs entered a steady and seemingly irreversible decline with aging audiences tuning into programming supported by commercials for medicines and health products. The tough challenge facing news executives is to create content that shifts the demographic and changes the product mix in the advertising surrounding the news:

> Network executives yearn to lower the median age for the news, which is about 57 or 58 depending on the network, and replace Immodium and Zoloft ads with ones for the iPod and Mountain Dew. If they cannot attract youth to the current brand of news, they think they can tailor news to be more attractive to youth.[23]

The goal of getting young people to watch news is a noble one. The real question is whether that news will be of much value after cheapening its content to suit the ratings, profit, and programming brand equation. One suspects that a better solution would simply be to recycle other Viacom products such as Comedy Central's *The Daily Show with Jon Stewart,* which is both funny and relatively informative.

Product Packaging and the Public Interest

The trend of turning news into a consumer-driven commodity swept the newspaper industry during its time of mergers and consolidation as well. As large corporations bought out the nation's struggling papers during the last two decades, marketing consultants were brought in to fix the bottom line. For example, the giant Knight Ridder chain (once one of the dominant companies in the newspaper industry) launched a "25/43 Project" aimed at winning back that affluent "demographic" (age group) of television babies who had drifted away from newspaper reading. Focus groups were selected to probe personal concerns and to find market angles that would appeal to new readers. A former editor at the chain's Boca Raton, Florida, *News* described the effort to make over his former paper as similar to "watching Procter & Gamble develop and test market a new toothpaste."[24] Reporters at other papers in the area dubbed the result "The Flamingo News" for its flamboyant Miami design, which included a pink flamingo on the masthead. Political reporting in the redesigned *News* was derided as "news McNuggets," and another former editor charged the paper with "pandering to people with the attention span of a gnat."[25] However, the editor of the *Boca Raton News,* who presided over the marketing makeover, claimed that the streamlined approach to news, along with more personalized features, was simply giving people what they wanted. Other Knight Ridder papers, with a few notable exceptions, soon followed the lead of the *Boca Raton News*, often to the dismay of their reporters.

Among the most surprising casualties of the marketing of news was the resignation of Jay Harris, publisher of one of the most successful and respected dailies in the Knight Ridder chain, the *San Jose Mercury News*. After the highly profitable surge of the 1990s (the *Mercury*'s profits ranged between 22% and 29% over the decade), the bottom line began to slide, in large part because the recession in Silicon Valley cut into lucrative employment advertising by technology companies. The corporate response was to slash the news budget severely to shore up sagging profits.

A memo from the president of Knight Ridder asked Harris to apply the standard formulas to make the cuts: "I would recommend taking a hard look at the recent reader research. If the *Mercury News* market is similar to our other markets, the research will indicate that the readers will want more local news. The *Mercury News* front pages are consistently local and compelling, while the inside of the A section is very heavily weighted toward foreign news. This may be something to reconsider."[26] Harris knew that a large percentage of his readers consisted of software engineers from other countries. Moreover, the computer business that defined the local economy was a global industry requiring international information. He also knew that corporate headquarters was unyielding in its insistence on maintaining unrealistic levels of profit growth. The inevitable result would be to watch one of the nation's best (and still profitable) papers deteriorate, so Harris resigned in protest. Jay Harris's resignation sent a sobering message to his colleagues in the profession, and he was soon invited to address the convention of the American Society of Newspaper editors. In his speech, he raised these crucial questions: "When the interests of readers and shareholders are at odds, which takes priority? When the interests of the community and shareholders are at odds, which takes priority? When the interest of the nation and an informed citizenry and the demands of the shareholders for ever-increasing profits are at odds, which takes priority?"[27]

And there lies the trouble: Whether in newspapers or television, the temptation is to produce cheaper news simply because the short-term profits are bigger. In the long term, however, audiences continue to shrink from the stream of mayhem, negativity, and empty stories. By the mid-2000s, Knight Ridder continued to suffer declining readerships among young demographics, and its profits fell flat, which angered large shareholders who forced the chain to be put up for sale. Knight Ridder was soon bought in 2006 by the smaller McClatchy group for $4.4 billion. McClatchy promptly sold 12 of the newly acquired chain's 32 papers in order to concentrate on the most profitable ones. And so the commercialization of the news business goes.

How Does Corporate Influence Operate?

As the above discussions suggest, executives at Disney or GE or Gannett do not issue many direct orders to distant journalists to cut back on serious coverage of politics and government or to run more sex and crime. The demise of serious news is a mere casualty of sensible-sounding business decisions. As a managing editor of the *New York Times* explained it,

> News coverage is being shaped by corporate executives at headquarters far from the local scene. It is seldom done by corporate directive or fiat. It rarely involves killing or slanting stories. Usually it is by the appointment of a pliable editor here, a corporate graphics conference there, that results in a more uniform look and cookie-cutter approach among a chain's newspapers, or it's by the corporate research director's interpretation of reader surveys that seek simple common-denominator solutions to complex coverage problems. Often the corporate view is hostile to governmental coverage. It has been fashionable for some years, during meetings of editors and publishers, to deplore "incremental" news coverage. Supposedly it is boring, a turnoff to readers, and—what's worse—it requires news hole. The problem with all of this is that government news develops incrementally. And if you don't cover it incrementally, you don't really cover it at all. Incremental is what it is all about.[28]

Journalist and communication scholar Doug Underwood has examined changes in business values of news organizations at the newsroom level, and he finds increasing limits on the content of news that stem from the manufacture and sale of news as a commercial product. Real press freedoms are limited each news day simply because, in his words, "MBAs rule the newsroom."[29] Assignments are made increasingly with costs, efficiency, and viewer or reader reactions in mind. Newspapers, in particular, struggle to survive in the video age; they are run with fewer and fewer concerns about informing the public. As Underwood describes it: "Today's market-savvy newspapers are planned and packaged to 'give readers what they want'; newspaper content is geared to the results of readership surveys; and newsroom organization has been reshaped by newspaper managers whose commitment to the marketing ethic is hardly distinguishable from their vision of what journalism is."[30] The paper that set this trend was *USA Today*, which has been dubbed "McPaper" and "the newspaper for people who are too busy to watch TV." However, in this era of newsroom cutbacks, *USA Today* is starting to look better.

THE POLITICAL ECONOMY OF NEWS

Economic pressures are not new. They have been steadily shaping the news for more than a century and a half. In the view of journalism historian Gerald Baldasty, the most fundamental transformation of news in the history of this country began in the mid-1800s when the political party press began to give way to a commercial press.[31] We explored these historical roots of modern news in Chapter 6. In a media system as heavily tilted toward commercialism as the United States, there is little escape from economic pressures on information quality. However, the question is whether the balance between corporate profits and other social values has become so lopsided that little else matters. The form and magnitude of economic changes in recent years have resulted in a remarkable period of change, making today's news very different than it was even a decade or two ago.

Audience size and common consumption patterns were two defining elements of the mass media. The fragmentation of audiences and the rise of niche media signal the twilight of the mass media era. There is, however, a sense in which the mass media, or at least a new variant, is still with us: the growing standardization of information at its source. If we add to this the declining commitment to producing hard news, we have a prescription for economizing in the industry: More information is produced in generic form, wholesaled to many outlets, and later dressed up or down, as the format of a particular channel and the demographics of its audience dictate. This seeming contradiction between multiplying channels and shrinking diversity and depth of news content is important to understand.

As the global media come under the ownership of a handful of giant corporations, such as Time Warner based in the United States, German-based Bertelsmann, or Rupert Murdoch's News Corp, the tendency is for the same centrally gathered raw news material to be delivered to more and more outlets in the "media mall." There are, of course, important exceptions: the *New York Times* in the United States, the British Broadcasting Corporation in the United Kingdom, *El Pais* in Spain, *Le Monde* in France, and the *Frankfurter Allgemeine Zeitung* in Germany. Although these independent, high-quality organizations seldom challenge the political or economic consensus in Washington, London, or Berlin, they provide detailed reports on important world developments, enabling citizens to have at least a chance of understanding events.

Economics vs. Democracy: Inside the News Business

As noted in Chapter 1, there is no guarantee of optimal information in any political system, including one that displays the First Amendment as a sort of broad guarantee of information quality. As a challenge to conventional wisdom, consider the argument of communication scholar Robert McChesney, whose historical analysis indicates that commercial press systems contain little inherent basis for public service or responsibility. McChesney suggests that if we lift the veil of press freedom, we encounter corporate interests that invoke the First Amendment less often to protect their freedom to publicize politically risky or challenging information than to defend their pursuit of profits against obligations to serve the public interest.[32] Today's catchphrase is *freedom of the market,* which means profits over social responsibility. Yet the raw pursuit of profits does not mean that giant corporations will necessarily prosper, however much they cheapen the product.

The Ratings Decline of Network News

In the case of TV network news, the ratings battle is a losing one. A rating point reflects the percentage of television households watching a program relative to the total number of television households, which the giant ratings company

Nielsen estimated at 115 million in 2010. Thus, a rating of 30 points equals 30 percent of all TV households watching a program. Advertising rates are determined by a combination of the size of the audience (ratings) and its demographic composition of ready buyers for the product. Also, because everyone is not watching TV all the time, the price of ads also reflects the percentage, or *share,* of actual viewers in a particular time slot who are tuned in to a particular program. While networks continue to experiment with different news formats, the audience loss has been precipitous. The evening news, whether at CBS, ABC, or NBC, routinely scores ratings in the 5 to 7 range, reflecting a steady decline from more than twice those levels since the 1970s. As recently as the late 1990s, ratings were in the 8–9 range for the network news, and less than 2 for PBS.[33] At the time of this writing, according to the Pew Project for Excellence in Journalism, the combined audience of the network nightly newscasts was about 22.5 million, representing a steady decline of about 1 million viewers a year since 1980. The corresponding decline in ratings now puts the 3 networks at around just 15 percent of television households.[34]

Why is it important? Consider just one aspect of what these huge changes mean. In the 1960s, an advertiser could reach 80 percent of women in the United States with just one ad spot. Today, that same spot would have to be run on 100 channels to reach the same audience.[35] This massive change means, among other things, that the costs of political campaign advertising have soared astronomically as campaigns spend more to reach fewer voters with messages that are less likely to hit their targets. In addition, consider the possibilities that much of the news today never reaches most people, because they are now consuming media that deal more exclusively with sports, gaming, food, or entertainment than with news. We are living through the end of the mass media, and it has important consequences for our lives as citizens, publics, and a nation.

Fragmented Audiences: The End of Mass Media?

With the exception of the Super Bowl and national crises such as 9/11 or the invasion of Iraq, it makes little sense to talk about a mass media audience any longer, at least one defined by large numbers of people gathering around televisions and watching the same information fed from a few sources.[36] In just one decade, between 1993 and 2004, the percentage of people who regularly watched network TV news dropped 34 percent.[37] Consider just a few other audience trends that have developed in recent years:

- The original three networks (ABC, CBS, and NBC) captured more than 90 percent of prime-time television viewers as recently as 1978. By 1997, that share was hovering at 50 percent and fell to 25 percent by 2010. By the mid-2000s, cable scored upward of 60 percent of prime-time TV audiences during summer seasons, and clearly trumped prime time audience share by decade's end.[38]
- Cable news markets are fragmenting. For example, the proliferation of cable news channels slammed cable news pioneer CNN's already thin audience share by one-third between 1992 and 1997, despite the fact that

the number of households able to watch CNN tripled during the same period.[39] As of this writing, the clear cable news leader is FOX, by far, with CNN a distant third behind MSNBC. Even so, with prime-time audiences for all cable news adding up to between 2.5 and 3.5 million and not showing much growth in recent years, the cable ratings race is taking place in an arena with limited spectators.[40]

- Perhaps even more disturbing for the idea of a mass audience sharing experiences in common is that news preferences are increasingly selected according to political ideology of the viewers, with FOX disproportionately drawing Republicans and MSNBC drawing more Democrats. It may be due to this political filtering that fewer people believe what they see and hear on television news.[41]

- People are less likely to make appointments to watch a favorite news program, preferring instead to tune in and out of various sources, and most people who watch TV news now do so with a remote control in hand.[42]

- Some of the slack in conventional news trends appears to be taken up by the Internet. By 2010, fully 44 percent of all Americans said they got news through some digital platform the previous day.[43] But there are by now many sources delivering information of uneven qualities online.

- More worrisome is that only one-third of the younger demographic age bracket enjoys keeping up with the news "a lot," compared with two-thirds of seniors. A national study that compared awareness of soft-news stories (e.g., death of a famous celebrity) with hard-news stories (e.g., Iraq troop pullout debate) found that 68 percent of those under 30 were aware of the soft news fare. Only 33 percent of the younger demographic was aware of the hard-news stories compared to 67 percent who were not aware of them.[44] The situation is summed up by scholar David Mindich as follows: ". . . across America, young people have abandoned traditional news."[45]

Are the Media Breaking Up Society?

Communication scholar Joseph Turow argues that the technology for targeting consumers and then marketing virtually anything to them—from the brand-extended lifestyle product lines of Ralph Lauren or Victoria's Secret to scary images of new health care reforms or the comforting idea of a more compassionate political candidate—all have the effect of breaking up society.[46] There is a "chicken-and-egg" possibility here that society is fragmenting for other reasons, and communication technologies simply follow the segments and further isolate them.[47] Either way, the segmentation of society into neatly organized consumer groups is great for individuals in pursuit of more emotionally satisfying lifestyles, but it may not be so great for democracy. Many scholars argue that such communication-induced social fragmentation reinforces personal, consumption-centered realities that inhibit mutual understanding, undermine the capacity for consensus, and inhibit the commitment to collective values and public projects on which democracy depends.[48]

In some ways, these new prospects for personal identities are liberating, and in other ways, they are stressful and confusing. One thing seems clear, however: personal relationships to, and uses of, public information are changing. The very things that people regard as news are changing. It may be that the latest 9/11 conspiracy theory site on the Internet is regarded by some as more newsworthy than the network newscast. With fewer people consuming the same news, there is less reality held in common. The effects of public consensus on how to define things, what to care about, and how to act appropriately may all diminish. The media echo chamber that recycles fringe behavior back into the mainstream may further undermine consensus on many things that are needed to conduct a democracy: civility, concern for common spaces and values, and interest in understanding the lives and problems of others— just to mention a few. In short the fragmenting media may also undermine the important idea of an "imagined community" that we can share, even as we may disagree on its directions or priorities.

If we combine the diminished authoritativeness of various information sources noted earlier with the personalization of information indicated in these surveys, a resulting information shift may be a tendency for people to more easily confuse their personal opinions with fact. New information technologies that target ever smaller demographics enable information to build realities that are more personal and close to home than to imagine social realities shared in common with large numbers of distant strangers. (For a frightening look at what this trend may do to news as we know it within the next decade, please watch the video available at **www.robinsloan.com/epic/**.) In some respects, the rise of the Internet as a core personal information source may feed this cycle, both by giving individuals increasing control of the realities they choose to participate in and by making it even more difficult to evaluate the quality or authoritativeness of information about those realities that comes straight and unfiltered from cyberspace. Many of these concerns are still speculative, but one thing is clear: The fragmentation of media audiences is occurring at a breathtaking rate.

Any appearance of a grand democratic design in such an information system may be based on faith that a free press and a free market create the most perfect results. Despite the growing arguments that we may need government to restore greater degree of media ownership regulation and public affairs content standards, many people may still believe that more channels and choices must be inherently better, even if they are owned by fewer parent companies and produce an ever more fragmented public that does not receive anything like the same information. Indeed, many people seem to believe that corporate profits are sacred and that no other values should stand in the way of corporate managers to maximize them. However, this argument ignores the many public goods that would not exist without government interventions: roads, schools, clean air and drinking water, security agencies, airports, and many more. Why not add decent public information to this list?

EFFECTS OF MEDIA CONCENTRATION: WHY GOVERNMENT DEREGULATION WAS BAD FOR PUBLIC INFORMATION

Opponents of restoring greater government regulation of the information industry point to the vast and growing numbers of information outlets that people have available to them. If viewed uncritically, the proliferation of inputs may appear to offer more choice and diversity than any individual could want. The problem, say critics such as Ben Bagdikian, former dean of the Journalism School at the University of California, Berkeley, is that although information outlets are undeniably proliferating, their ownership is increasingly concentrated, and the first effect of concentration is to push small media promoting noncommercial values out of the way. There are different ways to think about the effects of the concentration of media ownership on news content, some of which we have touched on in earlier discussions. Here are the effects most discussed by communication scholars:

1. Dominance by fewer players in local and regional markets distorts advertising rates, forcing small, independent outlets to quit, sell out, or change their formats—resulting in less diversity in music, news, and minority affairs programming.
2. The interests of corporate image and self-promotion means less critical coverage of the media industry in general and parent companies in particular.
3. News content shifts to infotainment formats due to the entertainment focus of owners and the economic efficiencies of soft news, "reality programming," and human interest features.
4. News is regarded less as a public service commitment or a prestige builder for the parent company, and it becomes just another product line in the race for profits.
5. Innovation in packaging and branding disguises declining information diversity and content distinctiveness.

The case study in this chapter illustrates the political issues involved in the government decisions since the 1980s favoring corporate profits over public values in the media.

▶ CASE STUDY

Ownership Deregulation and the Citizen's Movement for Social Responsibility in Broadcast Standards

The corporate concentration of media ownership was well underway by the mid-1980s when the government all but abandoned the mandate for the Federal Communications Commission to monitor and enforce the "fairness doctrine" which required broadcasters to present issues of public importance in a balanced fashion. For decades, this had been regarded as a reasonable protection of the public interest in exchange for granting commercial corporations the use of public airwaves for commercial gain. Increasing pressure from corporations during the Reagan era of anti-government sentiment and the promotion of deregulation led a Republican dominated FCC to abolish the doctrine in 1987. Many stations quickly abandoned news and public affairs programming, and new incentives for corporate concentration of formulaic media systems were introduced.

Yet the pressures continued from media companies for further reductions of government limits on ownership of multiple types of media (e.g., newspapers, television, and radio) in particular markets, and levels of cross media ownership in general. These limits were intended to keep small independent media companies alive in local areas, and to promote competition among local media, with the hope of stimulating content diversity and local voices. However, media companies had invested wisely in the campaign funds of both parties, and by the 1990s, both Republicans and Democrats had for the most part become advocates of free trade deregulation and the powerful idea of synergy in the media. Bill Clinton (who had powerful Hollywood backers) explained how enabling media concentration was a good thing because it would build capital for new investment, and make the U.S. entertainment industry even more dominant in global markets. As for competition and diversity, those questions were waved off with vague ideas about how huge conglomerates would have to encourage diversity and competition so their subsidiaries would not duplicate each other.

All of this culminated with the Telecommunications (TelCom) Act of 1996, which *The Wall Street Journal* heralded as "the first major overhaul of telecommunications law since Marconi was alive and the crystal set was the state of the art."[49] The most highly publicized aspects of the law promised increasing competition and lower rates for consumers in phone and cable services. However, the meat of the legislation was a maze of reduced barriers to ownership of a number of media outlets (e.g., stations, papers, cable channels), ownership of outlets in different media sectors (e.g., radio, TV, newspapers, cable), and the number of outlets that can be owned by the same company within the same city or media market. Along with these reduced regulations came what was termed a necessary relaxation in community service requirements for distant owners who can now operate multiple outlets in the same local markets. For example, if the entire program feed for a rock station in Boston comes from an automated control room across the country, there is little room for news or even local tastes in music to be reflected—only the cheapest program content that continues to deliver enough listeners to sell commercials at a profit.

Why don't listeners simply flee to other channels? With the sweeping deregulation written into the Telecommunications Act of 1996, most of the stations in most cities have become owned by a few corporate giants who gradually put the local competition out of business and replace high-quality and often diverse programming with the cheapest, most standardized fare that still keeps listeners tuned for commercials. An activist from Prometheus Radio Project, which supports community radio stations, described a typical situation when one company " . . . owns eight radio stations in one town, plus all the billboards and concert venues, and all the promotional machinery, suddenly they have a level of power that their competitors have no way to compete with. Once the competitors are out of business they have free reign to do just about anything that they please, that is the same just as any other monopoly."[50] Is that assessment too harsh or radical? On the

Continued

contrary, it is precisely the goal of many corporate owners, which is why corporate media spent so much money lobbying for 1996 legislation (and spent so little time reporting it to their audiences as news).

A few owners, such as Lowry Mays, who founded Clear Channel radio, will even be happy to tell you exactly what their business model is. As he put it to a *Fortune* magazine reporter: "We're not in the business of providing news and information. We're not in the business of providing well researched music. We're simply in the business of selling our customers products."[51] This philosophy was literally licensed and unleashed on the nation by the TelCom Act of 1996. As a result, Clear Channel delivers its brand of radio through more than 800 stations in 50 states, reaching 110 million Americans. The company's Web site claims to reach 45 percent of all people between the ages of 18–49 every day.

A noted above, ownership restrictions and community service standards were once regarded as firewalls for information diversity and competition in the American democracy. The old public responsibility thinking went like this: (a) local owners might be more responsive to community values, (b) different ownership of different sectors (types of media) was good for program diversity, and, (c) limits on a single company's control of a particular sector would prevent strangleholds on advertising revenues that might put smaller local companies out of business. The new business-driven thinking that was used in lobbying both Democrats and Republicans to support the deregulation went like this: (a) markets inherently create diversity through competition; (b) competition within each company's holdings will be created by the drive for audiences and profits; (c) therefore, even companies that own many media outlets in a community will be driven to diversify and reflect community values. As for public service, if communities want some sort of service from their media outlets, they will support broadcasters who provide it.

This easy reasoning ignores the fact that conglomerates enter communities with the intent of closing down local programming and piping the same music or talk formulas from central production facilities to hundreds of niche markets around the country. During the critical days after 9/11, many local people found that they could not get any information about what was happening in their communities because distant radio corporations had no provision for monitoring the local scenes in which they broadcast. Indeed, some had no news production at all and had to patch into CNN in order to provide communities with any news about the crisis. These realities of community service were glossed over by hasty and shallow debates on media regulation and deregulation.

Therefore, without much public discussion, Congress and President Clinton ended the old regime and announced the new. In what has been termed "The Full Employment Act for Telecommunication Lawyers," a consolidation frenzy was unleashed. This came on the heels of a decade in which few thought that merger mania could get any more intense. For example, before the new law, corporate giants bought out the TV networks (GE swallowed NBC, Westinghouse gobbled CBS, and Disney added Cap Cities/ABC to its portfolio of assets). The world's book publishers were also merged, stripped, and consolidated in breathtaking leaps. But the TelCom Act set the media world spinning even faster. The year following the new law was called the "Year of the Deal" by many in the industry, as indicated by just a few of the deals that the new legislation enabled. Murdoch's News Corporation (which earlier had swallowed FOX, HarperCollins Publishers, and *TV Guide*) bought New World Communications, making News Corp for a short time the nation's largest TV station owner. Westinghouse/CBS bought Infinity Broadcasting, giving it a chain of 77 radio stations to go with its string of other stations, creating multiple outlets in the top-ten markets in the country. Viacom bought CBS and all its media holdings, making it (until the later CBS spin-off) the largest TV and radio station owner. Time Warner and Turner Broadcasting merged into the world's largest media company, and, not long after, America Online bought Time Warner, making it again the largest. Gannett Newspaper Group bought Multimedia Entertainment to expand its newspaper chain to 92, its TV stations to 15, its radio stations to 13, and its cable operations to 5 states, and is still growing.[52] Typical of the big picture within most sectors, more than 10 percent (162 of 1,509) of the nation's daily newspapers changed ownership in one year.[53]

These stories unfolded largely as business and financial news, with the focus on corporate profits and growth prospects. The press (whose parent corporations lobbied furiously for the new legislation) seldom raised the question of whether the proliferation of choices would really provide the "diversity of voices and viewpoints" promised by Bill Clinton as he signed the bill into law.[54]

The level of media concentration soon became so worrisome that a grassroots citizen movement emerged (see, e.g., www.freepress.net) when the Federal Communications Commission (FCC) moved to relax ownership restrictions even further in 2003. Two of the five FCC commissioners voted against provisions that would have enabled a single corporation to own a newspaper, three TV stations, eight radio stations, and the cable system in a single market. Hearings were held around the country, and owners of remaining independent media outlets protested that the latest rules would surely mean the death of local media. A citizen lobbying campaign targeted Congress with hundreds of thousands of e-mails, faxes, and phone messages, and in an impressive display of bipartisanship, the U.S. Senate voted to block the changes. While the Bush administration regrouped around possible executive measures to restore good relations with its corporate sponsors, then FCC chairman Michael Powell went public with his shock. Robert McChesney described Powell's charge that:

> ...the rule-making process had been upset by "a concerted grassroots effort to attack the commission from the outside in." Seemingly unaware that a public agency like the FCC could, in fact, be addressed by the public, he expressed amazement that as many as 3 million Americans have contacted the FCC and Congress to demand that controls against media monopoly be kept in place. Capitol Hill observers say that media ownership has been the second most discussed issue by constituents in 2003, trailing only the war on Iraq. Following Brecht's famous dictum, Michael Powell wanted to fire the people.[55]

The citizen movement to restore social responsibility and public affairs requirements for media continues to gain momentum. However, even with the restoration of a Democratic administration in 2008, the FCC was scrambling to get a grip on the changing media landscape. More of the action in media was happening online, including news and other political information sources. Yet the Bush FCC had thrown a wrench into the agency's capacity to regulate the Internet by unilaterally declaring that service providers were not "common carriers" of information like phone companies that are obligated to provide service to all who want it within their licensed monopoly jurisdictions. This meant that giant service providers, such as Viacom and Comcast were essentially free to decide who could download what and at what charges.

Continued

Members of Free Press and other concerned citizen movements reasoned that if all content and users were not treated alike, then a company could promote its own products over competing content that might attract profits or clog its high speed bandwidth. Moreover, civic groups and public interest organizations that use the Internet to communicate with large numbers of members and list subscribers might be restricted or charged higher rates. The result is that content could be controlled to suit the business plans of the service providers, who are already highly profitable, and who have in many cases already been given effective monopolies in lucrative markets. Like the television and newspaper conglomerates that came before them in the days after the Telecom Act, they just want more. Although the digital media are new, the logic is much the same. The eternal belief in synergy that drove the old media to the brink of profit-driven collapse, the titans of the new media industries are also jockeying for dominance and control, and the Internet service providers turn out to be in critical positions to shape the game.

The early efforts by the Obama FCC to regain some regulatory authority in this rapidly changing mediascape was rebuffed by a court ruling that made the path back to public interest regulation unclear. Perhaps Congress needed to pass new laws made for the Internet. In the meantime, events and mergers were rapidly unfolding. Faced with a challenge to its own authority, the FCC invited giants Verizon and Google to meet and propose a plan for balancing profits with an open Internet. Not surprisingly, they were happy to propose how to regulate themselves, and they made reference to what citizen activists have called "net neutrality" or open and equal access to the Internet (with some provisions for restricting openly offensive or threatening communication). Yet the solution of letting corporations help set their own standards sounds eerily similar to what happened with the Telecom regulations of the last era.

Should the Internet be turned into a collection of giant shopping malls policed against political content that might reduce bandwidth and distract the shoppers? Should media companies regulate download privileges, file sharing, and enforce copyright policing in favor of their own and their partners' products? These are important questions that affect the future of the Internet and its potential for a viable public information space where experiments may enable citizens to discover the next form of public information to replace the currently crumbling news system.

Most cities now have media justice and media reform groups, and many of these citizen networks are currently pressing for "net neutrality," which would enable the FCC or some other government agency to make sure that service providers keep the Internet open for all users, rich and poor, political and commercial. No matter what one's main political issue or concern may be, media democracy is rapidly becoming a companion concern as citizens begin to understand the shrinking public communication space devoted to their main issues.

NEWS ON THE INTERNET: PERFECTING THE COMMERCIALIZATION OF INFORMATION?

Perhaps nowhere is the merger of news and advertising more advanced than on the Internet. For example, CNN and Barnes and Noble have created what the marketing director of Barnes and Noble called a "new paradigm that is not editorial and not advertising."[56] CNN sends the bookseller a list of its top stories of the day, and the book company loads up its books on the subject so that people who access the news site can click on buttons for relevant books to buy. Although this sounds like pure consumer benefit, there is a danger that news sites and, more generally, Web sites for many information-related services will filter and emphasize information according to the synergy it has with advertisers.

For example, information searches are far more likely to turn up news sources and information that favor companies sponsoring the sites where the information is provided.[57] The CNN site matches travel articles with reservation services and travel agencies keyed to those articles. A page on hair loss in the America Online (AOL) health-information service links to ads for baldness treatments. Amazon.com promoted particular books as "staff picks" after receiving money from the books' publishers. All that a person using the Yahoo! search engine needs to do to make plane reservations is click on "Travel Agent," but the link will go to an agency that pays to be the official travel service of Yahoo! A careful reading of Yahoo!'s own independent ratings of travel services (located in the back pages of the site) discloses that, in Yahoo!'s view, there are better services.[58]

An AOL executive casually dismissed the screening of content according to commercial criteria by saying "Our users don't care what the financial relationship is between us and the provider of the content they see." Another Web site executive said that "Anyone going online should assume that there is an advertising influence on most of the content they see."[59] This axiom seems to be true and the terms of use for standard free services such as Gmail, Facebook, or iTunes become ever longer, more unreadable and generally unfathomable. Most Gmail users know that their mail is scanned for content that may be helpful in targeting ads, and there are many tales of copyright snarls involving user experience with YouTube videos. Yet the basic tradeoff remains that we open ourselves to encroachments on our privacy in order for corporations (and increasingly governments) to extract useful information in exchange for "free" media use. Because consumers are generally unwilling to pay for information they take from or send through Web sites, almost all of it is developed in conjunction with advertisers. The increasing dilemma for information seekers is how to evaluate the quality and completeness of the information they get.

These concerns notwithstanding, the explosion of the blogosphere and the uses of social networking sites in politics in recent years suggest that a thriving information community is developing online. At the same time, much the content and conversation continues to revolve around news produced by the old media organizations which are in crisis. Yet, there have been few creative initiatives to reduce tension between news aggregators, such as Googlenews and the press organizations that it feeds on. Although there is talk of putting up pay walls and creating systems for collecting micro charges for viewing pages, these developments seem unlikely to save the root news organizations that were so damaged by the earlier era of media concentration. And even if a pay system is worked out, the product fed to online news aggregators and blogs is unlikely to be independent of official spin, which is part of the problem with citizen confidence in the media in the first place.

The future of a free Internet depends on the degree to which noncommercial information sites develop and find means of supporting themselves. In many cases, charitable foundations such as Ford and Rockefeller have sponsored the communication efforts of nongovernmental organizations (NGOs) dedicated to various causes, from the environment to human rights. In other cases, activists have donated programming and Web design skills to make low-cost independent political information channels available to other citizens. As we will see in the next chapter, foundations have also helped start independent online journalism organizations (many of which are staffed by reporters ejected from the dying commercial system).

TECHNOLOGY, ECONOMICS, AND SOCIAL CHANGE

Much of this book focuses on three core elements of political communication: (a) journalism and the news business, (b) the communication strategies of political actors, and (c) the information habits of citizens. However, we cannot ignore how a fourth factor, technology, shapes each of the others in important ways. Some of the greatest changes in news content were created by developments in communication technologies. For example, in the nineteenth century, the development of an overburdened horse-drawn national mail system,[60] followed by the telegraph, invited news dispatches to adopt a "just the facts," or "telegraphic," information structure, launching the "who, what, where, when, why" format for the news. In the twentieth century, first photography, then film, and, finally, television put the news emphasis on visual information, creating vivid images that communicate without words.

People talk of the twenty-first century as an age of technological convergence in which word, image, and sound will be translatable, storable, editable, and programmable on devices that will blur the distinctions among television, computers, and telephony. The electronics of a house, from TV to the Internet device, down to the art images on the walls, and even the kitchen toaster, may be fully integrated, interactive, and run from a single remote control the size of a cell phone. As of this writing, some 63 percent of all households in the United States have broadband (and 77% have some Internet access), although this does not put the US into the top 20 nations. It is clear that the trends point to increasing online information gathering (not to mention surfing, shopping, chatting, and data retrieval). In the next chapter we explore how these and the many other coming technological developments may change the news.

The potential for reinventing public information online depends on many factors, such as restricting large corporations from owning the Internet. If left to be relatively open, Jochai Benkler has argued persuasively that the Internet has fostered a very different and competing economic model based on sharing (e.g., open source platforms, operating systems, and software; a creative commons copyright system for public distribution of creative property under the control of those who created it rather than have corporations own it).[61] This economic model and the future of public information that may be based on it depend a great deal on how the Internet is regulated and whether big media corporations, such as Google, Comcast, Verizon, and Apple get to decide how that goes.

NOTES

1. Pew Project for Excellence in Journalism, "The State of the News Media 2010." www.stateofthemedia.org/2010/index.php. Accessed September 16, 2010.
2. This and the Bronstein quotes come from Maureen Dowd, "Slouching Towards Oblivion," *New York Times*, April 25, 2009. www.nyt.com. Accessed May 15, 2010.
3. Ibid.
4. Pablo Boczkowski, *News at Work: Imitation in an Age of Information Abundance* (Chicago: University of Chicago Press, 2011).
5. Dean Starkman, "The Hamster Wheel: Why Running as Fast as We Can is Getting Us Nowhere," *Columbia Journalism Review* (September/October 2010): 24–28.
6. Ibid., 28.
7. Bill Carter, "Chief of ABC News Is Resigning," *New York Times*, September 6, 2010. www.nytimes.com/2010/09/07/business/media/07abc.html?_r=3&hp. Accessed September 6, 2010.
8. See Neil Hickey, "Money Lust: How Pressure for Profit Is Perverting Journalism," *Columbia Journalism Review* (July/August 1998): 28.
9. Craig Flournoy and Tracy Everbach, "Damage Report," *Columbia Journalism Review* (July/August 2007): 33.
10. Ibid., 35, 37.
11. Ibid., 36.
12. Ibid., 36.
13. David Laventhol, "Profit Pressures," *Columbia Journalism Review* (May/June 2001): 19.
14. Matthew A. Baum, *Soft News Goes to War: Public Opinion and American Foreign Policy in the New Media Age* (Princeton, NJ: Princeton University Press, 2003).
15. For earlier episodes in this history, see Gerald Baldasty, *The Commercialization of News in the Nineteenth Century* (Madison: University of Wisconsin Press, 1992).
16. Christopher Harper, "Doing It All: Online Staffers Do a Variety of Jobs," *American Journalism Review* 18, no.10 (December 1996): 24.
17. For a detailed account of this period, see Dean Alger, *Megamedia: How Giant Corporations Dominate Mass Media* (Lanham, MD: Rowman and Littlefield, 1998).
18. www.freepress.net/ownership/chart/main.
19. See the *Planet Viacom Centerfold* in Mark Crispin Miller, "Can Viacom's Reporters Cover Viacom's Interests?" *Columbia Journalism Review* (November/December 1999): 48–50.
20. Several organizations have Web sites to help track media ownership. The most comprehensive is Pew Project for Excellence in Journalism, Who Owns the News Media. Viacom and other media conglomerate holdings can be tracked at www.cjr.org/resources/. Other issues connected to media ownership can be followed on the

Media Channel at www.mediachannel.org/ownership. By far the most comprehensive resource site is maintained by the media reform organization Freepress: www.freepress.net/ownership.

21. Paul Farhi, "In Television, Big Is Now Clearly Better," *Washington Post National Weekly Edition* (September 20, 1999): 21.

22. Quoted in Ken Auletta, "Look What They've Done to the News," *TV Guide* (November 9, 1991): 5.

23. Alessandra Stanley, "How to Persuade the Young to Watch the News? Program It, Executives Say," *New York Times*, January 15, 2000: C6.

24. Sally Deneen, "Doing the Boca: An Interim Report from a Reinvented Newspaper," *Columbia Journalism Review* (May/June 1991): 15.

25. Ibid.

26. Steve Rossi, "In Their Own Words: The Harris Resignation," *Columbia Journalism Review* (May/June, 2001): 20.

27. David Laventhol, "Profit Pressures: A Question of Margins," *Columbia Journalism Review* (May/June 2001): 18.

28. Gene Roberts, "Drowning in Shallow Waters," *Columbia Journalism Review* (May/June 1996): 55.

29. Doug Underwood, *When MBAs Rule the Newsroom* (New York: Columbia University Press, 1993).

30. Ibid., xii.

31. Baldasty, *The Commercialization of News*.

32. Robert McChesney, *Rich Media, Poor Democracy: Communication Politics in Dubious Times* (Urbana: University of Illinois Press, 1999).

33. Karen Bedford, "Public Affairs at PBS: The Pressure Is On," *Columbia Journalism Review* (May/June 1999): 13. See also *Broadcasting & Cable*, October 17, 2005; www.broadcastingcable.com/article/CA6273133.html?display=John+Higgins& referral=SUPP.

34. Pew Project for Excellence in Journalism, "State of the News Media 2010."

35. Henry Jenkins, *Convergence Culture* (New York: New York University Press, 2007), 66.

36. See Markus Prior, *Post-broadcast Democracy* (New York: Cambridge University Press, 2007).

37. Pew Research Report, June 10, 2004, www.stateofthenewsmedia.org/2004/ narrative_networktv_audience.asp?cat=3&media=4. See also "State of the Media 2010."

38. Nielsen data reported in Bill Carter, "TV Networks Are Scrambling to Deal with Era of New Media," *New York Times*, May 17, 1999: A17.

39. Pew Project for Excellence in Journalism, "State of the News Media 2010."

40. Pew Project for Excellence Report, www.stateofthenewsmedia.org/2007/ narrative_cabletv_audience.asp?cat=2&media=6.

41. "Online News Audience Larger, More Diverse," Pew Report, June 8, 2004, http://peoplepress.org/reports/display.php3?PageID5833. See also, W. Lance Bennett and Shanto Iyengar, "A New Era of Minimal Effects? The Changing Foundations of Political Communication," *Journal of Communication* 58 (2008): 707–731.

42. Pew surveys reported in Richard Morin, "The Move to 'Net News': Folks Still Want to Know What's Going On, but They're Turning from TV to the Computer," *Washington Post National Weekly Edition* (June 15, 1998): 34.

43. Pew Project, "State of the News Media 2010."

44. Thomas E. Patterson, "Young People and News," A Report from the Joan Shorenstein Center, Kennedy School of Government, Harvard University, July 2007, 17.

45. David Mindich, *Tuned Out: Why Americans Under 40 Don't Follow the News* (New York: Oxford University Press, 2005), 2.

46. Joseph Turow, *Breaking Up America: Advertisers and the New Media World* (Chicago: University of Chicago Press, 1997).

47. See W. Lance Bennett, "The UnCivic Culture: Communication, Identity, and the Rise of Lifestyle Politics," *PS: Political Science and Politics* 31 (December 1998): 741–761.

48. In addition to Turow, *Breaking Up America*; see also Stuart Ewen, *PR! A Social History of Spin* (New York: Basic Books, 1996); and Oscar Gandy, "Dividing Practices: Segmentation and Targeting in the Emerging Public Sphere," in *Mediated Politics: Communication in the Future of Democracy*, eds. W. Lance Bennett and Robert M. Entman (New York: Cambridge University Press, 2001).

49. From Neil Hickey, "So Big: The Telecommunications Act at Year One," *Columbia Journalism Review* (January/February 1997): 23.

50. Dante Toza, "Clear Channel Rewrites Rules of Radio Broadcasting," *CorpWatch* (October 8, 2003). www.corpwatch.org/article.php?id58728.

51. Christine Chen, "The Bad Boys of Radio," *Fortune* (May 3, 2003). http://money.cnn.com/magazines/fortune/fortune_archive/2003/03/03/338343/.

52. Hickey, "So Big," 24.

53. Ibid., 34.

54. Ibid., 23.

55. Robert W. McChesney and John Nichols, "Up in Flames," *Nation* (October 17, 2003). www.thenation.com/doc.mhtml?i=20031117s=mcchesney&c51.

56. Saul Hansell, "News-Ad Issues Arise in New Media," *New York Times* December 8, 1997: C10.

57. Saul Hansell and Amy Harmon, "Caveat Emptor on the Web: Ad and Editorial Lines Blur," *New York Times*, February 26, 1999: 1.

58. Ibid., A12.

59. Ibid., A12.

60. See Richard Kielbowicz, *News in the Mail: The Press, Post Office and Public Information, 1700–1860s* (Westport, CT: Greenwood Press, 1989).

61. Jochai Benkler, *The Wealth of Networks* (New Haven: Yale University Press, 2006).

All the News That Fits Democracy

Solutions for Citizens, Politicians, and Journalists

News from the Past
Where the press is free, and every man able to read, all is safe.

— Thomas Jefferson

News from the Present
The new market-oriented communications and information system . . . addresses people predominantly through their identities as consumers. . . . In the process, the system marginalizes or displaces other identities, in particular the identity of citizen.

— Graham Murdock and Peter Golding

News about the Future
. . . more than one-half of all teens have created media content, and roughly one-third of teens who use the Internet have shared content they produced. In many cases, these teens are actively involved in what we are calling participatory cultures. A participatory culture is a culture with relatively low barriers to artistic expression and civic engagement. . . .

— Henry Jenkins

Jefferson could probably not imagine the state of the contemporary American press. One suspects that he might prefer searching for information on the Internet, and participating in its creation, over the passive communication style promoted by corporate media outlets. As veteran reporter Walter Pincus has observed:

> Today, the mainstream print and electronic media want to be neutral, presenting both or all sides as if they were refereeing a game in which only the players—the government and its opponents—can participate. They have increasingly become common carriers, transmitters of other people's ideas and thoughts, irrespective of import, relevance, and at times, even accuracy.[1]

Indeed, being a perceptive observer, Jefferson would likely notice that there are at least two important public information models in play in the United States. The old press model is fading—both due to the collapse of its business model, and, related to this, because its product is no longer trusted or relevant to many citizens. The other model involves ever-expanding applications of interactive and social technologies that create networked audiences who participate in sharing and often producing the content.[2] We are beginning to see the importance of this second model in election campaigns, netroots movements, and the viral flow of often highly partisan information across desktops, phones, and iPads. These two political information models have parallels in many information sectors, from politics and business, to reference sources such as *Encyclopedia Britannica* and Wikipedia.

Even as old media die, experimental hybrids rise to fill the gap. The question, of course, is whether these replacements have the business model and product quality to sustain themselves. One story that illustrates the current era of experimentation involves a venture capitalist who reports sitting through a particularly "stultifying" meeting where representatives of a dying newspaper proposed running "more photos of pets and cute couples." The investor's growing concern was that journalism was never mentioned. He realized that in the golden era of papers, their large profits had subsidized some degree of quality political reporting. This rare case of businesses using profits to subsidize a public good began to disappear as the corporate takeover of news organizations squeezed the profits out to the last drop. Suddenly the venture capitalist had a revelation:

> That's when the light went on for me that maybe public-service journalism . . . is a public good just like national defense, clean air, clean water . . . [and something that] market forces, left to their own devices, won't produce enough of.[3]

After that revelation, the venture capitalist went on to help start the *Texas Tribune*, a lean online investigative reporting operation (www.texastribune.org). The *Tribune* describes its mission as "A nonprofit, nonpartisan, public media organization. Our mission is to promote civic engagement on public policy, politics, government, and other matters of statewide concern. . . ."[4] In addition to being nonprofit, the aim of citizen engagement is another departure from the longstanding dominant press model in America. You won't find either of these core principles in the mission statements of the *New York Times* or the *Wall Street Journal*. The case study in this chapter explores this and other experiments aimed at reinventing the news. A question that runs through all of them is whether the funding of such operations through private philanthropy and foundations is sustainable or feasible as a model.

In addition to shifting the news focus to investigation and civic engagement, the *Texas Tribune* has also pioneered a suite of interactive databases that give citizens direct access to public records. This has tapped a good deal of interest, as much of its audience comes to the *Tribune* not for the reporting or the blogs, but to access its interactive databases. Technologies increasingly enable citizens to have direct access to answers for their questions about the salaries of public officials, the sources of campaign contributions, school rankings, or traffic citation rates.[5] Indeed, a 2010 Pew survey found that fully 40 percent of adult Web users had looked for data on government spending.[6]

If citizens can become their own reporters by asking personally relevant questions and finding many answers through simple database interfaces, what does this imply about the future nature of publics? Perhaps social media such as Facebook or Twitter will enable people to share and act on such information, creating large and more active publics that rival the reach of old mass media. On the other hand, the result may be in many cases the fragmentation of public voices into more isolated communities of interest who are unable to be heard. Whatever may come of conventional journalism and its gatekeeping activities, the present information environment is a rich convergence of different information flows.

MEDIA CONVERGENCE AND THE LOSS OF GATEKEEPING

In the contemporary information system, these two models—the mass media fed by news organizations, and digital (interactive and social) media fed by many kinds of information inputs—often converge. That is, information content travels over increasingly connected pathways and different media platforms. Consider how the two public information models have operated in recent elections. When 2008 Democratic presidential candidate Barack Obama issued a response to President Bush's final State of the Union address, it received relatively little attention from conventional news organizations. Yet the five-minute response (painfully long by conventional news standards) was posted on YouTube and quickly received more than a million views—far more than the prime-time CNN news audience. In addition, the response was blogged on more than 500 sites and quickly traveled through Facebook and other social networks.[7] Even more impressive, when Obama delivered a lengthy 37-minute speech on race in America (a response to charges that the pastor at his church was a political and racial extremist), that speech quickly received more than 4 million views on YouTube and was mashed up in various shorter versions that also received hundreds of thousands more views. The participatory media audience for the speech was thus more than the total prime-time cable news audience combined. For the most part, the conventional TV audience saw only fragments of the original speech, laced with a good deal of punditry from the conventional news channels.

Emblematic of the participatory information culture among digital natives (younger citizens who grew up in the digital age) were many examples of campaign content that emanated from or circulated among the grassroots, rather than coming top down through the press or public relations strategists. For example, the so-called *Obama Girl* music video was produced by the startup *www.barelypolitical.com*, and starred a young woman who sang about having a crush on the candidate. It was viewed more than 10 million times before the election, and its iconic status has led to millions of view since. A more professional video from will.i.am of the Black Eyed Peas created a star-studded music video around an Obama speech rallying supporters after an early primary defeat with the refrain *yes we can*. The *yes we can* video received more than 8 million views in the weeks leading to the Super Tuesday string of primaries in February 2008 that were crucial to Obama's candidacy. By the time of the election, *yes we can* continued its viral travels to the tune of more than 25 million viewers (and likely far more, given the number of mashups circulating on various media sites). The Obama campaign also featured its own impressive social media networks, not least of which was the Obama Channel on YouTube, which won the ratings race the month before the election by topping its nearest competitors Beyonce and Britney. These examples of what Henry Jenkins calls *participatory media* are signs that new generations of citizens want to be involved in creating, sharing, blogging, rating, and mashing up the political media they consume.[8]

Obama's opponent John McCain ran a campaign that was not so multimedia savvy. Although McCain enjoyed an early honeymoon with the conventional press, this ended as the public opinion tide turned against him for seeming out of touch with the economic meltdown that was in motion during the election. His introduction of Sarah Palin to the national stage as his running mate temporarily sparked campaign news coverage, but she soon fell prey to news interviews that seemed to indicate a lack of knowledge and preparation. These interviews were parodied by comedians like Tina Fey who provided something of a national funhouse mirror on the campaign. Thus the election of 2008 involved multiple media layers from mainstream news to viral videos to political comedy, with each contributing to the judgment and participation of voters.

By 2010, however, Palin proved adept at using the different media systems to her advantage. Although she was not a candidate, she became a beacon for the Tea Party movement, and attracted a good deal of press speculation about a presidential bid in 2012. Her media advisors helped create a seamless interface between the two media systems, as when her foreign policy positions were announced on Facebook, which triggered responses from blogs and conventional news organizations. For example, her echoing of those foreign policy precepts at a national Tea Party convention in 2010 was then turned into a news story on FOX, where Palin also served as a "contributor."[9] Having established a solid communication circuit, Palin began lambasting the "lame stream media." This indicated that she would avoid future embarrassment with uncontrolled press situations and stick with her own communication network, which was by then both large and effective. Indeed, her sound bites often went viral in the media echo chamber, boosted by spinoff social networks such as a Facebook group called "lame stream media" which linked followers back to networks such as Palin, FOX News, and the Republican Party.[10]

In thinking about the future of mediated democracy, one concern is clearly paramount. Whether individuals consume their media from conventional or more participatory sources, they have the growing option to dial up the media realities they prefer, and thus isolate themselves from the information realities of large numbers of others in society. It is important to understand paths that may lead to broadening the numbers of citizens able to bridge their different information realities and develop intelligent public engagement with issues and ideas.

THE ISOLATED CITIZEN

The personalized potential of the digital information age has clearly captured the popular imagination. What is changing most about the conventional news, as many media consultants see it, is that our daily information handouts are becoming more personalized and tailored to individual consumer tastes. The first reaction to this trend may be to celebrate greater individual choice of destinations in our expanding information space. It may also be tempting to think that the more personalized the information delivery system, the better for democracy. But is this true? If only democracy were something that thrived inside the heads of each individual citizen, instead of in a shared public life, nothing could be more perfect than the trend toward highly personalized information described in the last chapter. However, critics like political scientist James Fishkin argue that even the best dialogue mechanisms in the current communication system, such as opinion polls and talk radio, are often counterproductive because they simply feed unchallenged beliefs and prejudices back to the individuals and isolated audience fragments who hold them. Fishkin argues that a better idea would be to apply the technologies of polling, persuasion, and focus-group deliberation to assemble interactive citizen juries who would be exposed to information and expert debate, allowed to question the experts, and then have group deliberation before announcing their opinions in public.[11] Despite several experiments indicating that these deliberative polls have worked in different nations, the political and media trends for informing people, polling them, and using their opinions seem to be moving in the opposite direction: toward less face-to-face deliberation and more personalized information delivery.

According to Fishkin, what is missing in many current schemes for increasing citizen input into the communication process—such as reporting opinion polls or opening electronic audience discussion forums—is that they generally lack conditions that facilitate new learning about issues. Some sort of focused citizen-to-citizen exchange is precisely what is missing from most current democratic political information systems. The predominant media focus on opinions expressed in polls and instant audience response emphasizes unstable private views that are not really "public opinion" at all, in the sense of being shaped by public dialogue and debate. Before citizens decide what the news ought to look like, perhaps they should be given opportunities to form more "deliberative" judgments.[12]

THE DELIBERATIVE CITIZEN

Fishkin proposes that instead of being encouraged to express raw personal opinions about issues, people first need to discuss them in interactive settings where they are challenged to consider new information. In his early public forums, people were first exposed to information delivered by experts and then organized in small groups to discuss what they heard before coming to any conclusions about the issues.

In a pathbreaking trial of this idea in 1994, Fishkin drew a random sample of 300 British citizens and brought them to Manchester, England, under the joint sponsorship of several print and broadcast news organizations. The target issue was crime. After reading various briefing materials, hearing the experts, and debating among themselves, the sample changed its views dramatically about how to approach the crime problem. For example, a preforum survey showed that 57 percent felt that harsher prison sentences were an effective means of fighting crime. After reviewing research and thinking more critically about the relationship between prison and crime, only 38 percent concluded that prison was an effective answer. Fishkin denied that the experience had converted people into liberals, noting that their underlying concerns about the importance of crime and the need to get tough on the problem remained essentially the same after their exposure and discussion. However, their policy views became more realistic and were less swayed by the kind of superficial thinking that is commonly heard by politicians and in the news.[13]

Based on these early deliberative models, communication scholar John Gastil recommended that states assemble citizen panels to deliberate on ballot propositions. Their recommendations and their ratings of the partisan positions on the various ballot issues could be delivered to voters along with their ballots.[14] Fishkin regards such experiments with deliberative forums as helping us learn how to produce "a voice of the people worth listening to."[15]

Many observers, including Fishkin, see the digital revolution as an opportunity to make deliberation more widely available to larger numbers of citizens. However, the expanding online universe may not be as easily adapted to focused interactive public experiences as many optimists initially thought.

Indeed, observers of online communities often note that the ways in which people organize online seldom produce ideal results: "Chat rooms, bulletin boards, news groups, listserves, blogs and wikis afford users considerable opportunity for talk, but that online talk tends to be undisciplined, intolerant and superficial, rather than deliberative."[16] The tendency to seek reinforcement for prior attitudes is also evident in face-to-face interpersonal relations. For example, Diana Mutz shows that most people avoid engaging in discussions with others who may disagree with them.[17] This chapter explores the future of citizen information, looking at both conventional news and at newer digital technologies with an eye to how active participants in the information process can avoid isolation and promote intelligent political action.

PERSONALIZED INFORMATION AND THE FUTURE OF DEMOCRACY

Perhaps individuals balancing the dilemmas of a fragmented, personalized media system against the potential of a digitally networked society will make their information choices in sensible ways. Perhaps people will not turn away from the tough problems in society and the world. Given the choice to construct increasingly private realities, people may choose to link to information sources that keep them informed about problems such as global warming that require great collective intelligence and action to solve. It is also possible that people will avoid issues that (they think) do not affect them, or that seem hopeless, or that require more thought and human concern than they care to give. Research on news habits and political participation patterns is not encouraging.

Studies of news consumption from the late 1980s through the turn of the millennium reveal steady declines in attention to national, international, and local politics. These declines are associated with decreasing likelihood of voting or even registering to vote.[18] At the same time, rapidly expanding networks of digital communication offer the potential for people to stay in touch with large amounts of distant information at relatively low cost. Perhaps the signs of renewed engagement in recent elections, particularly among younger citizens, reflect a promising shift in these civic trends.

However, the preceding discussion suggests that the quality of participation is as important as the quantity. A prime concern is that, left to their own choices in the current information environment, people may seek out only the points of view they already agree with and form virtual communities with only those people who share their religious, economic, social, or entertainment preferences. Can democracy in America survive more fragmentation and personalization of the political experience? A democracy of one? One aspect of this closing circle of information around the individual is that social reality itself becomes an increasingly personal production. For perhaps the first time in human history, large numbers of people actually have substantial choices over who they are and how they want to be identified socially.[19] As noted by many social theorists, a major reason for this is that the identities once attached to institutional memberships in class, church, business, social clubs, or community associations are weakening. As these elements of personal identity weaken, they are increasingly replaced by choices of lifestyles and communities of consumption.

WHITHER THE PUBLIC SPHERE?

The idea of democracy implies a public life, meaning that people think critically about solutions to common problems. The quality of public input into democratic decisions depends on people sharing public communication forums in which to express their concerns, try out new ideas, and see if they stand the test of everyday debate. The collection of these public spaces, from cafés and taverns to town meetings and book clubs, constitutes what the pioneering communication theorist Jurgen Habermas termed the *public sphere*.[20] Many contemporary observers sense that the public sphere is shrinking or at least splintering perilously in modern society and that, ironically, the expansion of personal communication technologies is responsible for much of the shrinkage. For example, sociologist Todd Gitlin argues that in place of any coherent public sphere, it makes more sense to think about the proliferation of tiny and shifting "sphericules."[21] These sphericules of interest can be extremely engaging, and they often offer a comforting escape from the pains of society at large. However, if people increasingly use communication technologies to construct and live in their own private worlds, where can people meet and share the concerns and the information required for coherent political discussion, much less for consensus to emerge?

To put it simply, the nature of our political communication process has something to do with how we act together politically—how we define our goals and chart our actions as a nation. At one extreme of national politics are the political crusaders who zealously fill the airwaves with moral ultimatums for everyone to follow. Their "flaming" on talk shows provides a low-budget media spectacle for the fragmented audiences who tune in, but they evidently set bad examples for the greater numbers who tune out. As noted earlier, many Americans today are more inclined to avoid politics, or at least to seek it close to home, than to welcome open-minded debate in everyday situations about common national concerns.[22]

Today's citizen, in the view of communication scholar Michael Schudson, differs from the citizens of past eras in the acute awareness of a protective armor of personal rights.[23] Prickliness about rights and related identity claims may have the ironic result of further driving wedges between personal lives and the public sphere. Some celebrate the liberation of individuals from oppressive public norms and obligations, while others decry the decline of coherent societies and nations.[24]

These changes in personal relationships to society and public life may explain some of the declining confidence in both national leaders and the press discussed in the last two chapters. Add to this the surrounding fragmentation of many social institutions, from schools and political parties to churches and families, and it is easy to see why many observers conclude that the authoritative basis of public information itself seems to be in decline: People simply have fewer common institutional bases for sharing and respecting the same information. These personal information trends are not helped by the politicians and news organizations who use communication technologies to tailor information more to popular emotion and consumer tastes than to challenging alternative perspectives. In short, when viewed from any aspect of the information system—whether from the standpoint of the press, political actors, the people, or technology—it is clear that the information environments in which we live are changing in important ways.

THREE AMERICAN MYTHS ABOUT PUBLIC INFORMATION

Understanding how to right the information system in the United States is made more challenging by the layers of belief and mythology that have built up to defend the very things that may be weakening news as the core of that system. As discussed throughout the book, common sense is not always the best guide to discovering how things work. We learned, for example, that the popular belief in liberal press bias is not only off the mark, but it may also actually keep people from recognizing more serious biases. The biases outlined in Chapter 2 run far deeper than ideology; they actively discourage many citizens of different political persuasions from engaging creatively with the political world around them. We also examined the myth that sensational news is what the public wants. This is, at best, a half truth, but its widespread acceptance gets in the way of seeing that cheap sensationalism is precisely the kind of news that satisfies corporate profit demands, even when large numbers of people tune it out. The irony is that the factors that have produced this disconnection between news and democracy are often pointed to as foundations of American freedom itself:

- Private (corporate) ownership of the media
- Popular resistance to government support for public broadcasting—compounded by the erosion of public responsibility regulations on commercial broadcasters
- The continuing belief by citizens and journalists that news should be objective or politically neutral makes it difficult to think about reinventing a journalism that better suits our democracy

These defining conditions of the American press are accepted with nearly religious faith by many Americans. Yet many of the same Americans also find fault with the journalistic product. Is there some relationship between these mythical defining features of our news system and the unsatisfying results it produces? Consider how each of these core elements of the American press system may actually limit the range and depth of the news.

The News About Corporate Ownership in the Media System

Americans too easily regard private ownership of public information as a good thing. Economic competition is easily imagined to produce informational diversity and quality. Yet markets often present opportunities for concentration of ownership and control, resulting in oligopoly or monopoly. This is why democratic governments everywhere regulate key markets—in order to protect the people from the many unhappy coercions of unchecked economic power, as when banks sold and resold poorly secured home mortgages during the housing boom of the early century that led to the economic collapse when the bubble eventually burst. Some government regulations seem more secure, enabling most Americans today to take for granted that they will not have to work in sweatshop conditions for starvation wages or that the new toaster they buy will probably not burn down the house. Government regulations concerning labor and product safety have become invisible guarantees of decent lives that few would argue with. Yet there is surprisingly little public concern about protecting the quality of ideas that ultimately define the quality of democracy.

As discussed in Chapter 7, the largely private ownership of the news business in the United States does not advance causes, such as the diversity or citizen-friendliness of information. When John Stuart Mill long ago discussed the importance of a *marketplace of ideas* for democracy, he thought about how to design election and press systems that would bring ideas into public debate and link them to governing.[25] Most democracies still think seriously about how to best represent and stimulate the thinking of the many diverse publics that make up complex societies. Unfortunately, the American faith in the rule of markets means that there is not much serious policy-level thinking about just what kind of press system citizens should have.

Even when scholars and journalists engage with this important question, there is little interest from government or most citizens in imposing public responsibility guidelines (beyond moral codes) on private media corporations. Public information standards in this age of free enterprise would be denounced by media corporations and by the politicians they support as dangerous violations of free speech and free enterprise. Most citizens would join the press–government choir in rejecting the idea of strengthening public service broadcasting.

The News About Public Broadcasting

The government regulates the quality of air, food, and water much more actively than it regulates the quality of political information. There is probably more truth in product advertising than in political advertising. People fear government intervention in the area of political information and cannot imagine government regulations that might actually expand the range of ideas in circulation. This hands-off approach to the press has been criticized by communication scholar Robert McChesney as actually limiting the range of ideas in American political debate. Compared with most other advanced democracies, the United States provides little airspace or financial support for public service broadcasting. Repeated government decisions to limit public broadcasting have served up the public airwaves to commercial corporations with little accompanying obligation to serve the public interest.[26] The journalism crisis of recent years promoted McChesney and John Nichols to think about how to restore public support for the most precious public good: information. They note that in the early days of the Republic, the main government expenditure after defense was subsidies for the exchange of information through the U.S. Postal Service.[27] If the founders felt that the government should find ways to support the flow of ideas, why is our public communication system so weak today?

Despite its bare-bones operation, public broadcasting in this country faces continual attack from members of Congress and from conservative commentators. In many ways, public broadcasting in the United States is not as independent as it could be because it is forced by limited government support to take money from commercial sponsors. As an alternative to this fragile public system, why not shift a tiny portion of the money spent on corporate subsidies or weapons of mass destruction to support an independent media system chartered for the explicit purpose of expanding the range of ideas and experimenting with news formats beyond those found in commercial broadcasts?

The repeated conservative attacks on public broadcasting alternately charge that it reflects a liberal bias and that it is dangerous to have such a system at all because it may be prone to government pressures on content. The irony during the Bush administration is that the Corporation for Public Broadcasting (CPB) board and management became stacked with Republican appointees whose mission was to insert more conservative content into programming—even though their own polling showed broad public satisfaction with the programming on both public television (the Public Broadcasting Service, or PBS) and radio (National Public Radio, or NPR). One of the first moves was to push out Bill Moyers, longtime journalist and host of the PBS program *NOW*, under charges that his program was liberally biased. Even if true, the idea that there should be no program reflecting a critical or liberal viewpoint on the air seems an extreme way to impose impartiality, but CPB, under its then Chairman Kenneth Tomlinson, insisted that this was how to handle bias. At the same time, more conservative talk and public affairs hosts were hired. Tomlinson's efforts to root out bias at PBS were finally rewarded with an investigation by the federal Inspector General's office, which concluded that Tomlinson had pushed a partisan agenda and failed to operate with the transparency required in such a public post. Although Tomlinson resigned under this cloud, the CPB management remained in the hands of staunchly partisan Republican appointees during the Bush years—an ironic outcome given conservative warnings about government meddling in public broadcast content.[28]

All other advanced democratic nations have far more developed public service news and entertainment media systems than the United States. Sweden even subsidizes local newspapers in areas where there would otherwise be no community voice. The most respected news sources in many countries are the public radio and television news services. Yet Americans generally have trouble imagining how government-funded journalism could avoid being a mouthpiece for the government itself. In thinking about this issue, it may help to remember that the current U.S. press system has not achieved such impressive levels of independence from officials, or set high standards for critical reporting, either.

There are many ways to insulate journalists from direct government pressure in public service media systems. A common model is to appoint oversight commissions balanced with representatives from different parties and political groups, along with members of major religious, educational, business, and labor institutions. These commissions monitor news content and negotiate norms and standards for journalism. The fight between the BBC and the British Labor government of Tony Blair concerning the government's grounds for going to war in Iraq suggests that public service systems can be quite independent of the governments they cover.

The News About Objective Journalism

When combined with a highly commercial and minimally regulated press system, the cultural ideal of neutral or objective journalism may be the greatest limit on the communication of political ideas. No matter how independent they may be, journalists who avoid introducing political perspective in their coverage all end up reporting much the same news. Worse, as illustrated in the case study in Chapter 6, objectivity may force reporting of one side of a story that is not true or well supported just to guarantee balance. Yet the powerful ideal of a free-but-unbiased press leaves most journalists and citizens unable to imagine another way. It seems that politicians, like the voters who elect them, believe that it is possible to separate the news from politics and arrive at something resembling objective information. Thus, Americans grudgingly receive a similar replay of the same events and ideas from virtually every mainstream news channel. Political communication scholar Thomas Patterson describes this as the "irony of the free press" in America:

> American journalists have concluded that the marketplace of ideas is
> enhanced when they are "free" or "independent," in the sense that they
> are not connected organizationally, editorially, or legally to any political
> institution or mandate. In this view . . . news decisions should be the free
> choices of unregulated journalists. . . . [Yet] when journalists are
> detached from political moorings . . . they tend to generate a form of
> news that, first, underplays political ideas and, second, is consensual as
> opposed to competitive in its content.[29]

The myth of a free press persists among journalists, politicians, and citizens, even as it muddles popular understandings about information and democracy. How can we get beyond this state of communication gridlock? A first step is to allow ourselves a more realistic look at the information system behind the myth.

NEWS AND POWER IN AMERICA: IDEAL VS. REALITY

In the ideal civics-book version of American democracy, power rests with the people, who are, in effect, the voice of the political system. Leaders are supposed to take cues from the people and express their voice politically. The journalist in this scheme occupies the role of the independent monitor who reports to the people on how well leaders handle the public trust. In simple picture form, this ideal version of power in America looks like Figure 8.1.

It is obvious that the reality of power in America does not look much like this ideal picture. As numerous examples in this book have indicated, leaders and organized interests have usurped enormous amounts of political power and reduced popular control over the political system by using the media to generate support, compliance, and just plain confusion among the public. Grassroots opinion drives various battles over rights and morals such as abortion and religious expression, but on matters affecting economic policy and other sensitive areas of state and corporate concern, the battle for public opinion is waged largely by organized interests and political elites using polling and marketing techniques to deliver images to generally inattentive publics. Which came first, the inattentive public or the blocked communication channels? Either way, the result is not encouraging for public participation.

The conventional commercial media also play a different role in the reality of American politics than the one they play in the ideal version. News organizations are more often political transmission lines to the people than they are monitors or watchdogs of the information they transmit. The news gates are opened most often to voices from below when government officials or other prominent newsmakers are already in conflict about an issue. Citizen groups seldom get into the news unless they first get on the government agenda. Figure 8.2 provides a more realistic picture of the place of journalism in the American political power system.

There are, of course, a number of obvious reasons the media do not monitor government actions in an adequate way. To begin with, the news as it currently exists is a profit-making enterprise (albeit an endangered one). As long as profits can still be extracted, even by dismantling the basis of quality journalism, the owners of news organizations have little incentive to change what they do. Those elite national journalists who still have jobs derive a large measure of professional success and personal satisfaction from their status,

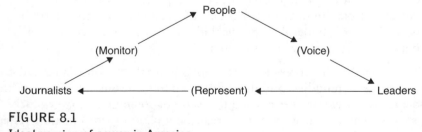

FIGURE 8.1
Ideal version of power in America

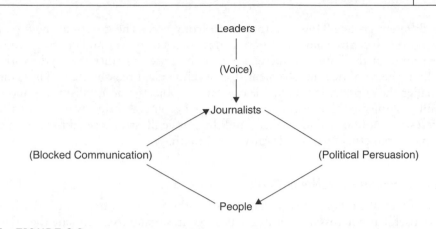

| FIGURE 8.2 |
FIGURE 8.2
Realistic picture of American political power

and have few incentives to rock the boat. In addition, critical watchdog reporting often brings social and political pressure to bear on reporters and their organizations. Even routine news reporting is constantly criticized by (largely conservative) media-monitoring organizations and by political and economic elites for not being sufficiently objective. Such media criticism has become an important lever in the power system by helping extreme voices gain greater credibility in public discourse. All of these distressing developments raise the question of why the myth of a free press in America persists.

WHY THE MYTH OF A FREE PRESS PERSISTS

Almost every citizen holds onto some inspiring images of the press. These images are based on the dramatic events and guiding sentiments of American history, such as these thoughts of Thomas Jefferson: "The people are the only censors of their governors [and they must have full] information of their affairs through the channel of the public papers. . . . [Were] it left to me to decide whether we should have a government without newspapers or newspapers without a government, I should not hesitate a moment to prefer the latter."[30]

Ideas like these have been passed down by every generation of journalists, educators, and politicians throughout American history and have come to represent the spirit of a nation and a people. The real meaning of those sentiments in today's society is hard to imagine, yet ideals that are given such powerful reinforcement and that endow people with such noble purpose often take on a life of their own. They are inspirational, hopeful, ennobling—giving substance to a national history that would otherwise become vague in the minds of new generations. Such are the characteristics of myths. Unfortunately, myths like the free press stand in the way of seeing the realities of power.

The myth of a free press and a free people and its guiding principle of objective reporting would seem to provide different but compelling benefits for different groups. However, there is an irony here: The groups at the top of the power structure gain the material advantages of power and control, while the groups at the bottom trade real power (because in reality the myth works to limit their political involvement) for psychological reassurances. Thus, the broader the support is for the idea of fair or objective journalism, the more firmly established the inequalities of power become. A brief overview of the interests of politicians, journalists, and the public illustrates the different (and even contradictory) bases of loyalty to the myth.

Politicians and the News Myth

The universal support of political actors for the free press/free people myth is both useful and necessary. It is useful because it is easier to deregulate the owners of media empires (who also sponsor politicians) behind a convincing show of support for truth and popular sovereignty. It is necessary for politicians to endorse the news myth because the American public would never tolerate a leader who lacked the outward appearance of commitment to democratic ideals. Even if interest organizations and the information agencies of government work overtime to influence public opinion, publics demand at least the illusion that their system of government represents their will. It matters little whether politicians are conscious of the contradiction between their public support for the myth and their political efforts to control information. The political benefits accrue as much to those who truly believe the contemporary relevance of the story of the free press and the free people as they redound to the cynical politicians who take the news myth in vain.

Journalists and the News Myth

The benefit of the news myth for the journalist is not power (at least in the conventional sense) but professional credibility. Without a public commitment to objective or fair reporting, the journalist could not claim professional status and political access. Even if this status is tarnished in the eyes of the public, it is supported by the values operating within the journalism profession itself. The news myth provides the reporter, like the politician, with a ready-made role in the ideal picture of American democracy. Because that role is so easily dramatized with the help of the politician, it would be hard to imagine many reporters not embracing the part. Reporters who become frustrated with mass media objectivity and other limits on daily reporting simply leave the major news organizations, perhaps to become freelance writers or reporters outside the mainstream.

Some journalists, like some politicians, may cynically mouth the news myth while harboring a fuller sense of its emptiness. However, most journalists conveniently fail to see the contradictions in their pursuit of news objectivity. At some point, most career journalists accept the fact that reporting what officials say and do is really the highest form of professionalism. When former NBC anchor Tom Brokaw was questioned about whether the press failed to raise enough questions about the Bush administration's case for the Iraq War, he noted that in the end, "Congress voted overwhelmingly to approve the war—and we had to reflect that."[31] When in doubt, the edge goes to the government. From this assumption, it is a small step from embracing the activities of professional, objective journalism to the assumption that these activities really are the keys to revealing the truth about politics. Telling it like it is can become equated, however erroneously, with telling the truth.

This does not mean that journalists do not worry about objectivity and other elements of the news myth. They do. The problem comes in finding a new journalistic stance that provides more critical distance from the power holders they cover. For example, after the invasion of Iraq, the *Columbia Journalism Review* ran a cover story called "Re-Thinking Objectivity." The story's lead idea was that "In a world of spin, our awkward embrace of an ideal can make us passive recipients of the news."[32] The lesson emphasized was the failure of the mainstream press to challenge the Bush administration's rationale for the war:

> In his March 6 press conference, in which he laid out his reasons for the coming war, President Bush mentioned al-Qaeda or the attacks of September 11 fourteen times in fifty-two minutes. No one challenged him on it, despite the fact that the CIA had questioned the Iraq–al-Qaeda connection, and that there has never been solid evidence marshaled to support the idea that Iraq was involved in the attacks of 9/11.[33]

The trouble is that the author did not propose a clear alternative to objective journalism other than better investigative reporting. As he pointed out, however, journalists did not need to investigate much beyond the already well-established contradictions in the administration's call to war. All they needed was some new professional guideline that gave them permission to go outside of the officially drawn boundaries of reality.

The People and the News Myth

What can people gain from embracing the news myth? To answer this perplexing question, we must return to the two pictures of power in America presented earlier in the chapter. In the second picture (Figure 8.2), which better represents the reality of power in America, the people are locked into a weak power position with their choices structured for them. Their efforts to respond politically are filtered through the gatekeeping rules of news formulas. In such situations, people often develop what psychologists call *learned helplessness*, in which they either withdraw from the source of their distress (in this case, withdrawal from politics and public life) or embrace highly idealized notions about their situation.

Those who seek to embrace idealized versions of power in America need look no further than the daily news. Both journalists and politicians continually dramatize the illusory appeal of Figure 8.1, the free press/free people myth, for the benefit of the public. They offer news stories as reports to the people about choices or problems that face them. Leaders appeal in the news for popular support and understanding. If people can suspend their concerns about such nagging questions as where media issues come from, how the proposed solutions are chosen, and what the limits of public involvement really are, then they can escape into an illusory world where democracy is operating just fine.

When the democratic illusion is shattered by the false promises of politicians or by the discovery that news coverage was too little or too late, people may revert to cynicism or withdrawal. However, even those who become disillusioned tend to think that the failings of the system could be fixed with more honest politicians and more neutral journalists. Such mythical solutions, while popular, fail to address the deeper problems with the national information system. The following discussion explores various changes that citizens, journalists, and politicians can make.

PROPOSALS FOR CITIZENS, JOURNALISTS, AND POLITICIANS

It is naive to think that some magic wand of government, journalism, or citizenship can be waved and all will be changed. Yet even small changes within each sphere can make important differences. Above all, it would help to recognize the roots of our communication problems and talk about them differently in public. At this dawning of a new age of electronic democracy, the opportunity exists once again to have a critical national debate about how we should inform ourselves and engage with politics. New information technologies through which citizens can interact with politicians, journalists, and each other may help us think creatively about striking a new balance of media power.

Proposals for Citizens

Citizens can make a difference by thinking more creatively about how information comes to them. Participating in public life without the illusions of the free press/free people myth is a good start. The next step is to begin thinking freely about alternatives. There is little cost to brainstorming about a more perfect information order. Should we encourage more partisan political reporting? More analysis in news stories? Celebrate the existence of perspective building political comedy? What about government incentives for news organizations that pioneer new formats for covering issues, elections, and chronic social problems? These and other ideas are worth exploring openly and in public forums without concern that they would somehow violate our mythical notions of a free press. Perhaps people should think more about diversity and other qualities on the output side of the communication equation rather than being so preoccupied with the ideal of freedom on the input side.

In addition to thinking more creatively about designing a better national communication system, people would also do well to learn how to better use the one we currently have. The critical analyses contained in this book can be used in decoding the news. If people learn to read between the lines and see beyond the images, they can reduce their frustration and confusion with the news. In short, becoming better informed does not simply mean reading more papers or watching more television. It means decoding the information from these and other sources with a critical eye. Becoming better informed entails more than just memorizing the who, what, where, when, and how of the isolated events of the day. Understanding the political causes and social consequences of public affairs is also useful for clarifying feelings and deciding how to respond. Armed with the basic introduction provided in this book, it is possible to recognize and decode the most common information biases in the news. The following guidelines should help in becoming a more critical news consumer.

Recognize Stereotypes and Plot Formulas   When new information is translated into old formulas, there is no challenge for people to replace their prejudices with new insights. Yet the easiest stories for politicians to tell and journalists to write are based on familiar images of the world. Unless these warmed-over schemes are detected and discarded, the news remains an unhelpful forum, reinforcing superficial understandings and old ideologies. It is important to detect and discard loaded descriptions and buzzwords. Calling President Obama a socialist only set off knee jerk reactions among conservatives who wanted to see him in negative terms, while angering progressive supporters who saw a wall against meaningful communication being erected.

Terms like *leftist, right-winger, big government, freedom,* and even *well-placed* or *informed sources* can frame information for very selective interpretations. For example, "well-placed and informed sources" are often high officials acting irresponsibly by anonymously planting rumor and innuendo in the news. Despite the dubious worth of such leaks and plants, their attribution to an informed, official, or well-placed source can lend them credibility. In general, more weight should be given to the sources who identify themselves than to those who anonymously spin the news. The exception, of course, is when sources fear for their lives or livelihoods by blowing the whistle.

The savvy news consumer should recognize that labels, such as *liberal, populist,* or *religious fundamentalist* are often planted by spin-doctors to undermine their opponents. Yet, such terms often stick as though they were objective descriptions. This is not to say that there are no leftists or rightists or other "-ists" in the world. However, news audiences often do not want to know more about characters who have been branded with such labels. The point here is not that we would end up agreeing with the statements of criminals, protesters, or terrorists, but we might develop a better understanding of how they think, why they do what they do, and what we should do in turn.

It may be true, for example, that some people really are the crazed, vengeful sociopaths that the word *terrorist* connotes. Surely the dictates and actions of Osama bin Laden and the Taliban were not defensible within the broadest spectrum of American views. However, declaring war on terrorism in general opened up political possibilities that were more questionable. Also, the emotional response to the terrorism frame enabled dubious foreign policy decisions to be sold more easily to the public. For example, the invasion of Iraq was sold on the seriously flawed factual premises, but the deal was sealed emotionally in ways that precluded many questions until it was too late. (If Saddam Hussein qualified as a target in the War on Terror, weren't there dozens of other unjust regimes out there that qualify for invasion as well?) In addition, the word *terrorist* was used to justify circumventing laws against torture and eavesdropping on the phone calls and e-mails of Americans without the legally required court order. It surely would have been more difficult for the executive branch to claim this power without having a loaded term such as *terrorist* to use when talking about the issue. At another level, the blanket declaration of "War on Terror" risks blocking understanding of disenfranchised groups who have resorted to violence as a last desperate measure to make themselves heard and have their problems addressed. As political communication scholar Steven Livingston has shown, the terrorist label is often strategically placed in the news by partisan actors pursuing policy agendas, and that label affects how those policy stories are told.[34]

Look for Information That Doesn't Fit the Plot   It is useful to remember the maxim that "There are lies, damn lies, and then there are statistics." Documentary evidence, including statistics and pictures, can be taken out of context to suit the image of the moment. Evidence often seems true or factual simply because it fits so neatly with a powerful image, a familiar plot, or a deeply held belief. An equally useful reminder about reality, by contrast, is that it is never neat and clean. Raw data are always messy and ambiguous. The ambiguity of data is their real advantage—they make us think critically and probe for new patterns. When facts and claims fit too neatly, they provide psychological affirmation, not a reality check. Thus, many Americans were surely prepared to hear that there was some connection between Saddam Hussein and al-Qaeda following 9/11, and few stopped to see if there was evidence to challenge this administration claim.

To counter this news psychology, the facts must be weighed carefully before accepting them. First, it is important to peer through the rhetorical smoke to see if there are any documented claims or only unsupported charges and assertions. Above all, the news critic should look for loose facts that could become the basis for an entirely different story. Building an interpretation around these loose facts can help illuminate the underlying political issues that are worth paying attention to. It is easier to focus on stray facts and see where they go when one is not trying to fit them into the surrounding news plot. Case in point: If the CIA found no evidence of connections between Iraq and al-Qaeda, did it really make sense to link Iraq to 9/11?

Seek Additional Sources of Information to Check Partisan Claims   This does not mean consulting *Time* as a reference on *Newsweek*'s presentation of the facts. Rather, it means consulting publications and documentaries that provide richer, more historical accounts that are told, above all, from the standpoint of critics, opposition groups, or disinterested academic observers.

The Internet makes it easy to gather huge volumes of information on almost any subject. The major search engines tap into different domains of news and information. It is important to recognize that not all the results of these searches are reliable, but it is possible to detect patterns of information from known sources that provide solid additions to what may be contained in brief news accounts. It is also a good idea to consult prominent international news organizations such as the BBC when thinking about international developments involving the United States. The BBC World Service can be streamed from the Internet, found on satellite radio, or downloaded as podcasts from iTunes. Moreover, it is easy to set up news tracking and delivery services (for free) with most of the major Internet portals. These tracking requests will deliver new information every day on running stories in the news. Some of these engines also provide user information on the quality and reliability of different information sources. In addition, searching the Web on a topic in one of the less commercially biased search engines (**www.google.com** is probably the best) generally produces a good deal of often high-quality information from interest organizations whose political agendas can be deduced and evaluated from their Web sites. Joining discussions of news reports on blogs can be entertaining and thought provoking. Finally, in order to tame the information tide, get an RSS (rich site summary or really simple syndication) aggregator. (Information about aggregators can be found at **http://en.wikipedia.org/wiki/List_of_news_aggregators.**)

Recognize Spin and News Control in Action   Sometimes there just do not seem to be any loose facts on which alternative interpretations can be built. Successfully controlled news has just the right number of facts to document the image intended by the political script. When politicians present their staged news events, or pseudo-events, successfully, the press tends to report only the documentary facts that were planted to lend credibility to the story. In this case, the critic must learn to recognize the characteristics of pseudo-events and decipher the political messages they convey. The first clue, of course, is that successful pseudo-events do not contain many stray facts.

When a president announces a war on anything, the news consumer should look for signs of staged political drama. Such political staging was plain when Ronald Reagan declared war on crime after nearly two years in office. He announced his support for a complete package of legislation that would make it tougher for criminals to get away with terrorizing law-abiding American citizens. The entire performance was designed to rally the support of a fearful, economically troubled citizenry around a strong leader. It was not incidental that it was staged just two days after Reagan suffered his first major political defeat (Congress overrode his veto of a major federal spending bill). Could the president's media team have prepared a winning scenario and kept it in the wings for just such an occasion? An attentive news critic should be able to detect the signs of scripted political performances and connect them to the political circumstances of the actors who perform them.

Consider in this light one of the stage props used by the senior George Bush in his remake of the Reagan War on Crime, replayed this time as a War on Drugs. The news prop was a bag of crack cocaine that Bush held up the night he declared war in a nationally televised speech. Bush offered the bag—purchased by undercover agents in Lafayette Park, across the street from the White House—as evidence that the drug problem could be found right across the street from his own home at 1600 Pennsylvania Avenue.

In a later investigative report, the *Washington Post* revealed that the dramatic moment was staged by Bush's media consultants. The *Washington Post* story, which received wide media play, opened this way:

> WASHINGTON. White House speech writers thought it was the perfect prop for President George Bush's first prime-time television address to the nation—a dramatic one that would show how the drug trade had spread to the president's own neighborhood.
>
> "This is crack cocaine," Mr. Bush solemnly announced in his Sept. 5 speech on drug policy, holding up a plastic bag filled with a white chunky substance. It was "seized a few days ago in a park across the street from the White House," he said, adding, "It could easily have been heroin or PCP."
>
> But obtaining the crack was no easy feat. To match the words of the speech writers, Drug Enforcement Administration agents lured a suspected Washington drug dealer to Lafayette Park four days before the speech. They made what appears to have been the agency's first undercover crack buy in a park better known for its location across Pennsylvania Avenue from the White House than for illegal drug activity, according to officials familiar with the case.
>
> In fact, the teenage suspect, when first contacted by an undercover agent posing as a buyer, seemed baffled by the request.
>
> "Where is the White House?" he replied in a conversation that was secretly tape-recorded by the drug agency.
>
> "We had to manipulate him to get him down here," said William McMullen, assistant special agent in charge of the agency's Washington field office. "It wasn't easy."[35]

After the cover was blown on a staged news event, Bush followed up with a staged reaction developed by the Bush media team as a tactical response to press criticism: from time to time, go ballistic with the press. Bush handlers had discovered that a bit of bristle with the press made the president look tough and committed. Shortly after the earlier *Washington Post* story appeared, the president took an image trip to a Maine tree farm to demonstrate his environmental concern. Rather than dutifully interview the president about his relations with baby trees, the press pack hounded him about the staged drug bust. The president suggested testily that questioning his methods in such a holy crusade made reporters antagonists in the drug war: "I don't understand," he complained. "I mean, has somebody got some advocates here for this drug guy?"[36]

Learn to Become Self-Critical   At this point, you may be concerned that these guidelines will turn you into a cynic rather than a critic. Who or what can be trusted? The goal of news criticism is not to reject everything—it is to think confidently and independently about world events in the face of a lot of pressure to think like everybody else. Nor is the point to distrust all authorities—it is to trust your own judgment.

This brings us to what may be the most important guideline: Recognize the importance of prior beliefs (and prejudices) in screening and accepting news information, and, wherever possible, challenge those beliefs with information that is at odds with them. The point of being self-critical is not to get rid of beliefs altogether or to tear them down as fast as we build them up. The goal is to make sure that our beliefs do not stand as a wall against reality. Beliefs are most useful when they help us engage constructively in the ongoing solution of social problems. When beliefs are proclaimed as absolutes to be defended against all evidence to the contrary, they become the causes of social problems. Because the news contains two sides to most stories, people can simply select the version of reality that comes closest to their prior beliefs and never change their thinking about the world. What if neither side represented in the news provides a particularly useful way to think about an issue? What if both sides have some merit? Escaping our current political dilemmas requires the will to challenge existing political beliefs, and there is no better way to challenge beliefs than by resisting the daily temptation to look to the news for confirmation of what we already hold to be true about the world.

Find Sources of Perspective Such as Political Comedy   As discussed earlier in the book, few people use political comedy as a substitute for other information sources, but as a way of putting information from other sources into perspective. When news becomes mostly spin, and reality edges dangerously toward the absurd, comedy may be the best way to straighten it out.[37] Perhaps if citizens found ways to join in larger participatory networks to take more intelligent political action, governments would be less inclined to stage events using conventional media formats that resemble dull reality TV. On the eve of the 2004 election Jon Stewart challenged his viewers to elect better politicians so his job of poking fun at them would be more difficult:

> Hey everybody welcome to the show! I'm Jon Stewart . . .
>   Our top headline tonight, as cities burn around the country . . . people furious that the electoral college . . .
>   . . . I'm sorry, I'm reading *Wednesday*'s headlines.
>   [laughter]

It is Monday, tomorrow is election day. Get out there and vote. Not because it's cool. . . . Cause it's not. I will tell you what *is* cool: smoking. Do that while you vote.

The thing is this: there will be long lines.

I suggest to you this: Be ready to waste a day for democracy. If the line is long, stay there. If you are hungry, eat . . . someone in line with you. Do not leave until you get your vote counted. I urge you to do that civic duty tomorrow.

On a personal note—I am a comedian. I make fun of what I believe to be the absurdities of our government. [pause] Make my life *difficult*. Make this next four years *really* shitty for me—so that every morning all we can do is come in and go, "uhhh . . . Madonna is doing some kabbalah thing . . . wanna do that?"

I'd like that. I'm tired.[38]

In 2010 Stewart and his Comedy Central colleague Stephen Colbert organized demonstrations on the National Mall in Washington. Stewart urged citizens to "restore sanity." Colbert's counter demonstration urged followers to "keep fear alive" by restoring truthiness and combating the "creeping reasonableness" of people like Stewart. Comedy may help, but the task of becoming an informed citizen would be considerably easier if the news required less decoding and provided more challenging perspectives to begin with. Mainstream news organizations are unlikely to proclaim their independence from formula reporting and the daily pronouncements of government officials. However, journalists can do a lot within the current constraints of the profession to improve the quality of their product. And the dual crises of economics and confidence that the current system is facing may create opportunities for innovation (as discussed in the case study).

Proposals for Journalists

Reporters and editors often argue that they would like to do more with the news, but time, space, profit pressures, and fickle audiences just do not permit it. In response to these journalistic laments, consider this challenge: It is the responsibility of the press to hold government accountable even when it fails to do so itself. Journalists may also aspire to prepare the citizenry for participation, or at least try to write news with citizens in mind. Here is a discussion of how to implement these goals.

Use Personalization and Dramatization Creatively

As suggested in Chapter 2, drama could help rather than hinder in communicating interesting and powerful messages about the world. Current news formats, however, are more melodramatic than seriously dramatic, sacrificing the enduring issues surrounding events for momentary glimpses into the trials and tribulations of political actors. Journalists could easily reduce the melodramatic overtones of the news by developing the historical and institutional contexts in which action is played out. This does not mean eliminating the actors involved—it is hard to tell a story without characters—but rather placing them clearly within the political context where the enduring effects of their actions will be felt. Thus, crime stories could be removed from the realm of the bizarre, grotesque, and sinister and placed in the social world of poverty, loss of community, alienation, group conflict, and psychological disorders. Budget deficits could be removed from the clutches of big-spending politicians and placed in the context of the bureaucratic and social forces that create them. International violence could be taken out of the personalized world of tough talk, bombings, belligerence, and mistrust and shown in the context of economic, military, and international institutional structures that sustain many conflicts. Virtually every issue could be thus enriched in favor of more useful social, historical, and institutional analyses. This shift corresponds to Iyengar's recommendations for less episodic and more thematic reporting discussed in Chapters 1 and 2.[39] Such journalistic shifts would make it possible for the general news audience to grasp the larger political implications of events without resorting to so much laborious decoding.

Many reporters and editors believe that more attention to social, institutional, and historical factors would only make the news more complicated and confuse people even further. It is not clear what, other than journalistic superstition, supports this belief. Most people probably could not be any more confused about the world than they are at present. It is also possible that this confusion is the direct result of melodramatic news formats that fail to provide intelligible contexts for developing events. Yet, news professionals opt for even more simple-minded coverage and wonder what to do with an even more simple-minded public.

Introduce More of the Journalist's Own Background Knowledge into Stories   This does not mean we need more cynicism or personal commentary on politicians' games and presumed political strategies. Rather, journalists should learn to use what they, as expert witnesses, have come to know about the workings of the situations they cover.

Current reporting practice leans heavily toward letting the actors tell the story. In these source-driven narratives, the reporter's voice sets the tone of a story. As noted earlier, this tone is often cynical precisely because journalists cannot find ways to say what they really know or think about the situations they are covering. Moving away from actor-centered narrative toward observer-centered narrative would place control over the development of a news story with the journalist, where it properly belongs, not with political actors, whose interest is in manipulating the story to their own advantage. The place where reporters could add most to stories is in the explanation of how different policy proposals were developed, why others were rejected, and what the competing proposals might accomplish if implemented. In her cogent analysis of news coverage of welfare reform, Regina Lawrence noted that during the extended period in which the various proposals were being debated between Congress and the White House, journalists mainly contributed commentary about the games and strategies. However, after the reforms were passed, journalists introduced an impressive review of the substance of the new policies.[40] Such journalistic discussions of political substance simply needed to come earlier in the coverage of welfare and other major issues.

Resist the Standard Plot Formulas   No more horse races in election coverage. No more "Is the president winning or losing?" in his relations with Congress. It is tempting to peg stories to plots that trigger instant recognition from the audience. However, the more standardized the plot and vocabulary used in a story, the less informative the content. Here is an experiment: Try rewriting a story about a personal defeat or victory of the president or some other prominent politician. Put the personal, dramatic, and authority-disorder themes in the background and emphasize the broader issues, institutional factors, and political consequences involved in the situation.

Define Political Situations in Terms That Appeal to Ordinary People   When reporters clearly define the terms and concepts in a situation, the news audience may begin to see what is going on. New information is hard to assimilate under the best of circumstances. In fragmented, fast-paced news, definition and repetition of new information are essential to comprehension. Pointing out that TV viewers miss the main ideas in two-thirds of all stories, Levy and Robinson urged a revamping of current formats. They concluded that TV news is "produced for people already in the know, it's filled with the jargon of policymakers and riddled with cryptic references to continuing stories. What TV journalists forget is that most viewers need some help in understanding the news, no matter how often the story has been told."[41]

When Congress passed an historic health care act in 2010, the Democratic leadership and the Obama administration did a poor job of explaining what was in the bill and how the new plan would work. Opponents filled the news with shouts of socialism and destruction of freedom of choice. Few news stories went beyond the political battle to sort out the actual details of the new law and make it accessible to people. Whether people would like what they heard cannot be known, since they were not given the information. However, what is clear is that leaving the news to become a spin contest—that the Republicans clearly won—resulted in a majority of Americans opposing the new law.

Remember to Explain Why the Story Matters   After plot formulas have been banished, background information enhanced, and key terms defined, one important reporting task remains. Although reporters may understand perfectly well why a story is important, the significance may be lost in a condensed presentation to inattentive citizens. A Pew Research Center survey of journalists revealed that fewer than half of television news workers felt that "providing an interpretation of the news" was a core journalistic principle.[42] Journalists should be explicit about what matters in a story. Levy and Robinson suggest that reports must pass the "so what?" test:

It's used implicitly all the time in the newsroom to decide if something is newsworthy. Why, for example, was it important that a space suit had been recovered from the shuttle wreckage . . . ? The TV journalists who covered that news knew the answers; they had to in order to get their stories on the air. But most reports in our . . . sample never explicitly conveyed that "so what?" element of the news. Sometimes it was there—between the lines. But in our experience, information reported between the lines tends to remain there.[43]

Journalists should be explicit about the highest social values and consequences at stake in newsworthy situations. For example, the term *human rights* appears frequently in reports about other nations, particularly those nations that receive U.S. assistance. There is seldom an attempt, however, to explain the relevance of human-rights concerns to U.S. foreign policy. A notable exception has been in reporting human-rights issues in coverage of U.S.–Chinese relations. Since the Tiananmen Square massacre of 1989, Americans have been introduced to the struggle between a hard-line Communist regime and those seeking to expand civil liberties and political rights. During the (first) Bush and Clinton administrations, and again in the Obama administration, the connection between human rights and trade relations between the two nations became a recurring theme of news coverage. Critics of the Chinese human-rights situation argued that the United States should use favorable trade policies to promote liberal political reforms in China. Pragmatists argued that Chinese leaders react badly to such political blackmail and would only turn to other trading partners in Europe and Asia, excluding American business interests from what is potentially the world's largest market. This active debate in the news has opened the foreign policy process to more public scrutiny and grassroots involvement than is commonly the case.[44]

Similar discussions surrounded both the tone of television coverage and official U.S. endorsement of the 2008 Olympics in Beijing while Tibetan protesters were being jailed. Yet commercial factors may shape how the issue is addressed in covering such things as sports events. NBC sought good relations with the Chinese government to secure future media deals and announced that its coverage would stick strictly to sports.

Involve the Audience in Producing and Sharing Content   The social media revolution makes is possible for individual citizens to produce and distribute often high quality and insightful reporting. As discussed in Chapter 1, the news about democracy protests in Iran depended on videos and messages sent directly form protesters inside the country. Blogs offer other ways for citizens to interact with journalists and stories. As the example of the *Texas Tribune* illustrates, the development of interactive databases may be the answer for many government watchdog stories that are increasingly hard to support in failing news organizations. These and other innovative approaches to public information are illustrated in the case study on Innovative Solutions and Public Information Experiments.

Innovative Solutions and Public Information Experiments

The growing crisis in the news industry may have a positive effect on new experiments and discussions about the future of public information. For example, one inventory of independent investigative news organizations not tied to large corporations and the related profit pressures listed no fewer that 15 major initiatives currently under way.[45] Some of these are longstanding operations, such as the Center for Public Integrity and the Center for Investigative Reporting. However, the rest have appeared within the last decade. Some of these are well-known operations such as the *Huffington Post*, which sports a variety of blogs and links to stories produced by other organizations about politics, the arts, celebrity gossip, and the environment, among other topics. It is a digest of a broad range of primarily progressive issues and viewpoints, spiced with its own bloggers and an investigative team that works on original reporting. Others are small startups such as *Investigate West* (www. invw.org), which does stories of interest to the western region of the country (power, environment, budget crises, prison populations, housing markets, homelessness, jobs, etc.). These smaller operations are often begun by top journalists from failing news organizations (the death of the Seattle Post Intelligencer, in the case of *Investigate West*).

In their sweeping look at the present and future of news, Leonard Downie and Michael Schudson note the explosion of new information experiments, but they also raise cautionary notes about how to support them and what sort of content they will generate:

> The question that this transformation raises are simple enough: What is going to take the place of what is being lost, and can the new array of news media report on our nation and our communities as well as—or better than—journalism has until now?. . . .
>
> Some answers are already emerging. The Internet and those seizing its potential have made it possible—and often quite easy—to gather and distribute news more widely in new ways. This is being done not only by surviving newspapers and commercial television, but also by startup online news organizations, nonprofit investigative reporting projects, public broadcasting stations, university run news services, community news sites with citizen participation, and bloggers. Even government agencies and activist groups are playing a role. Together, they are creating not only a greater variety of independent reporting missions, but also different definitions of news.
>
> Reporting is becoming more participatory and collaborative. The ranks of news gatherers now include not only newsroom staffers, but also freelancers, university faculty members, students, and citizens. Financial support for reporting now comes not only from advertisers and subscribers, but also from foundations, individual philanthropists, academic and government budgets, special interests, and voluntary contributions from readers and viewers.[46]

The key question of course is how to consolidate the best of these operations in ways that enable them to stabilize and grow? Downie and Schudson propose a number of ideas that should be considered both by citizens and policymakers. First, they suggest that any news organization that is substantially devoted to public affairs be able to claim nonprofit tax status. Some organizations, such as National Public Radio, are already in this bracket and can receive tax-deductible contributions from supporters. Broadening and clarifying the terms for inclusion in this category would help other startups find a sustainable path. They also suggest that foundations expand their focus to support more coverage of their issue areas and to open new programs to support public information. A third recommendation is that public broadcasting refocus its priorities to include more local news coverage. The fourth recommendation is for colleges and universities to expand the scope of journalism programs to do more active news production and engage in partnerships with various innovative journalism startups. A fifth proposal is to create a small license fee from broadcast license holders and cable service providers to create a fund for local news that would be managed by the Federal Communications Commission. The FCC already uses tax and fee monies to support various public interest communication initiatives, so this would be consistent with its current regulatory mission. Finally, they propose that both conventional and startup organizations (along with government agencies and interest groups) create easy to use interfaces for databases that enable citizens to get direct answers to many of their political questions.[47]

The news crisis is given an even deeper analysis by Robert McChesney and John Nichols in their examination of historical origins and contemporary solutions that turn out to be consistent with the views of the Founders.[48] One novel proposal in their discussion is for the government to create a *citizen news voucher* system that people would be able to use to support any news organization, broadcast or print, that is substantially non profit. This would enable citizens, not government, to support and monitor how organizations perform, and allow citizens to support organizations that cover the topics and viewpoints they find most acceptable. Funding for this plan would come from taxes on commercial media operations from broadcast licenses to cell phone services and advertising. With a citizen news voucher system, citizens, not government, would drive the public information marketplace.

What McChesney and Nichols also add to our understanding of the current news crisis is an historical overview of journalism in America, with the important observation that the Founders regarded government subsidies for public information as an essential part of a healthy democratic public. For example, the post office was designed with public information in mind. What would "strict constructionists" today say if they understood how the founders really wanted the American information system to work? Yet this history has been lost. What has happened more recently is that Americans have been propagandized against "big government" for decades by corporations, who understandably don't like government standing in the way of them doing whatever they please in order to maximize profits. As a result today, the United States spends about one dollar per citizen on public media compared to eighty dollars in the United Kingdom and over one hundred in Denmark and Finland.[49]

The idea of promoting corporate interests over the public interest is to be expected of business, but the fact that so many Americans have bought the sales job separates the United States from most other democracies when it comes to understanding that information is a public good, and that government is the only clear way to protect it. All

Continued

advanced democracies have encountered and addressed the problem of how to keep government from meddling directly in the content of public media. Some nations have done well with building political firewalls between government and the public media (e.g., Britain and Germany), while others have done far less well (e.g., the United States and Italy). The point is that, if given careful thought and monitoring, firewalls and systems like citizen news vouchers can be constructed and maintained so that government can support independent and competitive media.

Proposals for Politicians and Government

It is tempting to ask politicians simply to refrain from so much polling, news management, and political marketing in their relations with the public. If politicians did not try to appeal to the emotions and fears of increasingly isolated individuals and instead actually led publics by educating them on complex issues and encouraging them to make the sacrifices required for consensus and change, they might be more popular. Indeed, many politicians would secretly like to shift their public relations strategies in these directions but feel that they would be attacked by opponents.

An unfortunate reality of the contemporary communication system is that politicians who attempt to educate, discuss complex issues, or propose new ways of thinking about problems are routinely attacked as unrealistic, or worse, as big-spending, big-government politicians who would rob Americans of more of their freedoms and create more government programs that do not work. As a result, many of the most talented members of Congress from both parties have left government in recent years, frustrated at the inability to speak or act creatively in public. The communication system that has evolved in the United States seems designed to drive out careful, open, thoughtful discussion of public problems in favor of stereotypical and stifling appeals to fear and divisive emotions.

Appealing to politicians individually to change how they communicate may get some sympathetic responses, but few are brave enough to fire their spin-doctors and pollsters and step in front of the television cameras to talk openly about complex problems. What, then, is the solution for politicians? One approach is to put public pressure on government to referee the national marketplace of ideas just as it referees every other market to protect consumers from fraud, deception, and safety hazards. Why should citizens have less protection against public information "fraud" than against stock market fraud and faulty products? Following are five simple recommendations for government that would greatly improve the quality of political information.

Limit the Flow of Money to Politicians The news management required to get elected and to serve effectively in public office is extremely expensive. For example, polling and advertising costs amount to half or more of campaign budgets, and campaign spending has grown alarmingly with each election over the past two decades. No other industrial democracy permits politicians the legal fundraising channels available to American candidates. Cutting the money supply (e.g., by further limiting campaign contributions and the spending of elected officials on political communication staff) would force politicians to go public with fewer illusions supplied by manufactured images and staged news events. The campaign finance reforms passed in 2002 were a start, but in 2010 the Supreme Court issued a 5-4 landmark ruling that struck down provisions limiting corporate spending in elections. FOX News ran the headline: Founding Fathers Smiling After Supreme Court Campaign Finance Ruling.[50] Hamilton may have approved of this, but it is hard to imagine Madison, Jefferson, Franklin or many others applauding unleashing of the most powerful organizations in society to buy disproportionate amounts of propaganda to dominate already fragile public communication in the core democratic process. Denouncing the partisan ruling by the Court Republican majority was a 90-page dissent penned by John Paul Stevens for the minority said in part:

> While American democracy is imperfect, few outside the majority of this court would have thought its flaws included a dearth of corporate money in politics.
>
> The court's ruling threatens to undermine the integrity of elected institutions across the nation.[51]

Indeed, most Americans feel that corporations already have too much power in American politics, and that elected representatives represent their financial backers above their constituents. A 2010 poll showed that over 80 percent of Americans felt that big companies, banks, and lobbyists have too much influence over government and politicians, while a like number felt that public opinion had too little.[52] The solution is to continue fighting the disproportionate influence of those who represent already powerful interests over the average citizen and limit the flows of money into so many aspects of our politics from elections to lobbying. The trouble, however, is that as Washington becomes infested with corporate power brokers, it becomes harder for politicians to survive without their backing, and the battle to remain free of their influence becomes more difficult.

Develop Better Formats for Candidate Debates and for Coverage of Legislation

Despite voter enthusiasm for direct candidate debates and citizen–candidate exchanges, the debate system remains ad hoc. Parties, candidates, and news organizations hammer out shaky debate formats according to their various and often conflicting interests. There is no enduring commitment to a format that would require candidates and news organizations to present open and probing issue exchanges to the public.

During the periods between elections, political coverage of government is similar to sports highlight reels. Detailed coverage of legislative activity is limited nationally to C-SPAN, and at state and local levels it is limited to similarly underfunded cable operations. Increased funding for C-SPAN (and state equivalents) along with public school education programs to help citizens tune into these information channels might redress the balance of the currently superficial news coverage of legislative and other government activities.

Control Media Monopolies The consolidation of ownership of large numbers of print and broadcast outlets is detrimental to the diversity of information reaching the public. Antimonopoly laws and public responsibility standards once existed, and new ones could be written with the quality of information expressly in mind. Over the past two decades, government has all but abandoned its regulation of business mergers and has explicitly loosened requirements for corporate media acquisitions. Public debate emanating from government or the conventional media is notably absent regarding the political and social responsibilities of big business. On the contrary, many corporate opinion leaders promote the idea that the only obligation of business is to make profits for the investors.

It is not surprising that many citizens think that such freedom is good for business and jobs and that corporations should have few social or economic public responsibilities (which is ironic, given the perception that corporations have too much power). At the same time, the qualities of various aspects of public content produced by corporate media have declined: fewer documentaries, more mayhem news, less investigative reporting, dependence on officials for information, more cheap reality TV programming, increasing selection of news to fit audience demographics, and little programming for economically marginal audiences from ethnic communities to alternative music fans are best a few examples. It is time to look beyond the myth of press freedom and consider the actual quality of information being produced for public consumption.

A positive development in recent years involves the emergence of a citizen media reform movement (see **www.freepress.net**) that has put pressure on Congress to consider the public interest when writing media legislation and reviewing FCC activities. In 2003, as discussed in the case study in Chapter 7, Congress overturned an FCC ruling granting large media companies more control over the media in many communities. This surprising reversal followed intense lobbying by citizens and even politically conservative small media companies. While the battle over corporate concentration of the media is far from over, the front lines have shifted in recent years to keeping the Internet free and open to public content, as discussed below.

Provide More Funding (and a More Creative Mandate) for Public Broadcasting Current government policies on public broadcasting restrict funding and pressure struggling stations to be less controversial and more like the rest of the media. Instead, the policies should encourage public broadcasters to be what the commercial media are not—that is, to find ways to promote more diversity, more grassroots input, more minority views, and more opposition positions.

If all of this is too much to accomplish under one roof, split the current public broadcasting corporation into multiple organizations under the directorship of different public sectors: political parties and related interest networks (perhaps channels for Republicans, Independents, and Democrats), public interest organizations (e.g., think tanks, citizen watchdog organizations, and foundations), and social groups (churches, educators, arts and culture organizations). Alternately, government—prompted by citizen pressure—can ensure that the current public broadcasting organizations have boards of directors and political firewalls that open them to political viewpoints beyond the congressional factions that currently battle for the soul of public broadcasting—call it the *Public Citizen Channel.*

Above all, increase funding for public broadcasting so that it does not have to resort to donations and corporate sponsorship for much of its programming. Many other nations have designed strong public broadcasting systems to meet the public communication requirements of democracy. Continuing debate and scrutiny accompany those systems as they face government pressures and adapt to stronger private competition. By contrast, the United States has not had a serious debate since the 1930s and 1940s about the ideal balance between public and private media or the possibilities of more useful public information systems.

Strengthen Public Service Requirements for Cable and Broadcast License Holders Many Americans find it difficult to understand that the airwaves that bring them television and the local franchises that bring them cable are sold or granted by the government. Just as we expect transportation companies granted rights to public lands to provide some services to the communities along those right-of-ways, so should we require holders of communication licenses to have obligations other than to commercial advertisers and corporate shareholders.

In the view of communication scholar Robert McChesney, one of the great turning points in the American information system came in the 1930s when Congress granted the great proportion of the radio and television bandwidths to private operators with relatively few responsibilities to create public forums or cover social issues in any depth.[53] Over the years, the FCC, with the encouragement of Congress, imposed some modest public service requirements on licensees. The lobbying efforts of increasingly powerful communication companies, combined with the growing antiregulation mood in the nation, have resulted in rollbacks in operator obligations to run public affairs programs, community forums, and even basic news programming.

Another great turning point in communications technology and business development is now upon us. As governments decide how broadband cable monopolies and new digital spectra will be allocated, they have increasing leverage over what public service obligations (e.g., C-SPAN and local civic channels) cable operators should have. Local governments can extract subsidies from cable operators for high-quality local arts and politics channels that might promote citizen involvement in local affairs. Perhaps even more important, decisions are already being made about how to allocate and regulate the microwave spectrum that will enable the home television to become an interactive communication device. Should the interactive potential of television, personal computers, and other devices be used in the interest of commercial entertainment and home shopping, or should the democratic potential of the new electronic information age be considered seriously? These are just a few of the important issues that will affect civic communication in the next decade.

Even the openness of the Internet, which many people take for granted, is seriously challenged by deregulatory decisions that Internet service is not like phone or postal service that are mandated to be available equally to all citizens. Beginning with the Republican dominated Federal Communications Commissions of the early years of the twenty-first century, and continuing with court rulings more recently, Internet service providers have been reclassified as "information services" that can selectively discriminate in what they carry over their lines. This has triggered an important battle over "net neutrality" with many public interest organizations fighting for the Internet to continue to be a place where political communication and a good deal of other content can be transmitted without being relegated to more expensive or slower service by carriers. The battle over the freedom of the Internet is just one of the issues facing the future of public communication online.

THE PROMISE AND PERIL OF VIRTUAL DEMOCRACY

With the diffusion of personal communication devices, the production, distribution, and sharing of information can become richer than ever before imagined. Not only can citizens fine-tune their information needs with these technologies, but news organizations and new information services can also monitor use patterns and adjust their content accordingly. Because the electronic storage and delivery capabilities of such information are far greater than either printing or video news production, the potential exists for greater diversity of information to be supplied to relatively small numbers of consumers. The peril, of course, is that the personalized packaging of news described throughout this book may result in the increasing isolation of people from one another. This isolation may be bred by choice, technology, or demographic circumstance. For example, as noted at the beginning of this chapter, people may choose to subscribe to information services tailored precisely to their needs, tastes, and interests. They may choose to go online only with others like themselves, forming virtual communities of people connected only by an electronic thread of hobby, political issue, religion, or other specialized interest.

The promise of digital democracy, of course, is that citizens can also network with each other, using information they have gathered to build grassroots communities of interest that are at least somewhat independent of the media images and one-way political propaganda that plague the existing mass-information system. Government at all levels can be plugged into these networks through cable or streamed coverage of government proceedings, enhanced by e-mail, blogs, and video sharing to create interaction among citizens and representatives. Indeed, many states have experiments under way with various multichannel communication links between citizens and their representatives. E-government capabilities have sprouted all the way from the White House and members of Congress to local governments. One booster of this trend claimed that interactive media links to government "can restore for viewers, and voters, the kind of direct connection that people had with their representatives in simpler times."[54]

Another observer of this electronic scene notes that enthusiasts have become so charmed with the possibilities of electronic democracy that they see it as a modern-day Athens on a mass scale:

> . . . a new technocratic version of the participatory dream has emerged. Instead of entering the Athenian assembly, people fulfill their obligations as citizens through new electronic devices that enable all citizens to express themselves on policy issues but also to play a direct role in deciding those issues. . . . Modern citizens sit in the Athenian assembly of their homes armed with laptop computers. . . . Technology overcomes the problems of complexity and size. Technology makes ancient Athens possible today.[55]

Yet critics warn of trouble in this electronic paradise. The warnings strike at the very core of democracy itself. Will the private, personalized world of electronic democracy destroy what is left of the important idea of a public defined by face-to-face accountability and consensus, on which stability, legitimacy, and power ultimately depend? Will great inequalities emerge between technological haves and have-nots? Some citizens may become isolated because they lack the communication devices or the discretionary income to purchase connectivity or specialized services that others can afford. Communication scholars Graham Murdock and Peter Golding warn that a two-class communication society is likely to develop, separating those with full electronic access from those without the means, the education, or the technological support systems to become full participants in the electronic dialogue.[56] This problem is known as the "digital divide." A second divide may separate those who have technology access and use it to participate in a vibrant civic culture from those who see it primarily as a means of staying in touch with friend networks, shopping, and sharing entertainment content.

Other forms of isolation may emerge in conventional media because of the capacity to match content to demographics, such as race, income, ZIP code, age, gender, or occupation. The magazines or newspapers to which people subscribe may make editorial choices for them, sending some articles to some groups and not to others. On this possibility, consider a comment by Patrick Reilly of *The Wall Street Journal*:

> It bothers me that *Time* and *Newsweek* are working furiously on selective binding which, they say, will target ads and, more importantly, edit pages to an individual house or a row of houses. It's personally disappointing to read a story and sort of slap your head and go, "Wow! That was great!" and then realize that there are far fewer people slapping their head at the same time than there were last week because you're all getting a different story.[57]

Vibrant grassroots communication or egocentric musings from socially isolated individuals? The future of electronic democracy is wide open to the best and the worst of possibilities. The direction of electronic communication will be affected by the kind of public debate that emerges about what to do with new technologies. The greatest risk for the future of a citizen-friendly Internet is that many of the most important policy questions may be answered before many people are even aware of them. How will the Internet be used? Will it become a more vibrant place for citizens to gather, to form communities, and to work out new forms of government? Or will it become a virtual shopping mall-cineplex-friend networking scene, dedicated overwhelmingly to consumption and entertainment, with little space for public life or political communication?

These important questions are at the center of lively discussions among concerned "netizens," but they have received relatively little attention in the conventional news. For example, as a result of the FCC and court rulings noted above, Internet service providers may decide to charge large mailing lists and political networks for access to their subscribers. This would inhibit the growth of online activism by imposing virtual postage fees on citizen-action networks, while business partners of service providers would get preferred access at preferred rates. Indeed, as service providers become more interested in owning the content that their users are accessing (e.g., Comcast buying a controlling stake in NBC in 2010), they have greater interest to make other content less attractive or accessible. For insights about this issue of "net neutrality" and other communication policy issues of our time are, the reader may wish to visit Freepress at **www.freepress.net**. Other aspects of communication and civic engagement are on display at The Center for Communication and Civic Engagement (**www.engagedcitizen.org**), which the author directs.

BALANCING DEMOCRACY AND CORPORATE SOCIAL RESPONSIBILITY: A PLACE TO START

The digital future may lead democracy to new and previously unimagined heights. If the disorganized forces of markets, politics, and public withdrawal are allowed to have their way, however, future information systems on the Internet are no more likely to address the needs of democracy than the current conventional media system does. Indeed, the possibility exists that corporate domination of the mass media will drive digital democracy to the margins of society. Virtual huddled masses may grumble about having little public space to gather or few points of entry to a "shopping mall" cyberspace dominated by commercial values. One policy goal to develop the potential of digital democracy involves creating publicly supported communication commons in cyberspace so that people can organize and find resources to create and share information.[58]

As for more responsible conventional news policies, it is important to urge media companies to settle for more reasonable profits from news divisions so that cheapened news stops driving so many citizens out of the picture. Media companies once branded themselves around the prestige of their news divisions and expected those divisions to make less money than entertainment and sports. A return to the idea that news is a public trust would not seriously harm the bottom lines of giant corporations that do the majority of their business in entertainment programming anyway. The corporate claim that its only responsibility is to the stockholders amounts to saying that companies do not have to be good citizens. This bold assertion is valid only as long as silent leaders and silent majorities of citizens let it stand.

Corporations are conscious of their brand images. Citizens have learned to use this brand sensitivity to promote greater responsibility from companies in other industrial sectors from shoes (Nike) to food (McDonald's). The social and public responsibilities of media corporations today could become major consumer political issues, advancing the cause of citizen engagement in a vibrant democracy as a public value that can be discussed alongside profits. A climate of public opinion that expects good citizenship from corporations would go a long way toward helping companies think about branding themselves around social values beyond profits. Who knows, social responsibility might even be profitable!

Where would such a climate of opinion start? Perhaps it is the time for citizens, public interest organizations, and policy foundations to voice a call for both corporations and government to act more responsibly within the national information system. Citizens who are concerned about the future of democracy are already using the power of personal digital communication media to organize citizen communication campaigns aimed at getting media companies to behave more responsibly. The reader might wish to review these campaigns at places, such as **www.freepress.net**, **www.adbusters.org** and **www.mediamatters. org**. Many cities have their own media democracy networks, such as Los Angeles (**http://lamediareform.wordpress.com/**), Boston (**http://openmediaboston.org/**) and Seattle (**www.reclaimthemedia.org/**). If more citizens demand public accountability in the quality of their information environments, it just might be possible to design a communication system with democracy in mind.

NOTES

1. Walter Pincus, "Newspaper Narcissism: Our Pursuit of Glory Led Us Away from Readers," *Columbia Journalism Review* (May/June 2009): 55.
2. Steven Livingston, "The 'Nokia Effect': The Reemergence of Amateur Journalism and What It Means for International Affairs," in *From Pigeons to News Portals: Foreign Reporting and the Challenge of New Technology*, ed. David Perlmutter and John Hamilton. (Louisiana State University Press, 2007: 47–69).
3. Jake Batsell, "Lone Star Trailblazer: Will the Texas Tribune Transform Texas Journalism?" *Columbia Journalism Review* (July/August 2010): 40.
4. www.texastribune.org/about/. Accessed September 25, 2010.
5. Batsell, "Lone Star Trailblazer."
6. Ibid., 41.
7. Brian Stelter, "Finding Political News Online, Young Viewers Pass It Along," *New York Times*, March 27, 2008: A1.

8. Henry Jenkins, *Convergence Culture* (New York: New York University Press, 2006).
9. See Nick Wing and Erin Booth, "Sarah Palin's Foreign Policy Manifesto: Brought to You by Facebook." July 10, 2010. www.huffingtonpost.com/2010/07/04/sarah-palins-foreign-poli_n_632808.html. Accessed September 24, 2010. For the Tea Party story, see: http://video.foxnews.com/v/4006672/palin-on-foreign-policy-at-convention. Accessed September 24, 2010.
10. www.facebook.com/pages/Lame-Stream-Media/213732812039. Accessed September 24, 2010.
11. James S. Fishkin, *The Voice of the People* (New Haven, CT: Yale University Press, 1995).
12. See, for example, Richard Morin, "Thinking Before They Speak," *Washington Post National Weekly Edition* (May 16–22, 1994): 37.
13. Ibid.
14. John Gastil, *By Popular Demand: Revitalizing Representative Democracy Through Deliberative Election* (Berkeley: University of California Press, 2000).
15. Ibid. See also, James Fishkin, *Democracy and Deliberation* (New Haven, CT: Yale University Press, 1991).
16. Mark E. Kann, "More or Less Democracy in the Internet Age?" USC Annenberg School for Communication, networked publics blog, October 6, 2005. http://netpublics.annenberg.edu/digital_democracy/more_or_less_democracy_in_the_internet_age.
17. Diana Mutz, *Hearing the Other Side: Deliberative vs. Participatory Democracy* (New York: Cambridge University Press, 2006).
18. Stephen Earl Bennett, Staci L. Rhine, and Richard S. Flickinger, "The Things They Cared About: Change and Continuity in Americans' Attention to Different News Stories, 1989–2002," *Press/Politics* 9, no. 1 (Winter 2004): 75–99.
19. See Anthony Giddens, *Modernity and Self-Identity: Self and Society in the Late Modern Age* (Stanford, CA: Stanford University Press, 1991).
20. Jurgen Habermas, *Structural Transformation of the Public Sphere: An Inquiry into a Category of Bourgeois Society* (Cambridge, MA: MIT Press, 1989).
21. Todd Gitlin, (lecture, University of Washington, May 20, 1999).
22. Nina Eliasoph, *Avoiding Politics: How Americans Produce Apathy in Everyday Life* (New York: Cambridge University Press, 1998).
23. Michael Schudson, *The Good Citizen: A History of American Civic Life* (New York: The Free Press, 1998).
24. For an extended discussion of these ideas, see W. Lance Bennett, "The UnCivic Culture: Communication, Identity, and the Rise of Lifestyle Politics," *P.S.: Political Science and Politics* 31, no. 4 (December 1998): 41–61.
25. See Erik Asard and W. Lance Bennett, *Democracy and the Marketplace of Ideas: Communication and Government in Sweden and the United States* (Cambridge, UK: Cambridge University Press, 1997).
26. Robert W. McChesney, *Telecommunications, Mass Media, & Democracy: The Battle for Control of U.S. Broadcasting, 1928–1935* (New York: Oxford University Press, 1993).
27. Robert W. McChesney and John Nichols, *The Death and Life of American Journalism* (Philadelphia, PA: Nation Books, 2010).
28. See freepress.net, "Public Broadcasting Under Assault." www.freepress.net/publicbroadcasting; also Paul Farhi, "PBS Scrutiny Raises Political Antennas," *Washington Post*, April 22, 2005: C1.

29. Thomas E. Patterson, "Irony of the Free Press: Professional Journalism and News Diversity" (paper presented at the Annual meeting of the American Political Science Association, Chicago, September 3–6, 1992), page 2.
30. Quoted in Frank Luther Mott, *The News in America* (Cambridge, MA: Harvard University Press, 1952), 5.
31. "Weighing Anchor: At the Start of His Final Year, Tom Brokaw Takes Stock and Looks Ahead," interview with Jane Hall, *Columbia Journalism Review* (January/February 2004): 19.
32. Brent Cunningham, "Re-Thinking Objectivity," *Columbia Journalism Review* (July/August 2003): 24.
33. Ibid.
34. Steven Livingston, *The Terrorism Spectacle* (Boulder, CO: Westview, 1994).
35. From Michael Isikoff, "A 'Sting' Tailor-Made for Bush," *Washington Post* News Service, reprinted in the *International Herald Tribune*, Saturday–Sunday edition (September 23–24, 1989): 4.
36. Maureen Dowd, "U.S. Presidential Road Show," *International Herald Tribune*, September 26, 1989: 3.
37. Dannegal G. Young, "The Daily Show as New Journalism," in *Laughing Matters: Humor and American Politics in the Media Age,* eds. J. S. Morris and J. C. Baumgartner (New York: Routledge, 2007), 241–259.
38. *The Daily Show*, November 1, 2004. www.thedailyshow.com/video/index.jhtml?videoId=126947&title=vote. Accessed December 15, 2010.
39. Shanto Iyengar, *Is Anyone Responsible?* (Chicago: University of Chicago Press, 1993).
40. Regina G. Lawrence, "Game-Framing the Issues: Tracking the Strategy Frame in Public Policy News," *Political Communication* 17, no. 2 (April/June 2000): 93–115.
41. Mark R. Levy and John P. Robinson, "The 'Huh?' Factor: Untangling TV News," *Columbia Journalism Review* (July/August 1986): 48.
42. Cunningham, "Re-Thinking Objectivity": 27.
43. Levy and Robinson, "The 'Huh?' Factor": 50.
44. See Leonard Pratt, "The Circuitry of Protest," *Gannett Center Journal* 3 (1989): 105–115; and Donald R. Shanor, "The 'Hundred Flowers' of Tiananmen," *Gannett Center Journal* 3 (1989): 128–136.
45. Jill Drew, "The New Investigators," *Columbia Journalism Review* (May/June 2010): 22–27.
46. Leonard Downie Jr. and Michael Schudson, "The Reconstruction of American Journalism," *Columbia Journalism Review* (November/December 2009): 28–51.
47. Ibid., 45–51.
48. Robert W. McChesney and John Nichols, *The Death and Life of American Journalism*.
49. Ibid., 192.
50. http://www.foxnews.com/opinion/2010/01/22/ken-klukowski-supreme-court-amendment-mccain-feingold/. Accessed September 27, 2010.
51. Warren Richey, "Supreme Court: Campaign Finance Limits Violate Free Speech," *Christian Science Monitor* (January 21. 2010). www.csmonitor.com/USA/Justice/2010/0121/Supreme-Court-Campaign-finance-limits-violate-free-speech. Accessed September 27, 2010.
52. Harris Poll, February 16–21, 2010, Reported in *Polling Report*. www.pollingreport.com/politics.htm. Accessed September 28, 2010.

53. McChesney, *Telecommunications, Mass Media & Democracy.*
54. Daniel M. Weintraub, "The Technology Connection," *State Legislatures* (June 1993): 44.
55. Thomas W. Simon, "Electronic Inequality," *Bulletin of the Scientific Technology Society* 11 (1991): 144.
56. Graham Murdock and Peter Golding, "Information Poverty and Political Inequality: Citizenship in the Age of Privatized Communications," *Journal of Communication* 39 (Summer 1989): 180–193.
57. Quoted in the "Sound Bite" section, *Columbia Journalism Review* (July/August 1993): 13.
58. Stephen Coleman and Jay Blumler, *The Internet and Democratic Citizenship* (New York: Cambridge University Press, 2009).

INDEX